About the Author

Leyla Karaca was born in April, 1976 in Istanbul. She graduated from the Faculty of Arts, Department of Philosophy at the Middle East Technical University in 1999. She worked as a teacher in various schools. Translations, poems, articles, essays and short stories by her are published regularly in various journals and literary magazines. Presently, she is a member of the Temrin Thought and Literature Journal's Editorial board. She is also the Editor of Ferfir Publishing House.

Published works–

- Sonsuzla Sek Sek, *Poetry,* 2010 (Hopscotch With The Eternity)
- Göğsündeki Gökyüzü, *Novel,* 2013 (The Sky In Your Heart).
  It is the story of a mystical and fascinating journey. A passionate love and search for truth together. This novel was selected as the Best Novel of 2013 by ESKADER in Turkey.
- Kalbinin Müziği, *Story,* 2015 (The Music Of Your Heart)
  Presently being translated into German language.
- Kurt Ağzı, *Novel,* 2016 (The Mouth Of The Wolf)
- Tales for Children

The author has also presented a report, 'From the Collective Prejudice to Pure Consciousness' within the context of ISCAT 2015: First International Symposium on Critical and Analytical Thinking (Sakarya University, 10 April, 2015)

She has also given seminars in Writing Schools on the subjects of poetry, emotional intelligence, subconsciousness etc. The author also takes part in various poetry events in Turkey.

She is a member of YAZAK (Writing Academy Association in Turkey).

The Sky In Your Heart

LEYLA KARACA

Translated by
Ahmet Zeki Akturk

Originals
An Imprint of Low Price Publications
Delhi | 2016

First Published 2016

Publication of this edition was supported by
the Ministry of Culture and Tourism of Turkish Republic

ISBN 13: 978-81-8454-174-8
ISBN 10: 81-8454-174-0

Published by
Originals
An Imprint of Low Price Publications
A-6, 2nd, Nimri Commercial Centre,
Ashok Vihar Phase 4, Delhi 110052 (INDIA)
tel.: +91-11-27302453 fax.: +91-11-47061936
URL: LPPindia.com e-mail: info@LPPindia.com

Printed at
DK Fine Art Press Pvt. Ltd.
Delhi

PRINTED IN INDIA

Contents

1

I get a small and old photo shop of which window is full of colourful photos all along in no time flat. Inside the shop is quite cool in spite of the heat of the outside. There is no other voice than the television's at full blast. There is a Far-east movie on the TV with a fuzzy image on its screen. A woman's voice is tinkling inside. There is a beautiful, slim Japanese woman on the screen. She cries to a slant-eyed man with a strong look that "If you do not accept my help offer you will remain as a slave forever!" with a manner of empress. The man looking like a samurai with an old, mealy beret on his head answers that "I know, but I prefer remaining as a slave rather than coming with you."

This small and a little gloomy entrance of which walls are covered with photos smells cigarette ash. There is a small young man with grey hair behind the table ahead at the furthest end. The suffering expression of the steppe is fixed on his face. His face is colourless as if it lends all its colours to the photos on the wall. He says "Welcome" unperturbedly and turning his eyes away from the TV at a moment and then he looks at the TV with curious eyes.

I cast my eyes on the photos. Most of them are from 80's. They are photos of old couples side by side. I look at a black and white photo of a young woman whose forelock is about to go in her eyes. She looks at the objective over her one shoulder. She smiles like flirting. Who knows where this woman is now and what she is doing. She became a housewife most probably, even she put on weight. There is a photo of a child just under it. How he smiles happily with a football team t-shirt on him. I look at the photos of the brides and grooms. In a shot the groom takes the bride on his lap. The face of the woman is barely identified because of the make-up. There is another shot of another young couple just next to it. There is a man with a moustache, a happily smiling woman beside him, probably his wife, and only their heads and shoulders are seen.

"Hi, I want to have a photo taken." I say. "It will be a portrait. Can I get it instantly?" He stands up and comes to me.

"Of course" he says, "how many do you need?" The voice of the woman on TV is tinkling, it carries on tinkling, the woman cries angrily:

"I order you to come with me. The soldiers will soon be here, then they won't leave both of us alive, what are you waiting for?"

The samurai answers recklessly:

"I am waiting for dying, please, please go your grace..."

"Six is enough" I say to the photographer. He lifts the curtain with flowers on my right off and shows me the way. He points at a small mirror lightened by a cylindrical fluorescent lamp at the far end of the dark room and says "Make your hair here, I am coming, there is a comb over there." He goes out of the dark room. I look for the comb staring around. I get a quite dirty pink plastic comb. I had better to make my hair with my hand. I gussy up in front of the mirror for a while. I look around. My eyes catch an old, abandoned wing chair on a side. There is an old pouffe a few steps away from the wide plates. I go and sit on it. Minutes are passing. I look at the photographer sitting at the table lifting the curtain. He stares at the TV without gloating with a cigarette in his hand and his camera in front of him. He stays calm as if there is a mould layer between the world and his body.

I say with a low voice:

"I am ready."

He stands up immediately and starts to do his job.

I sit on the pouffe of which cover worn off because of sitting on again, but this time I sit up straight. The photographer turns off all the lights and two separate plates, both of them, start to shine with a white light. The photographer, who is behind the plates in the dark, takes a few steps to me, he raises my head a little with a timid manner and then he turns my chin to the right slightly. He pulls my collar completely to my neck. After he tidies my hair with the same timid manners, he says "Don't move and look into the objective soulfully." He walks back without hitting the bright plates and watches me still with the camera in his hand for a few seconds. "Don't hold your breath otherwise you look nervous. Please smile."

I feel a kind of anxiousness that I have in hospitals in this nervous moment. Just sitting there still... "Please smile," the photographer repeats. I force the edges of my lips to smile. At the same time the woman in the movie continues talking.

"Oh my God, the guards are approaching, I beg you Sadu, please come with me..."

A pair of hands blocks the lights of the wide plates first, I can see strong wrists are reaching out into me. The fingers of the hand starts to tighten my throat with hatred and rage, they press upon my veins to take me away from the life with all his power. On one hand I try to understand what is happening and on the other hand I catch his wrist with my two hands, I prick my nails into his skin, my breath dies away, first brokenly, then it turns to a growling. The owner of the unknown hands who understand that he cannot kill me tightening my throat now starts to hit my face with all his power, squeezes my arms leaving a great pain everywhere he touches. I tumble down with his last strike, he starts to kick me. There comes blood from my mouth.

The woman on TV start to scream,

"Guards, nooooo!" The clanks of the swords are heard, besides the painful moaning of the woman, the samurai cries: "Bastards! Leave her!"

The photographer calls from the darkness for the last time:

"Please stay still."

I am still dragged on the floor like an animal. Then, at a moment I get back my power, I don't know how, my eyes shine with a last will of life. I stand up, my fingers clasp the fingers of the unknown hands, squeeze them unceasingly, first my finger joints crunch, the power in my body well gets out after these strikes. I try to shake him pushing and bending my arms, I strive to run away from him. Once again he attacks with kicks, slaps and fists. I haven't got hurt like this before, I have fallen into a fire like this fort he first time. He punches me again and again, what kind of rage this is, this time he starts to squeeze my throat crying, the floor slips under my feet, everything starts to circle around me, I realize that I am at right beside him trying to save my head. He doesn't forgive, he starts to drag me holding the back of my neck, putting my feet down is useless, we come to the edge of the cliff. I understand his intention, he will push me down. I come with an ace of falling, and I realize at that moment that a man can do anything to survive, pain of life is not like anything. Desire to survive ignites all power in the soul. I start to bell like a wounded animal as my neck is dangling from the cliff, the only thing I want is to breath, my hands are looking for a space among his thick fingers for only one breath. His hands get more powerful as I scream; he tightens my neck much more.

The woman on the TV starts to cry,

"Sadu, oh my God, blood... Sadu, we will survive, won't we? Please don't give up, hold on!"

My shoulders dangle from the cliff; I must get rid of his hands before dangling from my waist. You cannot kill me, I say to myself. I resist his hands squeezing my throat with my whole body, I resist as if I rear up. I am helpless like a rodent in a beak of a bird of prey...

I hear the voice of the photographer:

"I am takiiinnngg!"

My eyes are drowned in a shining, puking light. A burning light crashes on my face. The time freezes for a moment, it covers everywhere as if it wants to swallow every lived thing. After a moment the light is drawn away, the photographer says:

"But we couldn't make it. You moved," and he comes to me. First he wipes away my eyes burst into tears due to pain without caring about my body about to dangle from the deep yard. He says "I am taking it again, you didn't smile," cleaning the fresh blood running from my nostrils.

He finds his place again without hitting the light plates in the dark room and he hides as if he takes shelter. The hands squeezing my throat with their all power grab my hair roots. My shoulders slide towards the bottom of the cliff some more. During the bitter struggle I do not even realize that my hair is torn from the bottom. Only a sharp pain cause my head lean towards the back. It doesn't seem that this unknown person, who ties his hands resembling paws to my hair, will free me. My eyes catch the eternal blueness shining over my head while my heart carries on beating as if it rushes out from my taut throat. For a moment I think that the sky will survive but this is my end. Two drops of tears runs towards my ears, as if they begging. They manifest as the fluid forms of begging. Once he frees my head, I will get down in no time flat. If he doesn't free my head, he will find my hair in his hands with my scalp. I grab his hands gripping my hair with my two hands; I grip him as much as his grip, may be more. I hear the voice of the photographer once again.

A little bitter, a little ironic smile is set on my face. I look at the blue sky forgetting everything. The camera flashes once more while the hands are dragging me to the blueness, my face is parallel with the sky and I am breathing deeply.

The voice of the TV fills the dark room; Sadu answers with a moaning and with his last breath,

"Yes, my darling, yes, we will survive, forever..."

2
Another Name of the Fire

Tuğrul gets behind the wheel, the key disappears in his big hands, and he leans forward a little looking at me at the same time. He is so impressive on me that if he says 'Dilruba you should die now,' I will say 'take my life.' If he says, 'Dilruba, we are going to die,' I will say 'let's go.'

He looks at me so, Dilruba let's die together. Dilruba, let's disregard life. I want to die with you. Are you in dying with me Dilruba... Your eyes are looking like a dagger on my neck Dilruba..

"Shall we go?" he says only. We set off slowly. His looks are talking slowly. Everything except Tuğrul disappears for me. I am jealous of even the window mirror that he checks rising his beautiful face slightly, of the road he is looking at, and of the letters pouring from his lips slowly as if flowing. I am jealous of even the tiniest detail that his being contacts with. I didn't know love is so. I didn't know crashing is so. If Tuğrul wanted to tie me at his door as a dog, I wouldn't object him. If he wanted to make me a mat under his feet, I would be proud of that. Tuğrul's voice tells me that heaven exists. Heaven is close. As I dive in his brown looks, the heavens that time freezes lies ahead of me. His scent resembling a magic sticks me to him, and I was racing to the pain like glow-worms racing to the fire. To the fabulous pain of love.

"Did you like the evening?" he said, he looked at me taking his eyes from the road for a few seconds. He was looking at me as if he was saying, 'I have cut your wrists, are they bleeding?' His sentence meant so to me. Or he was like saying that 'I have thrown you a hole full of millipedes, are you frightened?'

"It was so beautiful," I said.

"It is, I go to this restaurant very often."

"It is not the restaurant that is beautiful," I said. He looked at me as if saying what then?

"Your being..."

He spoke while he was moving up the gear,

"I am very pleased to hear that." He was driving so fast. The car didn't go on the road, it was simply flying. As if our emotions would have gathered speed if the car had slowed down. Tuğrul was moving up the gear steadily. He looked like that if he had stopped or slowed down he wouldn't be sure about himself. We needed to arrive at the dorm as soon as possible.

"You drive so fast," I said. I was talking to him in a more comfortable manner. I wanted him to slow down since I wanted to see him more.

"The road is empty, don't worry," he said, "are you really frightened?" He whispered without waiting for my answer:

"Dilruba... Dilruba... What a beautiful name this is... I must say this name continuously... I must call you without breathing... Dilruba... Dilruba..."

He was like murmuring by himself alone. Butterflies were flapping in my stomach; or the fish I had just eaten started to revive and move its tail after the sentence I hear. Then Tuğrul lit a new cigarette in a distressed manner. The flame of the lighter enlightened his beautiful face in the darkness. He inhaled the first sniff deeply, very deeply, and he exhaled with a distinct sighing. He threw the cigarette pack to the bottom of the front window harshly. The earth was sliding under our feet fast. The flat, shiny asphalt road was lengthening ahead increasingly. The lights by the road were reviving again on the front window in different forms.

Tuğrul's long and strong arms gripped the wheel easily, then he was dangling one arm from the window as if he was bored. Both windows were wide open. Again the same scent was mixing with the same ecstatic smell of the cigarette, and made me crazy.

"Do you know Dilruba, I have never been like this. Dilruba, you are looking like a gazelle." He said. He nailed his looks to my eyes ignoring the speed. I thought the car would go by itself. "I have no power, Dilruba," he said.

I was turning to a wound bleeding continuously. I would have died if there hadn't been his voice. If there hadn't been his dazzling scent, purulence would have been flowing in my veins instead of blood. Tuğrul was attracting me by a terrific attraction. I was about to lose my self-confidence. His breath was making me drunk next to me, right over here.

I heard that terrible scream at that very moment. I knew these flames getting closer screaming wildly. This was the Nafs. Tuğrul's whispers and looks full of desire gave it strength. Nafs was coming to me with its ugly body resembling a hyena and with its dragon wings scattering flames blended with black foams from its mouth. Hadn't I defeated it? In fact, hadn't Keşşaf knocked it down? How had it enslaved the Spirit again and captured the throne of the land of heart?

"Please stop Tuğrul, please stop. Pull over," I started to shout. I was thinking to sit at the back and get over these dangerous moments in safe. He slowed down immediately as if something happened to me, and pulled over signalling. He didn't ask if something had happened, he understood that I wanted to move away. At the moment the car stopped, everything calmed down suddenly. I got out of the car as if running away from the fire... There was a short way to the campus. The harsh wind made me get over. I waited leaning on the front of the car for a while. He came to me. He stood just next to me and leaned on the car as if he wanted to watch the landscape.

"Did I frighten you? You will be cold," he said. We were both standing on the edge of the cliff at that moment. We didn't lean on his blue car but something else on the edge. The earth could slide under our feet with a little movement.

"I just wanted to get some fresh air..." I was sniffing at the same time.

"Why are you crying?" he said quietly. "Did I say something wrong?" I wanted to say that 'yes, it was wrong. Your saying Dilruba was wrong, you shouldn't have say my name so sincerely, so warmly; your saying Dilruba in whisper killed me." Yet I kept quiet.

"No, no, it wasn't because of you.."

"I drove too fast and frighten you, didn't I?" Tuğrul was talking about the speed of the car. Life itself was fast.

"Life itself is fast, never mind" I said.

I was looking at the world at the end of a forked road. I would rather die having an accident than offend Keşşaf . He meant everything to me. Thousands of Tuğrul didn't worth only one word of Keşşaf. My thoughts became severe and were going to the right direction. I escaped myself from temporary and deceptive emotions in this way. Who was Tuğrul? I had met him a short time ago. How quickly I fell in with him! This was stupid... unreasonable... I again sat at the front seat next to him collectedly. If I had sat at the back, it would have meant that I hadn't trusted him at all, and myself at the same time...

However, I was again in the middle of the same burning emotions when the car started to go slowly. Tuğrul was looking at the road thoughtfully. He wasn't driving fast this time. He lit another cigarette. Again the same scent, again the same madness...

At last we arrived at the dorm, we arrived here safe and sound getting over hundreds of cliffs. When the car stopped in front of the dorm, Tuğrul leaned back; there were storms on his face. He leaned his head back completely. He hadn't finished his cigarette yet. He was smoking thoughtfully...

"Are you leaving now?" he said. As if I was setting sail, at least I was going up to my room.

"It's late, it's better I go," I said. There was nobody around. Lights were enlightening around behind the thick curtains of the dorm, but this street lamp at most that we were standing under. I got out of the car like a wire-walker leaving the wire. Tuğrul also got out of the car and he was walking a few steps behind me,

"Don't go to the bother," I said, "thank you very much."

"I see that you are at arm's length again," he said. He was smiling very nicely. It was very difficult for me to leave him there and go up. Again we stopped by the information cabin.

"When shall we meet again?" he said.

"Whenever you want..." I said.

"I will come again as soon as possible." He leaned again to my face slightly. I was drinking his voice like wine. I was inhaling his scent as if I wouldn't feel it again. I missed him even he was still with me. My heart was breaking and all the fish revived in me started to agonize. His hair got long, as long as to be fastened under his ears... A thin forelock fell onto his face. He shook his head slightly to throw the forelock back. Then he straightened it with one hand.

"To see you is very good for me, you cannot know this," he said.

"Me too," I said; I left him there and went behind the panel.

I wanted to cry as 'don't go.' I was hardly keeping myself together not to go down his knees to beg him not to go. Now there was a panel between us. Tuğrul went out by walking behind the panel and disappeared.

3
Due to your beautiful face

Let's tell the story from the beginning, very beginning. Tell about what had happened till the Tuğrul. I wasn't rated as a happy person during the period of my life before I met Safran. I was in my twenties and living in a huge university campus in greens resembling heaven, but my life wasn't different from hell; I had no idea that I could enjoy life. At the moments I stepped on Ankara after a long bus journey leaving my aunt who had grown me up and my city, an undefined melancholy was descending upon me. Something started to tighten my throat even when I was on the way; I was nearly choked as the bus was getting closer to Ankara. I cannot tell you that I had had a lot of friends before I met Safran. People I know, love and see frequently could be counted on the fingers of one hand. I was spending my days shuttling between the guesthouse and the faculty building, idling at the library, wandering about in the campus and see a few people I know. Furthermore there were also existential depressions on these monotonous days and thus life became worse. I was able to reach to the last grade in this way. Days rolled on without realizing how I got lonely as I was trying to comply with life among the young in this huge campus appearing as if they would stay young forever and trying to get used to it. Then one day...

That day I was alone in my room at the guesthouse. Moreover, there were only a handful of people in the campus. Everywhere including my room was buried into a discomforting solitude because of the holiday. I was waiting with a hope of getting a call from my father or my aunt. My father had gone on holiday with his wife and my aunt, before a widow, had just married; they both must have been busy to call me. Anyway, there was no other person to call me. Life was passing over me like a steamroller with all its weigh in this deep loneliness. This dim room in which I was watching at the horizon to bury into the darkness standing at the window was like an orphanage for me.

I usually sleep when I am unhappy. But this time I was unable to get to sleep. I threw myself outside. It was raining, the weather was cold. I was wandering about like Kays looking for his Leyla. The rain was pouring with such vigour that the rain drops left traces as big as a walnut on the ground they fell. One feels catharsis under such rain. The rain was washing me, I got wet to the skin. I stopped in the middle of the giant stadium; I opened my arms as if to hug the sky and pouring rain without knowing that this was the moment that changed my life. I was crying, my warm tears was flowing on my cheeks and meeting with the rain at the point that my chin ended. Then I started to talk to God being sure that no one could hear me. I was both crying and speaking to the sky.

"My God!" I cried. I started to shout out but the noise of the rain was suppressing my voice.

"You see, I am unable to cope with!" I stopped for a moment, I caught the eyes of the dark sky, my voice was mixing with the weather of the sky accompanying the rain. I carried on, my chest was heaving at a rate of knots, I was sobbing.

"O, the owner of the earth and heaven, please save me from this loneliness. I want you to do this, because who else can make real a human's wish? Give me a friend, let me find the true path, lighten me by a blessing from you, open my way by a light..."

I could only whimper the last sentences. Sinking to my knees like falling, I was continuously crying covering my face with my hands; the rain was fondling my hair. I took my chance again,

"The One of the destitute! Show me the truth, both let me out of this cage and bring me close to love! O, the sole owner of love..!"

It was a desperate pray; it was like the last prayer of the weak man who came to the end of everything, even loneliness. Then I rested on the grass with my palms, dropped my head to my knees and stayed there like a spot in the darkness smelling out the wet grass. All around was lightened by a light shattering the sky while I was crying jerkily. My voice died away with successive lightnings. I was cold, I returned to my room soaked. I wriggled on my bed. Then I sank into sleep during which I had that certain dream. This extraordinary dream was not of a kind that one can always have. One can have such dream only a few times in his life. I also did not know that prayers could be turned to so easily; life would whisper me that my prayer was accepted and I was about to enter a bright path. But what a path!

A few days later, once Hazel returned back, I told about the dream with a great excitement. Hazel was a rational girl staying at the opposite room. First she looked at me curiously, then she said:

"I know someone interpreting dream very well. If you like I will take you there."

"Of course, let's go" I said excitedly, "when are we going?"

"Tomorrow!" she said looking into my eyes. Caravans were passing through her green eyes.

"I was... I was just asking you about a dream..."

Safran! A saint woman!

On that day angels took me so close to you to show your beautiful face holding my arms and speaking into a language I never understood. Remember that day! Icons fell down one by one; all secrets on the earth revealed themselves with you. First you, raised your hand like a mirror which would turn my shaking image down and reflect it to me, as if to say "Hush!" My word remained hanged on the air and didn't know where to fall. Your hand sprang like a sparkle, it was white, whiter than white, I crashed onto its palm with my all confusion. Your hand was so white and that movement was so precise and strong leaving no room for doubt, my consciousness perceived the sudden movement of your hand as a weir blocking a river. The wild river froze to see what would happen with that movement, that blocking. In my confused eyes there was a reflection of your compassionate beautiful eyes at that moment. If I had tried to figure out, joy and hope would be unlinked from the knotted strings of that look.

"I know, no need to explain" you said, didn't let me tell about the dream and smiled only. This word was swaying with this pretty smile in the deep of a blueness toppling all the wisdom like dominoes. Your face was driving out my existence to the end holding from the beginning. The modesty accompanying to your deep perception, the solemnity in your deep big eyes knocked me down like a gazelle shot by an arrow. I wanted to run steadily with the hope that I found the response to my dream in this world even if I wasn't sure. For a short moment I looked for a simple answer in your eyes. You nodded your head slightly with the lights of your eyes shining like a sword. This was an approval, an approval of hope to find a root I belong to even if it was so thin after a long time. This image that I tried to hold from a dark strong poverty remained somewhere between dream and reality for a while.

Safran, remember! It happened in one of those freezing winters of Ankara. In that winter if all roads had jointed together they would all end in the same place: This small shanty! Remember that the strong wind holding my face and kissing my forehead called me to the endless wideness of the two-stair yard of your small house. My goodness, how did this endless sky fit into a two-room shanty at once? You, the one watching the pores of my soul, my consciousness, my mind, my whole existence on a brilliant mirror were like floating from one mountain to another, your long skirts were like hitting hard rocks like the coast. At your every glance, I collected a deserted moonlight from your face and joy from your eyes. When your white scarf you were wearing like a halo around the moon was flowing down your shoulders I let myself go freely to this calm riverbed. Your white hands, well-shaped fingers were gripping an endless heaven. Helplessness in your voice... Your voice was in a whispering corner as if it wanted to hide this helpless power.

Distinct cheekbones, a slightly aquiline nose, brave and mysterious eyes reviving that they penetrate everywhere they look and a sharp curved and polite mouth that can only be seen on wise people were drawn onto your face. You, dancing with the meaning; you, looking as purified from all worries and fears, moving her hands as if you were sowing or dabbling at the fire; you, pouring beauty from her voice...

Safran... There was something different in your movements, posture, manners that didn't belong to this world. Your fingers transforming the listeners, unifying the ones who saw you, aligning the life chains as meaningful rings in some invisible places was reflecting both joy and a heavenly consciousness. As your deserted but inclusive simplicity touched the skin of my consciousness of which conception decreased like hard, cold and rusty metals, faces of hundreds of events buried in the deep hole of the past in my mind was lightening, a scream prisoned in my chest was reaching out the daylight leaking into the cage.

The very day! Your existence lightening everywhere you touched was seemed like a brilliant oasis to the one that could not see where he was going and standing in a thirsty desert like me.

A tiny house surrounded by a low wall on one of the narrow streets of Balgat, large and small shanties nearby. My eyes catch the wooden door of the toilet outside. Glazed iron door of the house... Inside there is a sweet, joyful and assuring, damp smell specific for Anatolian houses. A seizing, swathing taste. The goods inside are concrete as well as they are unworldly. You go inside stepping on a handmade door mat. There are jugs on a stove in the middle. It is warm inside despite the sharp cold outside, warmness that grazing my face... An old glass case covering the whole wall nearby the door opening to the kitchen straight ahead. Books and artificial flowers in its cells... A divan on the other side, made carefully, and old chairs at the side of the wall. A few paintings covered with white clothes on the walls. Some parts of the floor have remained and stones can be seen partly, a big, large rug in the centre. I think the ceiling is low and it lowers and the stone floor remained as structure lowers and rises partly. A door opening to the small door on the right. The kitchen is as small as only two people can go in. The underside of the counter has been covered with a greenish cloth. Nearby a large flannel lifted from one corner on the breads in a plastic bucket. A small propane cylinder. A tiny window accompanying the counter with a curtain in dark colour. A narrow door opening from the kitchen to the bathroom. The bathroom is quite small and light-less.

One of the women with white scarves takes Hazel and me to the small room at the entrance. Two opposing divans in the room. A small glass case and a gross, old-fashioned television that I have never seen as turned on. Thick books in the side cells. There are two windows in this room, it is quite bright. Hazel and I are sitting side by side with a shy expression on our faces. Our heels touch the thick pleated skirts of the divan. The woman lets us in is short, plump, at her forties; she looks at us behind her glasses with a pretty smile on her face for a while. She has a manner of professor. She sits down the floor next to the divan.

This woman was sitting on the same place next to the divan during the time I frequented this house. She chose the words carefully when she speaks, cleaned her throat mildly, showed a maximum effort not to say something wrong and carried a boundless soul placed in her small body carefully. She seems thoughtful when she is pulling her glasses with the joint of her thumb. She is wearing a long dress and a light vest on it. She pulls the edges of her vest on her chest and she fastens her hands together as if she is cold.

She says styled:

"Safran is coming soon, please sit." It is obvious that they are close, probably neighbours. What kind of space does this house take up in this strange world? The strange state of this house, its voice echoing in my soul... I am trying to catch the silent and proud abundance brought by submitting in its every cell. Hazel and me are looking around, listening the sounds of the house. Sounds from the kitchen suppress the crackles from the stove. A coy wind outside, it is touchy as well as it is wild. After a short time, there is an image coming from a dream, she comes into the room like a murmur, a joyful tinkle; her steps are calm and unruffled, her long skirts are snow-white like the waves of an ocean, in foams.

"Princesses, welcome..." I have first met you then... Your face looks like a rose with a slight smile. We stand up. “Sit down,” she says and perches on the edge of the divan opposite us. Her voice is like a part from a touching song, it is sincere, misty, light, melodious. I expect her to ask “where did you come from? Why are you here?” but she doesn’t. She is in such a comfortable mood that her look and position is confident as if she is placing a lost part. She is in the face of us with her long dress, snow white scarf and face like moon. She is looking at us but as if she is watching beyond us. She hears us but as if she lays eyes on our souls. Without stopping smiling she says:

“How are you girls?”

We can say “Fine” with a voice like murmur together...

“May God give you health, it is so good to see you,” she says. Her speaking manner is an endless politeness blended with a hidden peace that nobody has. She is a heart that doesn’t observe the objects but the meaning behind them when looking. The tone of her voice is a melody brightening everything it touches. Everything both returns their own source and they break away from the tie of ordinariness. There is a thought that become distinct with that voice, giving value to you, to everything. The thought is completely far from the artificial, is innermost, starting to talk gurgling in the depth. The white scarf on her head lightens the feeling of devotion in her face. My soul is enlightened by her looks piercing like a hawk but staying still soft.

I heal with her melodious breath. I am falling from all lies I know to the only truth; rising bodiless, but I get smaller at the same time, I am falling apart. This unravelling, this frightening closeness with her is getting bigger and bigger, I cannot stop. My sudden arrival at this small shanty, I pour like cloudy waters on the floor. I throw myself to the ocean I find in those enchanted eyes. How can I tell her what? Words are empty, letters are inadequate here. Silence lands on my head. A giant agora is constructed on that three-step distance; lives are bought and sold. Who has the bridles? Nobody speaks. I can hear my own voice different from as it ever was.

“I would ask you only about a dream... We don’t want to keep you long, Hazel said that you understand dreams well. We, for that reason...” I am looking at Hazel as if telling her to speak. She keeps quite. Waiting. Everything is waiting.

“I know, no need to explain,” says Safran, and my voice crashes onto her palm once she raises her hand suddenly as if she tells me to be quite.

Only my heart snuggles silently. I came and saw you. Without knowing how I came. I was held! What do you have that makes me insane? This rhythm, this vibration. What's wrong with this place that doesn't let the grass grow under its feet? Tell me, who are you? How are you so? Take all my belongings, save me; I am on the verge of insanity. I am in the cradle of a wild, deep bottomless yard, of loneliness. Make me another you. Help for my weird states! A newborn breath for my addiction! Bring me a voice that doesn't have silence and mistake! A voice that doesn't know silence even if it is silent! If you are close to that mighty pencil that drew my skin and my face, don't stop, my life and my soul is yours. My flesh and bone sets off. I am all alone, I am desperate as if it was attacked by the existence on the way of life. Save me from me! Complete me! Give me myself so that neither life nor death exits. Show me your face during this sleep of sorrow. Throw a lasso at my life with Adam's wine, teach me that alchemy. Be my ancestor, let your ancestor be mine!

"Come!" only she says.

She catches me from my eyes. Here the attack leaving me breathless! There is nowhere to escape, I obey under the shadow of this plane desperately. My days, moments and life melt in that rhythm, this is a questionable siege winding up! I find an oasis far beyond the cage of these three letters. I undress from the wild I know as myself. A prayer in my soul, a trembling in my body sprouting all along. Now only Safran on the earth. Neither the lived past nor the expected future. This fire resembling the steel lied down on the anvil grants a joy to my soul as if there is no decay. I am about to die due to this closeness. I was not even a sound of this great plane resting its secret to heaven. I am silenced rather than I find my tongue in this relief. How can I tell my shadow about your existence? My existence is a tulip blooming with your existence, and my absence is a silence finding its tongue with you. You are both my tongue and my heart. Now I am here at this moment, I touch your solemnity spread to all times from end to end. Tell me, which great hand knotted me to you? Who is looking at me from your eyes? Who is calling me with your voice? Who is the one winding the fate like a clock at this moment that I go insane? Lo and behold! Mirage, lo and behold!

This fate circling between two of us touches the future like a boomerang. This silence, this waken form of propriety, right now, at this breath that the moment is rising through the moments like a chisel, at this place it wakes, even the air touching me cries out that you know that. The sky over us and the calm earth under our feet is blended with it. She is looking up and down me with thoughtful eyes, with a flying deliberate look on her face that is weak and glimpsing. She comprehends my state again and again suddenly, she hears the flowing dirty waters. A distinct hint in her face stops me. Her face is the most beautiful place to see in the earth. Now there is something cleaning and making true itself in this dirty water called me. A defect cleaned, covered in her presence. She makes me dive in a clean ocean but I don't know how to swim. I even run away from the water shouting and screaming. She looks at the ground for a moment, hesitates, I can consign all my life to this look. Actually she consigns me a load that I cannot carry with this look that destroys all doctrines, all '-ism's, all paradoxes, all philosophies.

Suddenly a solemnity appearing her on her clear face like a silent river and a joy accompanying it that she cannot hide. And her lending her snow-white hand to me. The sky is calling a hawk from the peak of a mountain,

"Come!" and repeated, "come!"

Now my head drops with a shame as my hands are knotted in hers. My hands are in a bowl of honey. Her voice is blowing my breath like a reed. It touches my purulent chest like an ointment. When I touch her hands a wind of mercy is shaking my soul as if they want to drop the decayed fruit. A turquoise river is flowing into my palms. Diamonds, rubies are flowing to its bed. An elixir is pouring from her hands that jar every bone in my body. A holy seal is impressed on my forehead. Her hands are pouring me from one bowl to another, throwing my heart to the smooth world. My back is rubbing on a placeless place beyond ancient tales, my feet steps on an immortal ground. She teaches an endless joy to words. Now love is in everything. The jot transforms to a crystal secretly.

This love swallowing the time and space mercilessly undressed like a black hole; space and time were bended. It collected me from my homeland. I will die of this love. I was altered with that love and transformed to an only moment with various faces. I put my worthless ugly head on the threshold of a suffering house. I didn't fit into the world, I shared the eternity for a short moment. I filtered my fate from a long scream. A pearl love case opened. I didn't stop and said what it said to me, I didn't stop, I became a cry as I had been a deaf mute and became silence as I had been a cry. I didn't know which mode I accorded, I didn't know which chalice I held with this shimmering wine. Ruby necklace fit on my breast. I approached to a name filled with love spears. I wore the sea on my head as a headdress. A curtain was lifted up between love and me, I was hung on its light like a drunk shadow. The twinkle, the light of this moment dazzled my existence, I took the past and headed to the future, I took the past and crashed it to the future. A pack of words opened, a forelock of mine touched a line. A gateway was opened slightly in the horizon, I went blind with its light. I predicted swifts in the twilight. I shook, I was about to die, I gave a soul and found the God.

"Come!"

May everything be my witness that I told it loudly, may earth and heaven be my witness, may man and bogey;

"Oh Beloved, my wish is your forgiveness, and I beg your love!"

On that day, we were embroidered by a counsellor in that atelier of love, Hazel and me...

***

My name is Dilruba. I walked on that path without knowing that I had dropped all the jewels in my pockets regarding life one by one with each step I take on that day. As a young girl at the milestone in her life, I was taking the hopes I had been trying to green in a hidden corner when I was going. I was swimming towards to a sequence of events that would change and transform my life and even the past on that way that I stepped out for dear life on that day. Neither Hazel nor I knew how much we would go further from the coast of life. We didn't know what storms, desolateness, offense and loneliness would hold us on this path. And when we turned back from this path towards Balgat without knowing anything would be the same as it had been. The seal impressed us on that day would be impressed on our whole life and these two souls trying to exist in a huge eternity as if it would never be erased. The truth of that our souls would never get better in another place would not change even if the film had been run back and we had turned back in the same rhythm. I would get used to this game in which existence and absence changing their costumes for all my life and I would watch this game with all its solemnity after long and painful days. Every time I extended my hand that construction of reality would be destroyed and it would give its place to more real, immortal and more complicated reality remaining the same.

I couldn't ignore Safran's utterance of "Come!" that great moment. Everything in my life was transitory; at the moments that I tried to understand the fate, there must have been only one answer both same and different for all those questions; one answer that could be the same when it was both this and that. Different reflections springing from one source and spreading to all directions like a light beam reflecting from a prism, and one true light source feeding those different reflections. These people living in a surprising humidity, these people away from greed and their silent states taking the material out of their heart and placing the spirit in the throne of their souls, this pure breath coming from the high walls, moment in the moment, thing in the thing, the perfection appearing their plain and modest states and the feeling of wholeness, the grace felt its footsteps on this wavy plane of this house, eternal happiness, foresight seeing the beyond of every being, that vibration felt in another way than all senses, that sense of justice. How they sounded me surreal!

While everything identified in the real world and the meaning I had known till that time had been based on the material, and I had been trying to open the door of a wealthy world with the key of material, I was buried in a horizon in which the priorities, truths, faults, shortly everything were upside down in this small house. I had first realized that some things are not hard and rigid in the circle of life in which I faltered. This balance, this harmony I couldn't identify with my imagination and finding the pure power clarified from all fiction between the seen and unseen and the true deeds caused by it was as difficult for me as lifting up a mystical curtain or dreaming about a land that I had never known if it had been exist or that I couldn't even imagine. Here, in this house, each day of which hours were adjusted for prayers was weighed on precision scales, and they were welcomed by trust and wisdom as if a river of divine light was flowing their gutters. These souls living their lives on the axis of a happiness thoroughly with the faithful peace of devotion to a holy truth were touching the light going on lightening them more and more with their hearts, and they realized this world and the other life after death separately like two circles touching each other slightly and they chose and explained the layers of the next world carefully while living in this world. The bond they established between these two worlds was so tied with each other that I would realize that they were travelling by the wings of both mind and heart with the help of real reflections.

Safran, this blessed person to whom every trace, every event, every situation in her life was a sign, was hearing the sounds and images on every day and night in a different way, unify the details of those including in a sign and did not waste any words she heard, even the blowing of the wind. Moreover, she didn't make an extra effort to do this, she was only listening the whispers of the secret love in every jot of the universe carefully. When these were happening she was reserving the possibility that every human she met in life could be Hızır in a deep modesty and devotion, so she valued everybody with a unique sense of justice. She acted impartially to a friend coming into her life with any reason without offending him, she kept the possibility that he was a medium of testing when it was time, she wrote peace and caution together in the same bracket of life.

The back of this blessed person, who looked out for God's consent although her every word, every step was temperate and well, who submitted the borders the justice had drawn to the full assiduously, turned to the words and acts that didn't touch her soul. To me, she was walking with a giant shimmering halo on her head and her faith penetrated in her flesh and bones, and blended with her blood.

This was a miracle. I can express what I experienced only with this word. I also ask myself what good it will bring to tell about this miracle. When I ask so, I go into a light opening in my consciousness forward like a flower. I am hosted in a place where the questions generates their own answers. I only watch. Watch the suffering and the joy wiping out all the sufferings... And perhaps the true miracle starts at the moment when you realize in surprise how you haven't noticed that you have been floating in miracles.

Discoverer! Now I accept that I always think about you since I tell about you. Please don't whisper the letters to me any more, knowing is horrible! I sheltered here not to know, not to hear. I escaped with all my power, I escaped from what I couldn't cope with. I don't get well from now on, I am half Majnun, half Layla on the earth. Even so I am telling, I wouldn't write without you, what would be left to be told? Without you... When I think how you captured me wholly there, no here, I am thinking about saying so:

Warn me where I should stop, don't let my tongue touch a wrong syllable. Don't let an exorbitant breath stop by here. Constrain me from the mouths saying "Me." Seeing that everything you have whispered me has been realized irresistibly in due time chains me. Wherever I head, the bond around my neck pulls met he place that you point. I hesitate to ask you something. What will you tell me about this time in the sky on your chest that I am familiar with, and what will you portray this time? How exhausting to experience this hesitation! When I turn to you, when I walk to you with a joy, I am dumbfounded like a frozen statue thinking what a storm will begin for at this time. A state of sticking, an ambiguity of perception. This.. This is a cry of saying "No, don't show me anything any more, I am powerless!"

Here is a place beyond reason. The place where I get tired from reading those words written by pearls vibrating on a glittering light. You cannot let me go and I cannot go away from you. I am a very helpless fugitive who cannot move, who stick where she is even if she seems going, who is repeating your words continuously. I am looking at the sketches of the portraits in my mind that you have painted with an unbelievable speed and intensity, the portraits of which one side is shade and the other side is dim. I hear clearly how the poetry in my soul and the lines I continuously listen have made me mature. I can see that I have been tested with loneliness, disease, poverty and injustice. I am like a stick running away from the wind blowing wildly, I lean on whichever side the wind wills, I run with all my effort where the wind blows me.

You are the most beautiful form of being human in this era. You told me, "Be careful about what you are thinking!" but you didn't need to say more; the universe were flowing through you with that perfect love. You, the most beautiful seal of love that I haver ever seen and will see! You were the pure gutter in which the magnificence stealing me away was flowing through! You, the one peeling my shells one by one and leaving me like a naked seed and then releases it to the fruitful earth!

4
Footmark on the Desert

Everything was still new so that I couldn't understand how much my life had changed. The routine life in the campus was going on. I didn't know that I was walking towards a passionate love that was impossible to escape from. There was only one thing that I felt, the colour of time flowing through life started to whiten and I started to hear an unknown voice shouting met hat everything had an end. Life quickened its steps and showed me those faint shadows circling in its circuit.

A few days after I had first seen Safran I found myself in front of her small and pretty house with a drawing that was impossible to escape. She welcomed me again with her clear and deep voice saying "Welcome!". This small house, this nice room was so alive that one could think that they would breath. The partly bent floor, worn corners of the thin rug, there were moments that every detail grumbled something and then kept quiet. This divan made carefully sometimes smiled at you warmly, it was waiting with a silence hinting that it understood you. You would feel that this house of which walls had been whitewashed was breathing together with you. The modest soul of this house shined suddenly in its simple and pretty look. As Safran was walking in this house, swaying, prostrating herself, as her blessed feet were touching on the floor, as her heart was beating in this house, the house filled with the divine light, it expanded, stirred and revived. As if the stars sparkled in the house and the sky listened voices of the conversations bending its head. The heartbeat of the universe echoed on your chest.

Safran's house was crowded on that day. My soul was running continuously and circling around a giant point until it was out of breath although I was waiting among the women shining like angels. Safran's soft and merciful voice was spreading through the crowd like a light. Tens of women in this small room calmed down and a calm and sweet sea appeared in their eyes with the start of Safran's speaking. Eyes filled with moist looks revealing the shores of this sea. Their faces were in the peace of blue sky, their lips were moving with pray and gratitude and their hearts were mystical inconceivably. How it was difficult to hide yourself in such an atmosphere! Safran stated that she knew your most inner passions, tendencies and even the darknesses that you even didn't know in a mode specific for her. This statement was definitely with love and compassion. You knew as if you loved a child, as if you're being meant all the world concluding that there was no place to escape from this giant mirror of which rain had been blended with mercy in the middle of the world.

Safran was sitting next to me with a smiling face, and the echoing of her voice to me was blinding from the edge of the divan I perched. Her voice wasn't smooth, bare or cornered like the voice of any human, but misty, sincere, mysterious and layered as if it was coming behind thick curtains. The perfect balance in her soul reflected to her voice, this voice was not only a "voice" at all; it was a case of the truth of love hidden and veiled in the tone of the voice. She examined the pocket of her jacket while I was looking her beautiful eyes as if flowing in a gurgling waterfall. "I will give you something," she said. After a while one of the women started to flutter as if the doors of the heavens opened suddenly or the roof flew away and she left in the flood. The state of the poor woman fluttering in her white scarf terrified me. However nobody interfered. Far from interfering, nobody looked at her. Only Safran stopped for a moment and waited the woman whose fluttering had interrupted her voice to recover. However the woman was struggling as if she was having an epileptic seizure, then she was releasing her voice with an unbearable pain. I froze on the very spot and waited not knowing what to do. At last the woman collapsed, it was clear that she was trying to take deep breaths under the white scarf quietly. The woman trying to hide herself with an eternal sense of respect wiped her face with rose water and calmed down. However, as Safran carried on speaking, the women were shaking like crops met by the storm on the field and this hot wind pierced through whoever it touched with the love spear like a gazelle shot by an arrow. Even if I didn't understand what was happening here, I felt that strange and hot wind on my body and soul and I was trying to avoid it as much as I could. At this very moment I heard a deafening voice:

"Hey, the people of Cabülka! Hey, the first stop of those looking fort he truth!"

I turn to the direction the voice is coming, but I cannot see anything other than the shining horizon. In fact the East, West, North and South is covered with this light. Lush black mane of my red horse is flying, it starts to run at full gallop, this black horse is harsh and wild, I tighten the reins, the saddle was about to fall, the horse rears up, I lean against its neck not to fall down, in vain! The more the horse struggles as I shout. I give up hope. I can breath hardly, can't see anything, reins slip down from my hands, the world is rotating around me like a top, I fell on my back noisily. When I lift my head with difficulty I see the front feet of a white horse moving calmly.

"Are you alright?"

The owner of the voice is none other than the veiled person on the white horse. Although I am sure that I have broken bones, I rise as soon as I hear this voice.

"Stand up hey traveller!" This statement encourages me and I stand up, he looks at me with big, beautiful eyes smiling behind the veil.

"Where are you headed?" I have no idea where I am going as well as I have no idea where I am. I can't say so but I just say,

"I am looking for the world of truth."

When he hears this, a merciful smile blended with surprise and pity appears on his face.

"Where is your food?"

Clearly he is making fun of me. His slim, delicate body is covered with a green cloth, he is wearing a head-dress on his beautiful head, his veil reveals his beautiful eyes. He has a sword on her waist ornamented with rubies and crystals. I lose myself because of his beauty.

I can't look into his eyes, if I look, I will die, but I don't die. His bolted big hazel eyes pierces my soul like a bullet.

"But I don't know where I am," I say.

"Here is the land of Cabülka!" His voice is coming from all directions, from my inside, outside, the voice enslaves me.

"Are you sure you want to move on? The valleys of this land are full of dangers for novices like you."

He asks that to test me, to test my intention. He controls his horse moving in situ with its bridles.

"Yes, I want to go," I stand out.

"Have you thought well? There is no turn from this way, the ones having got lost on the way haven't got better, and thousands who managed to pass over this land have been destroyed. Moreover you need to know that the doors of return will close once you set off."

"I want it," I can say with fear.

A mercy lightens in his hazel eyes.

"What is your wish?" he asks.

"My wish is to arrive in the country of love, if I am allowed," I say.

A glory appears in his eyes at this time,

"I warned you hey aspirant, if you are sincere with your wish, then hop on; we are responsible for taking those who desire love to the other side."

Once he extend his fair hand, my red horse appears just in front of me in its meekest way with a single act of him. There is whiteness on the horse's face down its nose in the shape of a comet. It sparkles as the horse moves.

"Are you ready?" asks the cavalry.

"I am ready." I say.

"The first test of Cabülka traveller is with his horse. If you want to understand your horse, first you need to understand yourself. The horse is sensitive for your thought. The first condition to be a good rider is to know yourself well, understand your own feelings well and to be able to control yourself. First think about what you want your horse to do with sincerity and seriously. Do you understand?"

"I think so." I said although I didn't understand clearly.

He pointed the horse in front of me and said, "Then forget everything you know and hop on." He was holding the bridles loosely with one hand and caressing the mane with the other on the back of his white horse.

"When you are on the horseback your body isn't only yours, the horse feels your feelings, remember! Trust its instincts, it will feel your thoughts. You should reconcile with it, look into its eyes knowing what you want. Don't make it anxious without knowing what you want. If you have a peace of mind, the horse feels this and becomes attuned. Talk to it. Slowly and calmly. If you understand and control yourself there won't be any problems." He said and added, "You should establish a firm trust with him. It understands your explanation for life and yourself from your movements. Take your time to understand yourself."

He must have understood that I didn't know what was the determined and confident position like on the horse, so he said:

"Trust your instincts and be relaxed." I hold the saddle gathering the bridles of this noble horse with red body and black mane and rode it in one move stepping on the stirrup. I was holding the bridles loosely. At the same time I was trying to establish a bond between it and me placing trust by feeling certain about myself and my feelings. Then I slightly tightened the horse's body with my legs, balanced my weight setting my feet on the stirrups and looked at he cavalry as if I asked him what I should do.

He bended his head slightly,

"Not bad for the beginning," he said and added, "The horse feels all your fear and anxiety, the more relaxed you are, the better it is! Now follow me!"

Then, the Cavalry spurred his horse and flicked the bridles, and I did the same: "Giddap!" We started to run with the wind like flying. I could smell musk carried by the fresh air and I wanted to cry for his help. I wanted to know who he was, but I kept silence thinking to ask this would be disrespect.

"Don't ask who I am, you will know in the future," he said.

We rode as if riding on the wings of the wind for a while. We passed through long, dark rivers and huge dense forests. We passed through marshes, deserted cities, mountains of which peaks weren't seen, we travelled far without having a break. It seemed to me that we had travelled so much that I couldn't finish all my life. How much longer would we travel? While I was thinking so, finally we stopped in front of a palace. First he dismounted, then helped me to dismount. He turned to me and said,

"We have still travelled very little." I got desperate exhaustingly. What kind of place here it was?

"Here is the hidden world, there is neither time nor space here. Haven't I told you to forget everything you know? So you haven't." He said.

"I am trying to forget." I said.

"Then forget that you forgot." He said. What was it like to forget that you forgot? After travelling some more, we stopped before a bling huge palace.

"Here is love palace of the people of hearts, you will go in there alone, give my kind regards to them," he said.

"Who sends regards?" I asked. His hazel eyes were sweeping me off of my feet.

"They will know," he said.

I walked through a thick light as if my feet stepping on clouds. A warm and sweet odour was attracting my soul. I knocked the door of the love palace encrusted with jewels. The gold foiled door at least ten times taller than me opened slightly with a noise. A scraggly dervish appeared with old clothes and looked at me with asking eyes.

"What is your name?" he asked.

When he saw that I was thinking, he started to look up my name on the edict he was holding.

"Your name is in the list, how did you come here?" he asked.

"I came with regards," I said.

"We accept regards with pleasure. Hey pretender, welcome," he said and the gold foiled door opened widely at this time.

"Take off what you love except God. No other than a heart full of love can go in there."

The inside was so beautiful that words could not express; it could not be put on paper. I walked following the dervish. He turned and said,

"Walk towards the voices, follow me!" I walked towards the voices I heard for a while not knowing where I stepped on, even not feeling I stepped on the ground as if walking on the air. I heard deep murmurs through the various joyful wood-notes. Then I started to hear prayers, I walked through invocations and whispers.

"Go inside one of these spheres and wait." He said.

Everything was occurring so nice and formless that I just went with the flow. I went inside the thing he called as sphere bending my head. Although I couldn't lift my head from my toes I could see this sphere was spinning around itself like a planet and lost itself. However, the ones sitting inside was only waiting as their heads dropped. I sat on a divan covered with pearls. Inside was so colourful that I had difficulty to identify the object. In spite of that all the world could be seen from this transparent sphere, even the other rooms of the big palace were clear. Even the beginning and end of Cabülka, its astonishing existence, rivers we had passed through on horses with the graceful person, deserted lands were seen. There was so many things in this sphere that I didn't know which one to look at. Everything, everybody was clear and fluid like water. I thought I was falling in it at a moment and I threw myself on one side involuntarily and fell onto a soft wing. When I turned to that way with relief, I realized a giant bird that I was holding one of the feathers of its wing. I knew it was phoenix without knowing how I knew. The phoenix turned its head to me, a sparkling crown was circling its head colourful with thin and feathers full of colour, and this crown made it more beautiful. Unbelievable! Also this bird was speaking. It looked into my eyes with a love that I had never experienced before and said,

"The feather you are holding on is yours, take it, you will need it," How kind-hearted and generous phoenix it was, I couldn't thank it enough. I had difficulty to see further due to the sparkling of this feather resembling a rainbow, but however Cabülka was seen very clearly. At that moment, a beautiful lady looking like a gazelle brought a series of many-coloured wine glasses on a pearl tray,

"Hey, pretender, here you are." She said.

When she saw that I was looking unwillingly,

"This is not the like the wine you have known, go on!" she said. When the wine dampened my lips, at that very moment, the journey ended and I opened my eyes. Safran was leaving a musky rosewood rosary ignoring my surprised looks with her smiling face.

"This is a treasure, count this in your heart and release your voice to the sky." She said.

5
Hearing Again

Countless waves arouses any moment
Not a drop lessens
The knowledge comes from there
Voice is its pearl (Shebusteri)

During the period I stayed at the guesthouse, I watch the stars sitting on the steps of the fire escape at some nights. There were a few places to be alone in that big building. Sometimes Kırlangıç and I chatted on the edge of the stairs. Kırlangıç was a smart girl with a clear mind. Sometimes she asked for hope behind her gloomy eyes. I went to Safran's with her many times, each of those short trips was a long adventure. According to Kırlangıç, her life was full of troubles and followed a difficult course. Of course I didn't have a lot of ideas about her life at first, but as I knew her better I could see that there was a deep faith behind her whimpers. The biggest similarity between us was the existence of unluckiness enslaving our lives. On those days it seemed us very difficult to graduate. Weariness winded us as if we would live in this guesthouse until the end of our lives. Matters such as endless tuitions, accommodation expenses, heavy courses, the difficulties of finding a job in the current conditions were jumping in our minds. Life was so difficult to us even in these early stages and probably we wanted to quaff from this pure water we found because of this.

Kırlangıç was an unusual silhouette in my social circle starting to change at that time. She neither lived exactly like a Sufi nor she broke with sufis. She was living in modes changing like wavy shores. Perhaps all of us were doing so, but she didn't have an exact devotion or she was hiding, rather she had some priorities in her life. Somehow she always had a state of deprivation. The state of falling behind and complaining was reflecting on her feature. The word of 'difficulty' was in the first place in her vocabulary, however she didn't want to reveal the other words of the vocabulary, she was tight-lipped in this way. She added some humour everything in the daily life including difficulties, a comedy covered by the sense of complaining was detected in her manners. Or sometimes humour was covering her complains, this strange tide was like the touchstone of her personality, she neither gave up complaining nor irony. Complaining eventually reached up a show of prank.

She didn't share many things about herself, maybe she couldn't, but when you got a little closer to her, a difficult childhood flowing behind the uneasy wiggles appeared. Her childhood was a life period that had been restricted by a serious disease and full of deprivations. When you were with her, your conscience breathing in the very deep of your soul remembered how life was hard and Kırlangıç didn't to say anything fort his, you heard a sad melody glimpsing in her slim body. A deep but quiet cry was heard in the impatient delicacy in her romp state and in the shadows of that defeated warrior sparkling in her eyes. This cry was undefinable and so obscure that one couldn't be aware of at first. It was like a clear and pure sound getting stronger as approached. Therefore she could hardly hide the tedium penetrated in her soul in spite of the joy she gave around. I was surprised that how she could stay as herself when she was hiding so much. This state was naturally pouring like the melody of her soul. Her quick-wit and readiness in solving problems puzzled me. A hesitation found only in very clever people disappeared suddenly and left its place to the existence of strong and sharp wit. I heard the strong and clear heartbeats of the questioning in her silence. She enjoyed life, laughed and her wit manifested with the details that only a few people could catch. It was wonderful to be with her, her extraordinariness, continuous wits and hints relieved you. She was like a unique painting in which the hundreds of different colour tones came to light.

A delicate head attached to her small body. Brown wavy hair. Matt, brown looks those were as so, in which sarcastic sparkling appeared and reminded steppes. The shadows of nebulous seeking crouched down behind those looks. A love that was always alive, true and unique in the roots of this seeking. A humour always ready under his tongue touching the bitterness of life. A balanced, quiet and rhythmic features, a thin and delicate bone structure. An almost abraded, note-less fragility that was hid by quick moves. A mild and unassertive expression. Dark colours hiding her colourful personality. Small black purses dangling one side with thin long handle. Her holding the handle of the purse a little slickly and a little strongly with one arm. A hesitant condition between pulling and not pulling the handle. The books she was holding like a baby in her other arm. Tiny, miniature shoes. Stretching out as "Anywaaayy..." with a matt voice between the conversations. The sharp clarity of the voice while it was stretched out. A quiet tone in this 'anyway' implying that she could stand up all difficulties in life but now got tired a little bit. And a feeling in my heart that defined Kırlangıç as "the shy victory of defeat."

I don't remember how we met Kırlangıç although I check my memory greatly. We must have met unawares when we were together with sufis and got used to each other. I must have seen her with Zümrüt for the first time. In fact she always imitated Zümrüt, Zümrüt tried to hide her laugh kindly covering her opening mouth with one hand, and she laughed until she burst into tears. They were very close friends. Zümrüt was brunette, she had a soft and sincere voice, her mimics animated her voice and she was unduly attached to the rules. Her most distinct feature was that she never waived. Her room could be seen when you pass the slope towards the next dorm building and the road surrounded by trees. White curtains flapping from the open windows of which two wings opened on the second floor welcomed you. When the curtains were flapping the neat state of the inside drew attention. Four beds on two bunk beds made up tightly, sabots put under the bunk bed carefully, tidy desks, chairs on the same line with desks as if drawn by a ruler, floor stones shining like a mirror... This room was like the royal suit of the dorm, this room always smelt sweet. I didn't want to be in this room too much, the cleanness disturbed me, I didn't know how to behave.

The Sufi circle in the guesthouse started to widen after Hazel, Kırlangıç and Zümrüt in a way that I didn't understand, I met another Sufi staying in the dorm nearly every day and surprised. In time I started to meet sufis from other dorms. We gathered in the middle of the night and went to see the sufis in the other dorm within walking distance. Perhaps we were only ten people coming together but these ten people accounted for hundreds of ten for me. The bond among us was so tight that now the dorm and the combine life here started to be a warm home environment that I longed for. Nevertheless the desire to own a home was preying on my mind in spite of the warmth of the energy here.

I must confess that I didn't know what I was doing exactly on those days, that is at the beginning of the submission, I abandoned myself to the waters of a sparkling and real river and I was travelling on this sweet and gushing river. My inclining was as natural as a thin, green branch extending its end to the sun. Those were the years that my thoughts sought the truth breaking into pieces. It was the seeking of my mind, heart and conscience for only one summit. I inclined to a love in which all the creatures melted in the same pot, I couldn't stop. I didn't want to stop. Besides, if you change in this way, not a lot of choices you will have, there is only one choice: Setting off.

On one of those days flowing with harmony like dancing Kırlangıç, Hazel, Zümrüt and I met at the time that we had agreed before and departed to Balgat. The whispers of a mysterious voice touching the lens of my heart were heard in this small shanty. A fate of which head the stars flocked, in which the sky and the earth emerged and water and earth busted with abundance was reviving for me gradually. A clear and definite sign of a love that I could touch was accompanying my every step like the blue sky I felt of which fresh breath on my forehead. It was impossible to hide from this love even for a second. I couldn't catch on the irrationality of finding a nook through the flowing moments on those days.

This love was a domino show in which a huge reality beginning to move from the end and from the beginning at the same moment was seen. The sound of the whole universe changed even on those early days when I submitted to the endless love. In fact the sound of anything started to change with my hearing of Safran's voice. Her voice was nice, merciful, humane and positive unlike the voices I had ever heard. The difference in this voice was that the tone that invited everything it touched to return their origin. Not only her voice but every crackle, every clinking and even every murmur from the world found a meaning. Every speed, every slowness, every image, every motion, every movement was a different way of reading. The sound of a falling leaf made me look at it as if I witnessed a miracle. Even the silence flowing through the noise of life was speaking in a special language. Every jot was loaded with a sign and waiting for me to perceive the messages about myself and the seeking; an exhaust sound, a door creak represented a call reaching me from far away. The tumult of the city was changed to a floodlit city, I was choked with the signs as many as the breaths of the people. Every happening, every flow became the music of an endless love; every rhythm, every move swarmed with loving shadings describing the reviving of this love gradually. Every look concluded with a mercy, and every prayer with an acceptance. Somehow the troubles of the past and future started to melt in the present moment, the passing time got off my back and my breath was spreading to all times as if snuggling to blessed good news. My feet was walking as if they didn't belong to me, my hands got rid of all chaos and it sank into a deep silence, my existence was wheeling about in a fluid and indifferent motion as if it got rid of all its obscurity.

That day Safran was very happy, she grew prodigiously, her features became more distinct with light, she became more distant as she came near as if she was looking from the invisible summit of a mountain. Zümrüt extended her head as if rose leaves was pouring on her brunette face, quiet and smiling with a happy look. There was no sign of Kırlangıç's teasing, she was waiting resting her hands on her lap seriously, and there was a pinkness and softness of the dough being fermented on Hazel's face. Smiling, calm, hopeful, fruitful. A strong energy among us... A simplicity touching me, Kırlangıç, Hazel and Zümrüt in turn, penetrating until the tar burrows somewhere deep inside us, moving the heavy stones of sorrow,reestablishing the letters we had identified with its existence and we were aware of and belong to as much as ourselves.

Safran's long skirt with dark coloured flowers are pouring down her knees, she perches on the divan as if she is about to stand, her hands are in her lap, her shoulders are slightly low, she tightens her scarf loosening as she talks, she pulls the edge of the scarf forward from her forehead, the sparkling halo of her face is completed with this last move. She is resuming on speaking. Her looks are just as clear as her thoughts and in the same seriousness with what she tells, an inclusive mastership in her body language being conscious everything she says. She resumes after she holds her voice in her nasal passage for a moment and thinks, her looks are so shiny and eyeful that we cannot look at her eyes directly. She feels the air as if she is touching the guitar strings,

"If you taste a little honey from the eternal hive of the love, don't think it is because of you, don't think so and respect the love. Be the enemy of the soul ordering evil! Take the love that hugs you from four sides as a blessing; it has been appreciated for you from all eternity."

Gül Hanım, sitting on her usual place at the point that the divan ends, has dropped her head to her right shoulder slightly, her face is turned to the left a little, she is there as if she is whirling.

Safran went on,

"Get clean like a breastfed infant. On the other hand wipe your face with the cloth of helplessness day and night, don't touch the skirt of existence, disappear in between so that love appears. Why will love appear in one having a big ego?

Kırlangıç has dropped the shadow of her long eyelashes on her face, is looking at her hands looking like a heart, it seems like she is hiding a ruby. Her eyelashes resembling hand fan lifts, her looks are like a long song. Like a painful song which wants to hold the source of the voice. As Safran speaks, a pink freshness appearing at the moment of the sunrise spreads to the faces, all portraits are painted behind a veil resting as if it will be pulled from the eyes. A silence tangling in our bodies unfastens, this room smells like an ocean. It pulls the silence from the edge with each letter, shines between us, we flow like water and we are added to strange dimensions.

I close my eyes with surprise. The choked gutters of time are dug, move with a deep cry, residues break up.

"Hey pretender! Here the meaning is important not the form, why are you surprised?"

When I turn my head after a short staggering I see that the talker is Phoenix.

"They accept the ones who waive to the world of love, those who don't waive their loved cannot come to this blessed door."

"Love of world?" I say with a murmur, then I remember the feather made of solid light it has given to me. When it sees that I am staring surprisingly,

"And you?" says, "One cannot come in to the house of the knowledge empty-handedly, what have you brought?"

I find myself in a dim tunnel. I walk towards the light appearing like a spot ahead even until the farthest point. As I get closer to the light I realize a group of people in white clothes watching a show with curious looks. The crowd so clamped together that I cannot watch the show but I can see only the head of a man further. People's backs block me like a wall, the shoulders of none of them move and let me pass. Somehow I find myself just in front of the show passing through the feet of the crowd crawling on the ground finally. Then I understand why all those people are watching like a speechless icon.

Rotating bowls full of water in two hands of a man that I can't see; bowls in each bowl full of water but rotating reverse side, my God, they are about to fall, but not only a drop of water is pouring. When the bowls below are rotating to the right, smaller bowls are also rotating to the left, moreover there are bowls over them with dancing clear water rotating to the right. Top it all, the man is whipping all these bowls like peg tops, my eyes staring at the speed of the bowls don't see anything else, all these round bowls and the water in them introduce such a marvellous display that the ones seeing them are rooted to the spot! The strange thing is that the young man whose face cannot be identified doesn't make an effort, the long strings attached to the bowls in his hands are felt even if they are not seen, that's enough to move his fingers as if conducting a puppet. He looks at me for a moment and asks the same question again, "Hey, you, have you paid for this show?"

I am ashamed before the crowd and try to return through the feet of the crowd, when I am out of the circle watching the show I examine my pockets. Thanks God! There is only one blackish coin in my pocket. I become happy, I have money to give, my heart fills with hope, so I can watch the rest of the show. He rises his head, I breath out, my soul breaks into pieces due to the beauty of his smiling.

I open my eyes, Kırlangıç offers tea on a round plastic tray. Safran's quoting voice pierces my ears like an arrow,

"Hey the Phoenix of God that the souls revolve around, thanks God you have returned back from the Mount Kaf!"

6
Meetings

> You get drunk with only one glass of water...
> How can you drink with a subservient who
> drinks but not gets drunk? (Sheikh Attar)

Here is a dream that the space is melt and an alive voice walks quickly towards the timelessness through this melting. A world of meaning that a warm joy spreads to the passing days, that a strange meeting of which subject is ambiguous occurs every time the world is covered with the veil called night. A chain of meetings that melt all the hardness of life and sharp spears stuck on my memorising are taken out one by one. A smiling whispering that every move, every image, every occurrence caught by my eyes and lie them down the rays as if taking out the material from the time. I was feeling this smiling to the hilt even if I didn't know from which source it was shining from, examining the relief touching my soul, I was waiting for a closeness from it in every direction I look at.

This smiling first appeared on Safran's face and it spread from there to the colourful flowers, to the harps and drums of which tone penetrated into souls, to the calm, quiet and clear rivers, to a clear sky and to the sounds waving through a silk atlas. This smiling attached to the wall of the endless happiness greening the thirsty and fragile branches of life and was pouring in my palms like a cheerful echo crashing its head to the horizon and turning back. This was the shadow of a hope heralding wisdom, submission and moreover revival while staying still like a dead. This smiling penetrating into the whole universe and the whole past like good news, was shaking the chaus holding my senses like a spiral day by day, caught my soul as if it wanted to show me everything could be as fresh as a daisy.

Safran used to smile as if someone had drawn a propriety sopped in blessing on her face. That elusive expression was walking around us like an abundance first appeared in her face and then flowed from heart to heart. That smiling was an alive, vivacious thing, it had a voice and a soul, I felt that it nearly walked.

Sometimes Safran told me to close my eyes and to present my state to Yusuf faced.* Whenever I called him, whenever I turned my face to him, he definitely responded me. Whatever I asked him, wherever my letters fell, he put them on the truth and turned the faces of the sentences to me. Again and every time he showed me hope.

He vacated an unsaid sherbet that I fired to my cells with of which taste down to my throat during the times when I sit with closed eyes, quietly and motionless, perhaps at a timeless moment. I supposed that the whole world, everything that existed consisted of this sherbet. There were such times I presented my state that he responded to my each state and listened to my prayers with an endless patient. At these moments of annihilation I was watching the things he showed me, or I heard what he said in a strange and obscure way. I had no idea where the voice was coming from.

I was wandering about like a drunk sank in incantation with my whole being without stepping on the ground, my day and night was overflow with his love and I was ready to die for this love. I looked forward to night especially, when the dark fell I rejoiced like a lover that reached his darling. I continuously talked to him, headed him, I couldn't spend a moment without him. This state lasted for a long time. At some nights he sent me presents from his face. At those moments my will melt away and I passed through states beyond all bearing. I was buried in an endless happiness putting my head on his feet when I lay to sleep, the heaven for me was the continuity of his existence. It was the irresistible fire of his love that penetrated every moment. Burning in this fire had been the greatest thing since the beginning of my existence.

Sometimes he didn't use letters when he talked to me. He only passed the images through my mind in an inconceivable speed and sharpness if one tried to say. Sometimes, even without doing this, that is without using images, he chose such a form to speak that one didn't manage to express. I understood what he said as if an elixir was dropped on my

---

* Through the story of Yusuf, Allah taught the believers that a person who possesses true Islamic character can master the world with the strength of their character. The example of the Prophet Yusuf shows that a person of high and pure character can overcome severe circumstances and be successful. So handsome/beautiful people of high and pure character are called as 'Yusuf-faced.'

cognition or I discovered a part of my body that I hadn't known how to use. He showed me clearly without using the elements such as shape, colour, manner, form, length, width. While I was about to die for his only word, he sometimes spoke at length and made me pass out. Perhaps he wanted me to understand that only word as if extending over centuries.

There was no end of sights he made me watch and I was wandering through peregrinations. The being eventually reached the freedom I dreamt about and eluded the record of place and time by courtesy of his beauty and his benevolent breath. Walls, all solid objects, sounds, goods, people, earth and sky and the flowing life were flowing like sparkling waters with his blessed light, and whispered met hat every jot was alive. However, I could identify only him from the sides that he turned my face with his loving hands in this half-opened magnificent door, there was no permission to see anyone else. The only thing that I wanted to see was that the lights of his palace of beauty that I wasn't able to cope with.

7
Miracle

"When a man is helpless, a light or a dark rises from that helplessness. The devil has been left in darkness due to his helplessness and the angels have emerged into the light due to their helplessness. And miracle does so; God's verses become so. They prostrate when they are helpless."

(Şems-i Tebriz)

On those days, when I first met Safran, I read in a book I found in the library that there were three stages of Sufism; according to the book, the firs stage is 'puzzle', the second is 'wonder' and the third is 'miracle'. Puzzle contained all these stages even it didn't reveal it at first. Actually the word contained all meanings these three stages met; puzzle, wonder and miracle. I was experiencing this situation in deed even if I didn't realize it those days. All these three stages contained each other endlessly in a mystical way. Each was both in and out of the other stages; puzzle was both in and out of wonder and miracle; wonder was both in and out of puzzle and miracle; miracle, the last stage, was in puzzle and wonder but at the same time out of them. Wonder contained both puzzle and miracle; miracle contained both puzzle and wonder. I thought what did this mean sitting at one of the wooden tables in the library, I know understand better what Hazret Inayet Han means with these three stages in his book. Actually all these stages existed in every step of journey of sufism; these three stages were hidden already in every breath you take during this mystical journey. It manifested itself and hid in turn; the road meant going through these three stages thousands and millions of time and departs from those three without leading away from the main road. It meant starting from those three at the same time and arriving at those three at the same time, and passing through those three at the same time. Life contained every form of these three stages during this mysterious process for which the language remained incapable. At all curves of this winding road the ineffable harmony of these three stages was portrayed, but every curve preserved its place in itself. Every direction you turned, every vibration to your ear, every piece of earth you stepped, even every letter your tongue touched on gathered the range of signs in itself in a way that the eye did not see and the heart did not understand and left you utterly 'helpless.'

A gift and beauty leaving helpless and marvellous miracles arousing amazement.. Rising infinite blessings again and again like the Sun.. Starting to breath the true meaning of the word 'miracle' which means 'left helpless' every morning.. Well, what was our part in this process exactly, only watching? To be able to wait calmly at the places going beyond perception, to be patient, to be able to drink the existence at the moment it transforms to poetry like wine.. This portrait appearing as one surrendered meant knowledge which became definite as one believed, was steady as a rock and without mistake.

Miracles which arousing amazement even at the earliest times that I stepped into the Puzzle and leaving one helpless in the end started to manifest themselves like a sun. I say Sun, because when you experience this situation the lights of the miracle of existence brighten everywhere in your universe, hidden seeds start to sprout until there is not even one dark or gloomy corner, your earth wakes and becomes blessed; you and everything included in your perception start to be floating for ever and ever in the capsizing of an astonishment. Beyond, waters flow over to the valley of wonder unceasingly.

I said Sun, because man cannot look to naked eye at the Sun, cannot stare at the Sun carelessly, is not strong enough to do this. This is impossible physically, the spectacular power of the Sun prevents this; you see the Sun above and you say "here is the Sun" looking up for a moment, its lights in great brightness reach even to a marsh, everyone sees this. The sky is brilliant, you raise your head, the Sun is screaming, the whole sky shouts, all flowers confirm this hand by hand, all seas open their skirts all along to be filled with the lights of the Sun. The whole universe, every place stepped on feels this, but they do not catch the Sun's eye; it is so hard, you cannot confront it with your barest state. You know the Sun, that draws away the darkness under your eyelids, you hear it in and out of yourself, from every direction, but you should surrender before it, it makes you helpless, you cannot look into its eyes. This hurts you, this looks over your soul, it cannot be coped with.

If you speak, your tongue gets burnt, if you do not speak you cannot conceive and you will go all around crazily like you fall in a hole of obscurity. The mercy of God and His closeness to His creature makes you helpless; undeviating magnificent timings cause you to believe again and again about that He is only and one. You walk on that thin and sharp sword between speaking and not speaking; and then you realize that aspirants already experience these miracles at any moments; non-aspirants always ask “Where is it?” even if they are in an ocean of miracles.

8
Love

"When I am away from your beauty, my body is like a wreck, and my spirit is the owl of that wreck.
Oh please, turn headstalls this side!" (Celaleddin Rumi)

That day Safran was speaking deeply, more silently, more loaded. Her voice was streaming. That day we listened to her at that small room with her daughter Didem, Gül Hanım and Kırlangıç.

"They gave a mouth to the Sufi suffering patiently for many years saying brave words. She is now red-hot as a continuously gushing volcano; this both happens by itself and is a rule of corporeity. The pot will start to effuse in time."

Safran spoke for another while. After a while, I didn't hear what she said. I let myself to her musical voice and had its pleasure. She stopped speaking after a while and turned to Kırlangıç and me and asked "Girls, are you hungry?" She turned to Gül Hanım who was sitting on the floor at the corner of the divan as usual, and said:

"Gül, have some food prepared for the girls". Gül Hanım runs towards the kitchen leaning on one of her legs.

Floor table is prepared in the twinkling of an eye. There are beans, rice, pickle and dried fruit compote in a white tray. There is home-made flat-bread next to the tray. Gül Hanım leads us seeing Kırlangıç and me playing hard to get, she lays the tablecloth on her lap and

"Come on girls, ..." She recites *bismillah* as if leaning her head on a steadfast mountain.

Here, meal is a blessed ceremony, each bite is pimping. I kneel in front of the tray as if sliding down from the divan. Safran cuts big pieces from the flat-bread and gives us, we take and put it near the plate. It is about to be mid-afternoon. Safran makes a pitch for eating from the bottom of her heart. Kırlangıç and I again were caught in current without making out anything about past and future. While handing up the pickle, Safran looked into my eyes with her deep big eyes, then an impish, happy look. I almost feel her breath from that distance. I hear melody of her face and hands. There is more than mother warmness in her breath. There is an attraction, whirlpool that holds, bundles up the person. She throws a lasso with her breath, memorizes with her words.

She says, "Princess, let's eat, don't hesitate".

Princess... Princess... The sound is echoing, hitting me, Kırlangıç, and the walls. Princess... I am pleased, this happiness is such wide that pleasure arising from this unexpected intimacy caress my face. Ropes of my heart slip and break... It is the time when darkness meets the light. That sound, that jingle of the spoon makes while putting on the tray implies the freedom of a chain breaking off its ring. Kırlangıç tells something, even though my brain hears, it doesn't understand it. She (Kırlangıç) spoons up the dried fruit compote readily as she is adapted. We catch each other's eyes; she touches everything gently with her thin well-shaped fingers. What a comfortable place, what a welfare table! Resting one of my legs to my chest, I spoon up rice with vermicelli, I relax as the rice melts in my mouth, and dried fruit compote leaves freshness. I forgot how to sit at a floor table; in fact I don't know how to sit. We are happy, there is an intimacy between us and the people we don't know but I don't know where this intimacy comes. I leave inexperienced me into trusty of my instinct.

I watch for the words that Safran will say. How will those letters integrate in the air, which words will they assume the form of? Which veil of the existence will disappear? Which secrets, which processes will I introduce to them. I watch as a soldier focused on the victory at the bulwark.

Safran seeing me still thoughtful touches my shoulder gently as if she wants to wake me up, looks at my face.

"Come on princess, what are you thinking? Why aren't you eating?!" When I look at Safran's face, I see the Cavalry with white head-dress in front of the love palace.

"Let's go, they are waiting for us!"

Once again we were going as if we are on the wings of the wind, black mane of the red horse flies for ever and ever, Cavalry doesn't make a statement, just says,"They are waiting for us, we don't have time." We again passed through green valleys, defiles, long rivers. We crossed cold, snow-capped mountains, shallow lakes, marshes. We reached a big iron gate. Knocker was made of melody. When it was touched, a pleasing voice was surrounding everywhere. Cavalry was nailing his beautiful hazel eyes to my eyes and was saying "Princess" allusively. "Remember that whenever you call me, I will hear you! Now, knock the door and if they ask you what you want, say them you come to get love!"

White horse reared up neighing, I was about to fell off my horse. Then, it disappeared.

I looked behind it in despair; it was running such fast that it wouldn't hear me even if I called it. My hand hung in the air and turned in to a lonely child holding a balloon. Ties of the white helmet of the Cavalry were loosened by the wind; its green skirt was flying. The sword in his waist band was flashing. It was like a green light flashing on the white horse. I caressed head of my horse moving anxiously, I looked around for awhile; there was no one or nothing around. I looked at the gate of the city with unhappiness, rider's living me here, this loneliness affected me. I dismounted from my horse slowly; I thought that I was good at getting on and dismounting from a horse. When I approached my hand to the huge and magnificent gate of the city a beautiful melody started. I listened to this melody for a time, then two door leaves were opened noisily. Embroidery on both leaves was made of gold and while opening, they were such shining that it became impossible to see what there was inside. While the light was flying like the gold dust, I held my breath, I held my palm as if I wanted to hold the light, yellow light was pulling me towards itself as a whirlpool, and glamour of this light was unbearable. Finally gold dust calmed down and a long amber haired, wheat-skinned, bright-faced young man welcomed me. His face was slim as if drawn with a brush. He looked at me for awhile. There were yellow lights on his amber hair. His hazel eyes were big and nearly black.

He said, "Welcome to leanness, my name is Keşşaf". I was repeating "love, love" in order not to forget the sentence "I come here to get love" at that misty time. This word was circling in my mind, but he didn't ask me.

After looking up and down for awhile, he just asked,

"What about yours?"

I suddenly said, "Dilruba". What a beauty was this face through this yellow light? Watching him was like trying to look at the brightness appearing after the moon leaves the sun. The sun was eclipsed through these yellow lights and then started to be seen behind the moon slowly.

He said, "OK, then". His voice was pulling me towards itself holding the halter of the "love" word.

He told me "Dilruubaa", when I heard this sound, at the time when I heard my name, I thought that this was something wandering about between dream and reality; it was neither a dream nor real. I must have been at the universe between two ends.

He smiled saying "Dilrubaa, are you the one cheering me up?" He was saying "we will see" with his eyes.

He said nervously and as if wanting to know what would happen to me, "You can't see inside, here is the place to hear before anything else, the ones who desire love just hear at the beginning, if you accept, come in."

I asked, "and then?"

"Then, you will learn to hear, to see with your heart. But I don't know when and how this will be."

Keşşaf held my hand and started to show me around. Firstly I started feel the rhythm of this big and imaginary country. This was a shadowy, obscure and seductive rhythm. Colour of the sounds was forming resuscitated body; each sound was blowing the gaff behind the tone. Sounds were mixing with the breath, rhythm of each breath was giving away itself freely and passionately; even the smallest melody in this huge orchestra was reaching to my ear without disappearing. All of these sounds were both holding and setting free the melody of each sound and hiding the creatures that they belong to skilfully. Here sounds were as fast as sparkle of a star, vibration was too layered to be true and each whisper appeared quickly. Keşşaf showed me the country all along and said,

"This part isn't even one step of the hearing world." I thought that this part was a country where all the sounds on the universe were hidden. Ever sound from the beginning of time were stored here, even a single vibration wasn't wasted. Moreover, steps of people, tapping of these steps, cry of a baby, sound of a *qa̍nun*, violin was going on here hale and hearty. These hidden sound bodies had vibrations like shining of a rainbow. A chorus in the in the tongue of a child, outcry of a bird, continuously run of water... Each one was occurring after separating from their place. Sounds of the furniture, a small crash, even an echo was full of life. I heard the all sounds other than ı know but I couldn't see their back.

Keşşaf told me "That's enough for now. I will blindfold. But don't worry, it won't give you any harm."

I had no other chance, I allowed him to blindfold with yellow light. As I couldn't see anything else, I closed my eyes. This whirlpool made me feel dizzy and I closed my eyes tightly. He said “Close your eyes so that love embroidery is drown in to pupil of your eye. Here, people learn to hear the sound of the jewellery, the resolution of the stones, the sound of an arrow in the air, the sound of the blood touching the arrow, the fate, the mountains walking slowly, the language of the flame. He knows why the water is clear.”

I tried to breathe quietly wondering what else could happen to me. He must have understood that I was in difficulty in getting into extreme conditions, he said

“This is difficult not only for you but also for everybody at the beginning” and added ,

“I didn’t have a name when I came here, when I understood that discovering a thing is more different than seeing it, they called me Keşşaf, now I’m proud of this name.”

“Does Keşşaf mean explorer?”

“Yes, you got that right,” he replied. I could hear her smiling while saying this. Cause of his smile might be his catching my feelings.

I said, “I have achluophobia, I can’t stay here long.”

He said, “It isn’t dark here”. A soft tone appeared and disappeared on the waves of his voice.

“Here, you see as you know yourself. This is hearing world but the best of seeing is also here. Hearing comes first until you understand what you see; your darkness is until you understand this. Actually, what could you know until now although you have seen with your eyes? Seeing is not with eyes, in fact, you are here to understand this. If you want to have another eye, close your eyes, you won’t lose anything.”

Keşşaf made me hear the voice again and again every day at the leanness. He was telling me about the sound continuously at a place similar to a classroom as far as I see, because the sound was echoing. One day at the love lesson, as he says,

“Do you remember that I told you that you will see the magic of the sound in the world of sense?” he said and added “But you have to see the darkness for this!” Although I couldn’t see anything else except the yellow light, I was alone in a dark room. There were sounds and vibrations all around me.

Keşşaf was teaching me everything I need to know.

“Sound” he said “consists of vibrations. Sound waves progress in the form of compression and expansion, sound is a pressure wave. Moreover, sound is an energy. A human being can hear the waves between 20 Hz and 20.000 Hz frequencies. Hz, Hertz is frequency unit. Frequency is the number of vibrations of a sound source in a second."

Keşşaf stopped speaking for awhile, I understood this when the sound stops suddenly, he took a deep breath and continued:

"We were saying the waves that a human ear can hear. There are also infrasonic sounds that we can't hear. They are infrasonic waves. For example, earthquake waves."

He sat at the table, and started to tapping on the table,

"Sound occurs as result of the vibration of the molecules of the substance. Anyway back to what we were saying, animals can hear above 20.000 Hz. Vocal cords on my glottis vibrate with the air and sound occurs. It isn't enough to just vibrate; the vibrating object must be in an environment like solid, liquid and gas to convey the sound. In other words, waves are separated into two categories as mechanic and electromagnetic. Electromagnetic waves can spread in the space too. They don't have a special environment; but mechanic sound waves need an environment to spread. As you see, mechanic waves can't spread in space. We said that sound is a type of energy, energy doesn't disappear, sound frequencies don't disappear in the universe but they only change shape. Universe consists of the repetitive frequencies. World of leanness is the place where all these frequencies, i.e. energies, are stored."

I said, "I see."

"All the frequencies from the vibration of electrons to rotational motion of the planets are here. And all the things which you see or not in the universe have vibration. Just as the sound having vibration. Yes, sound is vibration, in other words it is a movement."

E came near me, hold my two fingers on my right hand and touch his glottis.

"Do you feel the vibration of the vocal cords o my glottis?"

I caught a strange but cute vibration.

I said, "Yes, it's gorgeous"

Keşşaf was using different methods to tell me vibration. First he provided me hear the vibration with sax, then with violin and also with drum. I learned that the air in the instrument in wind instruments vibrates, sound vibrates eardrum and this vibration conveyed into the inner ear, when these conductions reach to the brain, the sound is heard. Air molecules, like sound were also vibrating in the air.

"Now, I want you to see the sounds in your mind. Your brain cells can do this if you think right."

I said, "I didn't understand what you said"

"In other words, how you feel yourself is a situation related with brain waves. A conscious brain transmits "beta" waves between 14-30 Hz at a routine day. When you start relaxing, now try relaxing, these waves decrease below 14 and you pass into "alpha" position."

I tried to relax as far as in me lain, but I was so confused that I just acted out.

"For example, when you are sleeping, your brain waves decreases below 8 and you pass into "theta" position. "Delta" waves occur at the frequencies between 0 and 4 Hz in deep sleep. Besides these, there is a wave called "gamma". Gamma doesn't occur at every people. To reach gamma waves education and some exercises are necessary. All the human beings know on this subject is this for now. They could only explore the gamma waves. However, the brain has infinitely many waves. There is a direct proportion between your brain waves and your consciousness level; how much you are enlightened, degree of your brain waves will be different and will accompany to your consciousness level. One day all thresholds will disappear."

Keşşaf was teaching me how brain waves change by different vibrations. I was listening to different instruments at every lesson and he was asking what I felt. He was playing all instruments well and he was blowing my mind. He wanted to show me the influence of beautiful sound on human body and soul.

He continued talking, "Beautiful sound has different effects on human body. It is effective on different units from heartbeat to velocity of breath, from brain waves to hormones. The reason of this is that the sound is moving."

He was playing every kind of instrument easily. I was getting goose bumps; he was good at all kinds of stringed, percussion, wind and bow instruments. Keşşaf also had intimate knowledge about the effects of different tunes on human soul. I listened to rest tune from violin, saba tune from reed flute for weeks, he wanted me to be familiar to all kinds of instruments. As I got to know Keşşaf, I understood what a perfect person he was and I was astounded. Where and when did he learn these things?

There are a lot to say about him. He recited each azan with a different tune. He recited morning *azan* in saba tune, midday *azan* in rest tune, afternoon *azan* in hejaz tune, evening *azan* in segah tune and night *azan* in ussak tune.

He said "all these tunes are in our cells."

I just listened in world of sense without seeing the rising and setting of the sun for many years. I eternally learnt that every creature has sound. Singing of the birds, sound of a mole moving underground, cavernous of smoke were solved, whisper of a sunflower turning its face to sun, wing-beat of a falcon came to my heart without visiting letter. During this time I sometimes got ill-tempered because of not seeing, the only thing that made me relax was listening to the sound that I didn't use to know before. I don't know how much time passed but I walked around with my voice and by silence in the world of sense. At one of the everlasting moments Keşşaf , with his hazel eyes, told me in front of the golden palace, "We will open your eyes, because you can see me although your eyes are closed."

"And, you started perceiving how deep power is sound. You learnt that sound never gets lost in the universe, each sound is kept carefully. You saw that how silver-tongued is music in love. You came closer to sounds as needed. Now I'm going to take you to a special place and I'm going to open your eyes there. I will untie the yellow light dazzling your eyes for years."

We set off a silent journey with Keşşaf , soon after leaves of trees let us know that we were in a forest.

At last, I could hear the sounds of the birds and screams of the birds, sound of slowly flowing water, sound of wild life accompanying lonely murmur coming from the forest deeps. After going for awhile, first I perceived the green covering the sky as a shadow, and then I completely perceived each of the trees linking arms. They were like strong, huge people with their thick bodies. Then Keşşaf gave a long and sharp whistle. Right after his whistle turned into a smart melody. It echoed and turned to us. Then he gave a longer whistle and this whistle again echoed. It went on for awhile.

When Keşşaf untied the yellow light on my eyes slowly, I started to see with my eyes and I thought for a moment that I was dead and in the heaven. The environment was so fascinating that I was about to be dumbfounded; breathtaking antelopes with their elegant steps, colourful peacocks moving their wings like a fan, tens of kinds of birds that I had never seen before were floating on the branches of the trees like a rainbow. A peaceful river through this riot of colours behind the thick forest aroused my interest. Its deep blue glimmer was mixing with the colours of the birds. Birds diving into the water, singing and screaming ones, rhythmic sound of a woodpecker. Verdant and soft grass under my feet, hard shells of the trees that I held, cheerful smell of this green that penetrating into my cells while walking, this beauty leaving a sweet taste in my mouth. While Keşşaf was moving along one or two jumps ahead paving the way for me, a beauty parrot carrying all colours and lights on its feather said "Hello!" with its high-pitch voice. Then mysteriously looked at me and asked pointing me "Who is she?"

Keşşaf just said "a guest."

We started to get lost between the colourful wings and continuously changing melodies as we moved ahead. Birds making advances at each other, by giving different shapes to their wings at the lower branches and by turning around themselves like dancing was glorious view. I didn't know where to look and was experiencing the beauty of seeing. Brilliant naive of meropia and magnificence of the eagles were marvellous. We started to walk faster when the thickness of the trees thinned out. Keşşaf turned back when a lily-white peacock that opened its skirt like a bride waiting for its wedding took my breath away and said, "We're almost there". However, I could walk through this beauty for years. Another peacock passed near it opening its green feather like a fan, its glorious wings was touching me. Hoopoes, goldfinches, sparrows, ortolans, European robins, kingfishers, turtledoves, kestrels, dunnocks, bullfinches... Long-legged buzzards circling on us, imperial eagles, hobbies... Pheasants swaying with it long tail, cuckoos, partridges... Keşşaf stopped, turned back and said,

"If you want to see a miracle, it is enough to look at the birds. I am going to introduce you to Lyrebird. If you want, you can stay with it."

I saw Lyrebird which is reminiscent of a pheasant with its long tail. It was holding its brilliant tail on its head like an elegant gauze hat and swaying gently. Keşşaf said,

"Lyrebird can imitate many different sounds; there is a lot that we can learn from it." Lyrebird uttering like a whistle came to Keşşaf and without feeling like a stranger stopped near him. Magnificence of its lyre shaped tail was taking one's breath away. Keşşaf was communicating with Lyrebird in a strange way. I thought that he could understand birds' language at that moment. I realized an intimacy between them as if they were living together. Lyrebird started to imitate voice of almost all of the birds in this strange forest. Sometimes it sang a part of complex songs of nightingale, and then the melody changed into something different.

We stayed with Lyrebird for some time. Keşşaf wanted to show me which sounds that lyrebird could imitate.

He was saying, "It can get all of the sound signals and can change them into sound again." Maybe, I realized that sounds had signals there for the first time. Lyrebird left us towards the evening and disappeared shaking its lyre-shaped tail. After that, Keşşaf turned to me and said,

"Every word, letter is state of a vibration turning into sound waves in the brain, Princess, don't forget this. I am going to make you listen to the sky."

I hear a terrifying rhythm in this sky. Although I couldn't see the resource of the rhythm, I could feel the lightning coming out after the songs of the birds wiped off. I was moving around this sky and listening to the words of each rain drop separately. Sound of the sky occasionally was stopping, and then was awakened again, this rising became evident first with whispers and then with heart beats, it was turning into continuous, strong and regular pulsations. When these pulsations came together a terrible noise was heard, each beat was like breath of a human.

Keşşaf said, "Inside of the brain is too silent, Dilruba. Main resource of the rhythm is here. This endless sky is in your chest. The things you saw are only a little part of your own sky."

Everything was turning around a thing as a giant whirlpool. Keşşaf picked up the rain drops falling continuously in to his white hand and said "let's drink!" When he saw that I was hesitating, he persisted on "Come on!" It was rain like a sherbet touching my mouth.

When I opened my eyes, Safran was giving me dried fruit compote with her own spoon.

Seeing me confused, she smiled at me and said,

"Come on, take it. Don't hesitate," and added, "Is it too sweet?"

Many questions that I wanted to ask her remained at the world of sense. And you couldn't ask questions here.

9
Gift

"What a shame, nobody has the power. World is full of sun, but eyes are blind!" (Şeyh Attar)

All universes, feelings, senses, joy, pain are together. There is a door in this complex structure. The person, whoever he is, finds me easily from this door but I can't find him. I am walking around with the feeling of being spied, I can't stay alone, there is a window which is continuously giving information about the things that I did. It draws and shows me what I did with its skilful hands, whispers that it knows of my every thought, every step. I know that it watches me from near and far, how can I escape from you? If I fall down a well, you know that I am in the well. If I drop a tear to my lap in the well, you show me my state in that tear, the picture reflecting from the wall of the well awakens in the tear. You are the one who sees all the time. You are the one who shows the things he sees. You are the one who sees the thing he shows to me with my eye. You are a beloved talking for ever and ever, you are love without being silent! Oh, delicate beautiful woman, I am your toy, I know neither the ground nor the sky! I know neither numbers nor correct the letters; I memorize a lot of coquetry! I am the ruined cover of that book! I am in lightened coquetries and they are in me..!

I am about to drink your breath, but you are still hidden at the ends of the earth!

There is a conversation, a conversation with our bodies, like this between us;

"What do you want to know?"

"You."

"Knowing me means knowing everything, if you know yourself, you know me. You will get answers for your questions, but I will claim a life.

I claim a life and give many lives. Here, you give your life and get your answers."

It is about to be 9 in the evening. Kırlangıç, Zümrüt and Nergis are talking in one of the empty rooms of guest house. They are in Hüma's room. I am looking around; I have my notes in my hand. We take pains with each other; this pain is not for ourselves, for touching our heads to the shadow of the same divine. Notes on my lap form a beautiful decor. I am arranging the paper; I hear the cheerful voice of Kırlangıç. She is making fun of Hüma's lying on the bed-less bunk. There is some surprise some admiration in this fun. Hüma takes the bed of her bunk and lies on the flat surface. There are books on one side of the flat surface and some rosaries next to them... Hüma has removed her pillow too. Kırlangıç lies on the hard bed and tries to make pillow from the books.

"That's it. These books make a good pillow. They are too comfortable!"

Zümrüt leans on the upper bunk with her hands and laughs at her condition.

"Kırlangıç, get up I will look, too. God bless you," laughing continuously.

"I won't, it's very comfortable, tuck me in thin paper. Zümrüt take some paper..."

Nergis, Hüma and I are sitting on the chairs, we have coffee in our cups. Hüma turns off the light on the table which is dazzling me, and then goes on telling the events at laboratory course, as the subject isn't interesting I am lost in the thought of funny Kırlangıç and Zümrüt.

Nergis... She was living like a puzzle a piece of which was lost; there was a picture on her face which cannot be completed. She looks at you from a pendulum plying between two pains askew on face. Making a sense of her, solving the strange puzzle being articulated day by day was impossible for me. She was confusing you, while she was a sad person, she suddenly became a grateful person, and there she had a shield on her face to her vulnerability and a silence rising at her words. She had a silent soul like her straight brown hair, she looked at everything behind a censer. There was some defeated some objective look in her brown eyes, she kept away from looking at your face directly, she turned her eyes away. Her wide forehead was shining like a white rose petal. Politeness and respect which every people didn't have was gleaming on her well-shaped face which was as if drawn by a pencil. Her wiggly lips which were in struggle for hiding on her white face were always colourless. Her cheeks got plump, tone of her voice rose and her soft look shone only if she smiled softly. Smoothness of her voice, calmness of her behaviours was like a clean stream. While she was standing against you with her dropped shoulders as if she wanted to get rid of the magic burden of life, she fastened her hands together as if she was cold. Her slight, bony hands were such calm that time slowed down in her hand, even it waited breathless. You got the feeling that she was carrying a little sparrow in her hands and in order not to harm it she didn't move her fingers. She was never in hurry; she was such cool that the one who looked at her would think that she had never laughed loudly, never shouted, never acted like a crazy. She never gave the lost piece in her image away; she walked slowly as if she wanted to be lost in this calmness.

Calmness of Nergis was sometimes disturbing me. She couldn't finish her sentence at once and I couldn't wait for her. I would like to come to end immediately. I got the idea that this much slowness was delay in such a chasing life. I was *ex nihilo* sorry. Then, I saw that life didn't mislead her or even didn't surprise her and was convinced that she was in safe. (In fact, life was full of errors and surprises for everyone.) Nevertheless, I thought that she was protected by well-secured castles; I wasn't sure about that there was a storm depressed loutishly behind this calmness. I was taking the pulse of the sadness that she covered with silence and examining the hidden fate in life. There was a deep questioning under this considerate condition. Maybe, her sadness was full of unanswered questions and she was caught with the possibility and hope of finding the answer. She was the successful and silent student of huge life class. She was away from all the naughtiness with the help of sadness. She was a heart which was shy about taking steps, which was trying to get rid of the siege of the pain. She didn't know the meaning of benefit. She was like a white notebook which didn't have doodles. Her calm language was shuffled to silence. And she made this silence wait at a threshold of a secret.

Indeed, it was difficult to be friends with a person who was full of invisible knots. Although this calmness gave confidence as a calm harbour that reduced the anxiety, you understood that you couldn't stay there at one point. While human being was a creature with many faces, you put a mirror on your face corresponding this silent sadness. It is tiring to keep in step with a silent rose. You can't serve explosive volcanoes in a transparent glass to a person who is making a clean copy of her speech. Thick walls between you lock you to yourself. Nevertheless, the purity in her silent sadness, inner humanity in her ego and devotion in her eyes were enough for the loyalty and lasting of the friendship. Hearing her questions which weren't asked but implied with body was as seeing the mirror image of a universe which I couldn't understand but percept with my five senses.

Although it is hard to admit, Nergis was giving me a lead to settle an account with myself. She was confronting me with my uncontrollable situations, with my enthusiasm, with my anxieties, with my dissatisfaction in life, with my complex soul, with indefinite streets of my existence, mind with unusual music although rhythm of which was definite. This silent, clear and soupy mirror she held me was touching all the cries of my soul with a breathtaking scream, was digging out the pyin I grew in my existence basket, was solving the shadows of my resistant soul, was displaying my passionate but unbalanced steps. She was bringing me together with my falling behind the life despite all my efforts, my collapsing with the winds, my evolving into cliffs while looking for a reason. While calling the dead-end streets, she was only and totally silent. She was slow. While I was trying to be strong, she was trying to stay weak. Life was always throwing me. While I was keeping my eyes open, life was always realizing her. Her sad silence was complaining about my inability.

Wasn't the resource of universe, life movement? Her invariable existence added to her indefinite sadness was making good time however fast I go. She was drifting with the whole universe as if she was banded together with everything, and she wasn't making an effort. I was plumbing the depths whereas she was going beyond the oceans with her inability boat. She was rising from dead while dying; I was dying while I was trying to rise. As long as I was against, she was on that road. Who I was as Dilruba, Nergis wasn't Nergis. When I was with her, I was a fireball which must hide its flame. As long as this fireball shone in her clear colours, I was hurt; I was getting into life as a dag stuck in itself. As a sharpened, sharp, cruel but a dull dag.

I was wondering what I was in her eyes. She was aware of the dilemmas of this friendship. She was meeting this with silence as usual. Maybe the most interesting place in my soul was disobedience habitat, my sustaining power fed by this disobedience and the address of my soul arisen from this. This side in my character was marking and dissolving the silence of her. If I was a stone thrown on dead water, Nergis was dispersing in circles. Although we completed each other, we were like chalk and cheese. However, our way was crossing at a humanistic place, at friendship. Moreover, when I thought about passion of the people, their greed, unnecessary anger and obstinacy, caprices, selfishness, I felt that Nergis had a different importance for me.

Hüma and Nergis, what a scary simplicity! Walking around as if peeled off, disturbing simplicity when zoomed out, putting on prayer while walking around without armour. How much these two people resemble. Nergis's simplicity, silence, and conserving a healthy soul in this simplicity and silence; Hüma's not having a shadow on her clear face. Whenever I look at Nergis and Hüma, I see a single pleasure waving like two lights which are reflecting each other. Both of them are like broken away a single peace. Hüma is incredibly calm and silent; I can call them "girls speaking slowly and below one's breath". Sometimes, silent people can also be selfish, but Nergis is not that kind, Hüma isn't, either. The commitment that I realized about Nergis became clear after I met Hüma. Indistinguishable expression on pretty face of Nergis became perceptible on Hüma's voice. In my opinion, these two girls, two subservients of the God, were far away from us. They were like as generous as earth, calm as the sky, close as running water, as luminous as fire; they were two lights on ugly world. They were liveliness on eyes of whom a blessed epic came to life. They were pictures showing what a heart going towards love definitively meant. They were free of greed and love of world as if a hand pulled away their ego from their bodies. Their eyes were away from the society, they were focused on that single point; they were wardens of their own hearts, they didn't have any other interests. They were on alert for witch grass not to grow around the Lake of heart. Maybe, for this reason they didn't have any energy or desire for fiddling for someone. They were competing only for doing charity work, they were sorry for the one who had problems. They were rare people who were doing with less at this era.

They were brush-strokes of an enormous balance aboveground, if Nergis was blue, Hüma was *eau-de-nil*. Let alone shouting, I had never seen them raising their voice or showing any caprice sign. Didn't they become unbalanced like us? Didn't they miss their foot when they ran into a pit? The dough of ones who were like Nergis and Hüma must have strangely kneaded with sherbet. Didn't a person go bitter? Didn't a person get angry and want to be cross with everything? It was unknown that how they succeeded being such subservient! Hüma was in front of me, it was like an extreme puzzle! She was on the chair in front of me, her letting her ends of scarf largely crossing at the neck, holding the cup with her two hands, thick socks on her feet, thin, ecstatic, elegant body, her face without any make-up; a purity without femininity, ornament, attraction and juvenescence, a heart dyed with paint of God, as if coming out of old pictures. She doesn't have an aim to be belonged to this time!

How she could come to this school, probably, she was solving problems in her free times when she wasn't worshipping. I can't think anything else. Her lying on a piece of board without pillow. Her effort to obey to the *sunna*! If only I had the opportunity to see Hüma's heart, could I perceive the pearls there? How does she live, what kind of a world does she live? She was starry-eyed Hüma! Ohh Rabia! She reminds me Rabia who didn't take two coins in one hand, taking two coins in two hands not to feel sick.

Nergis and Hüma... They would pass by you as the resuscitated soul of the legends in all books. Being with them was like walking around with angels on earth, their back was almost perceived, and the water they were drinking was almost seen. They were compassion from end to end; they were deep love every nook and cranny...

Suddenly, the door was opened and the most cheerful person of the world joined us like the sun. This is Hazel! Tingling the corridor with her laughter, her saying "Girrrrlllls!" while entering the room makes everybody looks at her.

She says, "At last, I could find you!" her voice slips like a soap. Hazel was the person who took me to Safran when I had that strange dream. Maybe for this reason she has a different importance for me; not only for this reason, but also Hazel reminds me of spring which is ready to shine with happiness. Her green-hazel eyes widen suddenly with joy and surprise, then squints with shame and veils with a strange look as if riding on a idea river. She is so clever and she loves meditation. She jeers at life with her laugh. She doesn't deplore like Kırlangıç, instead, she waits with patience. She is hard-working, she lives in the room opposite me but it is difficult even for me to see her; she always reads, writes, studies.

One of Hazel's skills is that she chooses her words even in her cheerful, laugh-filled, cute, and enthusiastic mood. Moreover her effort on not lacerating people causes her to go back. Deep compassion on choosing the words makes hesitation visible on her green-hazel eyes like yellow gleam. Her daintiness comes from her rightness. I am sure that while she is laughing like a cheerful girl, her mind is full of warnings of conscience, hesitation from divine, not exceeding the limits, reminding as-*sırat*. Of course, you couldn't see her cheerful behaviours outside. When I saw her on the street, there wasn't a shadow of her. There was a seriousness on her face surrounded with her scarf. Sometimes she got a thick scarf on cold weather, she passed by me heel and toe carrying her books between her two arms.

"I walked about all the floors, you weren't there. At last I remembered Hüma! I am exhausted, let me sit!"

When she saw Hüma's bed, she was surprised. Tussling, not sharing the bed scenes were successfully fictionalized. Kırlangıç gave in al last. A few minutes later, she tried to get up holding her back,

"God bless you, Hüma! How do you sleep here, every part of my body is hurting?"

Hüma didn't look as if she was bored with this pell-mell. On her face, there was light and happiness full of love of a sunflower which is enthusiast to sun, as if a birth announcing that she would reach to fruition.

10
Other Side of the Water

Separation is in the eye of you.
In fact, It's a single point circling around fast.
There is only one single line circling around from the beginning till the end.
Existence is this. (Şebüsteri)

It is December. I am happy that I am with Sufis, that I am close to them. But there is a problem, a painful problem. There is something that differentiates me from them like deboning the meat, something that puts me somewhere different; I am looking at things from the sharp-edge of the knife at least as much as that meat which is about to fall. This is uneasiness arising from knowing that no matter how hard I try, I won't be like them. Our ways break up at one point; I can't catch their purity and simplicity, their eyes looking with a sharp satisfaction. That brilliant aura surrounding them doesn't surround me. Uneasiness in my soul says this, my tides changing its mood continuously cry: You won't be like them. You won't be like Safran, Hüma or Nergis. The things you consider as real are all fantasy, they are your own fictions. Your imagination generates them. Your effort is useless! You are an uncontrollable creature, you are not comfortable at any place, you can't hold on here too! Look at them, look carefully! And understand that they don't have that chronic sadness, that terrifying dissatisfaction which you have!

I try to return to my uniform and meaningless life again with these in my mind. I don't look for a benefit nor gleam in life. Maybe there are a lot of life styles on earth, but my in-adaptability, my picture which doesn't fit to any place prefers this. On those days, flames of love started melting, water-leaves hugging me started to fade, while water-leaves of love started hurting my skin, it was losing its brightness. A lot of violins were being played in my mind at the same time, while my beats were trying to keep up with all of the violin sounds, it couldn't go beyond flittering. While love was a beautiful woman waking up to sun, she turned into a stained shadow dumped. Loneliness I was in and forgetfulness in dark guest house were making sound like a saw cutting my bones. When light started dancing a tango, I felt its thin and long steps in the middle of my forehead.

While walking, suddenly, my knees bent to sour, aromatic, sharp clay. As I wanted to hold, lean hope, it was moving away. I was walking around with disappointment. What happened? Why do I see black henna in my hands? I don't know what's happening? It is almost a month I haven't seen Safran. What happened to gathering and going? Sometimes I see girls going below the window like shadows. They are calling me insistently, when their voice crashes the window, it is broken. Generally they come upstairs to my room, they say that they won't go without taking me. I shield an excuse that I found on that moment. I am hacked to pieces behind that shield, on that dim darkness. I want to get in front of the sun again. I don't want to go anywhere, I feel like I was tricked. I am resting on a mouldy swing between going or not, resting is sometimes resisting. I am waiting for a gleam to break my resistance. A pray like zam-zam.

I must have done something wrong, I wish I could start over, I wish I could take out my footprints from myself. Where and how did I lose that casualness? I wish I could run away from this painful appearance turning around like birds of prey, from this separation. I wish I was pushed to the road again from the side I was covered with witch grass. I wish I could reach the stem of the tree branch of which I lost somewhere on the road. I wish I could resurge from the words in my mouth.

The things until now must be my fantasy! There is no relationship between the passing days and these events? How real can these live words between rigid time, cracks and fractures between the times, whispers touching my ears be? Why are the people playing around me and their shadows indifferent to sunrise? Then why I didn't go mad? Or am I in a big game and am I the only one I play tricks on? Furthermore, as life passes, how am I contented with just watching it? Why do I accept this?

I can't corner this sharp bend. Whether I will fall down the cliff or if you hold my hand and open the curtain, I will see the way. Don't leave me without seeing the future. Don't let the darkness laugh at me. Don't make me speak without killing my dead.

Days were passing continuously. Sometimes, we were spending time at the library after school, I was trying to find a reality between the high shelves, a word said to me between the thick books, a message that only I can understand between the lines, voice, a tone. But books didn't see me, words were passing by me as an arrow and hitting the targets except me. This idea was turning into a bridge that provides me going back to those old depressions. The treasure that I thought I found was changing into a night city turning off its lights and moving away from me. When I reached out to touch, it was changing into shining lights on the other side of the water, it was jumping from dream to real, lights touching the darkness, sea sparkle was knocking me cold. Each light was shaking me like a hand touching on my shoulder, touching my heart which was struggling to run on the water and to fly continuously, like a flame, was withdrawing sweeping away the darkness. While things in my hands were shining jewellery, it turned into love swaying like an obvious magic on the other side of the water. This love evolved to a total existence, which involved everything, kept everything alive, didn't leave anything out. As the sea sparkle went away, my soul became a victim who was stuck in for many years, it was trying to get out of there.

And I couldn't move.

When I thought about moving, I went down that dark water and in order not to be drowned, I was running like hell. I was begging for help when I was out of breath, I was dropping your name from my mouth while going to the light inside the picture I began to talk.

It was a free afternoon at a weekend when I was tired of these strange feelings. Zümrüt came to my room. There was a strange uneasiness in her blackish eyes. Maybe she didn't like my mood or she was afraid of giving herself up while trying to solve the reason of the everlasting separation in my eyes. She was trying to come near me from the bottom of the invisible wall.

She said "Dilruba" in a low voice, slowly. She was sitting on my bed and looking hesitance of a person who didn't know how to start. Referring that I know where she did and why she came,

I said, "Let me tell you in advance, if you go Safran, I won't come". She put her uneasiness in her look aside under my sudden and cold manner. She drawled;

"Buuuuut youu must come ... Pleaseeee...forr myy sakeee..."

There was some entreating some hidden order in her voice. In an effort to express that I was sure about my decision, transparently I said;

"I really don't want you to force me, I won't come." I was looking up and down without knowing where to look. I wanted to challenge and not to hurt her. She suddenly stood up and came to me. She started to tell with a soft voice that if I didn't go, she would be hurt, this was her first and last wish from me, hereafter she would let me alone but for that time she wanted me to go with her.

However, I would like to hear a sentence like, "Safran wanted to see you, she asked you". But it looked like nobody cared me. I passed her and sat on the bed.

I said, "Never mind, in any case there is nobody asking me".

She took the chair and sat opposite of me with a desperate expression.

She said, "But Dilrubaaaa, don't say so. She asked you without mentioning name",

"How?"

"You and Kırlangıç were absent for a month. She asked where the girls are",

"Really? What else did she say?"

"She asked if you were OK,"

"Anyway, I don't want to come."

She spoke pleadingly coming close to my face, her voice became such soft that it was softening my heart too, her voice softened me as if steel waiting under anvil.

I said swiftly "My not coming isn't related to you, be cool, really."

"Of course, it isn't related to me but please for my sake" she said sadly.

I said, "Excuse me!" I was getting angry.

She said, "I will wait until you came?"

"Will you wait for days and nights?"

"Certainly,"

"Whatever you say!"

There was an irritating silence in the room soon after. Zümrüt, is sitting at the bedside hopefully. She sometimes looks at me, and whispers "pleaseeeee". At this moment, rain drops lashing the window is repeating her words,

"Pleaseeee..."

When she sees that I don't care, she raises her voice, she repeats her word with a voice a little higher than before, "Dilruba Pleaseeee". I hear her voice again while rain drops are lashing the window.

"Dilruba, Pleaseeee..."

Time passes in this way. She won't give up, she will wait even if it's night. Rain won't stop, until I go, it will go on raining. We, two are waiting silently for the time to pass in the middle of the room. Rain is turning around us with the dark weather. I am moving away the bright side of the water more and more, darkness in the back is growing and growing, disappointment covers the room, silence of Zümrüt was spreading on the sea sparkle between me and the bright side like a headache. She was trying to throw a life saver but I was struggling to drown. She was handing me her voice for me not to drown but I was holding one of my arms and hanging down the other to drown in the dark water or even to show that I was about to drown. I said to myself, it wasn't the good time to get cross, as the love started. What was the thing returning me?

Rain was walking at a trot on the window, patter, patter, patter... This room of the guest house, tables, beds, wardrobes in the room was waiting silently. Time was stringing out in Zümrit's hand like a plait. Where was this place, the guest house where hundreds of people accommodate going? Where, in such a silence as walking totally with its foundation?. Yağmur starts running, knocking the window to enter, but it's useless.

At last, I couldn't stand her waiting on the rack, and I said,

"Okay, I will come but this won't change anything for me." I don't know what she understood from my sentence, but her face lit up and she fell into my arm, thanked as a successful commander.

Later, I thought about this situation extensively, Zümrüt was the only person among the girls who could persuade me. Kırlangıç not only couldn't insist on anything but even she couldn't suggest t go somewhere. Nergis and Hüma would accept my first rejection and go. Hazel was touchy, she would be hurt. But Zümrüt didn't give up, insisted on every subject, "No" means "Yes" for her, she walked towards that "no" in general, went through them. Zümrüt was the officer of the day to persuade me. Because of this reason, she was sent to my room alone and that day only we two went to Safran's house.

She must have refrained from my changing my mind that she offered to get on a taxi.

"It is raining cats and dogs, shall we take a taxi?"

So, we got there in about five or six minutes. A hand from the sky was imprinting like embroidery onto my face; rain was a whirlpool, liberation, a tear.

When we got off the car, my feet were dragging, I was making out what to say to Safran, I was talking through her and trying to bear the time spent on the way. I felt a shiver down my spine, I was saying that I was on a difficult way. When we passed through the dwarf walls of the shanty and reached the glazed iron door...

Zümrüt starts shining, rain drops get warmer on my face. Safran opens the door while singing "I never get angry with that love" enthusiastically.

The rain hearing her voice stops at the breast of the sky. The sky in my breast is washed, blue and clear. She says welcome with this song. From getting angry region to peace, from poverty to wealth, from darkness to light. This small house, this big world, immensity of my feelings. Safran is walking in front of Zümrüt and me. Happiness comes up and moves away as she ambles. Pulsar in my breath deepens at each stem. We go to the small room as usual. Her vest and long dress, her white scarf cover her solemnity, I feel like that at that moment. She betters as I look, she shines as I look. As soon as she sits, she draws the bow of the word, the arrow suddenly and angrily comes to me:

"We will cross over that dark water and reach to the shining side. İnşallah. We will go to the shining side."

While saying this, she sweeps the air as if she pushes the darkness. She looks into my eyes, I tremble, experiencing this shiver at this point of the universe... Turning around with the world at this very moment. I am rooted to the spot, I turn to jelly. Safran says, infusing into my heart,

"Let me tell you with Şems' speech. With his words. "It's a given that this river will be passed... If you fall behind, the bandits leave you weak... At the other side of the river, bandits can't attack you..." Do you remember princess, do you remember Dilruba? You are Dilruba, you are the one who cheers up, the one who pleases, the one who reaches to open heart... Love is healing for a human being, it isn't a trouble, does your heart know this?"

This time shower starts in me. It rains from my eyes, from the sky of my eyes. It runs down shamefully, consumingly. First, a silent river falls onto my face, then it babbles, I can't speak, immobility is this. I have a lump in my throat. My face turns into red. I know this from the fire. I look down, Is there anyone who could save me? Breath of love caresses my face, I am in shame, such a close particle, universe, her voice. I snivel, Safran seeing me in that condition leaves the room. "Long distance of my life, if only I could pass over... my eyes fill with tears... mountain yield me..."

I stare at Zümrüt. Her face gets pink. She stands up and goes out after Safran. I feel the smell of the God. I close my eyes. Cavalry with green cloth is at a distance looking at me on his white horse. He is smiling. At that time I know that he is Keşşaf large as life.

Oh love, I can't stand this, mercy me!

He appears near me holding the headstall,

Looks at me as if he is saying "You are right Dilruba! I am Keşşaf!" .

At that time, I think that the turning world is a walnut in my hand.

Keşşaf , turning his face away, says,

"if your fantasy is over, let's go on. Our aim is to reach, having fun here is falling off a cliff."

Which one is fantasy? Which one is real? Which one is Keşşaf ?

As if he hears my thought, e bends his face to my face and says,

"Love sometimes comes to heart mirror of the person as separation. In fact this is the work of Ruhu Derbeder. You will meet her soon. Separation isn't with us."

11
"Mystery, just inside you!"

"There is a goal, but no way. What we call a way is hesitation." Kafka

Müdrik said, "People think with their soul and body." Müdrik was a plastic surgeon. But a person having a chat with him for half an hour would think that he was a metaphysics expert. His fans were showing great interest in him because of his intimate knowledge on every subject. Müdrik Murathanoğlu was a close friend of my father that he nearly "charged" to control me in Ankara. My father who was a retired military officer requested Müdrik to look after me. Müdrik was controlling me regularly in every two or three months because of the respect that he had for my father. When he couldn't come because of his works, he would call me to his clinic. Whenever I went to his elegant clinic, I found myself in a different world. His clinic was a silent and class place like a space-port enriched with strange accessories, where were huge paintings on clean and bright walls. Here was a place of secrets that was full of women who were keen on their beauty and men. I waited for many hours behind the huge doors that I wonder what was happened in the operating room.

Talking to Müdrik was like being on a sharp sword. It was a hard job to try to find the by-pass between us. Because my every word might change and my father could learn it. I was waiting silently in this luxurious office in front of the window seeing the bright doors of the operating room. I was watching the snow outside thinking that each snowflake has a different shape. Today is the last day of the year. Shop windows were decorated as far as the eye could reach. There was a distinct joy on the people's walking and looks. As if we were going to be brand new people when entered a new year. I started this New Year meeting Keşşaf , I am happy for this. Oh right, there is not time for Keşşaf! There is neither place nor time. When I am with him, I am free of all the records. Among the people buying New Year presents, I have the most valuable present, a friend like Keşşaf .

Sweet herbal tea the beautiful secretary brings makes the ambiance more magical, the tune of the meal spoon in the cup makes me remember Keşşaf's words on voice. I realized that although Keşşaf told me a lot about voice, he didn't say anything about silence. He just said "Inside the brain is very silent Dilruba."

Müdrik flowed in charmingly pushing the air forward like a white angel between the leaf doors of the operating room. His strong head on his shoulders, tired-looking on his thin and expressive face come to life when he realizes me. What a miracle moment seeing him with white uniform! Smilingly he walks towards me, he states that he is pleased with my visit by saying with a flat voice reminding me that I am on the world,

"Dilruba, welcome honey," At about 2 in the afternoon, we go to a cafe at Tunalı Hilmi. We chitchat for awhile.

I speak of Safran. If I tell the things I experienced, he won't believe, so I filter my words. This is better. The waiter takes two cups of coffee with milk. Müdrik puts a cube of sugar and mixes his coffee, the steam of the coffee shadows his face.

I say, "I haven't been right in the head since I met Safran. What do you think dissuades me? Or will I believe in all these things?" Although he is tired, Müdrik enjoys talking. He says,

"Many people are deceived by the others' words but they don't hear the things they say to themselves. However, the things we say to ourselves consciously or unconsciously changes our life fluency to a large extent. Many people are not aware of how destructive and unfriendly they behave to themselves."

I am watching the people outside wondering about his next sentence. This is Müdrik's habit, first he makes an irrelevant sentence, and then he checkmates you.

"Do you think why you ask such strange things to yourself? What do these things you tell prove? Where do they take us? If you want, I can tell. Thoughts, which are not fluent, will drive us to bottomless space and meaningless connotations. Moreover, will you be creating all the things you tell by yourself? Maybe everything is normal and as it should be."

He is sharpening his words more and more to dig into deeper. I leaned back and I entwined my arms around each other, my body language was drawing a line between us. He continued.

" I think we don't have to search for the mystery in life, but if you enjoy this game, I don't know."

While I was inhaling the smell of the coffee, I said, "I think you are going to start judging me"

"Absolutely, no. Rights and wrongs are relative and there isn't only one true, of course I think like this. This is totally related to how you look and how you see. If your thoughts fetter you, I only want you to realize this. A person should wriggle himself out of all the obligations and necessities imposed. Freedom needs this."

"Then, why doesn't freedom wriggle itself out of these obligations and necessities, Don't you think it is a bit conflicting?"

"That's exactly what I want! I seek healthy thought. Thoughts wriggled out of obligations."

"Oh, you doctor, stop speaking confusingly and tell me a healthy thought. But, please don't say something mysterious (!)."

"As far as I understood, you are looking for an answer, but there isn't an answer valid under all conditions, Dilruba. I wish there were. But there isn't! As you know, no man ever steps in the same river twice. I only advise you to increase the rational answers related to life."

"I think I am not seen rationalist from where you stand."

"I don't like the idea that I can't control my life. As I said before, there isn't an absolute and stable! We just live adapting the social and cultural conditions."

I just said, "This is a bit cold and passionless life style...", I had a lot to say but this conversation was widening as two arms of a scissor. Müdrik pointed something turning in the air, opening his hands on the table like a tulip,

"Just contrary! I want a sensitive and an enthusiastic life. However, at least I want to determine my own emotional fate in my life. If there is fate, it is related with whether the person can control his emotions or not and the power to control his thoughts. While you are running after complex questions, you miss that the complex thing is the soul of the human itself."

He opened his blue-green eyes as if saying do you understand, leaned back, he was such confident that the meaning under this speech caught me. Although I didn't understand what it was, my fancy chased up.

"Don't look for the mystery out, mystery is inside you!"

"Can you clarify this, please?

"I say let's not believe in the stories we wrote. I say let's know ourselves." Müdrik took a deep breath, I can't help looking at the young people behind him. They were keeping to themselves as if they were waiting for excitement at the threshold of a different world. Müdrik ordered two more cups of coffee with milk, I was getting hungry. Müdrik ordered two *kazandibi* (white pudding with blackened surface) saying let's become sweet. Maybe he was trying to lighten the mood. I felt that he was going to tell something important from his features, in order not to disturb him I kept my silence. First, he took off his jacket and hung it on the back of the chair graciously. There was a smell of caramel, hot coffee, brewed tea, toasted bread, and oil at this cafe. Youngsters were throwing coins into the jukebox occasionally and then sitting back triumphantly. The triumph of listening to the music they wanted. I remembered the things Keşşaf told me about the sound as the music nestled in my soul and I was letting the strange limitless pleasure to capture me. The frequency of the saloon changed with the music and the people were calmed down with this fascinating smell. This small table turns into a huge arena and Keşşaf was running at full gallop from end to end with his horse, I was getting smaller, Müdrik and I was following the sea of which Keşşaf showed only one voluntarily or involuntarily.

What eye-catching was Müdrik with his white shirt! An elegant head on his shoulders, but above all, watching the coming and going of the waves on his face. Echoing of fragrant but sharp sound among the waves! His words were islands in the deep blue water.

"If you embark for some place, I don't want you to return empty-handed. This gives pain to the person."

I said suddenly, "Maybe, being on that way is the important thing."

Müdrik took out his wallet from the pocket of the his jacket hung on the chair and took out a photograph from the wallet.

He said, "Do you see the woman next to me? She is my wife I have lost recently."

There was a beautiful couple smiling to the objective with a blond woman in the photograph. They were in front of a wide-bodied tree. Müdrik put his arm around the young woman's neck, both of them seemed happy. A romantic photo as if taken at Ye□ilçam.

"I'm sorry, was she ill?" gullibly I said. I have known Müdrik for a long time through my father, even I heard his marriage but I have no information about his private life.

He said, "She didn't die. She left me!" A colourless cloud appeared on his face to hide the pain. Calmly playing music in the saloon screamed and quickened, the youngsters were shaken with laughter. A loud voice was heard from the kitchen. The cafe became crowded, waiters quickened their steps. I was under the impression that the people outside were putting first their noses and then their ears to the windows of the cafe to hear what Müdrik would tell, a noise was going on.

Müdrik laid down the photograph with a doctor manner. It seemed as if he was going to cut it into pieces and then re-shape it how he wanted with his skilful fingers, everything should be as it should be. What a holy thing it was! Somehow, he realized that it was impossible to intervene in the past and leaned back. Music in the saloon was getting faster, the youngsters at the back table started to tap out and dance. Door with the rattle was opened with a noise and a slim girl with long brown hair brown entered. Her little dog and some fresh air were following her. Sound of the girl's heel wasn't heard but felt and recorded to the subconscious of the youngsters at the back table.

Müdrik said, "Some day, she came to my office. Waiting room was bursting at the seams. My secretary was taking the necessary notes, giving appointments to the patients, she sat in the waiting room as a patient among my patients waiting to be beautiful, to change. She waited until the evening. I am generally tired at the end of the day, especially if there is an operation. Anyway... When I was about to go out, my secretary told me that my wife was still waiting. I couldn't make sense of her waiting me for hours. First, I thought that she came to control me and I didn't like this.

I said, "Was she jealous?"

"Not really, but she was strange. Sometimes, she sat still for hours, I had difficulty in understanding. That day, she suddenly entered my room and without saying hello, and said "Re-create me"

"She is a beautiful woman as I see."

"When she said that, she wasn't like this but she was beautiful for me."

My curiosity was increasing.

"How? And then?"

"First I didn't realize her strangeness. I thought that she was kidding and I treated as a joke.

Müdrik leaned back for the waiter to get the empty cups easily. My face was about to turn into a question mark.

"Then we went out to a restaurant. I continuously said that she didn't need any operations but she didn't believe in me, she was saying that I was thinking so because she was my wife."

I said, "She can be right in her way"

"She is right to some extent but when I look at her with the eye of a doctor I didn't see any defects. The defects that women or men realized about themselves are totally derived from lack of self-confidence. When I lift the women's eyelids, or when I lift their face or when they get rid of the fat on their legs, they feel as if they were re-born... The reality lying under this regeneration, their strange thought saying that when I look at the mirror I look beautiful old diffident me died."

"Then, what happened? Did you do what she wanted?"

"No, I didn't."

"So, you let her leave herself to another surgeon. Is that right?" Müdrik's face was telling me to wait. The conversation was going through a subject I was wondering very much. The main reason for my impatience was this. How do plastic surgeons look at their wives? How was the love of the owner of the hands giving shape to woman body? I was waiting for the answer? He continued,

"Next week, she disappeared leaving a letter. There were statements like when I came back, I would have been changed. She was saying that she would return. But I didn't satisfied with her explanations. She started meeting strange people. As I understood there was a man calling himself therapist, I think he was a dabbler. Anyway, he was moving spoons with power of thought.

"Yes, some people can do this, why did you say him dabbler?"

He lifted his eyebrows amazedly, his blue eyes become bigger, they were like a deep lake,

"For god's sake, could you tell me if moving a spoon shows that he is an incredible person? Let's bring the wisdom forward."

"In fact, no."

"His showing the movement of the spoons is just his moving the spoons, in my opinion. Nothing else."

"And, then?"

"Anyway, my wife, my ex-wife, was trying to change herself by power of thought, she thought that she succeeded it some. To tell the truth, she did what she said and she returned back rejuvenated. Lines on her face were reduced, she became slim. Of course, there is no need for bistoury for these! You do sports, apply masks and you get these results but she claimed that she did them with power of thought.

"I think your relation was in a bind. You shouldn't have taken it in stride."

"We were at the end of the road, she believed in such strange things! It couldn't be seen as normal, because she was pushing the limits of mind."

"Maybe, she went into depression."

"I was afraid that she was losing her vital functions, but she thought that she was starting to live. A person who looked at her could understand that she was in affective disorder. You needn't be a doctor to understand this! You know, brain chemistry changes in case of depression, but the person can't notice this in that condition, he is in a narrow circle. The people around him can observe the condition of his bond with life...

"Especially doctors", I completed his sentence. "She needed to enlarge the circle"

"She didn't accept this. About a month later, she left house. And what's more, she left a note writing that she wouldn't return."

Two portions of *kazandibi* on the table were about to melt.

"She was in need of interest, I think she did all these things for being loved." I said.

He took a deep breath, "I don't know what else she wanted, I already loved her. Oh, life is like this! While everything is perfect in your life, you find yourself in a scary knot. And everything tumbles."

"I think there isn't a direct relation between the things you told me and your wife's leaving you. Maybe, there is an indirect relation. There are people who get better by using power of thought, everybody knows this, what's wrong with this? There must be some other reasons..."

He tasted *kazandibi*, life was worth-living and good for him,

"Of course there isn't a direct relation but a person's using his power of thought must be somehow in relation with using his brain. Thoughts must walk in the riverbed. A person mustn't live only with blind and deaf thoughts eliminating mind. He mustn't take the risk. It is terrible! If he does so, then the private life will be affected, as it is in my example."

"We agree on this! Of course, mind, the supreme proficiency, must be the place to grow a strong vision and reasonable thoughts."

Müdrik, took the photograph on the table and put it in his wallet carefully.

With a serious tone,

"I told all these things to advise you to live the life you are sure about its existence! Don't dive into a deep water you don't know. Because you are not going to have a shower in that water. You will be drowned. Do you get it?"

I had questions that I wanted to ask him, but I didn't want to watch the pain in his eyes any more. I stopped speaking. It was five o'clock. As well as agreeing with the things Müdrik said about mind, I perceived the pettish appeared because of being hurt. In any event, being left by a spouse must be considered as a wound. Although it scabs in time, a wound is ready-to-bleeding.

Everything turned into a puzzle again with the things Müdrik said while I was considering that I found a clue regarding life, existence. I realized this after what Müdrik said this evening. Whereas I thought that I go forward, I was falling over with might and main, maybe , every minute was running against me. Moreover, maybe, there isn't that strange man who called himself Keşşaf! All of them, Cavalry with horse, Keşşaf, Anka are all scenes in my imagination. Self doubting, I returned to the guest house desperately. My feet were going without knowing where they went.

We came across at the bottom of the stairs with Kırlangıç. She was going out.

I asked, "Where are you going at this time?"

She said, "We are going to Safran with the girls." She didn't say anything except this. Without going to my room, I started walking next to her. I was both walking and speaking of Müdrik. Zümrüt and Nergis were waiting for her by the side of the road like shadows.

When we reached to Safran's house, it was dark and I was very tired. As we came here at this time of the day, there must be a message for us. I went with it.

When we arrived home, Safran welcomed us with a voice that was lifting all the weights on me. Her daughter Didem having a white pinked kerchief on her head was doing something in the kitchen. There was smell of butter, fresh baked dough in the house. I saw the flat-bread which was made by Safran and shining like moon. Happiness of the freshly baked dough. Zümrüt, Kırlangıç, Nergis and I ran away from the chaos of the world and benefited from the tea on the stove which was flaming with a gurgling sound. Hot tea and flat-breads. All these things, this suddenness in life made me suspicious. Müdrik's words were whistling in my ears. Words of Müdrik, words and incomprehensible look of the manager of the dormitory, wisdom of the teachers, complex relations that I wanted to establish between many things irrelevant to each other in this life, photograph of my soul away from clearness.

My helplessness turned into tears. Oil of the flat-bread in my hands. Slim tea glass trying to slip from my hand. Tea poured on me. The things I experience in this timelessness world. I called out.

"Let's tell me something. Don't stop. I smother as you are quite. Just talk to me. Talk like the *azan*. Like the prayers. Oh, Cavalry with horses! Oh, Keşşaf, you didn't tell me anything about silence. I can't bear this.

Tell me the sound again. Your voice. Voices. As if turning to me, as if dancing. Without stopping, like the letters."

Kırlangıç looked at me to understand what is happening when she saw that the bread in my hand was getting wet with my tears. To see, to learn, she asked. Smell of the bread was mixing with the smell of Safran, with the shadows of the aromatic corners of the house. I was flowing. Without stopping. Safran pulled her face over mine, sat near me, and said,

"Princess," she wiped my tears.

"Don't cry..."

I hugged her. Her neck. Until her white scarf got wet, until I was out of breath, my nose was running, I was out of breath, my face turned into red like the stove.

When I raised my head, my eyes were touching the beautiful eyes Keşşaf tearfully. He was neither close to nor far away me. My mind was coming and going in this closeness and distance. I tore myself away the sky of his breast as is flowing like rain.

He said, "Now, you started to penetrate. I am Keşşaf. If I unveil, you can't stand, you can't leave me."

This time, Keşşaf wiped my tears with his snowy hand. That's it! That's the time! That I the peak of the existence! The circle that all times turn around!

"You are surprised that I hear your, aren't you? Or even sometimes you think that all these are the things you make up. Our voices mix each other. You have difficulty in distinguishing which voice is yours. You become again audible in an ego hearing your voice. The words I whisper to you, the things I make you experience at the sky of your breast causes you to look at all the existent with a genius instinct. Your ego breaks into parts, then when you hold my hand it takes different forms. Read what is given to you! Listen to what is told to you! Watch as the doors are opened! Don't interrupt the universe while it, the endless reality, is talking to you! When you do this, you will understand that you are in that endless reality, your voice is spread over its voice. When you can't afford, turn towards and ask for help. When it is difficult for you, remember that you are approaching one more step to the peak of the mountain, you are climbing from the mountain of ego to peak of reality mountain one more step! Wait until they fins when you hear these words! Wait that word finishes the picture. The sky in your breast gets lighter day by day. Do you get it, princess?"

At the last sentence, he such laughed that one could see his teeth.

To come to myself from his beauty, the shape of this laugh took a long time. When I came to myself, Zümrüt was holding my hand and saying "wake up".

He said smilingly, "We are staying here tonight." His long black eyelashes shadowed his bright face.

"Do you mind if we stay?"

When I came to myself, Safran was reading a passage from the book she was holding like a baby. Again her white scarf was surrounding her forehead and bright face, she turned her eyes to my eyes like a barrel;

"Mind is desperate in seeing the divine light
Go on your way,
Search for another eye."

12
What the Night Says

"Now we are starting to tell about the talkings of the non-living things and their work. Wise people don't confirm this. How will I say the things I see now?" (□ems-i Tebriz)

The first half of January... There is still time for Ankara to unload the burden of the cold weather. Snow hasn't laid its smooth hands off us yet; the winter is warmer than ever, friendlier while the meaning of being cold has changed so much for me. For me an endless spring has started for me with the touching of Keşşaf's voice on my soul. Now I meet the trees covered with their white cloth, the sky, the hiding sun, the rain, the mug and each stone one by one all over again. How each of them is fresh and full of life. I say, for example, each tree sends the seasons without ruining its position. What a submission, I say. To stand like posing in spite of the snow and wind for years. What is it like standing attention, what is it like bending the branch for prayer and extending it to the sky, what kind of heart is it that a tree has? Trees turn green as the sing of the earth changes. The ground will be unable to contain itself as the earth revives again.

Kırlangıç comes inside while I am looking at the hard branches of the tree in the garden from my room's window. In this new year we are both more calm than the past. And also we are closer to ourselves and the friendship. Kırlangıç's friendship doesn't tire you, but it makes you rest. We are like water and fire. When I breathe fire she calms me, and put out the fire when flames catch the face of my soul; when she is dumbfounded like a calm river or slackens, my soul in fire revives her. Ours is the togetherness of the water and fire. Water's deceiving the fire is so unreasonable, and the ineffectiveness of the fire on the water is so clear that much.

Here that night... How many times does one have such a night during his life?

I was in a strange sleep that was sleepless. In my room. There were only you all day. I breathed you every direction I turned in this room, I filled with your smell like the sherbet filled my throat. It is due to your beautiful face. This face is nearly in the purity of oceans, your smile at every appearance of which in my mind I dive to the depths is a freshness hidden in the blueness. Whatever I say is due to your beauty. I know this thing, this unbearable fire between us only and absolutely burns me. Although you know everything happened between us, I don't know why you verbalise them. While the hand moving the pen is yours, you know, how can I look at your beautiful face, how can I be strong enough to do this? Looking at you is similar to disappearing dashes in the dark horizons, letting yourself go down that horizon and being out of breath in the water, or looking at the moon from a hand's-breath distance!

I was in a calm sleep of which one side could see. What a nice, light and transparent sleep it was! A sleep that knew that it was sleeping or a sleep that want to see that it wasn't sleeping. An eye was opened on the centre of my chest independent from me and I was watching my self as sleeping. Me and everything. It was watching every point that an eye could see, recording every sound, and saying only one name in the sleep with all its power continuously. This talking in the sleep sometimes resembled the suffering voice of a hurt person, it waved along its rhythm and finally turned to the still and calm whispers of a dervish drunk on happiness. During the night this rhythm changed form, I was watching this talking changing its form steadily with the eye opened on my chest all night. Jots reared up and everything was rotating around me like planets. Everything was continuously flowing and I was wading through these waves. The only thing that everyone and everything knows is His name! The night weaving His name like a lace-work, its breath doesn't stop even for a moment to exist with His name. As if it breaks away the rhythm if it stops saying this name, drops this name like dropping a jewel. It doesn't drip even a drop from its voice not to be inundated in the darknesses. It shouldn't fall behind even a step from the rhythm. Every little spot is a giant concert area. Everything that exists has become a sound. Boozily.

I see with the eye opened on my chest. My whole body has become heart, my beats are calm and strong. Then on top of the eye opening on my chest like a lotus, I also open my head eye. The night invites me to its depth, it lets me go in its secrets, its most private places. It hides me under its dark cover. I am waken up totally from the sleep of which one side can see –at that only moment- I rise and sit. I wander about the continents. Everything around me in this room is talking in the sleep boozily. Like overwhelmed, like having drunk all night. The table, books, pens, curtains, floor, closets doesn't stop. My God! The eye opened on my chest like a rose takes all these sounds on its lap. I hear with my ears, both I am flowing in the waters and I have become a voice, I have exiled from myself! Everything, everything one can think and see bands together circling with this voice. The sap of everything has appeared with this talking in the sleep! They die a thousand deaths from love talking your name in the sleep!

It has lost it transparency, misted from the speed, the table by my bed, here it is! It says your name with all its power. I catch the table's voice through the sounds mixed together. The voice comes as if this table has a body and a head and it is submitting. I cannot see anything rather than this voice, this talking. It has been saying your name continuously, endlessly as if it has been saying it from the eternity, as if it will disappear if it stops, it throws itself the fire of your name not to burn; it is talking in the sleep like a human. Its mouth say your name continuously as if it is a mouth on the whole. I have become a whole tongue and hear with my head ear. I see with the eye opened like a jasmine on my chest. I see with two eyes side by side on my head, with two ears. This is a voice falling from a nice and smooth waterfall of helplessness! It is dragging on with this name like a misty, shy slave following the orders.

Behind this talking as if a hive of bees are buzzing, or waves in an ocean has overflowed, raged, reared up; as if horses have boiled over from a green high valley to another, drums and clarions, as if it is a wedding party, talks are one within the other. They are rotating around me, we are rotating, this room, this city, this world... This is to go without pause!

The flow of everything with a tremendous energy. This, this is its disappearing in you quickly! Sleep lifts up its curtain from my eyes, and I am scared at that moment, very much scared, like terrified, like meeting the doomsday, the doomsday falling apart love, as if I fell just in its heart.

I can't move. If I go further, if I can't return back there; if I hear this forever, if my mind is burnt out? I wish I burnt until the petals of the eyes opened on my chest like tulips fell apart...

This process, this flowing everything to love crazily and boozily. The rotating of everything around themselves. That consciousness for a few seconds was a perfectness that I couldn't see again even if I lived for hundreds of years. To exist in and out of the pure timelessness that you opened my eyes simultaneously. Prayer of every jot in the universe for love with a terrific music and with a heading that broke hearts, minds and the whole conscious. We would have gone mad if we had heard this every moment, then you pulled me down that pitch and dragged me from one valley to another. Which one will I tell about, for which one will I have a power to tell about?

When I woke up from this half awake half asleep state completely next morning, I thought what would have happened if I hadn't been scared at that moment. I have never had such a few extraordinary seconds in my life again. I thought about this for weeks. The things that Keşşaf had told about the voice was flocking to my mind.

13
From the Dark Room to the Light Writing

15 days passed after the night that I had heard the talks of the goods and it was February. I hadn't seen Safran fort his fifteen days. When the mid-term break started the day that I would see her would fall apart. I was worried about that everything was going further so fast and I wanted to welcome life without intervening. Nor one should have been in a hurry nor proceeded very slowly; every event should have occurred in its own speed, and they already occurred so.

After spending a short holiday in my home town with my aunt, I couldn't stand this separation and got Safran's in no time flat. When I arrived, the girls were there, Nergis, Kırlangıç and Zümrüt and Hazel. As I understood Safran's speaking had finished and tea phase had started.

When Kırlangıç saw me,

"You have caught the tea phase, luck you," she said with a pleased laugh.

"Tea without me!" I said quietly.

Somehow I couldn't look into Safran's eyes directly, I couldn't ask her anything, I was satisfied with being there. She was talking to Gül Hanım and seemed quite well. When she saw I was joking with the girls,

"Princess welcome, where have you been?" she said.

I knew for certain that she knew where I had been.

"Here and there" I said, "at your elbow." She was content with smiling to this statement. I turned to Nergis and asked her what I had missed, "she haven't talked much yet," she said bending over me. "She only talked about the light shortly. She meant the light coming from the window, the light coming into the dark room."

"What light?" I said.

"Do you listen to the professors at school like this?" said Kırlangıç bending her head over me and covering her mouth with her hand.

“Of course, I listen.” I said.

“Tell it to your grandmother,” she whispered laughing.

This room, this house... Everything is clear, stainless, we have purified from anger and worry. We are passing through fresh and crystalline moments feeling and realizing. The feeling that life is unbearable cannot touch us, the bitterness of life hasn’t visited us, Zümrüt, Nergis, Kırlangıç, Hazel and be. Hope is very close to us, the flower of love is under our nose, sincerity stops over words, as if we take out the pearls of that beautiful lights from the neck of the obscurity bird, each of us is on the shore of the calm waters, our feet have never touched wild waves. Thick chains of being tested have not wrung our necks yet. It hasn’t choked and choked, we haven’t been out of breath in the middle of the sentences. It has never happened that we haven’t completed a word yet. We have never heard the footsteps of sorrow and being refused. The cruel hand of the injustice hasn’t held our delicate hands. We haven’t broken like thin branches. We are still in the first scenes of the film called love, even in the trailer. We don’t have a foresight for the other scenes except reaching. The objects have always smiled us in the shots entering the frame. We have never heard the crying melodies of the objects yet. The act of crying is only a consequence of love for us; not of separation or deprivation. Forgiving, being forgiven is all around us, we have never taken the name of hatred. There is a slackness of a hot summer night in our souls. We haven’t heard the existence of hard and cruel winters, we haven’t had pain yet, we haven’t felt dizzy with no reason. We haven’t known yet that the heaviest suffering is on our shoulders: Love!

The peace Kırlangıç feels shines in her eyes. Her moves talks even if she is silent. A glimpsing hesitation on her face. A look apt to the pain visits her face occasionally, touches slightly. A wisdom in Nergis’s way of sitting, a spontaneity, a feeling of being far from the eyes. In her way of sitting on the floor, an eraser has been given to her and she continuously erases her existence. Her head drops, her eyes are closed, her face is smiling. Her voice finds way to the earth from the lowest pitch. If it is possible, she will talk without opening her mouth. This is a kind of calmness that makes you jealous. A victory that seems like effortless. She is looking like a person that can give up everything if he loves. She has a talent of being nothing if she loves. Zümrüt is moving as if she wants to be loved rather than love: she has conditions such as ‘I love if I loved.’ She opens her heart to hear a compliment from the beloved. A calm silence has taken the place of Hazel’s cheerful laughters ringing in the corridors of the guesthouse.

Safran has finished her talking to Gül Hanım and a silence holds on in the middle. The light coming into the room by touching the curtains with flowers reveals it. The colours of the rug in the centre are speaking, washing with light, we are listening to the colours undressing as washing, we are watching how they are dancing with the light.

Long afterwards a thick cloud covers the light of February; the light has been out of breath. The sky becomes misty. Bloomy curtains get heavy and pout. The cheerful dance of the light fades from the scene, time passing at the double starts to breathe deeply leaning on its knees as if it is tired, tired breath of time is left. We are dumbfounded with shadows on our faces.

"The weather gets worse" Gül Hanım says.

Turning to Nergis, "What did she tell about the light?" I whispered. Kırlangıç is taking the floor, she looks at me as if she says "you know", and adds,

"It is impossible to tell the same, you know," "that is to say that it won't be the same probably even if we tell it word by word!"

Kırlangıç means Safran's mastership to tell something.

"Never mind, tell me anyway, I wonder" I say.

At the very moment, a strong cry is heard from far away,

A voice speaks, "Has someone said 'light' here?" I rise my head to the sky and recoil with fear, lightnings are flashing. Then as it come closer I see the white horse behind the lightnings. It runs so fast that the sparks from the hooves of the horse make me blind. The Cavalry with white head-dress slows down his horse, the horse stops in the end rearing up several times, he caresses its head to make it calm down. He says "Okay." The chest of the horse is heaving like a windbag. I step back with creeps. To hide my admiration even if just a bit.

I know he is Keşşaf. Again the veil on his face. His eyes are telling about me a love that I haven't dreamt before. He makes me know about the eternity with one look, good news are pouring over me. You don't know, I know, says his eyes, you are passing through a love that you haven't dreamt about.

He is bending from the horse a little, hop on, he says,

"I will show you the way to the light!"

He holds my hand and pulls me on the horse. It's been a long time that I haven't felt this moment. How I miss this magnificence showing up on this beautiful horse with his green clothing, this fresh breath of beauty coming into life. I am so close to him that I will nearly hear the sound of the blood flowing through my veins. I hug his waist. I press my face on his back tightly. He smells green and blue sky appears on my forehead. The skirts of his green cloth and the end of his white head-dress are waving as his white horse speeding. We are going towards the transparency, towards the land in which every moment is reborn. Which road entrance will he leave me this time, which palace's door will he seal me, what will I see just after now?

We travel as if we have wings. We pass through the paths hidden in the woods, we watch waters foaming as passing through rivers, we leave clouds behind as crossing the mountains. This travel without stopping and resting doesn't tire us. We cross the bejewelled door of the love palace and pass the world of sense. I know this palace, I hear all its sounds.

"Now," says the Cavalry, "We are going to world of seeing. Keşşaf will show you the light."

His voice echoes, sweeps my face through the misty lights in waves. The light has whishing tones, its circling and dancing around us becomes clear. The Cavalry leaves me at the threshold of a turquoise door.

"Get down here, the time is up!" he says. This is a mansion made of colours. All colours are waving, all colours are nested. Yellow, blue, red, green.

"Here is the source of the light and all colours, source of everything eye can see" he says. "Take here as your chest" and he adds,

"Remember this, I hear you every time you called me!"

I stand alone again. Only me silently...

I listen to the talks of the colours for a while. I watch each of them breathing, I witness how the colours that the darkness approach die; I am surprised how the colours that white touches exist. I step on the misty threshold of the turquoise door, my foot disappears, I am dyed endlessly as much as the colours touching my skin. The wide corridor and high ceiling glimpses in the plays of lights. Here the purity and permeability of the colours takes the place of the objects. Only the colour of the shiny chandeliers that I can fix my eyes on doesn't change, and also of the golden foils'. I walk through the light halos and colour twisters ever-lengthening.

A single step here means moving through a figure being arm in arm with the light spirals. As the curtains floating wavily slipping down the high ceilings give me way, another colour is pouring over me. When the rose-coloured curtain opens, the red wings as if it knows here is it's turn; right after it the orange curtain is passing burning with its colour. Whichever curtain my feet touch on, my face turns to its colour, I become talented to identify the secrets about colours, I discover that how each of them can be so sharp. I have just felt that every colour has a scent. I see how the heart of each colour beats with light. The curtains lifted up commodiously and calmly consist of only colours. I walk through the chromatic spectrum, yellow, green, blue, dark blue and purple curtains swallow me one by one. At last, behind a strong light his face is as shiny as the sun, this is Keşşaf who has told me about the world of hearing, his very self! Every colour touches his honey-coloured hair flowing from his shoulders separately, his hazel eyes turn to green, then to blue. The food bag on his waist catches my sight. It looks like a transparent bag from which every colour is leaking garishly.

"Dilruba, welcome to the house of light!"

I think that I was a good student in the world of hearing as I have managed to come here, otherwise why do I drop by here? I must have been promoted.

"Thank you" I say, a perfect smile sets on my face. I want to say that "Discoverer, you are the most beautiful crazy person I have ever met, perhaps your beauty is due to this." He doesn't get close to me, he speaks under the pulsating lights of the colourful mosaic pendants as if he is speaking from a rostrum. When I rise my head I see the breathtaking lights of the giant chandelier descending as if it is flowing over me from the centre of a ceiling. This chandelier is so big that it resembles both a tree and a sun. Its crystals are winking steadily; it speaks in its own language. I freeze under this magnificent view magically. Party-coloured pendants by it flowing like water. Thousands of colourful mirrors, stained-glasses all along, everything is colour, every jot is light. I detect a differentness, a strangeness in these lights. Each colour is deeper than I know, black is so bright that it looks like white here. Green is crucial and violet is so brilliant by no stretch of the imagination. Milk-white or yellow bright lights are rotating over me as if they turn to a tornado and want to swallow me. There is something more important that I just realize it. Colours I have never known, a terrific colour flow I have never seen before, a motion of light, my God! Green shows its white face shining until turning to black, then it becomes an ivy, red turns to dancing flames suddenly from a state like vapour or smoke. The white smoke rising until my shoulders turns to a white peony rotating continuously. These peonies rise to the chandelier beaming in party-colours with ribbons flowing its ends resembling crystal stars. Then suddenly they turn to white roses as they are rising. The spectrum of light is so complex and rapid I get out of breath completely.

Keşşaf is more real at every moment among these beauties!

"What are all these?" I whimper.

The glitters are slipping intermittently along his shoulders carrying his beautiful head. His honey coloured hair is washed by lights. I watch all colours in his hazel eyes. The delicate lines of his face are bright in the colour spectrum.

"What you see is the substance of the colours," he says.

I have the pleasure that I have ever had all my life. Keşşaf continues.

"The colours you see in the world are only weak copies of these colours."

"Oh my God, unbelievable," I say.

"Dilruba, the truth is so extraordinary that it is nearly unbelievable," he says.

I hear this incompletely. Something happens to me when he says this. First I go black and I feel exhausted, a terrible ache on my head and a strong sickness in me is melting. I don't have enough strength for this beauty. I faint in the arms of the colours.

When I recover consciousness, Keşşaf and I are in the middle of a deep blue ocean. I realize that it isn't an ocean but I am floating in the misty blueness flying about. Other colours of which I don't know the names accompany it.

"Blue brings you through and the others recover your consciousness," he says.

In spite of my weak state, I ask desperately,

"I will stay here, won't I? I won't go back. Come on, tell me I am here. Tell me I will stay here forever."

There is suppliance in my voice, he looks at me smiling.

"I thought I gave gained power in the world of hearing. He sighs long.

"I am sorry, this is impossible, time will resumes on for you," he says.

I also see this at the moment I hear. Everything is so transparent and clear. Images appear before the blueness, I am sitting on the floor in Safran's house, Kırlangıç and Zümrüt are beside me, Safran and Gül Hanım opposite. In the previous scene my going to Safran's house, I have just set off. Hazel is with me. In the previous scenes images of the past years open one by one. Again my heart is beating in my mouth, it is fluttering. It punches my throat.

"Would you like to see next scenes?" asks Keşşaf. I tremble, then the next scene opens, Kırlangıç and me are talking in front of the tall dressing mirror at the entrance of the guesthouse. A thoughtful expression in my face. In the next scene I am trying to cross the road with a ping rose in my hand.

"That's enough for now," says Keşşaf and he pulls down the photos in these scenes as if closing curtains. All these scenes tore like paper. The colour of the ocean, the blueness are withdrawn under us sliding at the same time and the colours of which I don't know the names disappear. I find myself in a big room with a high ceiling, covered with mirrors but again full of colourful pendants, various kinds of plants and shapes. There is a rectangle table between Keşşaf and me, and a rainbow lying on the table. He is like a dream appearing at one end of the table...

"You should listen carefully what I will say here," he says, "because at the end of this lesson I will give you a mission but this mission will not last short as you suppose."

He broaches the subject upon my curious looks,

"What do you know about photography?"

"I can't say that I have interested in it so much so far, I don't know anything about it significantly." I say.

"You will learn, be patient!" he says. He tells met he meaning of camera. "It consist of the Greek words 'photos' meaning light and 'graphein' meaning writing and drawing; it means lightened record, lightened writing or drawing with light," he says. He tells me about the history of the photograph. He talks about the stages of the first photograph known in the history that Joseph Niecephore Niepce's, a French man, took in 1826, starting telling about that Cabir Ibni Hayyam found the silver nitrate went black in the sunlight in the 8th century. Then he talks about the developmental stages of the 'camera obscura' that is the 'dark room.' The things he is talking about are so interesting that I am surprised that how come I haven't been interested in the photography before. Keşşaf starts to talk to me in my own language, this relieves me a little. I get rid of the mystery chilling me a little.

"I want you to think about a dark room. When light comes into this dark room from a little hole, the image will reflect the opposite wall of the room inversely." He talks about how Arabic astronomers used the dark room or dark box to observe the Sun in the 10th century starting from Aristotle, long before the photography invented. "European artists used the black box to reflect the images on canvas to make more accurate drawings in the 15th century." He says. Here he doesn't pass Leonardo da Vinci. "As you see, people had strived to catch the magic of the light and to tame it for centuries."

"Only light?" I say.

"This expression includes the effect of the Sun on the colours, naturally," he says.

He pulls the white satin cloth on the rectangle table swiftly. The cloth is flowing from his hands like water divided in waves,

"I want to say this, if you take the light from the photograph like pulling the cloth on the table swiftly, there is nothing left. Light is the must for the photography, it is the initial condition.

I am listening to him carefully and waiting what mission he will give me... "Human," he says, "is able to do anything he dreams about as long as he dreams."

I watch how the darkness under the cloth swallows and effaces the colours swaying around.

"If you come to think about it, the adventure of photography is parallel with the human's adventure of discovering himself. Don't be patient, I will tell you."

He pauses. His hazel eyes turn to iridescent green.

"After the 18th century, it was realized that some chemicals changed effecting by light. Materials covered with some chemicals recorded the light fell on them... Clearly the image of the object obtained by light effect was fixed. Of course you need a lens to do this, think that it is a seeing eye."

Afterwards he tells me about some techniques. Photoshoot of the moving or still objects, black and white photos, the depth perception needed in the photo, and balance, symmetry and asymmetry, contrast, spots, golden ratio, focus of interest of the composition...

When he understands I get tired, surprised and have difficulty to understand, he summarizes as saying "the reason of all I am telling is that I want you to hear the music of the photograph."

"I ask you to take the photo of your reality, but you have the right of taking only one shot, there is no permission to take the second."

I am confused and bewildered as a person who hasn't taken photographs before.

"That's why nothing is the repeating of something else in the nature as well as nothing is a copy of something else. I want you to learn this. Every moment and every thing in the universe is unique without repetition, when you want to take the second shot everything has changed. Even after only one short moment."

"But I have no idea how I will do this. Besides, I will do this with only one shot."

This is the photo in the lights that I already fail in the beginning,

I think. Only a few shots of photo I have taken so far includes only when posing people were looking around to find somebody to take their photos and I passed by them incidentally,they slipped the camera suddenly saying ‘push here.’ I have never frozen a part of nature or a person forever by the help of photography. Moreover, photography is absolutely not of interest to me.

When Keşşaf see my face has gone sour, he says,

“Don’t worry, you can do it. I have suggestion to you, while doing this assume that there is no such thing as photography. Free your thoughts as much as you can.”

The subject is going outside my abilities and knowledge.

He made the job more difficult,

“Why don’t you draw the sky on your chest? Or the eye on your consciousness?”

“I don’t have the faintest idea how this will happen.” I said. I started to get desperate. The plump pendants over me was losing their lights with my rising intimidation.

After saying “I will show you how you will do it,” Keşşaf first talked about how a photo should be ‘read’. As he told, I understood that the photo he was talking about was not the one in the meaning that I understood. He told me something in the language of photography. As if everything he said had double meaning, perhaps what he told was for photography studies in technical context.

“You will learn the balance, symmetry or asymmetry; spots or all kinds of plays of light in photography in time. If you look at a still, fixed object from different angles, you can reach different solutions as many as the differences you see.” And he went on:

“The first thing to be determined for a taking is the taking distance, perspective as you know. If the object you are taking is a still object, you can discover it turning around as much as you need. Here I want you to think irrationally as much as you can. If you want to take a photo of a moving object, you may need to move back and forward depending on its movements.”

The big room of this big building resembling a mansion was full of mirrors. There are pastel sparkling of the intertwining colours and lights that ever-lengthened endlessly. Keşşaf continued:

“If you want to take the photo of the eye in your conscience, you should take it at the sharpness as far as to the retina in that eye. It should be unique, different, you need to reveal its powerful aspects and make it speak. The photo of the sky on your chest should be revealed with everything, the whole universe, all seas, creatures, even absence. If you try to look at the sky I am talking about from opposite, from above, from below, from right or left as separate individuals, separate creatures, this makes you move away from it, and this is actually a strike to freedom. As you try to look at it you fall far from it. You should both look at the lens and the sky; you should both see it with all its nakedness and also your seeing eye in the photograph. If you try to take the photo of the sky on your chest in this way, you will understand that actually the loneliness does not exist, it only exist as long as you keep yourself behind the lens. The image of Keşşaf was vibrating in all mirrors at the same time and it blinded me. He went on:

"Actually the sky in your chest is so restless, so slippery, so immense, so complex and has so different shapes... The more you try to be free, the more you become worried and weak since the thought of being free isolates you. To do the things I am telling you, you need to go in the dark room in your own chest. This is the first condition! If you don't go into the dark room, you cannot see how the light reflects and how it reflect reversely to the opposite wall. If you can do these things, you will be able to watch the moving photos of your own sky on your own conscience and of all existent skies."

At those magical moments going on in the world of seeing, Keşşaf was talking tirelessly with his voice transforming to a melody. In a part of these long lasting lessons, he told me about the seeing of an eye and colours. "Our eyes," he said, "can see a little part of the all light types exist in the universe." Keşşaf showed me how light separated into different colours passing through a triangular prism and sometimes rain drops separated light as it is in the prism one day, and the other day he showed me light recombining the colours, that is the colour spectrum. Another day he revealed when a mechanism he called as colour wheel with different colours on it from red to purple was spun very quickly, it gave the light itself, and said "you see, white carries all the colours in its heart." Why hadn't I discovered before that my life was so colourful?

Afterwards he told that the colour spectrum continues beyond the two red and purple ends but it is impossible for our eyes to perceive this with naked eye. He said "the part that can be seen by naked eye is only a very narrow wavelength space.

He was telling me about colours in detail. He was teaching me tirelessly how light was similar to sound, and that light spread around in waves like sound. "The thing that changes the colour of the light," he said, "thickening or thinning of the light waves." And he added, "red is the colour having the longest wavelength." Then he showed me how all accent colours are formed by three base colours, that is red, blue and yellow. How orange is formed by red and yellow, and purple by red and blue... And the others respectively...

He said that purple had the shortest wavelength in the same lesson and added,

"Be careful about purple!"

One day, at one of the colour lessons, Keşşaf mixed red and white and he transformed the colour he achieved into a pink scarf and gave me. I thought the room filled with a pink smoke.

"I know you like the colour pink very much and even the reason of it," he said.

Keşşaf didn't miss even the smallest detail about me. I twined this lengthening, flowing pink scarf pouring endlessly on my neck.

After telling about all colours, he showed how black swallows all colours.

"Darkness is the place where the light and colours doesn't exist."

At the end of the same lesson, he said, "I want you to discover the harmony, accord and rhythm between colours and of course the play of the colours." He told this wit an implication.

During the moments while he was telling all these I was watching the continuously changing colours from all the corners and edges from the room covered with mirrors. I was surprised that the colour spectrum was painted into seven colours in that timeless space resembling a high ceiling. Keşşaf was relaying me interesting information about colours in a wide range, he said every cell in our body needed light. He passed from the energy of colours to the energy of body, and told that different energy centres in the body had different colours and every colour affected different parts of the body.

The tones of the green, deep blue, deep red moving with the vibration of his voice became clear, time froze in the world I had dropped somewhere behind me, and my body falling apart the space was turning to a dream completely.

"I know Dilruba! You want to take the photo of passion, love, purity, pains and pleasures crystallized in your heart. To do this, both your camera and the object should be moving. You watch for the light steadily without missing a moment in order to watch the foaming of the extraordinary colours, find out the perfect shot and frame it. You want to own it endlessly, you want to take out that one shot from the infinite number of shots and colours at an unprecedented pace. But be patient.

And wait for the light to reflect to your dark room. For this you definitely need to open a small, clear hole that light can go in. That single shot is to enclose the soul of the eternity, to free it at a rate of you capture, to flow babbling with that enthusiasm, to witness how everything loses their meaning there at your every look, even you know everything is meaningful there... Containing of the single shot everything crazily, while leaving others than itself outside, carrying all the sounds to its sky. Here you will do this! You will be this! When you own that one shot, you will own all circles, all triangles, all diagonal shapes. Perfect hexagons, ellipses and pyramids, the perfect face of each snowflake, molecules of the water, all ever-lengthening lines, all points rotating around themselves will talk to you. At the moment you can see that single shot you enter the road to reach the blessed secret of 'Jot is the mirror of the ash!' You will start to see how one atom imitate the whole universe."

Keşşaf went on telling everything he knew about photography through the moving shadows with mirrors of the mansion. As the days passing, I say days to describe the time intervals but it didn't fit the meaning of day we know, he asked me what I thought reflecting different photos of a mirror in the mansion, then he interpreted the photograph in his own style. There were photos among them taken in the countries that I had never seen.

One day he told me "photography is the poetry of the light, Dilruba." "And there is only one single light suitable for each photograph. One should wait for that light patiently, without hurrying, should trace that light tirelessly. You should also wait for the most suitable light to take the photo of the sky on your chest. There are such photographs that they reveal new moments in moments as if poetry discovers new and magical paths in the language. They nearly reveal the moments that eye cannot see. Here, they say, life is much more than you see. Just as music imitates the endless rhythm of the universe, a photograph shot tells us more than it shows.

As I sensed the terrific harmony, balance and rhythm waiting clandestinely in a photo shot that we just browsed slightly, perhaps inattentively, the doors of a new world was opening before me. I was watching each photo shot reflecting the mirror on the right moving wall of the mansion, on the left side space or floor in a new light in Keşşaf's hazel eyes turning to green at one time and blue at the other. I was watching the balance harmony in his angled, sharp features, in his dark skin, in his perfect face. While I was surprised how light reflecting from the prism over us was broken into pieces in his face,

"The focal point in a photo provides us to look at that life moment deeply," he said. "There are such moments in life that they don't have before and after. That shot is unique, from which direction you look at that shot, your point of view, the light fixed there, resolution or blurred pattern on the background, rhythm and texture or harmony, all of them are special to that only moment." Then he thought for a moment and added, "you know, every moment of life is so actually. Only we have given up sensing the differences between the flowing moments."

Then he went on with an admirable smiling on his face,

"If you want to see that perfect picture, first you should discover its existence. You feel it clearly as if tasting a candy, feeling the warm air on your face, or suffering from a physical pain. If the photo of your chest is blurred, it must be under your control."

"I think there is nobody not knowing about its existence," I said with surprise.

Colour spectrum flowing like a river around me slowed down as if they heard me.

"The world is full of those who haven't felt the existence of it in their own ego... You should winnow out unnecessary details after feeling it with its all warmth and all colours. There shouldn't be any unnecessary spots and shadows on the background. You should preserve symmetry and asymmetry how you like, and you should make it explicit at the rate of you wish. Light should speak there, and you had better avoid the figures overlapping each other there as it is in life. Balance and precision should be adjusted well as it is in life." I was watching the lights moving in his hazel eyes,

"Just so you know, in a photograph, especially in sky photos, the opposition of light and shadow provides us a texture purified from space. There is no space in the photograph as there is no in life, there shouldn't be."

Keşşaf continued to show me details from the life taken out of the time for weeks. There was such a moment that I felt uneasy about the timelessness in the photograph. I got tired of the immobility. All colours were on the move in the room of the mansion full of mirrors except photos, only photos started to be frozen and emotionless. Keşşaf must have understood so he said,

"Do you feel uneasy about this in a timeless place, it's a wonder. Don't feel uneasy. Time is not necessary for the photo. If you add time to the photo, that is if you make it mobile it is not a photograph anymore, but it becomes cinema." And saying, "the thing I don't want you to see is the flow. Actually I want you to see the perfect construction of the nature that doesn't accept intervention," he showed me hundreds of nature photos.

He said, "I show you one apiece of drop from the continuously flowing river, combine them and make them flow in you again. The mechanism of the eye is just like a camera's. Light is needed in the incident of seeing as it is in photography. Rays coming from objects constitute a reverse, that is upside down the image on retina by refracting on the cornea and eye lens. The image reflecting the retina is two-dimensional exactly as it is in the photograph. Then the image here reaches the visual cortex in the brain transforming an electric current and the erect image is formed. Actually there is no sound, no colour and no image in our brain, the only thing that exists is the electric signals. That is light cannot go in the brain pan, as you see."

I started to read beyond Keşşaf's statements thoroughly.

"You will take the photo of the sky on your chest that you have heard its voice in the world of hearing but looked at it from a tiny space. To understand this completely you have first been in the world of hearing, do you get it?"

I got very excited. So that night I had heard the voice of the table was only a moment in the world of hearing, my heart was fluttering. So everything I had experienced in the world of hearing or seeing had been revealed from a tiny space of my own sky. So Keşşaf also had known what I had experienced that night. Everything that I had experienced, my rolling to the valley of wonder suddenly, that magnificent moment without before and after... He had showed me the truth of hearing so that I had been able to cope with the magnificence of that moment. All those melodies, all those terrific rhythms, songs of the birds had been all for me to bear that one moment. To make me hear how furnishing, how every point in the room had moved boozily by love at that night. Now he was preparing me for another glory in the world of seeing. Once I felt the existence of the eye opened like a rose in the middle of my chest, he wanted met o see everything, to watch everything with that eye.

Keşşaf went on,

"So seeing is a miracle. And the thing that you think you see is only a copy, and there is no possibility to 'see' the genuine of this imitation with your eyesight. Actually there is nothing related to light and colour in the brain resembling the dark room! This is marvellous, think about it, thousands of lights, thousands of sounds and thousands of images pile in your brain resembling the dark room, but they are not there!"

I could say "wow!" with surprise.

"Then I need to ask this, why light is needed in seeing?"

"Seeing that the inside of the brain doesn't have a contact with light?" I tried to comprehend.

"I asked you to think unreasoningly," he said, "and now I want you think like this. Then, actually, there shouldn't be the light as we understand outside. So there is something else to stimulate the retina in the eye."

I was so confused. What about colours, then they shouldn't exist.

"Colours also don't exist." He said. "I think this is clear. In summary: there are only electromagnetic waves in the world except us, that is the energy! We talked about the wavelengths of the colours in the lessons about colours, do you remember?"

I nodded as if saying yes.

"Colours," he said, "are the electromagnetic rays at different wavelengths. A beautiful rose you see only reflects a different wavelength of the light. The thing you call as colour is the intensity of the light. Return to the moment that you learned that sound wasn't in the brain in the world of hearing and remember. There wasn't sound except us, there were only sound waves, sound didn't go into brain, remember."

At one of that lessons Keşşaf's voice saying "your brain is so silent, Dilruba" echoed my ears. He continued.

"Now I think the spiritual photograph that I want you to take is more clear. You should be able to see the core, the genuine of everything, you should be able to see the truth itself together with yourself there. Look at yourself going out of your brain. To do this, don't keep yourself behind the eye of your heart, behind the lens, include yourself in that movement, become both the one who see and the one who is seen. To do this, you should adjust your point of view well, learn to look at yourself from different angles, you should be able to snuggle all the passages of your ego. I am trying to train your looks with the example of photography. I want you to see every persistent detail, every balance for the dynamism in life. A photography master has a separative and distinguishing eye, he perceives any contradiction, the tiniest exaggeration, symmetry or the existent magic in the photograph in advance of the others. His angle is wide, his instincts can go deeper as much as possible, he senses the rhythm in advance of the others. I want you to become so."

My task was hard.

"I need your help to be able to do all these," I said. In my tone the appealing of 'I need you more at every moment.' He approached a little proudly, a little kind-heartedly as if asking me if I want to become like him. He was talking with the light in his hazel eyes;

"There are no such things as closeness and distance between us, closeness or distance occurs in the place where there is time and space, our togetherness is timeless and spaceless. If you love me the process going to the eternal start."

Then he shadowed the light in his eyes and touched with his voice again;

"Hereafter pay attention to the moments in your life. Examine your sky. Think how you make this sky clear with your thoughts, feelings and senses. You should catch the most critical moment to take the photo of a uninterrupted feeling moving to all directions continuously, and while doing this not to freeze that movement, not to offend the light. Sometimes our instincts teach us the way."

Then he stopped talking. He took a few steps towards me with an impish smile on his face. The long rectangle table between us had disappeared and a green, spoiled ivy with smiling roses on it appeared.

Keşşaf dived the food bag which had been hanged on his waist during the world of seeing, he seemed to be diving his hand in a lake at that moment.

He gave me a shadow, then, the thing he was holding...

"Do you remember this?" he asked. "You entertain very much looking at the pictures in this when you were a child."

He was holding a small hand slide machine I played with when I was a child. It was a small, pretty hand slide machine showing the pictures in it respectively with a sound of 'click' when the button on the edge was pushed. The broken, pretty toy I couldn't remember even the pictures and blown in the wind of the past.

"Where did you find this?" I asked with surprise and cheer.

"Remember," he said, "the only condition to see the pictures in this was to look towards the light!"

Keşşaf handed me the cheerful moments of my childhood.

"I want you to take that photo with this. First you can take hundreds, thousands, even by the bucketload photographs with this. Then when the time comes to take that single shot, you will feel it, but it takes a very long time."

While I was looking at the machine in my hand with admiration as being lost of words due to astonishment...

I boggled with the nice and warm voice of Kırlangıç, I was easy and carefree as I woke from a sweet dream.

"Light," said Safran, "extend your hand towards the sun to see the light." I had returned to the place I had been sitting on, to this small room, to the girls, Gül Hanım and Safran. I looked at my hands with the fear of losing in my hand, the small hand slide machine had left with Keşşaf.

Safran and I caught each other's eye. On the plastic tray on the floor in front of me there was tea again in the small slim glasses.

"Dilruba, your tea has got cold," she said smiling.

I didn't know how I had gone to Keşşaf from here and returned again, to know this was far beyond my power. I felt a swelter, tiredness and heat.. I attempted to take off my jacket. I rose while sitting, I realized a painting hidden with a white cloth over the door involuntarily. I was bewildered as if my face crashes on something cool. Why hadn't I wondered what was there in the frame before? I must find a way to lift up the cloth and look at it.

14
Inner Eye

"Dwell on the beauty of life. Watch the stars, and see yourself running with them." Marcus Aurelius

Heat started to fall with March. Today is a cheerful and warm day borrowed from the spring. At least it is for the morning. The weather started to heat, the night started to get warm are heralding the coming of spring. Trees are shaking with the surety of becoming green.

I am watching the people walking outside. The rest of the classroom is listening to the elective lesson teacher carefully. Togetherness of people from different branches. I am on a seat at the window side. I am watching the freshness of spring, the trees becoming green, lack of energy, the students entering and going out of the class, the people having paper cups talking in front of the classroom, the youngsters lying on the grass. A young boy passes by the window. He has books in one hand and his other hand is in his pocket. Then two cheerful and easy-mannered girls. Trees are more cheerful than them, they have happy land lords, birds... First, they are singing continuous songs and then as if someone has warned them, they suddenly stop singing, and then go on again like naughty children. What can be done in such a clear and spacious weather? People looks like pollens flying through the sunshine, they are chasing rainbows as if there is no gravity. We are the ones who are tagged while playing hide and seek in the shadow with light.

There is a pretty dizziness in the classroom with the coming of spring, a cute try to shrink from school. A movement, restlessness. The beautiful at the front row is saying the teacher that they want to have the class out, rest of the class support her. Voices are infatuated, time and place stretches because of these voices. All solidity of the place, desks, corners are searching for different corners to hide. The teacher stops these claims at first. Then he does a kindness and they go out altogether to the sun. We found ourselves at a green amorphous class.

We are like flowers on the grass outside. Attendance sheet passes from hand to hand. We found the thing given us through the twitters. The one who wrote his/her name gives the sheet to the other as if he/she evaded an important job. Before I get the sheet, the lesson starts. Teacher on the land looks like a statue stretching away to the sky. This statue is starting to rise from the dead with the warm breath of the sand. In fact, when his feet touch the sand, the person touches himself. He reaches the "what" state of wisdom. From my point of view, the teacher look likes a gardener who knows the language of the roses. As if he is a wise man who is going to take us to the back of Kaf Mountain. As if he is saying, "Come on, to the sky ,to the sky, flap your wings faster!". As if the teacher turns into a Hoopoe, and we are dove, dodo, partridge, nightingale, pheasant, turtledove, hawk around him. We are searching for Simurg. We are going to look for the reality on the track of our guide Hoopoe. While flapping our wings with might and main, we are listening to Hoopoe carefully. We are watching for that breath that will take us first to Valley of Desire and then to Valley of Love with his single words. The ones who didn't drop like flies are sweating for going to valley of skill, the ones who can reach the peaks of the mountains are sweating for valley of astonishment. While I am dreaming this, I find the attendance sheet in my hands. There are thirty people in the class and I am the thirty-first bird!

The teacher with his black pullover is standing like a black hole that is trying to absorb the light of the spring. However, the things he told are granting new, fresh lights to spring. New springs are getting out of his mouth. As soon as he tells, we bend our heads on the texts on our laps. Papers are our wings. We look like birds tidying their wings with their beaks. Some of us are tidying our notes, some are writing notes on the pages, some are looking for the things told in the paper dispersing around like sea foam. To let the wisdom of the people flowing like water to flow into its own waterless bed.

I am turning into a partridge bouncing from valley to valley with the things the teacher tells. The teacher goes on citing from Plotinus,

"Never stop sculpting your statue!"

When I hear this, I find myself at the head of a sharp statue. This is my own statue, image of my soul. I have to hit the stone such gentle that it must get its shape without breaking. My hand holding the chisel is in the air, the teacher is going on citing. The things he says are drawing the restful expression of the stillness on his face:

"Every soul is, and becomes, that which he contemplates!"

I understand that the chisel in my hand is my thoughts now. The teacher, turns one more page, my hand holding the chisel is still in the air. I need pure information about myself. To which valley can a person walk with this shapeless statue?

He goes on telling, according to Plotinus, everything in the universe is a result of overflowing of One. Only an object that twinkling of One touch can be beautiful. He says that Plotinus experienced "ecstasy" four times in his life. Ecstasy reminds me the woman struggling at Safran's house. Her falling down as if she lost her consciousness, I see her state again in the sentence (ecstasy is akin to passing away). First, the things the teacher tells us or the sentences in the texts we have are crashing to the sentences (we are only that of which we are aware). All of these point that the boundaries around us is the same as our awareness of selfhood, the same as being aware.

Then, the teacher says, "inner eye". I try to see the inner eye on his face looking to the wisdom. I translate these two words into all the languages I know. I am sure that the birds flying over us understand what he says. If there is something called inner eye, I see all the things are alive when I look with its eye. Or what the big tree shedding pollen over us whisper which picture with its huge branches... I listen to the sound of cute path sweeping from the faculty. I am looking for the word under the generosity of the sun shining on my head. The hot sand under my foot is calling us from its own world with its green hair. Meanwhile, the teacher is going on telling, he is turning around starting from "what" cleaning our inner mirror is. Inner eye... When our mirror is broken, when harmony of our body starts deteriorating, soul and its performance come to a full stop, in a sense, soul and its performance go on without any image. The problem was clear, it was closely related to how close you go to the reality which was called inner eye. This was the very thing that Keşşaf taught me!

He put an end to his speech with the sentence we all underlined:

"When you utter its name or when you think of it put all else aside, abstract everything."

The lesson finishes. We thirty birds brush our wings with our beaks. We tidy the pages bubbling on our laps, the one who stands up shake softly her/his lap, sheds the spring. I stay still watching the inner eye under the shadow of the huge tree. The thing Keşşaf told me, the things I experienced at the guest house... The things I witnessed at Safran's house... Inner eye that I front everywhere!

I again begin to suspect which one is real. These two worlds, this faculty and Safran's house, and the things Keşşaf told me. Oh my god, which one is true? Knowing disturbs me more, but the only thing I want is which one is true? I wonder if these three say the same thing although they are three different worlds. But how?

I must be a good student and mustn't cut the other classes. But I desire to go to Safran again. Leaving faculty and going Safran is something like being beamed up to thousands of years away. I say, there is no similarity. While drinking tea in front of the faculty, I think thousands, ten thousands of things at the same time, I go adrift. I resist the flow with a sip of hot tea. I am not a good student, I have never been! I swim in the flood of people along the way. I pass the lovers, I am about to touch their happiness, I say this is happiness, which part of reality does this stand? Maybe, they are aware of everything and maybe they are looking with love from the eye in their chest. I pass the library, restaurant and the long way to the guest houses. Walking in this way is about to turn me in an avalanche. Am I walking through the things in the text in my hand or totally opposite way?

When I reach A4 gate, I hesitate. I have the possibility to return. I can go to obscurity or return and stand myself an ordinary life. Do I have the chance? But in order to understand the things in the texts I carry, I have to go. Going now means staying for this reason, in fact. If I return, I would have allowed these invitations to break my mirror. I must walk through the light like the flowers turning their faces to the sun. If this light finds the way and ...

The things Keşşaf told me in the world of seeing appear in the mirror one by one. He told me to wait the light enter my dark room. He said, there is only one light suitable for each photograph, and added,

"Focal point at the photograph helps us to look at that moment deeply. There are such moments in life that it doesn't have before and after. That frame is single, where you look at that frame, your point of view, the light specified, clearness or unsharpened at the background, rhythm and texture or harmony. All of these are specific to that single moment. Do you know that every moment of life is the same? We just give up sensing these differences in those moments."

I try to see the photograph that I am in that moment at the gate of A4. There must be a single light appropriate for this photograph, that is probably my hesitation! What about the focal point of this photograph? What is it?

I stayed on the very spot. I was looking at the sky, the people, the cars and trying to saturate this light. In fact I was waiting for the light to enter the dark room of my doubt! I caught the eyes of the man at the door. He didn't like my strange behaviours, my looking at the sky, watching people. He was looking at me. I made a hand gesture in the meaning of no problem. He would think that I am mad if I said him that I was trying to feel the photograph of the moment. Only a single time later, I startled with the sound hitting my back.

"Dilrubaaaa, Dilrubaaaaa!"

It is Kırlangıç. She is going up the hill to A4 breathless. First her head, then her shoulders, bag and books appear in the frame. Focal point of the photograph is Kırlangıç coming through me sweeping the light on the way full of trees! Friendly face that I know in the frame fed by the tissues of the trees on the two sides of the way! Gorgeousness of uneasiness of little bitty body at the steep in the life. I watch for the rhythm in the tired steps of Kırlangıç in this eternal frame, the frame freezes in the life. Cars passing by the road, life swimming on the pavement, walking people stop their movement for this single moment. Trees hide their motion, sky pours out it all of its light to the stage!

I could catch the frame so for only this doubtful moment light in question entered into the dark room. The light I was waiting was this. The best answer for the hesitation between going or staying. The one setting the moments winded up that single moment for me and for all the others. There was an arrow showing us the way in our hard times when the life way gets complicated in our fate.

As she approached, she slowed down her steps. Her face was as pale as her pleated skirt. Her head was tipped hopelessly, there was a shadow of herself. She hung her bag crosswise, she was carrying her books and her big file in her hand.

She said, "I have been calling you from the centre."

I replied, "I am sorry, I didn't hear. I didn't hear her

"Where are you going?"

"I was thinking to go Safran. I am doubtful." However, I was on the way bravely when I started walking from the faculty.

She asked, "I hope nothing is wrong?"

"No, everything is OK."

There was uneasiness in my speech. Kırlangıç should understand me. This was her habit. I should be sure that she is the only one who understands me even tough years passes.

There was also uneasiness in her speech.

I said, “What’s the problem with you?”. She didn’t reply.

We started walking without saying a word. Although she didn’t say that she would come, she was walking with me. When she didn’t reply, I checked her face, her face was like hard rocks. There would be flash on her face at any moment. What the hell is this boredom despite the merciful magnificence of the air, the trees?

“Dilruba, life is full of pain, despair. Wherever I turn, I crash pain.”

I was silent in the meaning of go on.

“I can’t finish the school. I have to go one more year, again fees, expenses...”

She got hoarse, then she cleaned her throat and continues,

“Who cares? Somehow I will go on living as a unemployed with a degree. Of course, if I finish next year, it is also uncertain.”

“I care.” I said. “You know I am good at extensions.”

I know that extending school is not the only problem, she couldn’t tell this to her family.

“My mom called last night. She asked if the school would finish this year. I said it would.”

I said, “Don’t worry, we will find a solution.”

“Don’t say me solution.”

“I mean an excuse, you know.”

It got dark suddenly. The clouds that can’t pour out its soul were wiggling, becoming heavier, talking.

I felt melancholy. Sparkles were disappearing, strong dark green was taking its place. Kırlangıç and I walked for awhile without speaking. At first, rain was touching *sotto voce*, softly. When we reached Safran’s house it turned into hail.

I was scared of the crowd at the house. Walls, sofas, floors were covered with women wearing white scarves. Even there were sitting at the threshold. A woman we don’t know opened the door and welcomed us. When I saw the shoes at the door, I thought that we came on the day. The only thing I want was to be alone with her. I think it wouldn’t be for a long time. When I saw Safran, the crowd was disbanded, her voice sweeping all unnecessary details was healing my ears, my eyes, my heart and was making me breath. She was sitting on the sofa at the entrance; she was telling spreading her arms. She was like a huge tree. Although it was getting dark, the light reflecting on her face was giving place to bright shadows, she was playing puss-in- the corner as she wiggles her head. When she turned her face to left every point on her face got brightened. Her beautiful face. I would like to watch this face without moving for many years; sometimes it got bigger, sometimes it looked like clear water, sometimes it became a bed for deep smiles. The only thing that wouldn't change in her photograph was the light in her eyes! These eyes were a meaning nest which was full of life, I want to know all the meanings in them. To walk on the way going them and to touch that light with my hands... This was all I want. Everyone in this room wants this too. This was the thing pulling magnetically. It was certifying that there was an inner eye deep in her eyes which never got lost. As if we tried to see the third eye in our soul by looking in her eyes, in fact it was impossible to look into her eyes continuously, you took your eyes, as if witnessing her existence, we couldn't desist from the magic of this feeling as long as we were with her.

I thought that she didn't realized Kırlangıç and me in the crowd. We could hardly find a place at the threshold, she didn't look at us. In fact, it wasn't clear where she looked, while looking opposite, right or left, her eyes went away, then she dropped her eyes, sometimes she closed her eyes then watched the rest of the scene. You could see the attention and the meaning in her eyes.

Kırlangıç and I were on the blankets on the concrete floor. We sat down on the floor. This was what we were requested! Kneeling before this supreme meaning and moments. We were sitting sprucely between the crowds not to disturb them, holding our books tightly on our laps, and holding our bags on our shoulders.

Excitement was obvious to hold. Love becomes obvious here and we make love our friend here, ever than before. There were accounts, rivalry, greed, motive for survival outside. Demand for living, surviving directs people. There was only one thing at the schools, in the cities, towns, at the shopping centres, at the avenues where is traffic jam: the instinct of occupancy, possession. The more you possessed the happier you were. Fame, money, status, community, love, power... background of the photographs of these scenes or moments weren't important. Death... puff.. We would think this when we died, of course we wouldn't ran away, we would show humility to it like a rabbit caught by a hound, like an antelope caught by a lion. But this mustn't be important while living. Sometimes, someone dies and we put him in the corpse in the ground like putting a baby to her mother's breast and turn to our life as if nothing happened. We worry about earning and gathering. Even the ones who couldn't gather enough are guilty, our existence was evaluated over our possessions. This has been like this for many years. What is bad with it?

Safran was shining. Her look was crushing the light reaching first her shoulder and then to her face. The weather was live and cool, sharp as a glass. Her voice turns into a soft yellowish in gilded light; it strikes me that while talking like this she saw the things with her whole body.

"When we fall in love, back of our ego approaches the ground slowly. Growing up of the love is declining of the ego. It is a disappearance in a meaning. And unification, being one is impossible without love. Two objects can't be one unless one of them disappears. The one who loves only wants to see the one who he loves. Right?"

At the last sentence pupils of our eyes met. Curtains in the looks were drawn one by one. Fire in her eyes burnt me until my soul was naked and defenceless.

"When you utter its name or when you think of it put all else aside, abstract everything."

This was the last sentence I heard at the green garden in front of the faculty. Safran continued,

"First, your heart will say the thing you want to hear. Then, you will find it from other mouths. As if water from different beds flowing into the same sea. The one who want to see with the eye in her chest hear the music of every sound in the universe. Being blind is not blindness of the eyes, it is blindness of the hearth."

Safran was replying my questions; moreover she was confirming this with her look. Her eyes were training me,

"Power of love is destructive, you give up at last, when you disappear you reach your universal identity."

When she finished speaking, the women sitting still started to move and breath. The view which looks like calm cotton field with white scarves started to sway like felt the breath of the warm wind. Sighing was turning around. It wasn't clear where these sighs start and finish. Gül hanım was breathing out the air that an old woman breathed in. A young woman we don't know was breathing in air Kırlangıç breathed out. Breathing was invisible bonds of a wordless world. White brightness was surrounding us like lights. Fresh pinkness on the faces was shared from a red apple pulled off a tree. This pinkness was sometimes appearing on Safran's face, too. It was stamping the faces like symbol of happiness. I was free as a canary bird freed from the cage among the cute crowd moving like white chicks.

I was leaning on the door, trying t give way to the people passing. I was keeping an eye n Safran. There wasn't any sign of tension on Kırlangıç. She was teasing out the live colours of the real picture. Then she raised her head, her face became sharp, her chin was smooth and thin like the bottom of a cornered bowl. She speared her curious look like an arrow, and muttered,

"I wonder what is there in this picture?"

That picture! The one on my head! That big frame that I don't know what is there in it! I thought as if that crowd told me to uncover. However, I couldn't raise even my head.

I said "You mean this painting hanging on the wall, don't you?"

Kırlangıç said, "Yes, have a look at it"

As I raised my head, sateen cover of the frame drifted away like leaves of a corn poppy that wind blew, flew and severed all its ties with the picture. Then it fell down on my face like a white flag happily. Like covering the surface of the water with water lily, like the white moon covering the blackness ... I felt the coolness on my still face in this single moment. I was a white point in the cotton field with this whiteness on my head.

I put my hand on my face slowly like catching the birds, the whiteness was pouring on to my lap. I was afraid to raise my head and to look at the painting. Kırlangıç was struck with consternation. I was wandering between looking at the painting and knowing what to do by acting out like a casual moment, as if I realized the painting just at that moment.

I found him in the big frame above the door: Keşşaf!... He said in the World of seeing that our adjacency was timeless and placeless. Now, he was repeating his words by averting his gaze. Keşşaf was standing in the painting, walking with his gorgeousness, he seemed as if he was pressing roses on his chest. More importantly, he was smiling! Did Kıtmir feel like this after waking up from a three-hundred year sleep? The way I felt now.

Safran was as if she was sitting on throne while she was sitting on the iron-legged sofa. One side of the flower-pattern was seen at the pleated skirt of the sofa. These flowers were mixing with long skirt of Safran. Cloth which is a little pale, a bit heavy started to fly as if there was an earthquake. One of the women sitting on the ground was fluttering like a headless chicken, she was overflowing like wine overflowing its glass, as long as she wanted to stop herself, she was dispersing more, turning around herself and shouting. I somehow got used to this. But I was still astonished , petrified.

Safran ignored that woman, turned her look at me like a sharpened arrow, then drew the bow and ...

"Mood of a Sufi" she said smilingly and added "she was, what can she do?"

Kırlangıç was repeating her question like a *qanun*,

"I said that painting, what is there on it?" The painting was covered with white cloth and silent.

15
Slope of Perception

Kırlangıç and I are talking about the previous day at the breakfast including cheese, bread and tea in the canteen. Yesterday starts to seem like a dream now while we are watching the trees seen from the wide windows of the canteen. Although the soft tone of Safran's voice is still in our ears, every moving object, every motion we hear makes us away from the magical presence of yesterday. Our looks turn to the material, we involve ourselves responsibilities again. We remember that the flowing thing is life after those moments we flowed freeing from the ties of the mind. We stop to catch the life. Slowly...

I start to read the uneasiness in Kırlangıç's features. This uneasy bird flapping on her face has two wings as I know; failing to finish school and cool winds blowing between her and her fiancé. Perhaps it is unbelievable, but I don't know her fiancé at all. When I asked who her fiancé was, she said he was from the same department as her. Kırlangıç is so tight-lipped about private issues, she tells almost nothing about them. What is her fiancé's name, who is he, why is she in bad with him? Even I am unaware of these as being so close to her. This is Kırlangıç's darkness principle, nobody knows about her private life. This is a shield that she uses to protect herself against life. We don't talk about anything except the common points of our lives. So I know that I cannot ask her anything about it while she puts three cubes of sugar in her tea in the paper cup.

The tension in her angled slim face stretches oft her looks, she gives a look at the spread cheese on the broadsheet. She is inappetent as usual. She leans backward and lights a cigarette, "that's life, there you go," she says while she is puffing the cigarette smoke.

"For God's sake," I say, "how can you keep so many things inside yourself, tell me and relax."

"What will I tell? There is nothing to tell," she says, "that's all you know."

"But I don't know anything..."

"Never mind, forget it," she says.

She takes another sip from her tea. Her grasp the paper cup, the distance of her looks means that 'don't ask me anything.'

"As the poet says," I say, "to forget is being on the way going to yourself."

"I haven't heard this, who said it?" she asks.

"I don't know who said, I even don't know if it was said or not. I think somebody will tell in the future."

"Do you know," she says, "Zümrüt is the top student in the department again this semester."

"Good job! How do people become the top student, there is no such a success in the my history!" I say.

"And there is no space for so much knowledge in my mind, also," se says.

"Never mind," I say, "imagination is more important than knowledge." This statement belongs to Einstein hung on the wall of the entrance in Kırlangıç's section.

Just then, her eyes are at the door, "talk of the devil and he is sure to appear," she says. When I turn back I see Zümrüt walking like slipping with cheerful steps as usual. One can write a thick book only on walking looking at her way of walking. This is a kind of way of walking that overcomes life, it is a way of movement that flows easily at every step as if she is on a volant carpet flying the realities. This pacing means that this cheerful furtherance is in my nature, in my existence, life always comes to me with gifts and beauties; this means that I always choose the only clean and protected line among the life lines consisted of thousands of different spots, this happens spontaneously, unintentionally.

Zümrüt has a tone of voice that brings to heel even the wildest animals. She can form her voice into different tones, she can make it heard in one letter coating it with every tone of every colour separately. Her voice is like an encyclopedia of meaning, she attributes a different meaning to every letter. If you listen to her without seeing her, you can guess that she is a brunette. Her voice is deep, full, heavy; authentic tones generated from specific mimics take form just like the sparkles of the daylight falling partly on her brunette face. The stress of dominance in her voice comes from her self confidence. A strong sense of belonging reveals in this voice, she has had a happy childhood, she has a good relationship with her parents, she is the apple of her family's eye. Her relaxed and vibrant laughs contain distinct clues about her life. There are transparent unseen thick walls between us. These unseen transparent walls get thicker between Zümrüt and me; she doesn't walk on the edge, her life goes well as much as possible within the frame of certain rules.

"Girls, good morning," says Zümrüt as if she spreads her voice to a flower garden. Everything lightens as her voice is spreading through the flowers. This enlightenment also reflects to Kırlangıç's face, she is happy to see Zümrüt. She sits on the third chair of the table for four, just next to Kırlangıç.

While she is saying "Why don't you come over, where have you been?", she likens her voice a remonstrant, ingoing sea...

Kırlangıç says that we were with Safran yesterday as if she wants to make her mouth water, and gives the floor to her by asking where she has been above all.

"Why didn't you let me know, well done"

"We didn't agree together to go there," I say, "we went there unawares."

"Ah," says Zümrüt, "let's tell about it, how was it? Did she say anything about me?"

"What would she say about you? It was very crowded indeed, we didn't talk at all," says Kırlangıç in a devil-may-care manner.

This is Zümrüt's habit, as it is actually all of ours a little. We ask if Safran tell anything about us in order to hear something good about ourselves probably. We do this to keep calm about ourselves. However, Safran or someone around her never tells you anything good about you.

Kırlangıç wants to treat it as a joke and says "she said she didn't want to see you." Zümrüt takes this statement seriously and says, "ah, she is angry with me, isn't she? She says I am lazy, doesn't she?"

"Yes, she said you were lazy. She said she didn't want to see your face."

Once Safran told Zümrüt that she had been lazy, then since that time Zümrüt has reminded it on all occasions saying "she called me lazy."

"For God's sake! She said nothing," says Kırlangıç.

They continue to talk among themselves. I stand up to get tea for us. Just then...

Müdrik comes in. This is not a good coincidence for me at all. I understand that he headed to the canteen when he didn't get a result of the announcement for me in the dorm; he is looking for me in the canteen. I see him side face, we stand on the same line. He put his right hand in his jean's pocket as only his fingers are in, he is wearing a light blue shirt. I immediately turn back to him, perhaps he doesn't see me, perhaps he only associates and goes back since he is not sure.

I feel uneasy when talking to him for a while but how can I explain this to him? He has been helping me with everything tirelessly for four years. How can I tell this to the only person I have known since before in the city that I don't know, in the city of which climate, weather, people are totally strange to me. Above all, while I am sure that he considers what's best for me. I realize at that moment that Müdrik is the only man in my world surrounded by women. I realize that I haven't talk to any other man properly. Perhaps that's why there is something in his voice disturbing me. Yes, he sometimes looks after me, asks about me or I call him once a month. However I have realized lately that he started to interfere my life. Perhaps I give him the opportunity to do this by telling him something. The reason I tell him that I believe he can have a look at my life in a different way with an objective mind, that I am sure he will help me when I feel obstructed. At that moment I realized why I admire him: he is a citizen of world, he belongs to nowhere, he has a broad point of view, strong common sense and foresight. He goes abroad a few times in a year, attends symposiums about his profession, sees different worlds. He is free like the birds being able to determine their direction while he is flying for thousands of kilometres and he is also honest at least as those birds.

I was about to head our table with teas while thinking all these. Müdrik and I caught each other's eye. He waited for me to go by him when he saw me rushing towards my friends' table with teas. Kırlangıç must have realized the non-verbal communication between us, she said "I think you have a guest."

At that moment, Müdrik had took a few steps towards me and he had been hesitated to come by us. I went to him asking the girls to excuse me, I told him "welcome" sincerely and smiling. He smiled pleased with this sincere welcome. We sit at the table back in the beyond in the canteen. I didn't want other girls, Hazel, Nergis and Hüma to see me with him, but fortunately they didn't come to the canteen very often, to remember this relieved me. I was examining Müdrik's eyes, I caught the same relaxed looks in his eyes having a changing colour from blue to green. He sat as his back turned to the girls, Zümrüt and Kırlangıç, and crossed his legs keeping his body out of the table slightly.

"I just dropped by," he said.

"Welcome. Here is not a place to drop by," I say smiling.

"Thank you, yes, out of the city a little," he said. "But I have something to do this way. I think I have interrupted your breakfast."

"No, it's already been over."

"So, what has happened since we last meet? How is school going?"

"I think I can't graduate this year."

He opened his eyes as if he was surprised. His face was getting more mature ever day I saw him. Even he was talking in a way of father sometimes,

"This is not you," he said.

"Forget it, how are you? How is the world of aesthetics?"

"Good, everything is okay..."

He hesitated.

"Safran... Her name is Safran, isn't it? Have you seen her?"

I didn't expect this question. He must have been very interested in what I had told him at our previous meeting.

"Fine, as you know," I said.

"You don't tell me everything," he said.

"One cannot tell everything even himself, you know."

"He must tell," he said.

Kırlangıç and Zümrüt went out of the canteen leaving the table without looking at the side that we were sitting. Here, at the backmost table of the canteen, I was like in a tight corner.

"What will I buy for you?" I said with all my hospitality.

"I will take a tea."

I returned with two paper cups of tea and some sugar on the table this time. Müdrik leaned on the table slightly. The steam of the tea was cutting his face.

"Well, won't you tell me?"

I started to talk by saying "I visited Safran yesterday," I talked about that after the sentences I heard at the faculty, Safran repeated the same sentences literally and what these sentences were in detail. First he listened to me quietly and carefully. The tea was half finished. He leaned backwards, a sarcastic smile set on the edge of his lips. He was looking at me as if watching a playing little child and trying to understand the game affectionately.

"I really wonder what you think life is. Rise your head and look around. I see that you are looking for a divine love, but accept that life is an imposter."

"You are talking very frankly again."

His words was hurting me. He was leaving me alone as he was trying to protect me, he was sabotaging my reality as he was trying to show the reality he knew.

I could see the dorm's gate from the place I was sitting easily. I could see the people going in and out of that gate passing under the trees. Time was flowing as people were walking.

"Do you know Dilruba, your need a different kind of sensation. You want to feel some kind of things that nobody feels because this life doesn't satisfy one's soul."

"Are you telling this?" I said, without realizing that I was bending the edge of the paper cup of which bottom was about to seen.

"Yes, of course it doesn't satisfy, why do you think so many people come to me and want to become beautiful?"

"What do you mean by the need of sensation?"

"Let me tell you that a far cry of perception can exist only by themselves. The thing we most need while we are spinning on the line of existence is 'sensation'. We see that a rightful need of sensation enfolds us in its arms like an octopus when we descend the steps of the unhappiness stairs one by one. You know, serious perceptual disorders appear in individuals whose need of sensation is not satisfied enough. Of course here I am talking about the perception with five senses."

I nodded as if saying I see.

"However," I said, "I am not talking about material here," he interrupted,

"I'm sure you are not. Shouldn't one understand five senses first in order to understand the kind of communication without material?"

"Who has been able to understand fully so far? We have still been helpless to understand the process of seeing with all details," I said; the light of blue of his shirt meeting the daylight was combined with the blue in his eyes.

"For God's sake, we know about the subconscious," he said, "for all I care, perceptual permeability is experienced intensively at the rate of the fullness of the subconscious."

"Perceptual permeability? What is that?" I said. "Today you speak so strangely."

"Our perceptions are permeable. That is they often sweep with various associations with the object of perception. As I always say, human think with his mind and body."

I tock the paper cup that I covered with my hands like a cloth to my lips holding it as so it wouldn't burn my hand, and took a sip.

"Then this is also be true: it means that a man that starts out to raise the senses of the body is playing with the pans of the scale, with the terrific balance," I said.

"Yes, it is so in some sense. Drug addiction, eating disorders and obesity has revealed as the extension of the struggle of the body to raise its senses as a result of the lack of spiritual satisfaction. For me, the permeable structure of the perception is a treasure if you look at it with the right angle." Müdrik got serious as if he was speaking at a rostrum. His looks became hard and his features came to a state of angled as they revealed that he focused on the subject.

"Right angle?" I asked but he was going on speaking as if he didn't hear me,

"What you do, that is a man's struggle to exist himself over himself is a serious need of sense."

"Let's call this as the struggle of getting in touch with the reason of our existence," I said.

"Well, it can be called so, also."

"Because I think that the soul's course of sense adventure cannot be this a narrow field. I suppose you are not far from this idea," I added.

Müdrik stopped speaking then. I had never witnessed that he got close to the spiritual field that much before.

"You know," he said, "science and rational thought has not been the universal criterion of the perfection for a long time. All scientific models, even those seeming precise have carried their own limits with them... Everything can be a method, from dream to love or from nature to book during the process of human's discovery of himself. So the permeable structure of the perception is a treasure. The question is that how we will be sure? What if we are wrong? All in all, we have the chance of only one shot in our lives. We have no way back. What if we loose?"

Hearing this chilled me to the bone. Only one shot. This was what Keşşaf wanted me!

"To win or to lose are relative concepts. Then, one should ask what it is relative to," I said.

Müdrik put the end to the conversation so:

"Perhaps one should set off taking the risk of loosing. Loosing completely."

That day, Müdrik and I left the table in confusion like people who were able to reach the shore surviving through the waves. I later realized that he had meant sacrificing everything by loosing everything. Years later... Were we able to cope with sacrificing everything? That day neither him nor me could face that question...

I couldn't tell Müdrik but there was something I was sure about;

Keşşaf was talking to me continuously. At a moment that I was angry and withdrew he told me to be like 'wooden spoons', at another shot of life he advised me not to worry, another month we whispered some important information about life. While I couldn't tell all these even myself, what can I tell anyone else? I knew that Müdrik was not a someone else for me, moreover he was getting closer day by day, he was going beyond the distinct lines in my dream, he was leaning his back to the passages in my thought that nobody knew. My thoughts about him didn't become clearer in no way, I couldn't save myself from the arms of this flowing river.

In this strange place, this campus, this artificial place sometimes isolated with a great silence I had changed rooms a lot. If it had been thought that every room was four people, one would have met very different characters unavoidably, thought over the reasons of those differences, and then still surprised with the strange harmony between people. Here the loneliness that pours like black soot if one shakes himself makes you weak. Perhaps you are living with four or five hundred people at the same age with you, but here there are no children or elders, and perhaps that's why the real moments of life are like taken from the grey faces of these walls. In the evenings, especially during some periods, you always study lesson here, go for classes early in the mornings, always talk about the courses. Only courses, exams, grades here... They are like pollens flying about in the air. However, when you look down from the dorms in a summer evening, you see young people suffusing on the grass and you get out of your imprisonment, when their voices rise to you like flying you think what a beautiful place you are at actually. Couples usually walks hand in hand, when they are a couple they are as relaxed as they are at home. To be a couple here means only being two people; walking around comfortably as if there is none else except you...

As if there is a time gate at the road between the campus and Safran's house. It is impossible to know where exactly this sparkling oval gate is but there is one thing I know: this campus and Safran's house. Two different worlds that doesn't resemble each other with every jots and components. Shuttling between these two worlds makes me drunk and I am swaying about under the black earth like a mole that doesn't estimate where to go. The place where exactly I am at seems to me real, when passing through that time gate the other becomes dream. I am worried that everything I have experienced with Keşşaf, even Safran is just my fantasy.

While going in and out of the study room, seeing Kırlangıç, Zümrüt and Nergis did my heart good. It caused me to establish a bond between these two different planets. We were talking about Safran together at a corner... Other people in the dorm were going to the TV room as big groups, going up their rooms cheerfully. Nothing interested me. We were talking about Safran, the things she had told, and other people in the dorm going to concerts, joined proms, going swimming and sport halls. We were the negative films of this dorm as a handful of people. However, the truth is that nobody belongs to anything or any direction, we were all wandering through the continuously changing shadows; we always changed places, we always moulted. Among all the faces that we talked and moved in everything was renewing with those faces, non of us stayed as 'us' that we had experiences the day before.

The river of time always washes, differentiates, transforms human. Personally, I was also at the fringe of a serious transformation. I was dragged to a spiritual area steadily, I was trying to cross-check every sense of mine that I perceived by my five senses and felt I bagged in situ in a terrible clumsiness. I was talking less, listening more, I was even silence my steps in order to hear the signs I was hearing more simply and more strongly. As if a new, unique window opened for me in the horizon, in the horizon that all the light, all the beings piled up, and I was watching goings-on fixing my eyes there. Şems was right! "Here is the command of evil (Nafs al Ammarra)," he said, "nothing kills the soul that commands to evil like seeing the beauty of the heart."

Once human heard about this eternal beauty, he was all ears with every cell of him. As he submitted, he saw that thousands of wings were mounted to his self and submitted more. Since melting more and more, becoming only one drop would mean to melt away in those unique views, every kind of worldly desire started to wait at a corner quietly, a desire to transform to a drop slowly and silently got stronger in me.

I thought that I was very close to the answers that I had been tracing in life with all my naivete, even I had reached them. However, I was wrong, everything was still new; all findings, all searchings, questions and answers, still new... A love that I would struggle for hadn't lift up its veil yet, only it made me feel its existence and said 'come!' Keşşaf's all whispers said that there was another universe beyond the hologram images we called as the world but they didn't reveal what kind of universe it was completely.

A bigger life was flowing silently under the appearing life. This invisible life had streets, special colours, a magical atmosphere even dialogues. I was confused as I was shuttling between these two lives, went back to the drawing board in every journey unavoidably, was reflecting up without skipping over any detail. I hadn't even realized that shuttling, rise and falls had started to be the meaning of my life. I was living without being able to choose my direction drunk with the colours of the rose garden pouring in my lap; directions had disappeared, there was no right or left, down or up, I was driven away in an irresistible drawing.

I held on Safran's voice, held on the love continuously flowing in me with her breath. The existence of her made me hold on to the life, even if I didn't always see her, to know that she lived somewhere close to me made me so happy. Every sentence she said left its mark, I recorded every sign like a note I had been looking for, every 'alas', every smile, every look of her... Being away from her meant nothingness, it meant not knowing about your own existence, being lost in the middle of a dry desert. She knew, she gave out what she knew, then she hid, then she vacated everything happened in my chest on me with her looks, she made me giddy. All poems hidden in her voice, all sonatas. All virgin images in life were dispersed to the pens of the poets from her looks. Her chest was something eternal, as she spoke, her breath was bringing us gifts from the eternity like a windbag.

My life had evolved to a felicity that was swathed by extraordinary beauties generously. This felicity showed me a new face of it everyday, every night it made me hear about another fragment of love. Doors that I hadn't known about before opened one by one, I got smaller as I passed through those doors. Each door was more garish, more real and more magical than the previous one.

Whatever happened apparently in life, it didn't avoid Keşşaf to take me by splitting the space and time. However there were such moments that Keşşaf was waiting those moments as if he was on the threshold of a strange timelessness and placelessness, he disappeared leaving the word he would say or the image he would show in my perception like a photocopy. Those significant moments were those just before sleeping, we were about to abandon the consciousness in life and remained between submitting ourselves to sleep or not. The moments that we were about to wake up were at that kind of importance. If we thought that sleep as a long tunnel, he dropped a different state of consciousness into my mind at that short moment just we were about to go out of that tunnel, born into the body again and the environment was about to lighten. The most important aspect of this state for me was that the wakening state was known by him exactly. In fact, one wakes up a few times until the time he gets up, is conscious, turns left from right but falls asleep again. Keşşaf was waiting for exactly the wakening state as if he knew those moments were not the beginning of the day. The state of dropping the relevant consciousness or knowledge into the mind was so different from the speed that we knew. It was much faster than one's seeing a lightening in the sky. I was recorded to a giant electric network and certain signals were sent to me at arranged intervals. These signals affected my mind so perfectly and impeccably, unmistakable and incredible realities appeared when these frequency particles were combined.

When one starts to watch these incredible observations one by one, he starts to understand with a strange feeling that all these beauties are possible for all people equally. We only pollute our heart's sky by overload it, so to speak, we blacken the screen of our sky. We succeed this easily by falling into all negative and self-destructive feelings. When human perception steps on an ethereal realm, he understands that material is a darkness and earthly realm is a world of invalidity by destroying all the rules about information. He wants to go beyond feeling that there is a giant power, eternal love and a world of passions burning every jot by making them drunk under the visible shell of the existence. This also means having an ever-growing wound. Circling in a deep and wicked despair when a bunch of beams of this private love is not seen at every moment flowing in life. Watching for a vibration in every silence with the feeling of being forgotten... Being on the wrong track by thinking that everything happening in the private area is your fantasy. Moreover, breathing the trials that are more difficult than the previous one. Yet as the wound growing the love is also growing. The performer is the One, the one that signifies and doesn't signify is the One. The one making you change the states, pouring you from one container to the other, shaking the dirty rust of your ego with the fires of the trials is the One. Then, let us the wound get grower.

16
The First of the Worlds of Heart

"Truly it is not their eyes that are blind, but the hearts which are in their breasts. (The Pilgrimage/46

Another big day lessened in the pool of time for me. While the earth was spinning around the sun it also whirled around one more time, it whirled fixing its feet in the space sparkling like a diamond in the endless darkness.

Kırlangıç, Nergis, Zümrüt and I met at 3:00 at the skirt of the slope leading A4 as we had agreed last night.

"Hazel and Hüma cannot come, let's not wait fort hem," says Nergis. We get in a taxi immediately as if get on the wings of a bird by stopping it. We get out at the trail-head of the narrow, earth road heading to Safran's house.

A Sufi whose white scarf is hiding her shy looks opens the door. We are like the fish reaching water at the moment we pass the threshold. How faces look like moon here. There are ropes tying them each other with friendship and loyalty. Those strong ropes are far away from all lies and artificiality. Their looks, their looks are real at the most. Blended with pain, misty with being tested, covered with love. And blended with the core of hope. Words are washed by the clear water of love here.

Safran is talking as if she is reading a love book of which giant pages open in waves before her. This love book seems to be on a big lectern and a hand in the air is turning the pages. Words are coming with an unstoppable flow like babbling waters driving its foam. Every heart in this small room grows motionlessly like a tree, they wind the smiling face of the sky with their branches, and bend their head like sunflowers charmed by the sun. Every heart listening to the Word sculpts a reed for itself with the hand of this flute player. Safran's every stress, every tone of her voice, every good news running out of her breath pierces on this elegant reed. Those hearing beyond the Word and following it know clearly.

This must be heaven, I say. What kind of heaven I have come by, what kind of sherbet it is poured from, the walls of the sky come down. I understand what private means some more.

"The almighty Allah has ordered that internal deeds are the duty for hearts as well as visible deeds are duty for body parts. The duties of hearts are the true faith to Almighty Allah and opening the heart to Allah... The ornaments of the visible deeds appear in the heart. Here the "Almighty Allah, the Lord of the Universes, wants us to come into His presence with such an honest heart. All worries and sorrows about the world should be away from your heart being the sultan of the land of body, wisdom can be reached only by this way. Self's getting rid of its own natural determinants can be realized opening the doors of discipline to the heart. Love open the doors of discipline widely. This path is the path of rising by purifying the soul through self acquittal and heart refining. As the soul is rising curtains covering the precise information open one by one. Thus as the self is being cleaned, the heart rises to the world of truth. The taste that the soul tastes in the world of truth cannot be compared with any taste on the earth."

As Safran spore, the crowd listening to her silently first moved like a wheat field that the wind touched on, then waggled and bended their heads to their chests like full wheatears. I had never seen anyone in this blessed crowd looking in Safran's eyes while listening to her during the days I had been honoured with being with Safran and had listened to her very carefully. Every head bended aside, looks gave up all worldly things, everyone set off his own journey.

I must admit that I couldn't infer very much from these deep words, I couldn't make my life and inner journey meet these blessed statements. Of course this was my inadequacy. What I felt with all my heart was that my soul relieved like a desert Bedouin reaching water. My view got stronger as if oxygen was going into my brain's convolutions that I hadn't been familiar and my world of thought freshened by finding a focal point for itself even if I didn't understand what Safran wanted to mean. These words were the shower of the soul. Deep truths in those words surrounded my whole being, eased my palpitations and relieved my pain even if they weren't seen clearly in the clear mirror of my thought. Sometimes I didn't understand even a word of Safran's statement, but to not understand is not an obstruction for love. Sometimes instincts reveal the horizon with all its beauty on the course of knowledge. This drawing, this knot and this mystery was whipping me up, the desire of reaching unknown worlds was burning me. There was something there real, something I felt but I couldn't name, let me know about my being, an extraordinary universe of which language I wasn't able to understand.

Safran's words glared down on the wheatear field like a sun which was getting closer, they made me beg. She smiled. Again her face resembling a light garden framed with her white scarf sparkled. Suddenly she struck the right note. Harshly, just as harsh as the passion itself.. And suddenly meaning vibrated with glory. She exhaled as much as she could, first from her larynx and then her nasal passage. Thus we could see the way the voice was following and how it was blended with love. She opens the heart as much as we could bear; her heart was laid over the sky like the flying of birds of prey.

"There no another body and another presence except Him! Existence belongs only to Him. Human being doesn't exist actually, so hey human, don't be proud of yourself thinking that you are the reason of your existence! Know that me, you, these faces reflecting to the mirror are not real. There is no existence rather than the Almighty Allah! Existence is only God's, all universe including us takes its existence from Him. Only one existence in visible all around the world and it is God. You have such a part of flesh in your chest... And there is such a world in that part of flesh... Almighty God, ordered as "I didn't fit into the earth, sky and the ninth heaven, but fit into the heart of my faithful human."

Just after the last sentence, one of the women sitting on the floor, yes, that was the same woman, started to flutter with a bitter cry as if she was shocked on her breast. Intermittent breaths was coming from her tightly closed mouth as a result of the shake, deep wither of this quake coming from the inside of the body, the soul was heard. Poor woman continued to shake and flutter in situ dropped her head into her lap, her breath became quiet as if she died. Her clothes were in a mess, her scarf slipped from her head and she remained trembling.

Safran looked at the poor woman, she said "Gülistan," with a loving voice. This voice made Gülistan's trembling stop gradually. It made her fall on the floor in a half-stunned state. One or two seconds later, one of the women sitting near the threshold reared up as if she was shot by an arrow on her back, and she out-breathed with the sharp and harsh word of 'Allah', as if one was beating her body holding her arms raising to the air like beating a carpet. At that moment I saw the expression on her face, she was passing out, an expression on her face as if she was crippled by the bends was rotating and rotating. As if she became the target of bullets suddenly and was frozen just in the centre of that crucial moment.

Then, the crowd resembling a cotton field started to shaken as if they were attracted to a rotating whirlwind. I was under the impression that at the same moment, an invisible hand push the mines in this field one by one. One of the women on the divan was pointing far away as if pointing the horizon, raising her head as if struggling for breathing while swimming in the sea of sherbet with 'Huuu' exclamation and leaving her trembling body into the sea of sherbet.

I looked at Kırlangıç. She was ashen-faced and an expression full of astonishment froze on her face. We looked each other. I understood from her looks that she was scared. She became smaller in the corner she was sitting at, she almost hid. Nergis closed her eyes, she was like sleeping peacefully in the middle of this tumult. Zümrüt was looking at Safran, her eyes trying to understand what was happening on her brunette face was getting bigger and bigger. Safran started a nice rhythm softly like waterfalls pouring into an open sea, she started to tell a poem in murmur. Her eyes was closed, her eyes was turned to the valleys of love where the soul was wandering, her face was pink and very bright.

The palace that the God accompany us is heart
The place that He is seen, by gosh, is heart
Go, ask Him whatever you want
The noble place of the God is heart.

I was so confused. I again squashed between the reality and fantasy and was puzzled with the chaos of the existence I witnessed. I took a deep breathe. My lungs were filling with a beautiful, unique smell. I was dizzy, I was revolving, the earth was rotating. Suddenly a familiar voice cried with all its strength:

"Hey bewildered! Why are you astonished so much?"

I found myself standing. I was wearing a dress with mirrors on its breast end to end. Smaller round inlaid mirrors sparkling like lights on my skirts. Everywhere I looked at was sea sparkle, till the bitter end that eye could see. I was on a turquoise water.

"Don't be surprised so much! One having God in his heart walks in mystery..."

This is the Cavalry with his hazel eyes, green clothes and white head-dress calling from his his horse with foaming mane! His very self!

I cannot see the fur-flung, there is no fur-flung, no closest either; there is no line on which the clear sea and sky combine! Although there is sky, it is like a sea circling over us. As if we are in a round sphere and the water is circling continuously climbing over our heads with its colour of emerald. How can I stand in the middle of this ocean in which every tone of blue, green and white spreading in waves being riveted to the ground? How can I stand? All tones of blue, white and green translocate as the light spots resembling sea sparkle are playing on the water, and this happens at full speed! I breathe this beauty, deeper, deeper, deeper... This freedom is blending with my blood! This rich blue command spreading out by itself and eternity!

"What is this place?" I say, my astonishment rises.

"Let's say a world among the worlds at the other end of the ninth heaven," he says. My God! Who can bare the magnificence of the Cavalry? If there isn't his white horse like a light flashing on the turquoise water, I will think that he is a wild wave of this calm water with his green clothes. His looks makes me out of breath. His face is so transparent, so clear... Nearly the bottom of the water will be seen for cleaning at least like his face. The water doesn't turn to a dark colour as it becomes deeper but it turns to a bright light changing between blue and green.

The Cavalry tightens the bridle slightly and loosens, the noble horse moves its head. He pulls the bridle to the right and rowels slightly.

"This bottomless sea is full of pearls, coral and diamonds. Here is the sea of secret, don't try to see its bottom because it does not have bottom; does not have a corner, back, right, left and shore."

He sidled his horse, the expression in his eyes is unbearable, the fire of his beauty burns my soul. There is a tone of strict order in his voice, only his eyes are seen... What happens in the world happens in these hazel eyes. All this blueness, this sea fills his eyes. The hazel colour of his eyes turns to green. I am born in this eyes again, then I die to revive. In the absent bottom of the sea of secrets I am crippled by the bends without diving yet...

"Hop on!" he says, "Keşşaf is waiting for you."

I hesitate. He laughs at the astonishment in my eyes. Then he warns,

"You cannot stand on the water for a long time, you sink and not a part of you can be found. You should learn the heart to take a pearl out of the sea of secrets. Don't douse even your toe in the sea of secrets when you are alone, the swirl will swallow you, waves throw about. This sea welcomes only those returning their hearts to real owner by cleaning their selves. Come on, give me your hand, hurry up!"

Oh my God! My soles are burning as if I step on a hot plate. I feel a soft but hot earth under my feet, no it isn't earth, a density resembling melting soft dough is swallowing me gradually. I want to cry "help!" with all my power but I can't speak. He leans from the horse and grips my wrist suddenly, he pulls me from the surface of the water in one move, I get out of the dense water about to swallow me. I hug his waist. He spurs the horse rigidly; the horse started to run slashing and tearing the water. I hear the water hitting my flying skirts. My skirts get wet but my legs don't get heavy. Inversely I become lighter as I get wet.

Matter, I say at that moment, what a big imprisonment to be a matter, what a terrible bond!

"It is so," says he as if he has heard of me, "but for the one who knows," he spurs the thoroughbred horse again. As the horse picks up the pace, green skirts of the Cavalry is flowing on the same line with the water. The long dagger on his waist is flying in its inlaid case. The end of the head-dress on his head falling onto his back is flying crazily. The horse is running at full steam, the colour of bright clear water reflects on the horse's muscular body, the horse is running sweeping the foam back with its long white tail as if it is rising to a blue sky. Its honourable body moves along as if destroying the water with its head held high, its figure reflects on the water, I watch its terrific reflection looking like a falling star from the water. As we get faster so, we are about to fall. We are flowing through an endless crystal water leaving a milk-white trace behind.

After going for a while the surface of the water turns to golden colour, these crying lights make me blind, after a little time they become only white "What a calm and peaceful sea this is" no sooner than a storm waylays first. The sea of secrets starts to rear up as if it has heard of me and sway about as if it is looking for a rock to hit its head. Waves are coming down on me like giant pearls splitting from a string; we pass through these giant waves, water tunnels are formed, continuously moving, rotating tunnels.

"Don't be afraid!" says the Cavalry. "This sea is so restless, this is normal; when one of the dervishes' whose discovery opens takes out a secret pearl from the deep, such giant waves occur. The sea first heaves, then understands that it is a dervish taking out the pearl and calms down."

It is strange that the horse knows the way very well, it runs at full gallop without decelerating, shying from anything, moreover getting tired as if it knows where to go in this yellow horizon in which there is nobody except us. The colours of the sea of secrets are changing gradually, now we are flowing through a rainbow like water. We travel for a while, the storms blow over. The naked face of the water calms down. However, everywhere fills with fog just then, we can't see beyond the end of our noses, I can't see even the Cavalry's head in the white smokes. I hear the sound of boiling of the water beneath us. The sea is boiling profusely, we are drawn towards the whirlwinds consisted of wild foams, I was so terrified that I started to pray.

What a tough journey this is!

We are passing through whirlwinds, waves are looking like volcanoes waiting for their victims opening their mouths, raving fires come out of the sea, the heat of the flames is licking my face on the horse. I started to cry, "Please, save us my God..." My heart starts to run in situ as if passing the white horse.

The Cavalry says,

"It's time to pray, because this sea is not familiar with you. We cannot pass through the sea of secrets without saying His name. The sea is glorifying Him and wants us to do the same. Unless we say the name of Allah, it thinks you are a stranger and pulls you into the deep!"

I start to say all prayers I know, I burst into tears. I strive for my life. What if we cannot escape from here? What if this endless water, this wild sea swallows us... I cry sobbingly, with fear and with despair of someone coming to the last moment. First the sea hears my prayers.

The waves of flames are rearing up before us as if standing up. The horse slows down, staggers, my tears drips. My praying voice touches the flames... At last the Cavalry exclaims to the sea loudly,

"She is Keşşaf's guest, not a stranger!"

First the sea swallows fire balls; flame waves starts to die. Flying whirlwinds become compliance... The dark colour lightens slowly, lightens like the dawn breaking. I stop crying, thank God, water sets on its bed, on this endless sea like a wild lion stopping roaring and sitting slowly... It calms down as much as a white page.

"Here we are," says the Cavalry.

I tumble from the horse and fall in front of a giant door inlaid with green ruby. The wings of this door opened widely are endless. I go in immediately passing the threshold. Keşşaf... First I see his honey-coloured hair falling onto his shoulders. I find an allusive expression on his face, a sarcastic look in his hazel eyes.

"Welcome to the palace of heart, Dilruba," says smiling, "I see that you get wet..."

"Thank you. It was a very tough sea travel," I say. I am happy to see him like a child finding his mother. I want to go down on his knees.

"You need to get wet with the water of the sea of secrets, the water should touch your soul even as one drop."

I look at my dowdy look. First I see mirrors on my skirts, the lights of the ground I step on. I dry my wet face with my sleeves, I am bedraggled. I look like a street cat caught in the heavy rain. Keşşaf smiles with compassion.

"Close, Dilruba... The heat of your heart will dry you, close..."

My heart continues to kick my chest even if it slows down. I am still scared, I speak with a wobbly voice. I feel lucky like a person who narrowly escapes death.

I take a few steps. Safran's voice reading the poem echoes in my ears...

Go, ask Him whatever you want
The noble place of the God is heart
How can this happen, I say surprisedly.

"Safran's voice is ours, it touches hearts. You have a heart that practice the voices in the world of hearing, don't you?" says Keşşaf.

"Thanks God," I can say. I should give up being surprised or I will fail the course of heart.

I rise my head and look around carefully, this place is like the place Safran described in the poem, it is bigger than the worlds of seeing and hearing. Here is a magnificent palace with huge domes. I find all the beauties I saw in the worlds of hearing and seeing very easily. Varicoloured giant chandeliers, thousands, tens of thousands of spectacular pendants are flowing down like a music. I hear their sounds, every sound, every image having existed in the universe so far and the magnificence of all times are flowing like water here without touching each other; here is an ocean that different waters don't mix each other. A pink mist wraps me; this is musk! All skies of the world fit in the very little space of this palace. Here is the house of eternity taking your breath away. Keşşaf guides me around, I see so many place that I am exhausted,

"You haven't seen even a bastion of the heart. This palace contains eternal number of universe. Even if you walk around until the end of your life and thousands of life is added to your life, you cannot still manage to see all. Here is the world of heart. The very self of the eternity!"

Keşşaf tells me about the heart in the body in detail. First he talks about the parts of the heart, structure of it, how it pumps blood along the body.

"Do you know," he says, "the heart beats nearly one hundred thousand per world day and it makes eight thousand litres of blood get into circulation." Then Keşşaf tells about the auricles, ventricles and valves of the heart.

"The sound that we perceive as heart beating," he says, "is not the sound generated from the heart's contracting and unwinding, the sound you hear as pulse is the sound coming out as a result of opening and closing of the heart valves strongly."

Then he talks about what happens when the heart contracts and unfastens. The things he is talking about are so complex that I cannot understand the working of the heart. What a fine composition, what a perfect balance!

"Each chamber of the heart pumps the blood in it during the contraction and fills with blood when it unfastens. The heart, this perfect pump, collects blood from the body via vascular system, send it to the lungs to give oxygen to it and pumps the blood which has been rich in oxygen back to the body.

After he tells about the heart's working, I see the most spectacular, most unbelievable thing I have ever seen, the heart itself. A heart appears in Keşşaf's hand beating continuously, alone, without coordination. I bounce rearward horrified. It is as big as my fist, it belongs to a human. I see how this part of flesh moves in a bitter endeavour. I feel that a human is punching the inner walls of the heart continuously to go out of this shape resembling a bur. Or this is a sandbag beating itself from inside steadily. This is simply an alive thing! It's aliveness is self evident! Keşşaf articulates my feelings:

"Do you know Dilruba, the heart generates its own power. The power in the heart arises with the contraction of the heart muscles. Muscle cells contracting rhythmic movements have a perfect design making them contract when the electric current comes."

"I didn't know," I said shaking my head two sides...

The heart in Keşşaf's hand continued to beat as if it was being delirious, like an engine firing itself. It was fascinating to see this so closely saying the least of it! I felt helpless before this heart. It made me smaller not to understand its working, not to penetrating its perfection. Being so close to the heart but so far from it... Even so knowing this alive and perfect bur full of blood was in my breast made me happy.

"Well, do you know that heart can think? Your heart is a mind that can understand the metaphysical world. The heart is the door of an eternal universe comprising also mind. If your mind is the moon, then your heart is the sun. There are ears and eyes inside the heart, we said that data perceived by five senses was obscure shadows of which content wasn't understood, here the heart hears and sees the originals of these obscure shadows, it is capable fort his. What heart sees, hears and says is completely true."

The extraordinary music of the heart and Keşşaf's voice constitutes a terrific duet. He continued:

"Don't be scared! You will know the heart better in due time."

Right after the heart was wiped away in his hand, poured like water, melted and remained as a red drop...

"Don't worry," said Keşşaf, "this was only an image just like the images in your world. Now, let's get down to brass tracks."

What was the main point, what would I see more? When Keşşaf said "follow me," I started to walk stepping on his trace. "I will show you a land in this big universe, this eternity called as the palace of heart," he said. We arrived in front of a wretch, decayed door.

Keşşaf was walking in front of me, showed me the way, sometimes turned back with all his body and looked at me. He wanted to know if I could bear the journey.

We passed the broken up threshold of this decayed land getting covered with dust. Huge tiles were falling down our heads, I couldn't see more than the black sky and cracked ground. As if it had been an earthquake in this land and even one piece of stone hadn't moved for hundreds of years. When the black sky was lightened by the lightnings spilling out hatred, the terrible state of the around was appearing. Keşşaf started to talk while I was slithering behind him.

"Now, listen to me carefully because you need to know what I will say. Every human has two souls. One of the souls is dominant in every heart. One of them is Spirit and the other is Nafs. Here is the land of heart Nafs is dominant. Here is the land ruled by Nafs ordering evil. This is the darkest land of the material; all pleasures seen here get stronger and beat the Spirit, weaken it. Eating, greed for property, feeling of piling up and saving is at their big-time. All bad habits are about this country. Vanity, arrogance, jealousy and such traits captured the cities by vandalising. All lusts has been come out here. Thus the Nafs taking the throne rules the country as it wants. The Spirit has been captive, it has been helpless."

He turned to me and waited, I caught him. When I went to him,

"Now the Nafs can appear at any moment, be careful," he said. "If the owner of the land of heart doesn't fight with the Nafs, the land will always remain ruined as you see."

We were passing through the remains of destroyed old palaces. "Here," he said, "here was the palace of the Spirit. Now it is destroyed, and the Spirit must have been captive. Who knows where it has hidden."

We walked through the destroyed palace, the wreck. Ahead there was a giant black heart in the dirt... Vessels filled with blood had weakened and the red colour of the heart had turned to Brown.

"You see the heart," said Keşşaf. In the body captured by the Nafs this is the condition of the heart."

"What a pity," I said. The condition of the heart was miserable. It was so different from the heart beating in Keşşaf's hand, it looked very old, tired, weak and unwilling and it was trying to move scarcely.

Blood rivers were passing, snakes were wandering around the banks of these rivers hissing, every kind of evil showed up. A distress arose in me, I was suffocating. When would we go out of this land? Suddenly the black sky started to move, after a thunder fires started to pour on me. I couldn't see Keşşaf also. A terrible scream was approaching. It must have been the Nafs! It was approaching heaving and with wild clamours. At last I saw it. A double-headed dragon! My fears came to true. I stood alone whatever it was. I was spreading flames out of its mouth bending its heads backwards and approaching with its ugly body resembling a hyena as if it would swallow me. It was throwing its huge wings resembling the wings of a bat, then it rose them to the sky as if it would fly.

I am not a coward even if I am confused fast! I pluck up my courage and attack immediately. I have pleasure to push whoever or whatever the enemy is, but I'm afraid now this situation was over my head. First of all, we were not equal since this dragon was two rivals. It was at least ten times bigger than me and was continuously leaving me in flames. I poked about around. I started to run back when I couldn't find anything useful. I must have found something to use for weapon in the Spirit's palace, at least a sword! I quickly looked for something like sword through the dead magnificence, I found a mace. However it was so heavy that I couldn't even move it. I examined the torn cloth pieces and was looking for something to protect me. At last I found a knife like a wedge. It wasn't very sharp and it was rusty but at least it I would gain time. The double headed Nafs caught me in two steps. It was trampling down the ruins in dust with its huge, ugly feet, and tried to squash me with rage and anger.

I let out a yell to get back my strength. I thought my lungs exploded, my purpose was to scare it. Yet I wasn't able to think of protecting the fire. I was darting about, weaving; but the flames were still licking my face. The interesting thing was that I became a warrior and started to attack it. I surprised it passing between its legs, I was planning to knock it down by forcing it these sudden movements since I had realized the bulkiness of this huge body and heavy tail. Yes, it had a bulky body but it was nimble at the same time! I was circling at its feet like a mouse; it was also circling to catch me. I stuck the wedge on its foot thinking it was time. Black blood started to well out! I stuck the wedge again and again. I was sticking with all my strength, but it had no effect.

"Hey, big baby," I cried. I annoyed it! "Bend your head and I will kiss your face."

It understood I was mocking of it, it hit with one of its front feet that it threw me meters away. Fortunately I fell on my back. I got up moaning. I didn't feel the pain. I flew at its left leg. I was sticking the wedge. Then I thought to approach from back. I started to climb its tail. I couldn't turn back, swinging two sides. I climbed some more. I was close to its head. I stuck the wedge in the back of its neck with all my strength. The Nafs cried in pain. It was throwing its head to the back to get rid of the wedge. It was throwing about its head so fast that I found myself on the ground again. I was defeated in any case. I saw Keşşaf's feet from the ground that I had lied down.

"Child, think carefully," he said to me, "think carefully, what is the solution?"

Did have time to think? I couldn't think any cunning. Then suddenly the magnificent views I had witnessed in the worlds of seeing and hearing. If I managed to draw the origins of the sounds and images and reveal them as the Nafs could see... But there was a problem, that black heart ahead, what would happen to it? It needed to be lightened, to generate power again, to contract properly... The tired beatings and this miserable state resembling a sad face of this heart should have changed, it should have revived.

I realized that moment that the flames coming from the Nafs' mouth burned my face but didn't hurt, moreover it didn't give any harm to my skirts. Inlaid mirrors on the skirt reflected the fire back. I had got wet in the sea of secrets and this wetness lessened the strength of the fire very much. Firs I removed the mirrors on my chest one by one. I would use them to reflect the images coming from those two worlds. I didn't think anything else.

I piled the small mirrors I had removed on the heart blackening more and more. I started to draw the origins of the images and sounds little by little by focusing deeply. Keşşaf had taught me how to do this. I drew all these reflections to the heart. Magnificent lights reflecting on the heart and wonderful melodies making one become listless were first flowing to the heart, they gave strength as they were leaking through the mirrors, then reflected to the Nafs' face and made it blind.

I drew all the light and clearness to give strength to the heart with all my strength. Rays reflecting to the heart as a beam gave strength to the heart and reflected from it to both heads of the dragon, muddled it. The dragon being dazzled and went blind slowly went down on its knees. A crying sound was coming from it, it was groaning. It was entranced by the beauty. I reflected it all magnificent beauties I could remember from the world of seeing, it went crazy. It was moving heaven and earth hitting its head to the ruins and purulence was coming from its mouth. At last the Nafs lied down weakly. It just fell down in the shape of a foetus.

I turned to the heart in a manner of a heroine knocking down her enemy. I wanted to see how the heart was. The origins I had drawn from the world of seeing were not on the heart! It was Keşşaf's face lighting there. I had deceived myself, defeated myself, had been beaten attributing power to myself. The Nafs had seen Keşşaf's face. I bowed before this face in shame. Then Keşşaf came to me,

"Do you know, you had hurt it by the Spirit's regret wedge," said he as if he consoled me.

He looked into my eyes compassionately and went on.

"I don't want to upset you, but this is just the beginning... The Nafs will confront you much more."

I looked as if I understood everything.

"We have a hope as long as you are here," I said.

Keşşaf had disappeared. He had gone.

I dropped my head. I was exhausted. What did he mean by the last sentence? I had fought with all my strength. I sat on the ground, I was a tired warrior. I took a deep breath, victory was mine. Victory was the heart's. I understood that I was nothing in the absence of Keşşaf. I struggled with Safran's voice reading a poem. The crowd in the room was the same as I had left, time hadn't flown here at all...

A building from jewellery in my heart
I saw there a red ruby gate
Going in and going further in an instant
A ruby palace was manifested

I gulped. I was thirsty and hungry. I had paled. Afternoon *azan* was being recited. “Let’s go for prayer,” said Safran. Then her soft looks touched on me, Kırlangıç, Nergis and Zümrüt in turn... Her voice resembling the silk satin was coming so nicely.

“Girls, get ready,” she said, “we are going on a trip at the weekend. The time is up, a traveller should be on the way.”

Then she locked her eyes to mine.

“Those who are tired will rest well,” she said.

I felt rested when I heard this. The road was calling me.

17
Set Off

Then only then,
Light of intimacy reflects to your forehead
Freesias of this garden speak,
Narcissus sees (Shabistari)

Good news about trip four days later brightened the dark and silent rooms of the dormitory like a sharp glimmer of hope. Whatever around me, the place the hope touches is turning green. Going to classes is all turning in this plan; exams are becoming distinct mosaics of an impatient waiting. I look for a distinct love on the teachers' faces and I find love signs easily. A wedding turned over me is approaching.

Moments are lengthening out more and more. What will I see?

I know her, Safran, as much as she showed me herself. She said me that her name was Keşşaf. I saw her as a Cavalry on a thoroughbred horse, she was hiding her face with a niqab. She was carrying me away the entire world. She was taking me form Cabülka and dressing my wounds, whispering the secret of existence; she was showing me the originals of the colours, sounds and images, we were passing the secrets sea all in one breath. Being with her... Being with her meant to watch at the dimensions time, place melted. Keşşaf's world was so wide that I couldn't see at once. It was perfect above my head.

I was approaching the idea that the things I experienced with Keşşaf have a reality in the world of seeing. She was occupying a field in this world, there were people, her family around her. The idea that she was not a dream was nailed on my brain. I was going to follow the reality of the things that she told me. What if Keşşaf moves away from me when I see her reality? What if she becomes ordinary as she wraps herself in reality, if she becomes the subject of love which is hard to get when she was that she has a life on the ground? Her corresponding and reality in life is a big obstacle. The best thing was to stay as I know her, as Keşşaf!

Nevertheless, I should have gone, I should have seen her. I should have gone to her all in one breath and shouted out that all these worlds aren't lie, they are not my fantasy, there you are, that is you. I must throw myself to her and I must say save me from myself. I can't stand staying here anymore! I don't have the power oh sultan! I don't have the power of love! Oh Keşşaf who made me find myself! The one with antelope's eyes, oh Gül-I Rana! Oh owner of the light burn me, let me hear your voice; Let that voice echo in the sky and drop the suns into my heart like an ember. Oh the one filling my medulla with musk, if you stop speaking, I can't hear my own voice, I can't fly behind your eyes. Seeing that you are so close, don't move away... I will come you fast as long as you don't stop, don't stop, wing me from a country to country, roll me from a universe to universe, whisper me all the secrets, make me *majnun*, talk to me unceasingly, say me. Don't stop speaking! Your silence is my death.

I must cry, beg, and shout out. I must speak to her with the most beautiful letter, I must be the most precious words itself. If I can bear, I must look at her face, if necessary, I must die there. I must be right beside her. I must go there to say you are my mother whose smell I didn't feel, to say you make me find my real hometown abroad... I must say you are my father, my ancestor, my love, friend. How can I bear all this distance! I must go, I must go, she is there, she is there!

It was four days later. Everything was going to reach fruition! I was going to see her! This was an irresistible draw! How the women seeing Yusuf cut their hands helplessly, how they could not help but they were drenched in blood before that beauty, how beauty of Yusuf became flame and flew them... I should also be covered with love after seeing my own Yusuf. I must find him!

We meet at the end of a wreck street at the darkness of the night, beside an old *masjid*. We, Kırlangıç, Zümrüt, Hazel and Nergis, are little shadows waiting for light in darkness. And Safran appears grandiosely, comes near us with five or six people. She surrounds us with her soft and naïve voice.

She says, "Girls, did you come? We are taking the road after evening prayer. But some more people are also coming, let's go together, let's not come off"

We have bags with us. There are veiled women waiting at the corner in dark, familiar faces that aren't perceived. There is a strange taste. An old bus is approaching, stopping in front of us like a thick wall. Noise of the motor slows down and fades. At last it stops with a *tısssss* sound. Smell of the exhaust surrounds us. Some men with cap get off the bus looking in front of him. After putting our bags, we enter the mosque. We drop shadows from our forehead to the cold ground of this small mosque, our faces are on the ground. This moment is worth everything. We greet the angels among this elegant community.

This cleanness, this feeling of purity, putting everything aside for love and setting off surrounds us. Darkness caresses our cheeks like an elegant veil. We get on the bus for a long journey. This is a fate embedded into our breasts! The lights of the bus are turned on, our reflection is on the windows. Safran checks whether the passengers are ready or not. She controls us. We say "We are OK." "Everybody is OK." We are sitting at the back seats with the girls. Hazel and Gülistan are at the front seats side by side. Gülistan, the woman who was turning like a fireball. She is turning back and smiling, and then she is trying to amuse her little daughter on her lap. A curtain is drawn two or three rows behind the captain on the other end of the corridor.

Kırlangıç sitting next to me referring to the curtain says, "We are going to watch a movie soon." Say, "What next?" Kırlangıç started to chat, she is such happy that she is about to jump. She says, "Wow, at last we are going, too". Bottom of the seats are full of supplies, as if it is a long journey which will last for weeks; we have taken all of the food and drinks. Zümrüt is spouting to Nergis who is sitting next to her, then she checks around and goes on talking. She has a floral kerchief. Safran is sitting with Gül Hanım two or three rows ahead, her grandness is overflowing the seat she is sitting. What a mystery is this! The captain dips the lights. First sizzles come from the microphone and then the captain speaks "Let's not forget the intentions. May Allah accept." Then prayers are said. Wheels start turning with mutter slowly. The voice at the microphone says "Bismillah (In the name of God)". We start flying like birds flying to their nests. To a new life on old wheels...

At last we could set off. This old form of the bus starts going like taking wings. Safran says to the one sitting in front of her, "We are going to take some people on the road, tell the driver to go slowly." The one sitting in front of her says the one who is sitting in front of her. People greet and sit on the empty seats. Some of them are wearing black abaya, slippers and have their little children with them. They are happy. The captain steps on the gas. The things they speak can be heard from the microphone. They are talking. The fire in their heart reaches us increasingly. Then they stop speaking and hymn starts playing and the microphone is turned off.

A plate full of stuffed vine leaves is reached to me. She says, "Take it Sufi, eat it with pleasure". I take some and give it to the front row. Kırlangıç says "We are at the right place." Before we eat stuffed vine leaves, they hold pastries, cakes. As if there is a kitchen at the back, we are filling the plates and emptying, spring rolls are passing from hand to hand. Kırlangıç and I are the naughty children of this bus. We are climbing the walls, I wish we could sit silent like Nergis. Kırlangıç says, "I hope next thing is tea." Tea is served in plastic glasses... Kırlangıç says, "Is this domestic goods week?" We enjoy the moment.

The way flows under us, the time flows. The captain again turns on the microphone. Then, he starts telling. He says, "The ones who goes there for the first time, first intend. Listen for the God." He speaks clearly. He tells the rules to be obeyed, the things to be considered for not returning empty-handed. We listen to him carefully. Then, some people come to Safran. We immediately run and listen to her.

Safran says, "Politeness, in any case, politeness. Do not hurt anybody there, please and take care of the patients, olds, children. Know yourself lower than any others. Do not look down on people, otherwise you will come and go like a tourist! Be patient at the ablution queue; do not take the others' turn. Do not worry about the place t sleep at night, pad down some place, do not look hostilely. Do not evade serving, compete in serving, know that it is a felicity."

We look at each other with Kırlangıç and nod in the meaning of course. These are important, we shouldn't hurt people. Safran goes on,

"Do not think ill of anybody. No matter what happens, do not open the door the devil. The devil will nauseate your heart, make your words dirty. Do not push someone around, take what comes to your destiny. There are hidden saints in the public, maybe the one you look down on is a friend of the god, whoever it is it doesn't matter, be respectful."

About an hour later, we are taking a break for *salah*. We are getting off the bus in rows like beads, we are taking the road to the mosque orderly. Everybody is waiting for their turn, we are giving way to the old and the ones with children. We are holding their bags, we are rummaging about around. Sometimes we are sitting at the foot of the wall and smoking secretly. We are afraid of being seen by Safran. We are sure, if she sees us, she will criticize us and prohibit us this. She will say smoking is not your business. She is enfolding us in her arms like a mother, she is looking at us mercifully, she always speaks from heart. She is quiet suffering like a mother, she gathers the breath when she touches affectionately. There is no place for grudge, hate, passion in Safran's dictionary, she only delivers love to the earth.

We are coming back to our bus like children having candies in their hands after the night prayer. How meaningful our life is. We are not wasting time, our saddlebag is clean our water is fruitful. We are aware that we are being controlled every time; every time is melting in the meaning ocean.

The things we do are echoing in the placeless universe. Bow of the love is stretched to dig Sweet's (Maşuk) arrow into the deepest point. Shadow of the bus is on the road. The road is flowing under us in the opposite direction like rebellious rivers. Turquoise reflections appear among us. I am spinning my hope of seeing Keşşaf with the love yarn; I lean my head to the Cabülka once more,

I see Nafs falling flat on the floor on the window. Hot water of secrets' sea is burning my sole. Cavalry is passing us on her thoroughbred, at full gallop. She passes so near that the skew-back of the saddle can be seen, shadow of the bus touches his head-dress; shadow touches the reality for a moment. A hand is scrubbing my temporal bones with attar of roses. It is turning into hand and holding my hands. It is turning into words and washing my words.

Hour hand of the clock is about to show the new day. It is going to unload the heaviness of a day. It is going to take the new day on its lap. As it is swinging the new day in its lap, the moon in the sky will go on fading, will look as a jealous sister. But now it is shining like an oil-lamp on us. It is going as we go, it is in step with us. Soft light of the bus fades, seems like thin blue thread. Some people are passing through the narrow corridor holding the head of the seats, as if they are silhouettes...

Someone is talking at the front row of the bus, the philosopher captain is taking to the person next to him silently. Suddenly, an "ahh" sound disturbs the speech. A strong, sad "ahh"... He worries about his own Keşşaf, he is stepping on the gas. I am closing my eyes again, a thin sleep settles into my eyes...This time I hear a cry... I am looking at Kırlangıç, lke asking "What' happening?" She is opening her eyes curiously. She is standing up and looking at the seat in front of us and saying "She is on air". This is Gülistan...

Mystic communications settle into the days, nights incomprehensibly. Sometimes you have a feeling that the Beloved left you alone after the divine attraction. It is if your material eye is opened, spiritual eye is squinted. Time slows down, the place stays the same, people around turn into baby doll. You crush the floor of loneliness harshly with pain. Everything remains the same on the other days. In fact, this is so in your eye. A blessed hand has immersed that hard iron of love, your ego that you think non-flexible into glowing fire, is forging it on the anvil with might and main for you. By this way, a strong armour is being prepared for you. Seeds were spread on your fallowed heart land without your knowledge. A heart that can carry that strong armour is being with the poisoned water of loneliness. One day you will understand, time has hurried up during the days and nights, because time obeys the divine commands without any hesitation like all the other created things. When time is up, gate of the patience cage is opened, suffering basket starts weakening. This mysterious process is one of the testing valleys of the Beloved who is always alive.

Before beginning this journey, I feel that I was preparing for this special journey on the way of life. I was waited for the equipment that could meet the unique tastes and troubles of this journey. I was wavering in a deep loneliness after Keşşaf's taking me out, I was walking about at the desserts where it is impossible to content with the things seen or heard. I lived with the delusion that everything was my fantasy for a long time. We were said nothing related to the inner journeys in life. Most of them were silent like mute. Struggle to earn a living, pains of secular separations, material dreams were wasting our time with very limited part of existence. Maybe we have cogent grounds. Only some people realize that it's a kind of weird and trying to know themselves. Questions like "Who am I?" or "Why am I here?" were nonsense for most of the people, they were just living the moment. In my opinion, in fact, living the moment was the most terrible fetter. Heart that can loosen the rings of the moment can enjoy the life and existence. Moment is the narrowest cage. The ones who open the door to material pleasure, who remit the spiritual one, the desire to live the moment was going up like an indestructible wall in front of the perceptions.

The ones on the bus... The ones who left their comfort to get out from their narrow caves and set off. The ones who realize that they are in a cave. The ones who set off to get out of utter darkness. The ones who emigrate to find the homeland of their spirits. The ones who tire their bodies on this road... the ones who lend their days to reality and find the hidden cause... the ones whose headlong, whose heart eye doesn't see anything other than the land of Beloved. The ones who see the reason and result without looking among the ones who look but don't see.

Most of the ones in this bus are poor, culturally disadvantaged people. Most of them don't have even shoes. You could understand this by just looking at the children in the bus. The children were quite thin and their clothes were quite old. Eyes of these children look at the felicity of the life from a distant. They don't know junk food. As if brownness of their life shadowed their faces, made their skin dark. But yet, when they smile, the earth moves because of the beauty of their smile. Your heart will sink when you look at their shining eyes. Mothers carry them for hours without complaining. Their children are like a part of their body, they haven't separated from their body yet, it is such a good maternity. They don't show any tedium to their whine. Sometimes the children in their arms don't sleep, that time, a blanket is laid on the corridor, the mother swings the child on her legs. She lies her head to the seat and zonks out.

These mothers always smile. These women whose husbands are mostly workers are noble women who avoid raising their voice when they are near their husbands or family elders. They don't laugh loudly, they don't speak except gratitude and prayer. They don't complain about the shanties they live, because their palace of heart is wide. They don't ask many questions about life, their amenable spirit isn't complex, it is calm and still. Their stance, glance draws the picture of obedience. They didn't go to school properly, so their mind isn't dirtied with suspicion. But they struggle for making their children go to school. They study at the hard and pitiless schools of life, their books are poverty, their pencils are firm belief. Their situation is worthy of astonishment; they save themselves from helplessness called depression by means of the love in their heart, gratitude on their lips. They know that the world is testing land. Despite their hard lives, these beautiful people know to give for love. Financial difficulties don't keep them from helping. They are happy women whose spirit is friendly, whose look is sincere.

When you look at the bus taking our breath away, you will think that it is as old and tired as it can't bear long distance. Some of the seats sway on its place, you can't lie back easily, they are as if skinned. Its doors are such old that it can't easily opened or closed. It smells old. This is an old but ageless smell. It doesn't tire you, instead, it's like a refreshing melody. It is like a melody that refreshes the person who is on the bus even once. This is a gratitude bus, this is the place where the people knowing to be satisfied are.

I look at Kırlangıç. She is as if she wants to sleep happily. Sometimes her head falls to her right, then she tidies herself up as if to say where I am. I catch clear deep of her heart when I look into Kırlangıç's eyes.

There is no trick in her look, she reflects the things inside her. Sometimes indefinable pain settles in the apple of her eye, it is something like a search for hope similar to waver. Hundreds of questions appear on her face. It lasts until a hand catches her existence with all its power. Kırlangıç is looking for that hand which clears the cloudy water. She is asking that hand from near and far; that hand has kept, withheld her spirit from all eternity!

Now, there are similar questions on shadow of her face. She is breathing slowly. Nergis's head falls one side, Zümrüt is watching outside. I bend and whisper, "Why are you not sleeping?" she replies smiling, "I am not sleepy, what about you?". I say "I am excited. She says, "Me, too." Being inexperienced is difficult...

A fat and old Sufi sitting behind me stands up, lays a blanket on the corridor, and lies down on the floor. When she realizes me looking at her, she says "I wasn't comfortable, deary. My feet swell up on long road trip." She lies down quickly on the floor. I smile tolerantly.

Almost everybody is asleep. Safran is still. Gülistan stop crying. Hazel is in front of me and her head is about to fall between the two seats. I lean my head. The bus is swinging us like a cradle. What a beautiful thing to go, to be able to go. Going from a point on the earth to the other sliding, like flying. To reach like a sound, like a shout... Towards the sun; towards burning...

I fall asleep. The sleep I fell is the deepest sleep of my life. It is endless. A sleep like diving into the world of absence. Peace of a country where non-being is lost. My spirit moves away from my body than ever before, this is a sleep like diving into the bottom of the sea. I am lying on a bed which is pulled off clouds, cotton of which is beaten by the angels. There is a pillow made of moon light under my head and a soft darkness on me from end to end. It covers my dirt. It is preparing me for an utterly different light. My face is about to touch Keşşaf's face. It takes out tiredness of whole life from my soul as if taking out butterfat. Each organ of my body is a day dream; each particle of mu soul is washed with the water the cup-bearer pours. The absence is lighter at each breath... I swim on my mother's breast that I have never smelled. I am silence of a huge father. I am registered into the land of welfare, my copy is taken out of my body, I am flowing in an endless space. I am curled in foetal position to the sleep that is going to bring me again into the world...

My soul returns to my body again with Captain's voice. Squeaky sound says "It's time for Fajr Prayer, sufis". The ones on the bus wakes up quickly, they stand up. The bus slows down, stops shaking, with a tired, long *tıss* sound. When the back door is opened, refreshing *azan* and chilly breeze of morning fill in the bus. Darkness in the bus is dispersed. Kırlangıç and I can't wake Hazel up. Safran says, "She is in a deep sleep, she is being cleaned." She speaks of sleeping on this way purifies soul. At last, she opens her eyes... The ones who tidy their clothes get off the bus one by one, a crowded shadow is on the way of the mosque. Bodies got numb because of sitting during the night relax. The dawn hasn't broken yet. The dogs are howling from a distance. This little mosque seems like a deserted place. There is a chilliness that shakes a person. Because of the cold, everybody is walking like hiding their heads in their shoulders. There are only trees around, dark green. I am waiting for my turn for ablution. I feel very sleepy. I give place to the old woman slept on the ground during the night. She is praying, her lips are moving, her cheerful face hasn't awaken yet...

The modest lights burn our eyes in the mosque. We blossom like roses. Foreheads touch the old rugs on the floor. Coolness of the floor holds us, the place is happy to see us... Performing prayer with crowd sweeps the loneliness particles in us. Voice of the Imam becomes a long love...

The bus sets off again. With the buzzing of microphone, revival starts. The captain says, "we are going to have soup soon". A hymn starts... Everybody looks at his hearth like bending over a deep water... When the day breaks we reach to a *dergah*. This is a modest building with two or three rooms. Inside of the building is so simple, there are only tables and chairs... there is a kitchen at the end of the building. Big cooking pots can be seen through the door. They take us hot soup and bread. I learn that this is Mecca for the ones on this journey. They serve everybody come by here for love.

I can't wake up without drinking tea. Kırlangıç, neither... we two are looking around like waiting for tea. After the soup, hey serve tea. We are glad to drink tea. Hot tea goes down my throat. The day starts with this first sip.

I ask Safran if we are about to arrive there. She says, "If god lets, we will be there in the afternoon." What a long way... We again sit our places happily like the babies who are full up. Captain turns on the microphone, this time another one starts telling. He is repeating the things to do there. Then, they turn the volume of the hymn up. Hazel goes on sleeping. I feel enthusiasm in my heart. The women start dancing the *halay* in the narrow corridor. Back and forth. Gülistan is taking the lead with a handkerchief in her hand. It is a silent *halay*. Kırlangıç and I rush out and join the *halay.*

"I wish I was apprentice to a master; Far will be near; I wish I make my bone comb; For earlock of the lover..."

We drink the lyrics of the hymn like wine, torture moves away us. We don't so care about the world that I am suspicious that we are mad. Shoulders move faster, we catch an unbelievable rhythm in such a narrow corridor. Rivers are rippling in this rhythm. Cool water takes our soul away in waves. Breath of rhythm falls backward and forward. Safran says smilingly, "Sufi, be quite". She smiles such beautifully that I want to hug her. Although we don't speak, this is the song of our soul.

We are almost there, if god lets. When you wait for something impatiently, you can't shape it in your dreams. What kind of a place is it? How is its ground, water? What about the people? What do they look like?...

The weather gets hot more and more, we were drawing the thick green curtains of the bus to avoid the causticity of the sun. I was half-opening the curtain constantly and looking where we came. So the sunlight was cutting the darkness in the bus like a yellow knife. I started seeing valleys like endless desserts. There weren't any plants or people. It was drought all out. Everywhere the eye could see was bright yellow, arid land. The bus was going on a asphalt road in a dessert slithering like foam between a yellow colour. I realized that we reached to a virgin, forgotten place. The road was too long, the land seemed like long yellow carpets which were washed by the sun in waves. The weather inside started to take our breath away. Sweat was licking our face and went down our neck; hot weather was clenching our feet like fetters. We ran out of water in this blistering weather, we started to wait for the time we reach. We were half-opening the curtains impatiently and checking outside.

I was saying "My soul is drier than those bright yellow carpets from end to end, of Keşşaf", Keşşaf was listening to me. I was saying, "Here I am, we are almost there." Keşşaf was smiling. Cavalry with his niqab on his face was passing on his thoroughbred white horse. Skew-backs of his horse were shining, chattering. Transparent flames were arising on the asphalt because of the heat. Cavalry was running at full gallop like a mounted Bedouin who found mirage in the dessert and showing the way to the captain. He sun was fascinated in the dagger in his waist. Ends of the white head-dress was rising, skirt of his green cloth was flying with my heart. I saw his brunette hands holding the headstall. Mane of the white horse was pouring into his hands like a milk waterfall. The bus was taking the corners fast. The seats were swaying from side to side. Cavalry was looking at the bus with all his solemnity; I don't know who I was in love with, this horse or the cavalry.

Then, high rocks appeared around us, the asphalt road was giving way to rough, arid and sandy road. We were going in dust cloud. The cavalry was going leaving dust clouds behind him, flying sand like gauze. There was an unendurable spiritual hunger and dust smell inside. At the bottom of the high cliffs, sound of tambourines celebrating this visit was heard. A shadowy image was beating the drums with might and main. The dessert under us was turning into a bright yellow sky; the bus was flying.

Keşşaf turned into a sweet who doesn't hear the cry of the lover; he was ignoring her lament and wasting her time pitilessly, he was delaying the meeting time. He was still behind the blinding light; I was saying waiting is severe than fire. He was releasing the flames on me. I was saying "Please, take pity on me", he was saying "Don't say 'me' here".

The bus entered a narrow village road. It stopped at the end of a street consisting of bungalow roofless houses and several shops. This village was like a place out of the world. There were some alone and shrubs, some small houses like matchboxes which were mortared randomly, some people wearing white from head to foot. There were randomly parked cars. We found a place between them and parked there. We stopped with a thick and tired "ptıss" sound at a nook place with exhaust fumes.

The group stepped on the ground like a mirage in the middle of a dessert. I felt the fine sand, it was burning my sole. Broiling-hot was disrupting my breath, bright light was blinding me. The one taking his backpack got off the bus calmly, and started to wait. There were bird calls among the shrubs. We started walking towards a thin road, towards the high iron doors like portcullis.

Wings of the high iron doors were half-opened. A group of women bags in their hands and children stepped outside. They walked calmly looking back from time to time. These iron doors were rising like hiding a city. As the wings of it is opened and closed with sound, it was whispering that there was a huge life behind it. I walked at the threshold of the door like a voyager approaching to the axis of equator. When I pass the threshold, the climate will change, the water will flow in the reverse direction... The act of living behind these doors will get a slap in the face... Love will let itself go. Secrets will be concealed. It is the first step to pass to world of absence.

Kırlangıç pokes me. We haven't passed the threshold yet. She says, "Look at this" looking at a distance. When I turn my head, I have my heart in my mouth, my breath is taken into a swirl. I see a cavalier on a red pacer with his white cloth and head-dress... There was a spot blaze on the forehead of the horse, there was a comet shining on the place between the blaze and its nose... But this is my horse! Yes, while I was going to land Cabülka, the horse next to him when I first met Cavalry. The horse the Cavalry in other words Keşşaf taught me how to ride it, the noble horse that I drilled for the first time!

"What a strange place!" I say.

Safran turns us and says "Don't idle around" she looks around in a hurry. She hits the half-opened door slowly. There is no one. There is a concrete slope downward... There is a high oriel building cutting the narrow walkway. There are intertwined large and small, low houses.

Safran says whisperingly, "Sometimes Keşşaf stands behind this oriel, and looks at the people coming". Outgrowth like a balcony is covered totally with wood oriel. I clean my act up immediately, tiredness goes from my body, I return to life. I glance at the behind of the oriel. It is dark and hidden back.

We reach to a wide yard after passing through the low houses with intertwine flat roofs. Water is rippling from spring into two small pools in the middle of the yard. Everywhere is very clean, it has just washed, and stony ground of the yard is shining. We tend towards one of the stairs going up. We enter one of the rooms in rows. There is nothing else than rugs on the floor. Safran says, "we are going to stay here. Leave your luggage here and have a rest." We crouch down. Backpacks are opened slowly, I still have the murmur of the road in my ears. We start eating something.

Another group come to this room without window. They enter happily. I don't understand the language they use. They wear their most elegant clothes; we are so weak when compared to them. Their clothes look like kaftan. Kırlangıç says, "How do they wear these heavy clothes in such hot. But they are beautiful..."

I feel like I went back in time. There aren't hardly any signs around from the century I live. The group wearing their Sunday-go-to-meeting clothes is as if they popped out a history book. There are tattoos on their faces and hennas in their hands. They set a big table in the middle slowly and they also invite us. One of the women encinctures the end of her indigo-blue scarf from her neck and pin it down her cheek. She rolls her inlaid wristband up and hands me fatty pastry with a smile on her face. She says something I don't understand. She is such comfortable and happy that it is impossible not to be jealous of her. There is refreshing expression of pushing the world and her feelings aside on her face. She says, "Hodeş derazibe" or something like this. Her large brunette wrists are such thick and strong that she looks like the women in fairy tales. They eat their meal cheerfully for a while

Sun goes on walking towards the peak of the sky. Safran says, "There is little time for midday *azan*, let's depart" We pack up and go downstairs, women in the other group also pack up with us. Lavatory is downstairs. When I look down the stairs, I see that the yard which was empty when we entered is full now. It is an incredible crowd... we crowd into the lavatory. Everybody is in a hurry, Safran says, "There is little time for azan". I toe the line. As I try to be quick I crash people. At last I can perform ablution. Safran says, "upstairs, upstairs, to the other side.". Everybody is in a rush. I have no idea about the reason for this rush. My feet are knocking together for fear of losing the group. I find the stairs gliding through the crowd.

There is a smaller yard upstairs but it is still wide. As if I am in a small doomsday rehearsal. The crowd scatters from side to side, when do these people come here? I can't see my tiptoes, tens of face crashes my face in a minute. Wherever I turn my head, I am in a cage of a pair of eyes. Oh my God, what a place is this! Why do these people gather here? I am scattered through a woman in the wheel chair on the yard side. She is there as if she wants to protect herself. There is a young woman next to her. After smiling them, I dive into the crowd again fearlessly, I look for Hazel and Nergis. Oh I wish I saw them once... Everybody is hidden in her scarf, I can't recognize them. Then I see the group with shining clothes, and Gülistan is next to them. I hardly pass the people and reach them. Gülistan says, "We can't go further." Suddenly there is a mess. A sound is heard from the front. A high pitch is begging "Sufi, go back, go back for God's sake". People go back unwillingly like muttering waves. When they find the opportunity, they again go towards. We continuously go back and forward. They push me back and forth. On tiptoe, I raise my head in order not to be drowned in the crowd.

A mechanical buzzing calms down this crazy crowd. A sound through the sky rears ups: *Allahuekber*! The *azan* starts, as if the muezzin is among us, his voice comes from such near. After the *azan*, the crowd again starts moving, I can't stay where I am, I fall back and forth. A voice in the front says, "Coming" bodies freeze in a silence which makes people deaf. "Don't look, bow your heads, close your eyes, Sufi for the god's sake..."

a woman next to me says *sotto voce*, "I come from Germany, how come I don't look?

Smell of rose covers the yard; air doesn't mix with the weather here. This smell of rose passes over the air layers, as if it is going to cut the head it touches... I know this smell, this is Keşşaf's smell! He is coming mixing with a flood of light. Bodies staying where they are tipping like the grass caught in a storm; they turn into scythed anther. A scary murmur surrounds everywhere. I look at the other side of the yard as all inexperienced do. First, I see a giant corona, it takes white colours from rainbow, flowing like milk... We are petrified in this picture. Time stops, the place is rooted to the spot. Each of the women is petrified as still as statue.

First, an invisible fireball is approaching to me, then I perspire suddenly. Firs I see his stick. He is swimming in a smooth light. Then he appears; it is Keşşaf, his very self, he is rising on a great tower of divine glory. Centuries flow in this single moment. My all life is nailed to the spot. He shoot me in the chest. His beauty wreaks my spite. After his stick, I see his hand. He has a bunch of roses in his hands... His face... His face... his face is so beautiful that one can die for it... My life is worthless now. He goes one step forward slowly, then looking ahead he goes one more step. Stepping my heart.

Aww... Keep out of my way for the God, give way... Please do not interrupt us while Yusuf yüzlü is so close to me. Oh reason of my existence, turn and look at me for the God's sake! Stop! Why are you passing by like a stranger oh my heart, what happened to the things we lived, those words, why are you so away, why is this dashed coldness? Stop or I will throw my heart under your feet... oh the one I sacrifice myself for, please stop for the God's sake...

My mind slips under my feet. I am scared of the solemnity of him. His beauty fears me. His eyes... Eyes of Cavalry with whom I travel countries, worlds, with whom I pass secrets sea all in one breath. This is the face which knocked down the Nafs with his one glance. The moon in the sky takes its light from this brightness. His head-dress makes all white colours ashamed. His head-dress is such white that it burns my eyes. Expression in his face takes the form of glory. I see him until the stairs on the right end of the yard.

His smell is on every road he passed. The crowd is shocked. They are like drunk people who drink wine. Some of them starts turning like moths to a flame. Nobody can approach Gülistan; Gülistan is salamander burning in fire. I kneel down in the middle of the crown the node in my throat turns into sobbing. I cry like a baby who lost her mother.

When you burn yourself, at first you don't feel the pain. But this pain gradually increases, burns you ceaseless. I feel that all my body is burning with a sweet painless flame, I let myself in the arms of flame. This fire took me to the pools downstairs. I was washing my face with the water flowing from the spring, but I couldn't get over. At last, I embedded my head into the pool. The water which was as cold as ice started to extinguish my fire. I relaxed.

I sat at the side of the little pool. I felt in unnameable pain. I was nothing! I said, "Who do you think you are? Look at these people, what are you in this crowd? What is your value for Keşşaf? Nobody... he didn't even realize you. You are a groggy poor person in the doomsday.

People were passing through the yard. Children, young people, old people. Patients walking hardly were passing. There were some women, I saw the mounting evidences of love, commitment, loyalty on their faces... People were speaking different languages but were burning with the same love. They eat at the same table, and then they go to their own homelands. Only the humming of this huge crowd was sweeping the orphanage of the person. Here one starts hearing his own voice after the first half hour. The old ones having a nap were sleeping as if there are in their beds.

The woman who served me pastry upstairs at the *dergah* came in colourful clothes with a little girl next to her. She was like a walking rainbow. The little girl was also wearing the same fancy clothes. There were light embroideries on each span of their clothes. They look like peacocks in these clothes. The woman first washed her daughters face, then give her some water. She caressed her daughter's hair with her wet hands. She leaned over the spring flowing in streams , washed her face with her hennaed hands and guzzled the water. Then she looked at my face, tattoos on her face was shining more than before when it was washed. Lines from her temporal to next to her mouth were look like dark green ivies. Her chin was full of a lot of complex shapes under her lower lip. She smiled and said something that I didn't understand. I looked at her face wailfully. She gave me pat on the back. I asked her name. She drew a no to the air with her hand as is she was saying I don't understand you. Then showing herself, she smiled as if to say okay. Her thick and muffled voice was coming from the deep of laryngeal, her breath was smelling oleaster... She said "Hevida".

Oh Hevida you don't know. The place I came from is so different from here. Do you know which one is more real, which one is dead in this chaos, or which one will never die? The answer for this is hidden in your shy look, on your face which is totally eluded from guilt. But I don't understand your language, juts as I don't understand the events around here. What about you... what does the place you come from look like Hevida? Are we ill, Hevida, are we mad? How time slows here, do you feel that? Your heart is as clean as your look. You are like cranes flying with hope. There is shambles downstairs, you have a look silently and pass. Who is who, what does the sky to these, Hevida? It is difficult to be downstairs... Being down stairs is agonizing. Our lives are lie out of this threshold... Isn't it Hevida, don't look at like that...

It seemed that many people like me, like Hevida, came here, souls were flowing as rivers. Everything was arranged according to this flow. Greatness lavatory and the words walking from end to end were whispering this. The attendants' aligning the crowd with *hoky-poky*... I was getting lost among thousands of people. What worthless was I... What a disappointment? What kind of pushing out was it after attracting? What a fearful loneliness was mine...

Intimacy between me and Keşşaf wasn't a physical intimacy, it was out of the question. I feel this reality on my every breath. He was taking me to a luminous way, he was continuously dragging and training in his way. I was bounded to him with invisible link. Not having a visible intimacy was hurting me at the beginning.

Which I why he told me, "our adjacency is timeless and placeless, Dilruba". It means, our entities walking on the earth can come close. My mind was crashing the wall with this painful reality. Is it necessary to sacrifice material for meaning?

During my sitting at the pool side, hundreds of people passed from the yard with their crystal looks. Some of them were carrying food, the attendants were in a rush and were looking around fast with eyes that want to do all the work on time. We Kırlangıç, Hazel, Nergis and the others were in a game until the evening. Each of us was trying to do something, by this way we were learning around and meeting new people. Kırlangıç and I were running in the foams and carrying water for washing the yard when it is mid-afternoon, big cooking pots were carried to the yard, hundreds of people were delivering soup. Hevida and her group were sitting at a side of the yard and having their soup cheerfully.

The evening *azan* was being recited. The yard upstairs was bursting at the seams, shaking heads were swimming in clean lights. Lights... It was enlarging in circles and surrounding us in a way that didn't left a single twitch out. Purity, clarity was such extreme that the smell of it was being felt. The sounds were such clear that they were like drops coming from mouths in a way that the bottom of it could be seen. Divine light was raining continuously, when I raised my head I saw that rhythm of a dance flowing like swimming in a cool weather on a starry sky. The sky was hanging down our head more freely than ever before. If I gave my hand, I was going to pick a bunch of stars. A bunch... just like the flowers in Keşşaf's hand. Hot and blood-red.

We all were orbs turning in Keşşaf's orbit. We were waiting for getting covered with the dust of Keşşaf's foot. We were jealous of the flower in Keşşaf's hand, we could die for a thorn of that rose. *Azan* came with cutting all these good things like scissor; *Allahuekber!* The God is great. By the way, this is the first time I heard these words that clear. The sound of *azan* was coming from the person's heart, from the deepest point, not from outside. By scattering all the materials, by reversing the existence, by shouting out who has the real power. The sound was echoing rusty, sharp and free. First smell of Keşşaf disturbs this glory. The darkness was absorbing this smell until it looks like drunk. This smell was passing through our vein opening the dark, hard, blood blister parts. Blood was passing through our veins many times and was sending new signals to the maze of our soul. It was forming marvellous links, bridges between the soul and body. It was rubbing the neural crest like shining and passing over all of our sensitiveness for hundreds of times. Then we saw the Keşşaf's beautiful face which looks like a moon. His noble shoulders were coming dragging a light flood, all the languages we know lost their meaning. We were leaving all the guns that we turned to ourselves; we found the most powerful gun... Being without gun...

Love was shared to each of us; we were fighting as if we don't know this. More love meant leading a life of pleasure, twinkling to the real existence by this way.

In fact, we didn't see Keşşaf . We just perceived a light reflecting to cataract; we were saying "that is Him". None of the things we saw was Keşşaf. Everybody thought that the one he saw is Keşşaf. He didn't resemble any of the ones we saw. Everybody saw his own wish on the curtain; heard the sound of his own perception geography. Sky turned into a mirror eluded from the secrets slowly. Every heart was watching itself from this mirror.

Which one was the real Keşşaf among the ones I was until now? The one who made me hear the originals of the sounds? The one who showed me the back of all images? The mysterious one whose horse I got on and who had hazel eyes and was hiding his face with niqab? Was Keşşaf the inaccessible freshness that I saw on Safran's face? Was he the waterfall falling from the faces of Sufis climbing on the walls while waiting at the yard shining like glass? Was it this swiftly flow which surrounded me and was on the peak every time? Face of the material is continuously changing, meaning was hiding itself.

When the crowd disbands, I am walking through his door. This is the door that Keşşaf went out. Two insanes are sitting at the threshold. I sit next to them on the floor, on the cold floor. I see a little sparrow's nest on the line where the opposite wall and the ceiling combined. We are looking at each other turquoise with the sparrow. I lean my head on the wall and my eyes are closed. People disband for prayer, I hear the soft steps moving away slowly. I realize cold gnawing my flesh finely. Silence explodes like a fatal gun in my ears and continually echoing. A troop of dove crashes my face, this deep loneliness turns into that soft music of their wings... This is one of the most desperate moments in my life. Oh beautiful! I am on the very threshold of the door. How tangling are my soul's feet in front of him. My forehead is the place where the arrows that found the target have a rest. As long as I begin to talk like you I won't move. As I said before, your being silent like this is my death. If you don't speak ... If you don't say anything now, everything will be silent forever. My face is burning like a sheet dancing on the fire. It meets with a hotter tear. My heart in my chest is kicking like a bad-tempered child.

Oh Sheldrake that I sacrifice myself for its height... I have nothing to tell except you. Neither a place to go nor a land to stay. While passing by me like a stranger, you take my life, you crumble me up. I don't know a word other than you... I see the trees, the clouds falling in love, sounds turning into groaning in your absence. O my god, this is madness! I am counting everything into your hand for you to throw away. I have learnt what being drunk without drinking means. What dreaming without sleeping means, what leaning towards a distance without moving means. Thanks to you, you went silently and I learnt. I wish you turned for once and had a look. But the lover doesn't have the right for expectation. There is only one Layla on this world, rest is all Majnun... What is left from you is a huge space; a deep, bottomless, deaf, blind cliff...

Earthshaking neigh of a horse is heard in the silence. Doves are flying and disbanding fast leaving white spots in my dream. His voice is gradually close, gradually familiar, takes a breath next to me.

Hands pull in the headstall hard.

"Give me your hand Dilruba ..."

I see him. I find myself on an arid land fractured. He is looking at me with his irresistible look on his white horse. I fall into the same whirlpool in his hazel eyes. He is showing me the red horse behind of him with his hand in inlaid sleeve. This is the horse we saw when we were going to the *dergah* with Kırlangıç; I recognize it from the blaze on its forehead and from the white spot like a comet on its face. Its my horse. Elbow of Cavalry draws a bow in the air. Showing my red horse with black mane, he says

"Let's get on your horse, hurry up".

There are hopeless times in life that we say "This is it", your ship is up a gum tree, the ocean is like moving away gradually. Then a hand comes and slowly pushes you to the water. This hand is like rains touching your soul in arid dessert. Merciful and generous; active and noble... I stood up like reviving from arid land, like ingoing waves. I gathered the headstalls and hold the saddle and got on my red horse in one move. I put my feet in the skew-backs and balanced my weight. Cavalry who taught me all of these things was glancing at me. I tightened the horse's barrel softly; at first the horse started trotting, soon after we started galloping.

We were flowing along the foot of cliffs and over the thin, colourless sands of the thirsty steppes. This road looked like the one that the group was following while they were coming to the *dergah*. I felt that I had passed under these cliffs before. On this road resembling yellow carpets, we were leaving a thin dust cloud behind us as the hooves of the horse step on. After going ahead like the wind for a while the rocky part was left far behind us. Now this wide land till the bitter end that an eye can see resembled a desert. We were like slipping waves in the curves of this very yellow land. The sun started to descent from her throne, our shadows were gradually getting longer but the road didn't end. It must have been a little after mid-afternoon. The hot weather was taking my breath away, transparent flames were raising on the thirsty earth ahead.

"This road walks over the deep yards, I am with you, don't be scared" said the Cavalry, he turned back on the horse, checked me. Actually I realized that we had been passing along the edges of the yards after a deep rocky valley. Apparently we were bearing down on the mountain meadows, we started to climb up gradually. Wide highlands welcomed us. We passed by the high peltry tents standing side by side and settled amongst yellow grasses and hard bushes. Travelling through this severe nature made me thirsty and tired. The road passing over the highlands ended at a vast plain, and then it was reaching out towards the hills. I was again circling in a dream. In the middle of an endless valley, we arrived beside the crowded riders. A very crowded group of people, wife and children out of a wide field, was watching the riders trotting on the highland. There were no other plants around than sparse, thorn-like plants, tragacanths. Birds of prey were diving over our heads as if they attack to the water of the sky with their wings. The Cavalry pointed at the wide field and said "Here is the arena."

There was a thin dirt surface inside. Crowded riders were wandering around steadily, and some was holding big white flags. The riders gathered together, the horses was flicking their tails, they were fidgeting. A rider with a white flag got out of the crowd and fooled around for a while raising the flag. The cheer and applause of the crowd was roistering. There were blinders on some horses' faces, and thick headings that I hadn't seen before on the others'. Some had saddles from goat skin; some had colourful beads on their necks. All the horses in the field were dressed up as adorned for a festival. A voice divided these riders into two groups. Riders took sides as seven each. The rider beside me was a Cavalry, he was holding out long clubs to me steadily. I took one in my right hand, and I put the other in my saddlebag at the back to reach from my left easily. Then the earth retreated into the silence of battle. The steppe was so silent that you could hear the breaths of the horses. On the arena, on this highland, the sky was so close that you could sweep the clouds with your hands. I looked up the bright sky; rain clouds were gathering at the horizon. There was a smothering heaviness in the air. The distress of the earth became the distress of the earth of my body.

One of the riders taking side across us got faster, passed the middle of the field, threw the javelin in his hand towards me yelling "Dilrubaaa!" and spurred his horse back towards his group. He was clearly challenging me. The javelin was stuck to the earth one or two meters before me. Weak, rusty voices arose from the audience outside the field. "Come on" said the Cavalry, "it's your turn!" I rode my red horse quickly to the field. The black mane of the horse was washing with hot yellow lights; his breath was mixing with mine. I raised the javelin like a sword, I was holding the bridle with one hand and throwing the javelin to the air with the other; I threw the javelin to the rider just like he did to me. The javelin fell to the ground like a weak, tired matchstick. Another rider from the opposite side started to ride towards me; I understood that I must have run away. I turned back immediately, I was trying to bend my head to the horse's neck and lie aside, but the javelin hit my back. When I returned to my group, the Cavalry started to ride towards the rider hit me. At that moment the earth was lightened by a lightening tearing the sky all along. The face of the sky was torn into two by shining swords; some horses reared up because of the noise. The rival rider was leaning till the belly of his horse and lying aside to protect himself from the javelin of the Cavalry. The Cavalry was riding his horse to the target fast leaving a thin, nice dust cloud behind him, he was fairly entertaining with his rival's acrobatics. He arose the javelin like a spear and threw it directly to his rival's back to ensure his balance. From this moment the riders of the two groups started to face off against each other. Lightnings were flashing one after other, continuously running horses was sparkling from their claws. The one throwing the javelin withdrew, one from the rival team stood out to the field, the arena was filling with continuously spinning riders. The horses was running at full gallop at full speed in the dust thickening steadily, javelins was flying in the air, I was riding my horse from here to there without knowing what to do. I was getting javelins from my left side on and on in this tag fastening increasingly, trying to hit the players of the rival team.

It was about to get dark. The heavy air was flashed by a terrible bolt at this time. Everywhere was lightened as if it was morning; the horses were shying as if a lantern was flashed on their faces, every moment of their running resembling poetry was falling into place. As if a hand from sky was taking a photo of us; flashes lightens steadily, one after another. Cries were arising from the crowd watching the game, these cries was mixing with the horses' neighs. The game turned to a noble dance; where and how every rider rides was identifying the movements of this dance; we were embracing the earth and sky with lively movements and spins, indeed we were challenging to ourselves. Actually we targeted our own rebellious ego with each javelin and arrow we throw to the rivals. The Cavalry with a veil on his face and with his flamboyant eyes leaned on his horse, caught all javelins in the air with his agile body, an earth-shaking uproar started at that moment; this noise became the follow-up of the lightnings. The sky started to puke in a moment; it was raining cats and dogs as if it was trying to clean a dream. I was washing the air with might and main to pull each of us out of our dreams; to make the images clarify. The Cavalry was leaning right and left and the belly of the horse to avoid the javelins, he was picking up the javelins thrown on the ground when he was on horse. When he was attacking he fastened his horse, then eased down suddenly, shunted suddenly, he had my heart in my mouth. Everybody got wet completely; nobody had an intention to leave the field. Manes and tails of the horses was soaking wet, collarless shirts of the riders fastened on their body due to the heavy rain; long boots were full of water. The audience was trying to protect themselves from the rain by the thick covers they stretched over their heads. The Cavalry was riding his horse steadily throwing his javelin one after another. At a moment, a challenging rider from the rival team was holding his javelin like a dagger, he approached to a degree to bar him; this meant breaking the game rule. The horses staggered due to the rain were nearly knocking together. Drops from the wet manes of the horses were cutting the direction of the rain. The Cavalry could throw the club in his hand to the chest of the rival rider at any time; but he didn't. Two riders looked each other, the Cavalry's club holding hand was like hanging on the air; it froze under the heavy rain like a rearing arrow at that moment. There was not a sound to be heard on the arena, everybody was waiting for the Cavalry's movement with excitement, and not other noise could be heard than the groaning of the sky. The end of the javelin was flashed by the lightnings; waters were coming out of the shirt sleeves of the Cavalry. He was so close to his rival that he could knock his rival down with only one move. The head-dress of him was soaked, got heavier due to the rain, he was sparkling in his clothes turning dark green. The colours of the ornaments of his dagger on his waist were releasing its eye-catching colours as lightnings flashed. The Cavalry changed his horse's direction with an expression of mercy on his face. This meant clearly that "I forgive you."

The game was about to be over. The ones whose javelins hit the rival's horse, who dived into the rival group with a greed and passion, crashed his horse to the rival's on purpose, hit his javelin to the horse on purpose and threw the javelin to his rival in a close-range was losing point in this game. All these lifted the curtain before me like spiritual images each.

The Cavalry brought victory to his team in this small battle. Now, on the arena, he was touring around with a wet white flag in one hand and greeting the crowd. He was greeting each riders one by one, he was looking at them like a commander respecting the defeated. I thought that he was the most extraordinary person in the world.

He rode his horse to me; he was looking at me with smiling eyes. Rain was flowing on his temples, wet black eyelashes was turning his hazel eyes into a colour of shimmering green.

"You see Dilruba," he said, "how love is pouring on us. How it is generous."

I knew that Keşşaf was behind that niqab. Keşşaf was only showing his face among the lightening. I was tracing love with the horses running at the full gallop. Wherever I looked I saw Keşşaf. His voice was like the God's voice for me. I had the hope that I would hear the God's voice in my own voice as long as I heard the God's voice in his voice. Keşşaf was transferring me the God's music with his voice. I felt dizzy. Everything was continuously turning.

He approached to my horse. He took a blood-red rose that had wet petals out of his chest and held out without saying anything. Rain drops stuck on his eyelashes were falling down his cheek like a fine line. The entire universe was sound instead of him. Everything was opening its mouth to say one thing, always the same thing.

When I regained consciousness, I was still sitting next to the insane at the threshold on the floor. Two steps besides the Keşşaf's threshold. Sparrows were playing with each other in the bird nest at the corner of the opposite wall and ceiling. Suddenly door was opened and a young girl got out of the room; it was understood from her clothes and behaviours that she was attendant. She smelled a bunch of rose in her hand. She was about to go but she stopped and gave me one of the roses in her hand to me. Petals of the rose were sopping wet.

18
The Light of the Night

And love already
was pointing that
Closeness is a mistake
(Hallac)

I ran to the *dergah* with the blood red rose in my hand. I was going down the stairs to the lower yard two at a time as if flying. People in the *dergah* was preparing for the prayer. I was holding the rose like the sign of love; I wanted to shout at the top of my lungs. Keşşaf was obvious no matter he hid herself; he was with me with all of her being even if her body wandering on the earth was not by me. He was talking to me in a manner that only I could hear, revealed herself only to me. He was extending her hand to my heart without being seen, heard and known by anyone else. However, I was transforming to someone who was getting thirsty as he drank salty water, all these meetings had been expected to comfort me but they were drawing me to a more desperate longing; I was looking at everything from a terrible fire. With this drawing fettering me I was looking for love turning around it.

The small of the *dergah* got crowded after the prayer. Tables were set. We would stay at the same room with Hevida and her group. Hevida and the sufis with her ate their meal in a silent chat. Tea was made, then the place started to be filled with a happy noise. Kırlangıç and Hazel were chatting eating fruit, Zümrüt was listening to Safran's words looking into her eyes. The calmness of her soul was balancing the fire of my soul. On the other side the old woman having slept on the floor in the bus all night moved into a deep conversation with other sufis. There were slippers and shoes piled up at the entrance; packs constituted a small hill in a corner of the room.

What a carefree night, the only thought of the people was to submit love and spread their wings to the beauties that love would bring. The earth and tumults in it seemed to fall even further behind. Here was a place of healing; pomades were delivered for the wounds in the hearts; *saki* was delivering healing water for the symptoms in the souls. Here life was eluded from all routines, sounds and images were changing at any moment as there wouldn't be the same again.

After a while voices started to raise from the yard. Kırlangıç and I raced to down. The yard was like a three-ring circus. Women constituted a big, wide ring, were circling with murmurs swaying slightly; this wide ring was circling like a giant ring. There were women in the ring signed by love on their abdomen, women that didn't look like each other and came from different places. Those from Hevida's group was among them. A magnificent harmony was constituted while their long and bright skirts were swaying, it made those looking at it dazzled. Hazel, Zümrüt and Nergis also went down behind us, all of us started to watch the women dancing the *halay* slowly in an ecstatic manner. I thought that these people did not have sex in this magical moment, they imitated angels. Their scarves that they had covered their faces until the edge of their eyebrows hid their expressions ingeniously. They were pure souls disguising in the swaying bodies in full clothes. Murmurs started to laud and the ring started to fasten; it didn't matter how much these murmurs were low, they continuously echoed in the ring since they were said altogether. Swaying the shoulders slightly pushed this world made of material even until backwards, flying skirts constituted a small wind in the ring circling steadily. Each woman looked like a fire ball which was impossible to be stopped. They slid their steps sideways to catch that single moment in the moments, and thus became distinct in this rhythm.

Women in the circle raised their voice some more, they were singing a hymn, those watching them were accompanying this echo and nodding their heads as if approving the words of the hymn. Some joined *halay* splitting the ring, the ring was getting wider and wider. This was a ring of peace, people from the east, west, all directions in the world came running and grew the ring. That moment, I realized the rose in one of the women's mouth in the ring. The stem of the rose was between her teeth. She was embracing *halay* with two hands, at times she was holding it between her fingers. I stood up. A approached to see her face better. The yard was washed with light blue, water coloured lights, and the stone ground was shaking with the rhythm becoming stronger gradually. Stars blazing over us were shining in the eyes of the women.

I approached the accelerating ring. I grasped the arm of the woman holding the rose in her hand. She caught my hand with the rose in her hand and pulled me into the rhythm of the *halay.* The swirl in the centre of the *halay* was revolving us fast. Breaths turned to only one voice being one. This was a groaning voice suffering from joy. My weak voice was melting in this strong breath, my feet were moving by itself. We started to get faster, we couldn't walk as we accelerated, we were simply flowing. Our hearts adapted only one music as if tambourines and drums were played by the ring. I was dragged in a terrific dance, heads dropped to the same shoulders, shoulders were moving in the same way, arms were locked like an extended rope, our feet were leaping; we resembled a rainbow covering the horizon swaying in light halos. We were circling as if we wanted to free our souls hidden in the body, as if we wanted to save them from the body cage.

Each woman in the ring got quiet suddenly. The speed of circling decreased and feet got heavy. One of the women in the ring, it was Gülistan, continued to sing by herself. She was pouring her breath finely and warmly, her strong voice was rich like waters springing from the earth. Then, Gülistan got quiet. One of the women in Hevida's group started to sing in her own language; everybody knew the meaning even if languages were different. All women continued to sing the hymn from repeat. We isolated ourselves from the world as we were circling, we were going further from ourselves at every step for a new self, a pure unity.

The voice of the women was melting as they were singing, first it was softened like a soap under the sun, then it dispersed. Breaths took place of the voice gradually. That moment I became sure that these breaths were originated from a pain similar to mine. Here everybody was in pain for her own Discoverer. Everybody's face was covered with a silent prayer and a sincere reproach.

Hu: An ancient name of Allah. Saying 'Hu' is a part of Sufi prayer.

I closed my eyes. Many women's eyes were also closed but there was no disruption in the rhythm. I sow the Cavalry, then Keşşaf, I was wandering between these two and lost in the same face.

At last the voice stopped decreasingly, the ring circling like a beg-top was slowing down simultaneously, movements were getting smaller, swaying were decreasing. In the end, the ring parted slowly like rosary beads, drunk souls were spread. I didn't feel my feet, my heart was beating fast, blood was passing through my vessels quickly. As if a giant cliff opened on my own chest and I was looking at myself from the sky.

The yard started to become quiet and people started to freshen for the night *azan*. Night was long here. One felt that such a night wouldn't end and continue through a bottomless eternity. When I took my place at the upstairs yard with my freshened soul, I was as light as the birds I had seen in the sparrow nest. Now I was more sure. This flowing was making the secrets of existence flow together with itself continually. The future was real at least as the present and it was experienced; it only covered with a veil called time. When this mysterious veil we called as time took the veil from the face of existence we called it as 'present'. It opened only one face; in fact, there were a lot of invisible aspects of present.

While the night *azan* was recited, the crowd was moving like waves impatient to come ashore at he upstairs yard. The light of the lamp just above us was embracing the enthusiasm of the stars, the transparent shadows of the clear flames in the middle was penetrating into my soul like the groans of a violin. Again the same voice was telling us to go 'back, back more', again I was pushed from the front to the back, tired bodies were leaning like wheatheads flying in the wind. Keşşaf was walking through dim, pretty shadows. Her light made all twinkling smile, she was passing over us as if giving the good news of a joy and snuggling into our souls. She was walking looking at only front, teaching us what the solemnity was like a nobility figure, and was passing by hiding the blessed truth of being human.

Keşşaf was passing by... Like a stranger, as if he was alone in this yard looking at the end of his baton, calmly. He was walking in the same way that the first human had walked; her breath was as far as the breath of the last human in the earth. He was walking with his baton as if he hadn't seen us in her life, he wouldn't see us in his life. His baton looked like touching the furthest point of life, as if pointing somewhere that we couldn't understand. Keşşaf looked like dropping the mask of life with that baton. How much he was far from me... How much he was close... I was weaving between this terrible distance and burning closeness. I was burning in winter frostiness; cold flames were scratching my face like the paws of a leopard and making it bleed. A one hundred years of solitude was lying between me and this walking; there were cold, invisible walls. This distance weakening me was killing me. It enfeebled me, shouted that bitter despair called as material. However it was teaching me the meaning; this silent going and the thing called as closeness was only a bottomless distance in the world of material. Atoms, molecules, the tiniest structures were in a cycle gurgling to the ultimate union and calling to unity continually. What about material! What was the hard, rigid structure we experienced? Objects looked like cages, bitter looks of someone having been away and returned now set up in my eyes.

At the wee hours of the night everyone withdrew to the corner of their own hearts. Breaths slowed down. I cowered somewhere in the downstairs yard and was discovering the light corners of the night. There was a long time to morning. The desert was cruel. It took the heat that it gave during the day back at night. It sucked all the heat it borrowed me with its ventose and made me freeze to the marrow. Night was so cold as it was hot during the day. Suddenly freezing, harsh winds started to wander on my face burnt by the sun during the day. Kırlangıç was sitting on the floor by me with a heavy silence in her eyes... There was the shine of a jade stone in her looks trying to understand what was going on. The edge of her lips were moving as if she would cry. The tiredness of the journey was on her face. Then Nergis and Zümrüt came to us from the upstairs yard. Nergis looked as if she had been living here for years. She adapted very quickly. What a beautiful thing to have a calm soul, it untangles the knots easily. Zümrüt is talking about what Safran talked about in the small room of the *dergah* in detail. Some women from Hevida's group are passing by us with their shining skirts. The place they are in turns to a festival area. Kırlangıç says that she would look around with the girls.

A new and different day is about to come now. I feel lighter as the colour of the night blackens. There is the difficulty of youth in my heart, the fearlessness. I am looking at the two-storey, single-storey houses with flat roofs linking their arms around the yard. Lights on the windows haven't lose their vitality yet. Soughs are coming from the *dergah*s. The pool of the yard fills and drains away, its cool water flows in streams. I just realize the third pool next to the two small pools. It is disconnected with them, alone. Waters overflowing from its spring are pouring to a loophole near the ablution room from a thin, deep pit. I am leading to the ablution room at the basement. There is a small construction similar to a fountain in the centre and a tiny room on one side. Just at the entrance, near the stairs going down there is a wide flat stony place, it looks like a place for sitting, I sit there and watch the passer-by for a while. Women with children are coming and going after they perform ablution. Some women are coming then, they have tattoos on their faces, they are walking gathering their skirts. The severe weather blowing in the yard cannot reach here.

"I will hear you when you call me, don't forget," said Keşşaf. "What if I stay here, with you?" I say, he says "you should go back." I feel sad. There is no life here belonging to me. I can just open a hole to breathe for myself, that's it. Where do I belong to? I say. I am looking for a meaning in all his answers. Where do I belong to? If not here, where? "Let me stay here with you," I say, "No" he says, "no, you should go back." Where will I go back, how much of the place I go back is mine? I am staying only as a guest wherever I go. Is there a continuity in my life? How long will I drag from pillar to post? Like a bird looking for its home, how long? What else colours will I be dyed?

I see him when I close my eyes, I see his state on his running horse. Every time my mind touches his brunette forehead. "you don't want me with you" I say. He looks at me as if melting the silver. As if saying "understand", I don't understand. The pain of leaving here hurts me deeply. "Say something, do something, don't send me away."

"Princess!.. Shhh, princess!"

I open my eyes, this must be Safran, because only she calls me so. There is a slim woman before me, this is the woman having rose in her mouth before the night, the woman holding my arm and pulling me to the *halay*. The scarf on hear head slipped to the back of her neck, she looks like being about to perform ablution. She has rolled up her sleeves to her elbows. She is wearing slippers. She is holding her skirt with one arm, she pulls her skirt from the wet floor.

"Do you want me to give you a secret?" she asks and she just say ignoring my surprised looks,

"If the one who comes here for the first time has a bath with the healing water, he knows the eternal secrets of love, but every point of the body."

"But I haven't seen anybody having bath here," I say naively. I am worried, she is talking as if she knows this is my first coming.

"You don't talk like one who is curious about the secrets," she says and adds, "this is your first time, isn't it?"

I continue talking assuming this is a joke. It looks like the joke played on the newbie in the dorm. Unless I hadn't witnessed her state in the *halay*, I would have say that she is clearly fooling me. It is a good idea to be cautious in case she knows something about be.

"Yes, but how do you understand?"

"It's obvious from your surprised looks" she says. I think being experienced is something great. I must admit that it seems a very annoying idea to have a bath in this cold night of the desert. I want to ask how I will know she is telling the truth, but then I give up thinking this statement will hurt her. But she understands this.

"Try and see if it is true or not," she says, "If you like talk to him as you have just done, ask him!"

I chill. She looks at me in the way of the one who loves. She hasn't lost the spiritual drunkenness in the circle yet. She sits on one of the small stools in front of the fountain, takes off her watch and put it by her. She starts to take off her socks.

I stand from the stony place and go to her. I sit on the wooden stool next to her. I feel the same smell in the ring when I get so close to her, I must confess that I envy the clearness in her breath.

"Okay," I say as if I want to understand the mystery in the nonchalant looks, "Of course I will. With pleasure... Is there anything I need to be careful?"

"Just be sincere while doing this and don't talk to anyone," she says. She turns on the tap; the thin water pouring in her palms comes to life.

The most distinct feature of Sufi experiences is that it takes the one's will from him. In this way it seems to somebody shouts you that you are not independent as much as you think. Your being is surrounded and there is no way to escape; it looks like your right of choice is taken from you. At such times you get closer to the knowledge of that human faces with his fate. Human is a being that wants to go beyond his fate at any moment of life, so to say is trying to overcome it. At this very moment that I face with my fate, that ongoing attraction opens a new stage for me.

I see. This is a precious clue from Keşşaf. He wants me to follow the trace of the signs. This is a unique consolidation from him as response to his answer "you must go back" upon my wish to stay here just after moments. It means "you will go back, but being a new you." This is the hope to commend the space cycling in these bottomless hunger to a true love after saying "no, you must go back," as a response to "let me stay with you." This is the first scream of the seal of love he will impress my forehead after my begging "do something, say something, don't send me."

A wordless conversation starts between us. The meaning of turning my head and turning my eyes away is revealed. His passing by looking only at the end of his baton there in the up yard is drawn in a wordless word heaven. I am dragged in this love that I don't remember the beginning of like a thin stick in a river. I am pouring from the waterfalls, I am swimming in solid revival every moment.

I experience the existence throwing everything to wind. I wake up trembling at every time I pour the water. As if I have nothing in cool waters. Everything is flowing. Everything, continuously. The water changes everything I have. I transform every drop. Cold water beats me like a whip until my skin turns to delicate rose leaves. It softens. It knocks me around until I don't feel anything but only the music of the water. That severe whistle on my ears until I hear only the words of the water behind all sounds...

I watch a small lake is pulling me in until a real love of purifying is worked on my heart and the light of the clear and strong water enlighten my chest. Then the going away of everything becoming a river. The water turns me to my state of foetus. In the water... I am born again from myself with a clear breath.

I lead to the stairs passing the down yard. I started to go up the stairs fast. Then I stop as if I am stuck on the floor. What if I have forgotten to wash my face? It's impossible, how come... perhaps... I turn back to the water. Cold water attacks me to the hilt as if I go under a waterfall. I remain defenceless again under this attack. Again I head the stairs passing the lower yard. This time the doubt of missing something preys on my mind. Then I returned to the under the water again. Coldness increases its severity at every time. Once more I head to the stairs escaping from the water. Well, has my arm holding the water bowl got wet enough? I again returned to the water. I submit my soul and body once more. I put on my clothes moistened thoroughly. This time I am sure that I have wet as if I have swam in a river. Again I head the stairs passing the lower yard. Almost there is nobody in the yard.

I look for my bag before snuggling somewhere among the people in rows on the floor. There are a few dry clothes in it but it seems to be impossible to find them in this tumult. I say 'good luck!' finding somewhere among the people pulling the blankets on them and lying in rows. I snuggle finding a place a little further from the entrance. I try to fit in a small space. I pull my legs to my abdomen and I rolling into a ball. I wish I stopped this trembling due to being cold and sleep. I think my bones have interlacing each other, my teeth are screaking. My feet are as heavy as a piece of wet cloth. I wish I relaxed... My wet hair makes my job difficult. I look around half-opening my eyes in the light leaking from the door. The poor woman having lied on the floor during the journey by me has pulled the blanket to her neck and is about to fall asleep. The women on my other side must be from Hevida's group. The girls must be at the back of the *dergah,* I cannot see them from here. There is nothing to warm me up except my breath. I look for a blanket lifting my head a little. I cannot see anything except crowded shadows. I use a bag I don't know to whom it belongs as a pillow and The gnarled things in it hurt my head.

I bury my head to the hallow of the bag. First the light leaking inside increases and the door is half-opened. I lifted my head to this light cutting the dim atmosphere of the room. I see Safran before me. She comes in with a blanket and a pillow. When she sees me she gives the blanket and the pillow to me. When she sees I hesitate,

"Take these," she says, "I will get another one for myself." And she goes out to get another from the storage. I wrap up myself with the blanket like swaddling. I snuggle to the softness of the pillow as if leaning on a soft chest. I am better now. Much better. Only this trembling doesn't calm down. I say to myself, "you will sleep even if you want or not. How you are fond of your comfort." The poor woman lying so close to me is looking at me as if she is uncomfortable with my trembling. Or I think so. Perhaps she will tell me to go and find another place to sleep. Perhaps I should go before she tells; I can find a bigger place to lie in the other rooms. She doesn't say anything. She looks at me with the kindest looks I have ever seen. I think she is my mother for a moment. Or I think she will give her blanket to me. She does something that isn't expected from a stranger. She pulls my freezing feet to herself and holds them in her soft palms. The heat of her hands penetrates my heart. The heat of human makes me recover. My tissues relaxes calmly as if I am in a sauna, I fall a deep, sweet sleep with all my relaxed cells.

I am on a crowded bus, I am standing. I am on a night journey. I don't know how, but I see a beautiful baby in my arms. This is a baby girl. An intensive make-up on the baby's face. She is looking at me smiling with her big and bolted eyes. How big her eyes are. Her cheeks look like pink apples. A red rouge on her lips. I hold the bars with one arm. I struggle not to drop the baby, her beauty fascinates me. Her eyelashes are like embroidery. But it is strange that there is no meaning in her face. Once I realize this she laughs and she looks like Satan with this laugh. She takes a deep breath and say only one word: "keşşaf", then she exhales, her head drops aside, her eyes closes, she dies with a white face. I want to say, "Oh my God, she is dead, she is dead!" I cannot speak.

I wake up with a murmur around. Sleeping woman beside me have already got up. "*Azan* will be recited, come on," says Kırlangıç. Everybody is running around. I get up and head to the stairs. I am still in the shock of the death of the baby. I cannot forget the sorrow and pain in her face at the moment she died. Have I killed her? I try to remember every detail. First I turn to the baby's shining face in the dark bus. Then my fascinated looks at her. Her death. That word she said while resisting the death, the last breath by stretching her body: "keşşaf." An unidentified sorrow in my heart again. It gets hold of me. I am nothing here, I move away from myself in this murmuring crowd gradually. Turning around in an unpleasant despair and go further from myself with each step. This great crowd scares me; people walk very quickly as if they want to save their lives, nobody looks at each other, and so they don't see. Feet become fast ; everybody is trying to save themselves, in spite of this there is an astonishing collaboration.

I feel the cold and severe breath of the night. It's about to dawn. All lights are on in the interwoven houses on the side of the yard. Here, at this time, every soul become fast some more to enlighten before the day. Leaving this yard, the sadness of going away under the washed lights like a shadow is loaded on our shoulders. Even my shoes looking like slippers now since I stepped on their back are still wet. Time doesn't stop Dilruba, I say to myself. I am only happy when it stops. I get the up yard in no time flat following the crowd performing ablution. I again meet that woman on the wheel chair by the wall. The same crowd pushes forward and backward as if slipping over my shoulders. After azan the treble voice saying "back, back," is remaining. I first see his gazelle eyes. The harsh wind of the desert night gives us the smell of rose generously. Again the heads are bowed like wheat heads leaning aside. Now there is the gloom of going in the middle of the crowd. Keşşaf is passing far from the crowd looking at the end of his baton. As if he hasn't known us, as if he won't know us. As if he is passing by far lands. My dream of closeness crashes on the hard walls and returns to me. The waves of hopelessness rear up. Here one learns the name of the despair again and how it is bitter.

There is a dynamism in the *dergah*. Attendants shout as 'groups are leaving!' They say "Ankara group, all aboard!" Everybody is packing up, then I watch my reflection on the pool for the last time. I see the dream called as life in the flowing water in stream. We have come and are going, I say quietly. I caress the clear face of the water, "take care."

Groups that are about to leave gather in the yard. Hevida and her group are by us. They start to shine with the heating weather. We get on well each other by exchanging glances even if we don't speak the same language. I call Hevida. She looks at me with an interest, I wave hand while leaving.

When our bus departs, everybody is in a deep silence. Perhaps nobody has been able to woken up yet. The bus starts to sway slowly and break up the sadness. I feel myself as a forgotten, worthless small stone. My sharp corners stick to me. Everybody is too sorry to say a word. I look at the rocks moving away slipping and barren land looking like yellow fields out of the window. Life buries its meaning to this barren land; my feet tangle to a strong lie.

The journey back home seems very short. We take a break for breakfast. Separation appears in the middle of my forehead like an identity, but what a big mistake this is. It is with me it has never been before. If I reach out, I will touch its real being. Separation is good for human, my heart gets closer as I leave. I understand that separation is only in our perception as this separation blows to the cinders in my heart. Distance is in our look. Wasn't it Keşşaf itself saying "Inside our brain is so silent, Dilruba!" All this journey, the quiet flowing of the group is a repetition of what he taught me. I am trying to gather the all pieces together in my mind, the only result I reach is that the things I have experiences are not fantasy. The presence of the people in the group appears like the cross-check of this obscurity equation. Looks confirming every result I reach are all around me. I split hairs in every form; everything crashing onto my breath shouts: "Keşşaf is real." Our insolent reality veils its reality. The mystery in the statement "there is no self here" is cleared up; it takes the load of your own existence from your soul that put the will away and give it to the real owner. It was only possible for human running after his desires like a wounded wild bull in the arena to get rid of his replicas by touching the paint of a blessed love. Every pain suffered on this way was a sum of the studies that first shook and then destroyed these replicas. Human was running after love with this motive like a glow-fly running after the light in order to reach the originals of everything especially his. To be able to melt together with his own face in the temporary subjects of love, to touch the real light with his heart by pulling the curtains down.

I was surrounded with people suffering from love. One trying to pass the narrow corridors of the metaphoric love must have passed through his own corridors first. The soul itself would be hungry of the rain of love and was looking forward to the storms breaking out in its own sky as the difficulty in transforming to a loving subject was diving over the black spots on the heart like bird of preys. The only condition to be able to escape the imprisonment in the body was to reach the sharpness of the commands it imposed and then to ignore them with all strength.

This cliff becoming deeper gradually between a man and himself would forked with every breath and eventually man would be realize the contrasts in his being in this way.

I was reading the pain in the features of Kırlangıç who was in bad with her fiancé. I was watching them while she was having her soup with the wooden spoon silently. She got lonely and turned in on herself as she was thinking that an obscure future was waiting for her. Separation was about to take out the most precious subject for her from the picture of the future. All her dreams were pulling the pin of the sequence of the reasons that embittered her. She was able to find thousands of reasons for this separation. Why didn't it happen? Kırlangıç didn't hear what the separation talisman told her, the pain she felt was veiling it.

There was something known by everybody: pain of separation was as delicious as the pleasure of regaining. Otherwise why do people continue separation? Pain of love unburdened the load of self on one's back and provided him to wander about the subjects freely. One was in love with the traces of the love in the shape of himself and pain of love was proceeding on these traces. It looked like with each step on this mysterious path that love was constituting its throne on an eternity when thought was focused on only one subject with a deep aspiration. As a man started to watch himself and everything existing, there came a moment that everything was burnt out including himself. The remaining was only the loved one. The groans of the lover made everything invalid except this love; all rules were destroyed, every deed turned to this love itself and transformed to it. An eternity expanding gradually! Man was looking only for this with the metaphorical love, even seeing your own helplessness against the power of love became a great pleasure! One tasted the sharp difference between soul and body; soul escaped from the material record with the fire of the pain of love, and its imprisonment in the body ended as it had this pain. For that reason alone the attraction of love was irresistible; however it was, love was the first rule to exist.

I knew that the distance between Keşşaf and me was only material. In the world of hard, rigid objects... In spite of this, even after everything he had taught me this artificial distance ruined me, he walked over the remaining bits of my being with his passing by like a stranger. I meant 'you don't exist.' However this meaning changed from head to toe with a right look; knowing something wasn't enough to read that thing properly. Even, sometimes the deed of knowing put one far away from what he knew; knowing was a foetus growing in the womb between man and himself. The arrogance of one's belief of he knew was a blind mirror, and getting out of what you know and being that thing itself was a magic which caste the tain.

I hadn't been aware of yet that I was following Keşşaf like a slave whose hands and feet were tied. My will had taken from me completely and my self was like bought by him. All doors was closing except him one by one, but I hadn't realized it yet. I was dragging falling in his face naively, even compliantly like it was in a silly way. I wasn't in a state to understand where life would go in this way. The lights of his beauty made me blind, I had lost all sounds when I was in the unique tones of his voice.

Safran was having her soup at this large and empty table, and how she seemed to be happy when she was getting the bread. This chaos we called as the world was spinning in her hands like a peg top. Love destroyed all the rules and made everybody submit its normlessness. I sank into a madness, there was only love in my front and back, and all my being was a pleasure consisted of pain.

I didn't understand what was happening as well as I didn't understand what kind of soup I was having. I just warmed up myself with the soup, I got warmer and lighter with every spoon of soup and I felt at home as I hadn't felt before. This home, this castle was protecting me from myself. This sheltered spiritual state made me away from everything happening in the world, and I was melting drop by drop in a feeling of crowd that I hadn't experienced before.

The group set off again. We were landing on branches like migratory birds, our skilful bus driver was again talking enthusiastically; Nergis was watching outside with all her calmness, Gülistan and Hazel was talking in murmur, Kırlangıç and I was talking cheerfully ignoring the tiredness. How beautiful life was now! What a unique taste to be able to go, flow continually, lean your back on an invisible door. Our feet were like getting rid of the gravity, the flow of the cool rivers were rising in us, our breaths were escaping from their ties, our looks were restraining the wild horizons. The pendulum of my soul was swaying continually and fast, and the hand of a muralist was touching between existence and absence. I saw. I was also swaying with that pendulum steadily; I was looking at myself from a swing coming and going fast as if swallowing the air, as if tearing the air.

When we had a break for prayer I believed that everybody in this group is my true family. That poor woman who had warmed up my feet all night while I had been trembling from cold was not different from a mother. For Safran, we were needy to be protected like little chicks. Gülistan was giving away what she had in her food bag, we got astonished with this interest and affection that we did nothing in return. We understood later that this honouring was not only for us, but for all people; all people who carried the breath of the Creator in their souls.

After the journey took all day we returned to the point where we had departed. I felt we returned suddenly, I woke up suddenly. I woke up from that strange dream suddenly. The bus stopped by that small mosque slowly. My body started as if it woke up with the last quake. We got off the bus one by one as if we were hung in the heavy and gloomy air of this city, as if we were left in a deep solitude. My soul was falling apart in parts. Returning back here was like being insulted. The great difference between two cities made me dizzy at the moment I got off the bus. Ankara, this tired city pulling one in like a swirl with its grey air was pulling people in with a intensive sickness.

I was like a fish out of the water when I returned back to the dorm. I was moving my gills and was in the throes of death. I felt peckish, had a difficulty of adaptation, I was wobbling between these two worlds in doubts about which one was real. I lay on my bed leaving my bag on the floor. I watched the weak light on the ceiling alone for a while. Keşşaf should have taken me now. He should have taken to himself, he should have show me the essence of everything again.

19

"Knowledge is a clear question, and love is like a secret answer." (M. İkbal)

The next morning I woke up as the happiest person on the earth. I was looking in mirror as if I had a sign of peace on my forehead. I was in a purity of a pearl just coming out from the oyster. My thoughts were as clear as a still water and I was full of confident. Everything was happening by itself, I was walking by myself, laughing and feeling by myself, being me by myself; as if no stress, extremism or difficulty had remained in my life. I was simply flying escaping from all physical rules. Darknesses in my heart was dispersing, and a peace was pouring over me with all its beauty.

I forgot everybody.

A guest coming in the evening the next day interrupted this flow for a while. It was Müdrik. His voice was full of complaint and worry. He was telling that he had been looking for me all weekend and he had been worried when he hadn't found me. We sat at the backmost table as usual. We were sitting by the wall below the painting named "Scream." Everything, all of us were here as the imitation of ourselves same as this painting was an imitation.

"Well, tell me the fugitive, where have you been?" said he. Hard, dark shadows had appeared on his face since I last saw him. I saw a distinct uneasiness in his fine features. His eyes changing between blue and green looked like wild waters.

"Let's say I was on a short weekend trip," I said.

"You were with him, weren't you? It seems you still believe in the stories that you have written. Well, how was it? Could you find what you expected?" This was a severe beginning for me.

"Who do you mean with the third person singular 'he'?" I asked.

"You know who I mean," he said. Müdrik was sitting opposite me like a knowledge envoy. A little later he would advocate that the knowledge that couldn't be tested wasn't knowledge.

With a reserved tone of voice,

"He has a name, Müdrik," I said "but if you continue to have these blaming eyes, you won't learn it." This small challenging made him compose himself.

"You got me wrong, Dilruba. Why do I blame you? I just want to know what you have experienced, besides, how do you know? Perhaps I also need such a trip" he said.

"Do you want to hear the details to tell my father?" I said clearly. We both know very well that my father wouldn't like what I had experienced there in the *dergah*. For my father, people who has religious tendencies are under the effect of opium. My father starts a speech telling about the miserable states of the Islamic countries when such a subject is started and eventually he ends the subject with the reality that only hard data of the mind can make one happy.

"I informed my father about my trip."

Müdrik made a u-turn obviously, and he said,

"You should know that I don't talk to your father about these issues. A circle has been constituted between us that even your father cannot go in."

It would becoming clear that what Müdrik wanted from me. He thought that I would go on an adventure and he would lose me. What was the reason of this interest that picked up steam suddenly?

"No need to worry," I said while leaning back in a relaxing way. A sensitivity settled on my face. What offended me was Müdrik's reference 'he' while he was talking about Keşşaf. However, Keşşaf was somebody that wasn't talked about with any pronoun. It was a good idea to change the topic.

"Well, you tell me.. What have you been doing, is everything alright?"

He smiled, my question didn't work. He was looking at me like saying 'I expected that you had told me about the trip,' but he couldn't express.

"Good, good, everything is as you know, women are still trying to become beautiful. Everything is as you have left," he said as if he wanted to let things slide.

"You are talking as If I haven't been here for years," I said. Suddenly he extended his hand to my hand on the table with an unexpected move, as if he wanted to hold... I felt the heat of his hand, flames on his skin. I withdrew my hand with a sudden reflex. Müdrik came close to my face as his hand was in the air.

"Dilruba, I don't want you to do anything without me, if you go, let's go together," he said. Müdrik was pouring the words ignoring my surprised looks. He hesitated,

"If you like, I will take you wherever that place is. It's not a nice thing to disappear with people that you don't know at weekends. A young girl at your age need to know these things." he said, "because you have been commended to me."

What was happening? What if I was commended to him? I wasn't registered on him.. I gave him the right of calling me to account by telling him what had been happening. I was dumbfounded as if I stopped on a forked road. I didn't want to hurt him, but I couldn't let him control my every action also.

"I am aware that you are thinking of me," I said first, "but there is nothing as people I don't know, I know all of them. I am at least sure that it is a community trying to purify. I don't do anything bad, there isn't any danger as you think," I said.

"These are very ordinary statements. I don't know if you are aware of that but you are here as a student. You have a school to finish..."

I interrupted him. This was too much. I thought to stand up with a sudden movement and to run to my room leaving him there and saying 'hell with the school, but such quick-tempered actions hadn't been good for anybody since the world began. Besides, it would be disrespect to one who came here from a long way to see me wondering. However, we were both aware that Müdrik was threatening me. It was a big mistake to tell him that I failed. If he had told about it to my father, there would have been the possibility to stay penniless. Although I stayed with my aunt in summers, my father was covering my expenses at university. And there was also the step-mother factor. I knew that she was pressuring my father not to send me money. Müdrik reminded me that I should have got my feet on the ground with his small, implicit threats. However I had neither desire nor time to be engaged with these small things. For me I had found a treasure and drunk with it; I didn't want it to end.

"You are so clear today," I said. I interrupted him, continued.

"This father thing causing us to meet makes our friendship go in a dark and mistrustful ground. Let's give up holding this over each other if you like. This will be better for both of us." Now, I 'warned' him, I was threatening him to put thick walls between us as he continued to do this for a response of his threatening me.

He tried to make it right immediately,

"You have completely misunderstood me" he said. His face lightened, wild waters in his eyes calmed down. His stiff shoulders loosened, he loosened the collar of his dark blue shirt as if he was waiting for me to say this,

"As I said before," he said, "we have a friendship that doesn't related to your father now. I am not a messenger to send messages to your father. If you see me like this, I will be sorry. I care about you only because of you, only because you are Dilruba, not because you are the daughter of our old family friend Haşmet Uçmaklı."

His voice slowed down, calmed down. He took a deep breath. I saw the signs of a deserted prayer, of loneliness and desolation...

"You might think that I come down on you very much. If you think so I am sorry. My aim is not to sorry you. Also I don't have a mission of bringing you to yourself. Only..."

He hesitated to continue or not. Then he started to talk with courage,

"I think I have grown on you, even I have been attached to you. I don't know how this has happened. Dilruba, do you know what I thought? In my new house..."

I must have interrupted his speech quickly.

"Have you moved to a new house?" I said.

"Yes, it is more beautiful than the former one. You know my office, the house is two blocks away."

Müdrik hadn't got used to be alone since his wife left him; this was obvious. He wanted turn over a new leaf and he seemed that he wanted me in his new life. I didn't know what to say.

"Let's live together in my new house," he said.

"You must be kidding!" I said like a reflex. Müdrik was talking as if he didn't understand what I had been experiencing, he didn't understand me. I was trying to find a light way for myself; he was clouding this way as much as he could. Who knows what else he had planned for 'us'. He asked me to live together while I was thinking to enter the service of a *dergah.* As if he was giving me my death warrant. He was going too far. I stopped talking in a deep disappointment. Müdrik made me remove from Keşşaf and everything about him.

"Why are you keeping quiet?"

"I think I have been keeping company with the wrong person, the person who I had been telling about myself hadn't understood me at all," I said.

"No, no, I understand you. Everything will be as you want. We will do whatever is needed, civil marriage, religious marriage.."

"What a strange proposal this is, it's very you!"

"I want to give my life to you, I don't want a relationship of giving-taking like the others," he said.

I raised my tone of voice.

"Enjoy your new house, I hope you have good time there," I said. "Now I must really go, I am glad you have come, thank you."

My last words were broken, I stood up,

"Don't go like this, please, you are cross with me, look, I will say something, did I say something wrong, what did you offense?"

He was talking quickly in a panic. He had begging eyes telling me not to go, he was extending his hand to hold mine. How strange the people are! There was a surgeon there, Müdrik, who I always admired, who always talked like a competent psychologist, who I had always found close to me, I had always believed that he had understood me. Now there were deep ditches between us. When the words crashed on the wrong place, sizzles started between us; it was about to be blackout. His voice was moving away gradually. The painting just behind him; the scream. Only the human resembling that ghost screaming terribly in the painting remained. My pain was similar to that man's in the painting. I wanted to scream exactly like those screams. Müdrik's desperate eyes were like included in the painting. His face intertwined with the dark colours of the painting..

"Müdrik, I am not such a person that you can offer to live together. But I think you don't care this."

I took a few steps. Müdrik caught me, stand in front of me like a mountain as if he wanted to stop me. He held my arms with his two hands, first I thought he would shake me.

"Dilruba, believe me I meant no offense, if it is a crime wanting to be with you all the time.. Yes, I admit that crime."

I was hearing his breath. I could see his blushing neck under his dark blue collars. His face looked confused. What happened to that calm person? What happened to that shiny voice saying "Dilruba, welcome to my life"? Where had the great wise man looking sparking in his white shirt gone?

"Let's continue this later if you like," I said, "I cannot think anything right now. I don't know why but I feel offended, perhaps I am still tired because of the journey." I was trying to express myself without offending him. However, I was so confused that I moved away with staggering steps in a state of not knowing what to say. I heard that he was calling me,

"Okay, take a rest. I will come again."

I felt I was slapped terribly. I thought about the meanings of what he had told me during the following days. I couldn't be with him; yes, I admired him, even I cared about what he said. However at one of the sharp bends of life that I was about to take, there was a strange mismatch between us; our ways was breaking up after somewhere. One could talk to him only about science and philosophy easily; I started to hear the bells ringing when I stayed him alone. He didn't have rules in his life. Sensibilities needed to be followed were like excess for him. Müdrik had a little hedonist structure; he cared pleasures even if he knew that these pleasures would give harm to him one day. I needed to find a way for myself without him, I needed to remove from him slowly; from him and the shadow of his wife having left him. It must have been a painless end. We needed to stay as two acquaintances. He mustn't have known anything about me any more. Knowing was so far from understanding; the darkest object I have ever seen.

20

The first day of April... I started to wait for the visitor coming after the evening prayer. Although all troubles of this campus life I was sitting still as if waiting for good news. I was about to see the oasis which was about to appear on the edge of the testing desert. Everything was shining, the weather was clear and my hopes were endless this evening. The aura of everything was more lively and full of life.

The girls coming to my room and asking hard questions made the stress of waiting increase. Kırlangıç was steadily asking questions about the one who was about to come, I told I didn't know every time.

Zümrüt, sitting on the lower bank took the ground,

"Is he a relative of Maide's?"

"Why is he coming this evening? Have you ever talked on the phone?"

"No, we haven't," I say.

"What's his name?"

"How do you know him?"

Hazel is joking,

"Tell him to wear a clove on his collar."

I had had a call about two weeks ago. The call was from Maide who I had met through sufis and who was also a Sufi. Maide was totally out of the university circle and he was living in a remote quarter of Ankara. He invited us, Kırlangıç, Zümrüt, Hazel, Nergis and I, for dinner especially in Ramadan. We stayed in her house for a few times except dinners. She told us about her experiences in detail and the details of Sufism. About a month ago she asked me if I wanted to marry or not, then told me she wanted me to meet someone. I ignored what she said then. Two months later she called me again about the same subject and she got the same negative answer. However her calls didn't stop. At last I accepted to meet the guy she talked about upon her call two weeks ago. This might have been a nice beginning for me; perhaps all her insistence would cause good news for a new life. It was meaningless to resist.

It is hard to draw sufis out, since you know that they don't talk by themselves. There is someone to draw them out as well as there is someone to make everything speak. Hidden causes under their words appear as you grub. There are some other hands holding the ropes making them move behind the shadows on the curtain. Everything has been fixed, every detail has been considered and everything is for a reason. That's why I couldn't refuse Maide any more. Rings were intertwined each other in Sufi life; without breaking, another stage was reached. I told her I accepted to meet him probably because I wanted to arrange my whole life and my whole being according to the Sufi way of love that I had been tracing. The reason that of my answer was that the guy I was going to meet was a Sufi, of course. Being inexperienced in something is difficult, but trying to be accustomed to a new and unknown world makes you live the most difficult states of being inexperienced. That's why I expected perfection whenever I heard the word 'Sufi'. The main thing I considered and cared was to be close to Keşşaf when it was possible. This was the main reason of that I agreed to meet him. If I got married to one of the followers of him, I would be closer to him. I could learn a lot of things about Him thanks to my marriage; and life would go on in a perfect way for me.

The next day after Maide's call two weeks ago I visited Safran. That day I heard one sentence Safran said, the sentence I needed to hear. "Beware of sufis in opposite sex," she was saying, "if you come across one somewhere just pass by without looking his eyes." That day Safran told something else that I didn't hear: "if you catch his eyes..."

Asking questions gives courage. I had started to loose my courage since Keşşaf forbade me asking questions. Why didn't Maide meet the one she was talking about? I was listening to Kırlangıç while I was looking into round mirror on my desk.

"Everything should be done according to certain rules," she said.

Then I remembered Maide's statements on the phone: "you can see each other only three times, after three times you should reveal your intention." "Yes, it must be done very carefully," I said while I was fastening my silk scarf on my collar.

After about ten-minute waiting, the announcement for the visitor echoed in the room. It was one of the hundreds of ordinary announcement for the clerk. "210 Eda, visitor; 506 İrem, visitor; 213 Hale, phone call; 430 Devrim, phone call... 406 Dilruba, visitor." The voice rang in my ears as strong and sonorous to destroy the special vibration of the room. The vibration of the voice swayed about the room in circles and it became a giant circle taking me in after the short time passing until it reached to me.

The weather wasn't dark yet. A nice, volatile dimness outside made you languorous; the young were playing guitar sitting on the grass at the entrance of the guesthouse and they constituted pretty images. The heavy glass door of the guesthouse was opened and closed steadily, living here, at this very point of the earth was gurgling in its utmost enthusiasm. Voices of people were overflowing from the canteen in a deep murmur, some residents of the dorm was wandering at the entrance without any purpose, some was looking for some coins for the biscuit and coke machine, leaf doors opening to the floors were pulled sharply, and serial and joyful steps towards the visitors were heard.

I stood up slowly and calmly, I went down the stairs of two floors picking up my long skirts like a princess. When I stepped on the ground left as a doorway with panels, my consciousness touched on a shadow standing next to the announcement cabin. He was wearing a dark suit, left two hands on two sides randomly as it was obvious he didn't know where to put them, and he was like aleph with his tallness. The took a slight step when he saw me and decided it was me he had been waiting for and nodded his head as if saying yes. It wasn't too long for me to decide staying still there or moving. I took two steps and said hello without extending my hand and doing any other movements. Just a hello existed in the air first. Then a new hello imagined in a different form was born again.

"I'm Tuğrul," said he in a state of not knowing what to do.

I didn't think anything to say except welcome. Tuğrul, who I didn't know at all and knowing nothing about him except his name, said "will we go out if you like?" He felt uncomfortable being there at the entrance where people were going in and out. I didn't understand his utterance 'going out', but I couldn't ask questions also. We went out through the heavy glass door being two silences. The perfect weather outside could be deemed as relaxing for one in such a state. I felt I was melting in the noise of the world, and a kind of calmness settled in my cells with this feeling. Tuğrul was like a giant tree pulled away its roods. The branches of this tree extended to the sky over my head like a shade, and it was protecting me from himself again. After a few steps in the fresh air, I tried to say something like, "I was waiting for you, Maide had told me you would come." I would be useless sentence. I kept quiet. I walked watching the ends of my tiny shoes under my long skirt. Some familiar faces were looking at us in the crowd of the outside. One of them that I didn't remember her angled difficult name was Zümrüt's group and she had been talking about that she hadn't attended the classes because of her scarf in recent days. I recognized her face in the dimness beginning to get dark, and she was looking at me and my company so carefully that it was impossible to notice. She was trying to understand who my company was and why he was with me. Because of her careful looks, the others with her turned to see us. Tuğrul was the secret of the night not only for them but also for me. We went down the three steps that raised the short concrete road in front of the dorm. We took nine or ten steps until the road which was between two opposite dorms. I couldn't look at the face of Tuğrul walking next to me; I just saw his feet as much as I could.

He opened the door of his car parked by the road between the two dorms by the remote control. I waited for him to direct me not knowing what to do. There were tall green trees in front of the two dorms and the group playing guitar was singing 'Akdeniz Akşamları' (Mediterranean Evenings) now. The voices of the girls and boys were mixing each other and the magic of the spring was painting a transparent existence around us with these voices. I didn't know Mediterranean evenings, but this evening Ankara was so beautiful. When Tuğrul attempted to open the door for me he said 'please' with a dimmed voice. He said this with a voice that only I can hear. This 'please' meant 'please don't be shy, relax.' There was Keşşaf behind my perception of this 'please'; there was Safran and Maide also. I made bold to get in the car trusting them and taking them as reference. I was sure that Kırlangıç, Zümrüt, Nergis and Hazel was watching us from the window of the 406 numbered room at this moment that Tuğrul opened the door of the car politely saying please and I got in this luxury car with a noble manner.

Tuğrul started the engine. He had parked the car to depart directly without needing to turn around the roundabout heading the stadium. He must have guessed that he asked "where would you like to go?" Was it necessary to go somewhere? I was worried since I didn't know what to do in such as situation and I didn't want to go anywhere with someone I didn't know at all. "Ah, Maide," I said to myself, "you brought this trouble." Tuğrul said "it's only a dinner." He understood that I was worried. He continued to talk probably to calm me.

"You have a nice school, very big."

"Yes, it is," I said.

He was trying to say something like 'how are you' but he couldn't start a conversation since he was trilling. Blinking lights and lots of indicators in the car appeared clearly when it got dark. Then an alarm started to sound insistently.

"I think the seat belt..." he said. He couldn't complete his sentence.

"Ah, yes," I said. It must have been on the right. I fumbled for the seat belt but I couldn't find it. Alarm was getting stronger and my panic was increasing with this sound. At last I found it and managed to stop the alarm.

His hands holding the wheel were big, his road-holding was relaxed and his voice was a little weak unlike a man's, perhaps soft. We saw students hitch-hiking when we started to drive towards the exit from the roundabout in front of the cafeteria. We went on as if we didn't see them.

"There is no need for a big thing," I said. This sentence went out of my mouth suddenly. I didn't want a long dinner. "There are nice places around here for dinner."

"No way, I will take you to a nice restaurant," he said.

I felt heat burden without knowing what to do. Actually the seat was so comfortable and the music was so soft... One could travel in this car slipping like a soap on the road for a long time without getting bored.

He drove into a luxury restaurant of which neons dazzled on Konya road, he parked the car and gave the key to the vale. The vale said "yes sir," while he was taking the key. We went up the stairs rising as if going up a high castle slowly. When we went through the large door, passed a giant stained glass panel just at the opposite and raced to the stairs going upstairs. The restaurant upstairs had a really high ceiling and a chandelier as big as a room was dangled in the centre of it. There were so many chandeliers that here was like Keşşaf's world of seeing. Inside was as long and large as a horse could run at full speed. Carefully organized tables, ornamented chairs, glass wall from end to end opening to the terrace. Behind this glass wall, big green leaves were sweeping the glass. Waiters and waitresses in uniforms were rushing around; two attendants wearing suits were waiting in front of a small stand and were ushering the guests.

"Welcome Tuğrul Bey, your table is ready" said one of them when he saw us. He walked before us and directed us a big table with leather covered chairs. On this table there was a white card with a writing on it 'Reserved Tuğrul Soylu'. The attendant bowed with respect when he took the card from the table as if I was the young princess of a civilization in welfare; he said 'enjoy your meal' smiling.

Tuğrul took care of pulling my chair. He was very polite as he had opened the door of the dorm. All these were very unfamiliar to me! All this politeness, this magnificence, this speed was very far to me. This dance of civilization didn't fit my frequency. Even so I tried to look polite sitting on my chair resembling a throne. Tuğrul was sitting just opposite. I continued to look around and be fascinated probably because I tried to look at his face as few as possible. Groups included stylish-looking men and women sitting at the large tables by the glass wall constituted nice images. At smaller tables in the middle there were groups of two or three and families. Attendants showed special interest to the children sitting on the high chairs, and an instrumental music like Turkish classical music was heard at the background softly in this large luxury restaurant that every detail had been considered carefully.

I would look at his face necessarily at a point of no escape as I was here. When I directed my eyes to him our eyes met. First I saw the naivete on his face. A flossy skin on his face resembling satin... A shadowy power in his light brown eyes. Then I heard the repetitive notes of a crazy wavy music. These looks struggling to impress me as much as possible... It was as sharp and obvious as the wildness of a hawk floating from the peak of a high, very high mountain. The purity spread along the moment was hiding under the large wings of this hawk and when appropriate it was diving on me.

Conversation didn't start in any way. At last he looked into my eyes and smiled; he moved his wide shoulders as if he tried to secure all his power.

"A computer was asked," he said, "what was going on."

He must have been joking, I smiled.

"What was the computer's answer?" I said.

"I think its circuits fused," he said and added, "what is going on?"

"Fine," I dogmatized. "What about you?" I asked then.

"A fascinating beauty," he said.

I blushed to my ears. I should have changed the topic immediately and prevent this wild but nice water to flow towards the waterfall in this speed and emotion. However I couldn't say anything. As if I scored an own goal. He must have understood this so he prevented the water before me.

"You are at the third grade, I think, Maide told me so," he said.

"No, last grade," I said.

"Hmmm, which department?"

"Sociology."

"Very good," he said.

I didn't want to bother him with my questions from the first moment. He would tell me if he wanted. I didn't want to seem so interested about who he was, what he was doing.

"I am also at the last grade, I will graduate this year I hope. I study international relations. At ... University. I live alone. My family lives in ... city. As you understand, I am also far from home. Maide's brother is my close friend. Where do you know Maide from?"

"We met via our common friends. She has had us in her house a lot," I said.

The waiter came to us. He poured the water to the glasses in a polite and quick manner. He gave us the menus saying 'here you are.' I started to have a look at the menu as if I could eat hungrily. I didn't know many meals in the menu, I chose something randomly. Tuğrul said, "same as always." An army of waiters started to set the table and we preferred to keep quiet until one asked "is there anything else?" As I guessed, Tuğrul was eating with left hand; he was holding the fork with left hand and the knife with the right skilfully. I was holding the fork with right hand as I knew without touching the knife, and appeared to participate the dinner not knowing how to eat.

"Maide told me that you are Sufi," I said.

"Well, yes," he said as if he remembered an unimportant detail. "I visited the Excellency a lot."

I relaxed as if I drank litres of chocolate when I heard this.

Then he asked, "have you ever been there?"

"Yes," I said, "I hope I managed to go." I meant with this sentence that I didn't know if my visits to ethereal realms were accepted or not.

"I hope," he said. "Very beautiful place, isn't it? Quite different... I have stayed there for a long time."

There was somebody sitting opposite and saying he had stayed at a place where I had been fascinated. I started to have a crush on him as if I was going adrift.

Tuğrul realized my weak point from my looks. He told me the interesting events he had experienced there and his memories about sufism for a while. I was fascinated as he was telling, asking questions continuously and looking into his eyes to tell me more.

We talked until the end of the meal. I couldn't admit but I didn't want this dinner end. This evening I was discovering the different lands of the world opened before me with meeting Safran. That world was so large that I couldn't see and understand at first glance. I was getting close to the idea that my experiences with Keşşaf had a reality in this visible world at each moment of this evening. Others were also passing through these processes like me; and Tuğrul was one of them. I saw with my own eyes, there was a space in this world that Keşşaf held, there were people around him, he had a family. I was sure that he wasn't a dream. Here someone who had stayed with him for a long time was telling me his experiences. Tuğrul's words confirmed what Keşşaf had been telling me from the beginning. As Tuğrul told I thought that Keşşaf was a relative of mine. Even I was jealous of him sneakingly; I had to share him with a lot of people; the world was full of people loving him. As Tuğrul told, Keşşaf I knew was moving away me, but then he again trailed into a different reality. Keşşaf had a life on the earth as a subject and it was impossible that he only belonged to me. His equivalent and reality in this world and being loved by a lot of people with such a passion became an obstacle for me as great as I couldn't expected. I had had such a feeling in its sharpest manner when I had been in *dergah*; I had wandered around among hundreds of people as if I had lost my worth. As if I had been left in a corner...

The waiter in a chic uniform brought us tea without spoiling his stand at attention; he pulled the white dishes in front us with fleet actions like a magician. Then he put the dishes one after the other in tray held by another waiter at the back. The expression of respect on his face was hardening on his young face like a mask.

Tuğrul wanted to ask me questions about my family; question marks were wandering in his looks. Without giving opportunity him to ask, I said;

"My aunt have brought me up. I live with her in summers."

"Has she?" he said as waiting for the rest.

"My mother had passed away when I was small, and my father got married to someone else."

"Such things can happen in life," he said with thoughtful looks. His smiling while he was saying this was relaxed and warm.

"But he is a very good father," I added. At that moment I remembered Müdrik. I remembered his tone of voice full of wisdom. What would he think if he saw me tonight?

I was still feeling the smell that burned my nose starting from the very first moment that I saw him by the announcement cabin at the dorm. The scent didn't die away, on the contrary it was getting stronger. As if Tuğrul was feeding and growing the scent as he breathes. When he bended his head slightly to say something I realized how his hair was thin but strong, and I was attacked by this mysterious scent surrounded my soul. I felt the steps of this scent as Tuğrul's looks were wandering on my eyes and face. The scent was like a net on me; this thick net was making me immobile, restricting my point of view, confusing my mind. Tuğrul's hands were shining, his clothes were sparkling and his look refreshed steadily with this scent. How could a *parfum* become integrated with a man? How could it become a power that cut one's soul like a sword and greened everywhere as cutting by mixing his warm breath and turning to a breeze then. The air I had been inhaling since I first saw him was falling in my cells with passion, it was changing me. My skin was burning in flames and the scent was pouring in me with every breath I took.

You can resist a voice, a beautiful face or another factor like them, but scent is different. You have to feel it as long as you breathe and surrender. The scent object gains power instead of dying away with every move. Eventually it became a focus of desire by itself.

This scent, this mysterious invisibility coming from Tuğrul and surrounding me from the inside and outside, quite sharp, whispering all desires and closeness of the metaphorical love, bubbling inwardly like a geyser, this pearl-grey fire which is about to overflow. This cycle presenting me a mottled rainbow as my breath touches this silver. As greasy as sticking the unguarded aspects of my being with its ventose, as cruel as leaving my soul naked against a whirlwind circling before me, as aromatic and flamy as burning my chest, having flames as aromatic and charming as causing me to faint. This strong magic is performed on the stage where I see various illusions when I look at Tuğrul steadily. It cuts me, and then reveals as a whole again, it gives me different shapes in colourful labyrinths, then it shows me myself in all these differences suddenly. Then Tuğrul, then me, then me, then him. Tuğrul's being turns to a big fiction, a play appearing with me.

The molecules of this scent are rough like a cruel order: Love! This scent beating my being completely was cracking my perceptions, and it included all motions and vitality existing in the world. It was not a floral scent, not delicate, it was actually a greed aiming power. It was an arrogant melody drawing a hard, rampant horse indistinctly, taking the being of one to the climax, and having said that the existence was such kind of thing. A little slippery, more alive, something like elixir of life! It was an attraction addressing all particles of human, refreshing one's life and filling with love. It was opening the black points inside me waiting in knots one by one and filling me. I was getting hungry as I was filled, and I let this speed and pleasure enslave me. This was a rain pouring in the dark, a lightening making you blind, unidentifiability circling in the air. It was a cool coast and the wind bringing the mystery of the mountains. It was the apparent state of the frequency flowing between human and the universe, it was secret, it was a symphony heard among beings, it was the garden of Eden seen suddenly.

Tuğrul lit a cigarette. With his white, thin, long fingers like pencils. He was holding the cigarette with a careless manner, he was bending his fingers slightly. He was inhaling the smoke deeply and exhaling the poison touching every corner of his lungs with a great pleasure as if he wants to get rid of something. All these scents, this atmosphere and Tuğrul's experienced and a little cunning looks were making me dizzy. I gathered my thoughts, and I said "thank you for everything, it has been a very nice evening," as if it was an ordinary night.

"I thank you," he said while he was setting the cigarette at the edge of the ashtray. He had put his elbows on the table and bonded his hands.

"It was a different night for me." He squinted as if he was watching me behind a transparent curtain and couldn't see properly. I felt that he would say something about meeting again.

"We had better go," I said to prevent him speaking. He looked at the watch on his left wrist. The watch was like fastened on his wrist, he slid it down.

"It's still early, a few minutes past 10. Is it late for you?"

"Yes, quite late," I said.

My ears was pulsating due to the noise of his being. He asked for the bill with a hand movement. The bill was paid at a blink of an eye, and Tuğrul smiled warmly. We went down and passed by the light of the stained-glass. The lights were shining, scents, sound. They were clarified from their dirt and became purified. As if all beauties in life were waiting at the entrance of this restaurant. To be here was resembled touching a tale for a moment.

I relaxed with the breeze touching my face outside.

"The weather is wonderful, isn't it?" said Tuğrul.

"Very much," I said.

"Let me order a coffee for you for the sake of this beautiful weather," he said. I didn't want him to realize but my knees were still trembling. "I hope another time," I said to escape. I regretted saying this as soon as I the sentence finished. It meant I wished to see him again. I should have made it right.

"Let's hope for the best, we'll see," I said this time. "I really thank you."

He laughed at my confusion so much that I could see a dimple appearing on his face in this large space in which neon lights were echoing in the dim light of the night. The dimple was like a flower blooming on his angled face. Now Tuğrul was much more relaxed; I could see the slackness of being able to talk. His vibrations slowed down and calmed down.

The vale brought the car. Tuğrul continued his politeness and he opened the door for me without letting the vale do it. I wasn't accustomed to such things, so I was astonished at every time and was embarrassed. I would hit something, break something or do something stupid at any time. Fortunately I didn't do such a thing, and I sat on the front seat of the grey car as if I had been used to it. Tuğrul opened the windows as soon as he got in the car; now hard times started for me until we got the dorm. When two front windows were opened, a hair-raising flow emerged and I smelt only his dazzling scent in this flow. Suddenly I heard the alarm sounding intermittently as if it got hurt. Tuğrul turned to me while he was holding the wheel with one hand; he was leaning back and put one arm out of the window.

"It liked you very much," he said.

"Ah yes, seatbelt," I said. Again I pulled the seatbelt on my right and fastened myself on the seat.

"It doesn't like everybody," he said. I didn't think something to say. Tuğrul speeded up the car, my ears was howling due to the flow inside, I was looking at to road flowing in front of me under the enslavement of the scent.

This was unfair. This scent! He had no right to do this. I could have used scent as a weapon, as a centre of attraction in the same way, but I didn't even think so. I didn't need to do that. However, he liked to wander about the peaks of life as I understood. I didn't know him but when I looked at his life style I could see that he liked comfort and luxury; he was self-confident, courageous and challenging life. He was like fearless. He seemed that he didn't care anything. An expression of nonchalance was read in his face. There were mysteries in his brain that I didn't understand. He accepted the holiness of something but he desired to live as he wanted. His hands were telling this mostly. There was a hidden bratty-ness in his manner of putting the lighter disappearing in his hand on the table after lighting his cigarette. His hands were talking mostly when he was driving. He was touching the wheel as few as possible, sometimes he fixed one finger on the wheel and put his hand in his lap, and he hung down the other arm from the window or he bent his arm as his elbow stayed outside. These careless manners of him showed that he was living the life as it came. He was such a person dancing with life.

At the entrance of the campus he showed his guest id he had been given when he had come and after the permission of passing he started to drive slowly on the empty road. I couldn't look at him but my right or front, but it didn't prevent me to catch the moments he was looking at me; as it was exactly right now. If I turned and looked he would understand that I understood he was looking at me; it would be necessary to say something and the thing to be said would be painful with the effect of the close distance of this moment. I didn't care. He turned the roundabout in front of the cafeteria and headed to the dorm region. I wanted to know deadly that what he was thinking right now.

When we entered to the dorm region, the crowd we had left when we were going became rare and there were a few people around. Tuğrul passed by the young chatting on the stone benches and parked the car slowly. He leaned front a little while he was turning the switch and the switch key disappeared in his hand... He looked at me with his most emotional look of the evening while his hand was touching the switch key. The sound of the engine had stopped and it was silent; only his looks were heard. As if he was telling the moment of separation hurt him with this look. We just stood there anxious and like two branches about to burn. When I headed the door,

"Thank you again, it was very nice," I said. I looked at his face resembling an endless and white horizon with admiration.

"It's my pleasure, Dilruba," he said. How he pronounce my name. Letters constituting my name suited his mouth very well, and they transformed to a terrific and irresistible melody while passing through his lips. How my name was burning on his tongue, Dilruba. It both fired his chest and mine with its form of broken from his chest and made me crabbed. I could listen to my name in his voice forever. Even if I didn't have a name and he would give one..

He got out of the car with me and walked by me with his hands were in his pockets looking at the front like a tramp. He again opened the glass door politely. We arrived at the beginning point, by the announcement cabin. I needed to rise my head constituting a 45 degree angle between my head and chin while I was looking at his face when we stood face to face. My head could touch his chest only. Immediately I moved myself away from this crazy idea as if I was escaping. I was standing there as my eyes were locked on his deep brown eyes and fascinated. Neither him nor me could turn our looks for a few seconds. Unless the attendant making the announcements had asked permission to pass by pulling the half door by saying "excuse me," we would have stayed in that position a few more seconds. Tuğrul let her pass by moving back. The woman floated between us with her small, plump, pretty body and headed to the canteen.

Tuğrul got close to me, closer and closer. Here it was his burning scent with his breath over my head. He leaned his head quietly without touching me, and asked as if he was whispering,

"Will I see you again?" I was like a freed prison with this question; he wanted to see me. I told him what my mind ordered me to say slowly as if I wanted to protect that magical moment as it was forever.

"Let's hope for the best," I said again. Tuğrul leaned a bit more in a state that he didn't get the answer he wanted.

"Of course hope for the best, but I will see you, won't I?" he said.

My face was burning under the sun of his face. I saw the movements of the skin and swimming of the colours on that skin when he was so close to me. Under his eyes were slightly dark and they became clear under his almond eyes, and this fit him very well. They were like a little mature, a little wobble and a little outcast images on his face. His distinct, ordered and a little weak eyebrows were harmonious with the symmetry of his face. He had a shaped, nice nose and angled, self-confident face. His eyes in the thousands of warm tones of brown were drawing the tides of the breaking dawn. His head stood on his large shoulders as a nobility.

"Why not?" I said. I must have confess that I was crashed tonight. Why would it be actually? This was the question needed to be asked! What was it to create such a powerful effect between two souls? Tuğrul hadn't been in my life until this evening, but now, from this evening as if I fell ill. My strength started to lessen and my thoughts started to break against the vital threat of being without him. I was drowning in the worries as if I caught an infectious mortal disease suddenly, I was trying to understand what would happen.

It was very difficult for me to leave him there and went upstairs. While I was leaving, something hot, sticky and aromatic stayed on me. My mood was very different from that when I had been going down these stairs a few hours ago. The meaning of Sufi in my mind became wider and smarter. One would be so, then. So there were these things at one side of that pure and clear world I had seen in Safran.

Five long days passed. These five days passed by attending classes and reading with the girls in the evenings. Five days later, on Thursday something very strange happened. After class I came into my room. I attempted to open the closet leaving my handbag and books on the table. I was alone in the room. I put the small key in the keyhole of the stained wooden door of the old closet and turned it unconsciously. I felt that scent poured on my head, my whole body and all my cells as soon as the door of the closet was opened. As if a hand had been waiting in the closet for me to open that door. As if thousands of scent capsules had been left in the closet and blossoming of the scent leaves had been arranged to bloom at the moment of the closet was opened. I froze as my hand in the air still and surprised at that moment as if I got a slap in my face, even as if I was sworn. I stared at the untidy clothes and the scarves fainted because of the scent in the closet. The scent was Tuğrul's that had been left over me like a net that night. At that moment I felt that I became so helpless to understand anything with my weak cognition. I staggered as if a hand pointed me a gun and was trying to captive me. First I was as alarmed as I saw Tuğrul but then while trying to understand what was happening and inhaling the dazzling scent at the same time... I slammed the door of the closet quickly and a little angrily. I stared at the door of the old closet with my hands got as cold as ice sitting on a chair shallowly as if I was watching a ghost. When I calmed down, I got the idea that this was a sign. My God, how ridiculous everything was proceeding. It was unreasonable. I ran to the bathroom to get over, I washed my hands and face. The scent messed with my hands. I could smell that sharply. I soaped down my hands again and again, I looked at them as if they were messed with blood. I watched them as if I committed a crime. I took a deep breath when I saw that Nergis had been come when I turned to my room.

Nergis, the mildest, calmest person I have ever known. Everything would back on the track and all this illusion would end.

"I understood that you were here when I saw your handbag," said Nergis with her usual clearness. I wanted to say a lot of things to her that moment.

I wanted to say, "ah Nergis, I wish I were like you. As normal as you, as peaceful as you; but my life is getting balled up every moment," but I kept quiet.

Instead, I said, "Welcome, you can't imagine how nice to see you."

"Yesterday evening you were so quiet, I have been worried," she said. "You didn't say a word, is everything all right?"

She couldn't clear up the last sentence, she was saying that she had been worried about me. I was looking at her in front of the ghost closet without knowing what to do.

"I'm fine, fine," I said, "business as usual." I turned to the closet with a new attempt. The same thing couldn't be when I was with Nergis. But it happened again. The scent attacked to my face more intensely as if it wanted to get revenge of the previous closing. The scent transformed to a horrifying hand and it was scratching my face, making it bleeding, opening the thin, peevish and bloody traces resembling the traces of the paws of a wild animal. The scent was overflowing the closet like a crazy volcano. The closet was vomiting its lava like a volcano that awaken from hundreds years of sleep and seeking for a victim. It was getting furious like a raving sky on my earth cracked of thirst. This sky was penetrating in my body finding a way in all veins. It was making all my cells drunk and capturing all my points vandalizing without mercy. It was capturing me as it was penetrating my cracked earth. As if it was saying "come on, admit it, love, be, say, tell yourself you have been beaten. Tell what you think. Let yourself go. Let yourself flow. Let yourself love. Say that you were thinking of him continuously without missing a moment. Look, I'm here, by you. I'm love, I'm in your head, in your chest, in all your being, and I'm everywhere. Here."

I turned to Nergis and looked for a sign on her face if she smelt the scent or not. "Has something happened?" she said.

"Do you feel that?" I said, I must have been sure.

"What?"

"Do you smell the scent?" She was looking at me as if I was mad.

"I don't smell anything. I think you're very tired. Get some rest. I will be downstairs, if you come," she said kindly and went out.

I couldn't believe in myself and this moment. I sat on the lower bank. Then I curled like people having nothing to do helplessly. I buried my head on the pillow as if I wanted to escape everything. I covered myself with the thin, ragged blanket. Now I was like a poisoned bug resisting dying. A bug that was so pleased with the poison it had had, assuming itself lucky to be messed with this poison and considering this poison with eternity. I was pulling the blanket resembling torn paper over my body to inhale this poison fully. To be alone with this poison. To witness that how this poison called love made me drunk. To transform the scent every note of which was constituted of passion under this blanket, this patchy darkness. To become the scent itself every corner of which taken from pleasure, every brick of which was borrowed from a heaven called Tuğrul.

I was far beyond of the ridiculous and meaningless feeling of happiness. I was wandering far from the visible material world, somewhere out-of-the-way, in the transparent streets of an invisible universe that wasn't understood by language and heard by ears; I could disguise in everything I wanted, I touched my head to every zenith of love, I could hear every melody, I found a faceless beauty every time I felt it. It seemed to me that Keşşaf had a hand in this fast beginning Tuğrul story. Even Keşşaf was standing in the centre of this story with his whole being, and he wanted me to see his reality with precise evidence. Even so it was too early to make sure about that. He had told me "you will take the photo of your sky, Dilruba." I was trying to gather my perception that had broken into pieces, and I was going too far as I saw Tuğrul in the photo of my sky. Why not? What was preventing this?

This love must have been a present after the hard tests I had been experienced in the worlds of seeing and hearing. It must have been a consolation. There in both worlds I had learned to use my senses to the full, and I had seen the beyond of the sounds and images. What I had seen that sounds and images had had no limit. Keşşaf had said, "inside of our brain is so silent, Dilruba."

I was trying to combine the things Keşşaf had told me in the world of seeing. How I needed a new lesson! A new lesson that enlightened all this chaos. I fell asleep while thinking these. I woke up with a voice echoed in the room. The voice was yelling with sizzles and calling me. "406 Dilrubaaaa, telephoneeee. 406 Dilrubaaaa, telephoneeee." Upon this voice, this announcement taking back my soul to the room the telephone started to ring in the silence of the corridor. I threw the blanket and got the phone cabin in no time flat running out of the room. I picked up the receiver with excitement and strong heart beating.

"Hello?"

"Hello, Dilruba, hi, it's me, Maide. How are you? Where have you been? I have called you a few times."

Maide's rough voice sounding like she had adenoid was touching my ear with sarcastic tones as usual. A little ironic, a little relaxed. Maide was an ironic person, she hadn't been to school and had learned life from life itself.

"I have been around. Have you called? I haven't heard." I said with a casual manner. I didn't want to reveal that I had been waiting for phone call.

"Look, what I will tell you; but first answer my question; how did you find Tuğrul?"

"Fine, an ordinary person. I don't know, I couldn't understand well."

"He is calling steadily," she said, "but I cannot reach you. He wants to see you tomorrow evening. He has just called. He is waiting for an answer. He asked your phone number but I didn't want to give it without asking you. What do you think?"

I took a deep breath. I relieved, everything was getting back on the rails, there was no need to worry. Now everything was looking at me smiling. All letters were carrying good news and they passing through the way called hope by running. What had they talked exactly? What utterances had Tuğrul made?

"What day is it today?" I said.

"Thursday," she said.

"Tomorrow is impossible," I said instantly.

"Why?"

"I am preparing an assignment, but he can come on Saturday, Saturday evening." She shouldn't have thought that I flew at this offer. I was a busy person, I didn't have much time to give him. I wanted him to think so.

"Okay, I will let him then."

"He can call me if he wants," I added.

"Okay, I will tell him," said she and added, "do you know what he said? He liked you very much as I understood." She waited me to ask what he had said, but I didn't, I couldn't.

"O! Thank him," I said, "he looks fine."

"He is an honest man, I suppose you didn't like him, did you?"

"No, what can I say? I don't know him yet." I only said, "he seems to be a good man," not to reveal her that my whole being softened like a ball of dough.

"He is good, very good, very hard-working. I'll call you again. Now he was waiting for an answer. Bye," she said with pleasure.

I was feeling that a terrific, dreamy love had started. Tuğrul was thinking of me. During five long days he had thought of me as I had thought of him. I was sure about that. He had been thinking about all details of that evening, and he was experiencing every look, every mimic, every word, every syllable. From the moment that we had first met, a silver, transparent aura had been surrounding us, imprisoning us and making us prisoner in each other's breath. I remembered his last look, he was confessing everything by the last look and saying a statement that enlightened the whole future. That statement was waiting for the moment to throw itself to the fire by circling around all the words like a lightning bug. I went out of the wooden telephone cabin as if I went out of a celebration, a carnival. I whispered as "Saturday evening." Saturday evening... How these two words sound nicely! They were shining like a moon in the sky, turned to a rainbow jumping rope on the sunflower fields, touched the earth with their fruitful hands, and distributed love, light and abundance to the sky. These two words... Saturday evening... They enlighten the dark face of the sea like a lighthouse and hid the darkest wave with their light.

Friday dragged. I thought how love whirling fast like swirl in my chest changed place continuously all day. First I had fallen in love with Safran. I had understood that I wouldn't have been without her in the rest of my life when I had firs seen her, I had started to look into her eyes getting deep as being looked like a slave, and I had passed over the peaks of the mountains in one breath with her smile. Safran. Then I understood that there was no difference of her presence and absence or being with and without me. She was always with me. When she was absent, her conscious surrounded me. She was following me from far away, examining where I was and what I was doing. To be with her was the same thing to watch everything existed from the wings of a white, pure and merciful bird. I thought how the dorm had been so small for me during the days I had first met her. The walls had fallen down one by one and drawn as if saying 'go to her.' All roads lead her; every moment of my life was adjusted to her automatically like an alarm clock; every word I know praised her and my every move was imitating her automatically.

Then I moved on the upper stage of love and in fact of pain also. Every love stage turns to pain a little, and it was articulated to the pain of being the watcher. It rolled up itself to the dissatisfaction of the desire of going more beyond. Everything had been upside down when Keşşaf had taken me, and I had witnessed how material had been an unimportant quality. Keşşaf's hands had been attached ropes to this lifeless puppet, this nothingness and played with it as he wanted. All being had been made up of Keşşaf. There hadn't been left any alive jot except him; every object that hadn't been looked at by him had been dead forever; every horizon on which his nice smiling had been seen had revived in an eternal life. With only one look of him, love had been presented as sherbet springing out suddenly in the very centre of my heart. How easy it had been to exist; I had been leaking from time and space as if I had been flowing from a strainer; I had been wandering about the lands consisting only spiritual joy and unutterable pleasures. How easy it had been that only a prayer, a tending had been a magic by itself.

Love was a poison like nitric acid melting the matter! It spoiled the hearts that it passed through burning, it deformed the heart as if it said 'this is the real life, what is visible only consists of this,' and destroyed it. When that ugly skin was peeled with pain, unique and eternal records appeared, and the essence and mysteries of all frequencies and perceptions appeared. Burning was needed mostly for this; to clean up the dirt. Excesses was pruned as burning, flames of the fire penetrated the lungs like air and granted human a new soul for a new life.

How it was easy! Five times a day you met the Beloved, every state was presented to Him, palms begging after the lofty presentation covered the face like a rose petal, and everything was commended to the real owner after every amen. That was not all. Every time I closed my eyes, every time I referred Keşşaf he was asking about me similar with a mother's interest to her child turning his beautiful head standing on his shoulders to me. He was caressing my head, listening to me patiently, he took me his side or he sent his voice from far away. How easy it was to live like this! Even the sleep that people committed themselves to the forgetting cave became a meeting, privacy and an ultimate union for me, and I was curled in the bosom of the mother called as love. He was teaching me what I had known starting from the beginning, revealing the originals of the sounds, colours and images, showing the summary of my creation. My soul was trembling like an aspen leaf from that obscure and indescribable pleasure every time he took me from here, and the pleasures of the body became much more inferior than waste or clay.

I was thinking sitting on the prayer rug. This prayer rug I had laid on the floor in front of the ghost closet... All these loves rolled into a ball in my heart, they twined like DNA spiral, and they united indivisibly. The most painful aspect of the situation was that if Tuğrul started to get a place in this spiral, it would be very difficult to pull him out of this complicated construction. He was touching the thing being divine for me. He was touching with his eyes, with his words... And I was preparing a background for him by the things said in his absence without seeing him. I was doing this unwittingly. With my entire naivete. I was placing him in a giant photograph Keşşaf was included in. Tuğrul was existing as the shadow of his shadow's shadow and was getting closer to him. He was looking with the light he had taken from Keşşaf, he was crashing me steadily since he had a record in Keşşaf's notebook, his looks became the Cavalry; that is Keşşaf!

The hour hand of the clock on the table stopped where it was instead running crazily to reach Saturday evening, and it waited as if it was imprisoned in time. Kırlangıç and I was smoking leaning back the wall in the corridor and talking about Tuğrul. Time wasn't elapsing. We went down the canteen, bought tea in paper cups, and smoked again. We were talking about how the school year lengthened like a chewing gum, and I was saying 'never mind.' I was never frightened of life during these drifting periods, living was spreading in the eternity like rings widened on the water, and echoed from the future being a strong sound with a safe and carefree tone... Here I found it. The truth I had been looking for, I had found Safran, Keşşaf and the way I would follow. I was singing this love as if singing the repeat of a song a ravishing one in the middle of the chaos called life. I was singing it passionately, crazily and as if dying for pleasure. Or for love.

It was exactly one week passed after the first meeting, and my room again echoed with the same announcement: '406, Dilrubaaaaa. 460, Dilrubaaaa visitooorrr.' The voice exploded in the room like fireworks cracking the sky. It flashed and died cracking the sky and sweeping it with its lights.

"I think it is him," said Zümrüt. Kırlangıç was talking again while I was looking in the round mirror on the table at that moment, and she was giving advice such as "never be alone with him, ask whatever you wonder about, don't be shy, have an edge with him." While I was wearing a different pin on my collar from the previous one Zümrüt added a new advice by saying "but you must be careful about that..." I went out of the room as if sliding from the chaos. I went downstairs with my wings. I was so fast that if I had jumped from the window I would have been there in a longer time. Someone was laying red carpets under my feet, another one was pouring confetti over my head, houris or angels were tidying my skirts up and looking at me with envy. This was what I felt. The sky was lightened again and again for me, it was prepared for me and Tuğrul, the earth was waited for the moment we would talk and look at each other, love was poured on us generously, and the world was decorated all along with the extraordinary, unknown colours that I had seen in the world of seeing and didn't exist in this world.

Those magnificent sounds in the world of hearing was ringing in my ears, the whole earth was waiting for the moment that it would hear those unique sounds, fascinating melodies and the symphony of the birds of paradise. This was what I felt!

First I saw him there from the small space constituted by the panels. I looked at him as if looking through a key hole. His being was shining there. Something was passing by him with the speed of light. This time he seemed to relaxed as if he had come out of his shell, this time he was wearing a white shirt of which collars were shining in a lighter colour of suit. I was proud thinking that all his care was only for me. His wide forehead finished all autumns and started an endless spring. A silky satin was walking on his features; when this satin waved it painted the picture of the most beautiful emotions and it started a weird contact between us. I got close to him seriously, and stopped,

"Hello," I said, "welcome" with a warm smile.

"Hello," said he.

Dilruba was again getting confused in the drunkenness of being so close to the scent caressing the orphan corners of her soul affectionately, inhaling this aromatic scent madly, and she was dragging falling into a river gurgling continuously while trying to stay calm.

Tuğrul was staggering with the astonishment of finding this null subject called Dilruba before him as full of life; he was struggling to curb this very moment starting the flying time fast when he was with her as if he wanted to hold golden sands in his hands, he was looking at the zenith called love, at her eyes.

"Shall we go?" he said. We passed by the shadows of the people laying under the trees in front of the guesthouse. We were escaping from the light of the inside to the dark of the outside; the light inside made us weak. We went out to become blurred and turn to obscure spots. We were both aware of this. We couldn't bear so strong vibrations at such a sensitive moment. Looks were peaching on us in the light. I relaxed again when we went out and I took a deep breath. Secretly. Everything cleared again.

Where was I going? Where was this road starting with my meeting Safran going? What was this adventure beginning only one dream? Perhaps I should have listened to Müdrik and I shouldn't have dived in unknown waters. He had told me, "You shouldn't take a shower in that water, or you will get drowned." May be I should have looked ahead and lived the day. I should have been a good student and turned my face to the future. However, I didn't have strength to review all these things. I didn't have any strength at all at this moment. Above all, it was impossible for me to turn back after the things Keşşaf had showed me. Turning back from this road was as ridiculous as telling 'don't see' to a person after he started to see when he had been blind formerly. Yet what happened happened; I had seen, I had heard. How could I fall asleep again after I had had a teacher giving the light to the sleepy eyes slowly like Keşşaf? He had woken me up step by step. He had peeled me as layers, and wrapped me with the cloth of the reality stage by stage. Wherever or however this adventure of Tuğrul would happened, it would happen as Keşşaf wanted me to and as in a manner not to offend Keşşaf. However the die was about to cast!

Which hand could turn back it when the die was cast?

I slowed down at the slant stone path when we passed the three step stairs. Tuğrul talked while he was continuing the pleasant action of walking with me. I thought there were so many operations between his tall physical body and the ground. The soles of his shiny shoes was stepping on the ground steadily and slipping automatically and self-confidentially.

He said, "It's very nice to see you again." His voice was warm, his voice was like a flame. I hadn't had difficulty to remember his voice and appearance during last week. I had found his voice or appearance very easily, I had revived all the records related to them whenever I wanted. The tones of the colours on his face had been at my disposal. The colours had been like my soldiers. However, I must have confessed that I was avoiding using the things that had been taught to me in the worlds of seeing and hearing as far as possible. I must have avoided doing that. The reverse would be disloyalty and betrayal of the truths that Keşşaf had taught me patiently. I avoided this deadly. Yet the faculties awakening in my mind had revived his voice and appearance automatically like a train driven on the rails fast. Of course there was something different when I was so close to him. Being close to his body meant snuggling the labyrinths of this soul. It was getting close the compound of the body and soul at the same time. I turned to him,

"Really? It's same for me. How was the last week?" I wanted to know if he had thought of me or not. "It was very difficult," he said, "I thought it didn't end."

I looked into his eyes with admiration. The castles of fear fell down one by one with his words, and the crystal mansions of love stood instead of them. My chest... My chest was turning to a sky. Tuğrul's voice was being laid in my heart like blue clouds as I breathed calmly. My heart became so large that it carried everything on the earth; all movements remaining on the ground turned to obscure and unimportant spots; I could see everything from here, I could hear all sounds. Was my soul rising? This blueness and whiteness was dazzling, and I understood that every particle was drunk like me.

"I was going to call you last Friday, but I didn't want to disturb you when Maide told me you were preparing an assignment," he said. My long skirts was hitting the air voids by Tuğrul at every step as if waves hit the shore; waves turning back to the blueness with the effect of the wind were flying, and they made me feel wonderfully.

"Ah, yes," I said, "We have a lot of assignments, we are so buys, there are exams soon." My Goodness! How busy I am!

"I take your time," he said regretting.

"It's weekend, a break is needed sometimes."

In fact, I was uninterested in the courses. Courses meant escaping for me. It meant losing through the pages, and founding what I had owned once and lost through the words. The lesson in which I found the talisman that I didn't know what it was wasn't a lesson any more, it became a reality integrated with life. It wasn't a lie, I closed myself in the study room, covered a table by the window, and I continuously read night after night. The first paragraph of a new book made life a little more delicate, it shouted a new thing I hadn't seen before through thoughts, and untied the knots preying on my mind one by one. Sometimes it was difficult for me that all the courses were in foreign language, a dictionary of which cover had been torn and pages had been lacerated, and that was as thick as two bricks became the fixture of my desk. I turned back from the library with so many books that I hardly carried when I had assignments; I aligned them on the desk in my room carefully, and first I looked for who had been the latest person reading the book. Names and dates were written on the inside of the back cover of the book. Sometimes I saw that the book had been read by one of my professor and I became happy. My name would be under the name of the professor. Sometimes I borrowed the same book four or five times successively. Then I was pleased inwardly. I liked thinking that I occupied the book for a long time. Then I piled them on my desk, and I started to write fixing snow-white sheets with paper clips. The performance of writing gave me a deadly pleasure. I lit a cigarette, and turned on the music. That was a flying moment. That was an extraordinary period of time imitating an artist who was creating his artwork excitedly. I liked reaching the impossible connections between thoughts and events, I put two unrelated people together, and I started a strange current between their thoughts. I was fascinated with my handwriting as I was writing, and I saw every letter to revive on the sheet. I took important notes on detail paper, and I looked at them as if they were prescriptions of life. I thought I could learn love from books. However, I had been delayed everything recently. I had been reading only one book called Keşşaf for a few months; I was looking for who had read the book the latest, and I always Safran's name in the list.

Tuğrul and I walked to the end of the road. As if the stone path was touching a secret distance stretching out eternity by each step of ours. This time Tuğrul had come by another car. I was surprised. It was blue and its model was different from the previous. Again a short, thin and light sound enlightened the headlights of the car. The headlights opened their eyes wide as if they woke up suddenly in this dim road and they blinked with the voice of the opening.

At that very moment there was something more real, much more real than these happened. The Cavalry appeared with his veil at the slope going to A4 door like a dazzling dream appearing in waves. He was the one who had come to take me to Keşşaf for a lot of times. At the same time he was Keşşaf's very self! He was looking at me under the green trees, from the darkness. He didn't say 'let's go, they are waiting for us' this time. He was only looking. I was reading his being from far away and from his upright head and back. His position was telling me to be careful. A cavalry in the dormitory quarter! A reality from dream among the dreaming young. He was on his white horse splitting the darkness like a sword, the light his green clothing reflected the sky. This time he had a reddish scarf on his head and a veil on his face. Lightening was flashing in his hazel eyes harshly and crazily. This solemnity, this splendour! Should one fall in love with the beauty of this white horse or his fabulous aesthetic position on the horse? That dagger which was always on his waist was again on the edge of the green belt like a black sharp hose. The power walking on the dagger frightened me from far away. These wild but familiar looks, this burning mystery! Oh God, what should I do now? Why do I see him here, what is he trying to tell me? Is Keşşaf calling me? His order happens precisely. He doesn't wait, he doesn't make one wait. This is only a warning! A warning for me to be careful. This is a warning meaning 'I see what you are doing, I am watching you.' Yet it is impossible not to know this. There is something else here that I cannot understand.

I know that the Cavalry is Keşşaf. He is only one of the forms that Keşşaf takes. I last saw him in an arena in the middle of a highland; he fascinated me while running at full gallop with a javelin in his hand.

Tuğrul is by me, and I am looking at that slope helplessly. Should I leave? How a crazy situation this is! How a shouting and screaming silence this is! He pulls the bridles to himself on the white horse with foaming mane, and spurs his horse. He is pulled into the darkness like a storm up the slope. The white horse is shining on the black road leaving a trace, and disappears through the dark green trees sliding like a comet. Quickly.

I gulp a node in my throat, a giant and thorny node. I stare at Tuğrul motionlessly at this speechless moment between going and staying. His face sets everything to rights.

"Shall we go?" he says. He smiles. Front door is opened again. He touches excitedly what I touch. He gets behind the wheel quickly. Again the seat belt! It is ringing brokenly. I interpret everything favourably when I am with him. I talk to myself as if I tell about a dream to the dream. Here it is, I say, Tuğrul has come, and also the mysterious rider; the Cavalry! Is it bad? I remember the journeys that I passed by forests, rivers and mountains burying my head to his back and I felt the blue sky on my forehead with all its aliveness one by one. My heart hurts. I remember Cabülka and the first moment I fell down from the horse in brownout. I remember the Cavalry's look at me when he asked if I was all right. And his utterance of 'no way back from this road.' I hear the voice again saying 'I will show you the way to the light.' The smell of sherbet is flowing into my throat once again.

Should I go with Tuğrul or with him? I want to do both.

Tuğrul is looking back from the window mirror. Then he shifts his look and sees the back from the left window once more. He touches a key among the complicated indicators. Music revives inside slowly. I identify the sounds one by one from the motifs waved with notes delicately. Each note, each sound exists again and again, and it gets more powerful after each moment. They pull my dreamy mind out of the depths.

"You are so thoughtful this evening. Have I come at the wrong time?" He turns his head to read the expression on my face, only to do this; I turn to him and smile as if saying everything is all right. This smiling is a little forced.

"No, perhaps I can't find many things to say" I say. This is a firm confession.

"Do you mind if I call you more sincerely?" As if he asks to eliminate the unnecessary barriers. This short sentence tells me a lot of things. I feel the will to talk. His voice is plain, without layers, and it is flowing.

"Not exactly," I say, and added, "No."

He says "if you don't mind, of course."

"No, I don't mind," I say barely.

The music overflows the wide open windows. Tuğrul's left elbow is dangling from the open window. This is an extremely relaxed and careless position. He is looking as if saying how the being is nice. My God, what is happening to me, I said in this dim light. I touch the invisible wings of the wind via Tuğrul's scent. This scent. Is there any other scent on the earth that turns the emotions upside-down? It enamours you. It knocks me down like a strong punch from my left side. This is one of the most powerful effects I feel. These slightly oily and circling molecules like a pouring elixir completed something in me. The scent overflowing from the ghost closet last Thursday. Now I understand that it was a signal coming from Tuğrul. Perhaps it was a reflection of the intensity appearing with Tuğrul's thinking of me, but it wasn't an illusion. It was as real as the trees we are passing by, even more real than those. It was the first speech of a language between us that is difficult to be identified. The first words of it. The first tone.

Going together with him sliding in the darkness... As if flying. Here the action of going fast doesn't contribute the scene in fact. The speed of his being is enough. Feeling these vibrations makes one shifting place enough. It makes you slide over the continuously flowing points.

Again we pass by the cabin at the entrance where the identity check is made and start to travel out of the campus. As soon as we go out, neons, continuously flowing traffic, different buildings, houses, that is the sounds of life being more real than those inside revive. It means freedom. You remember again that you live in a country and a world in which normal people, children and elderly live. After arriving at the real ground of life through the buildings constructed for a specific purpose, Tuğrul said,

"I will take you a very nice place this evening, a restaurant in Tunalı Hilmi."

I got worried when I heard 'Tunalı Hilmi.' Müdrik's office was also in this street and he had told me he preferred having dinner hereabout. Moreover, his new house was also hereabout. Müdrik had phoned me a few times after that shaking conversation and tried to make peace and soften me. I had talk to him calmly. I had tried to tell him how our lives were different from each other. He hadn't understood me as if he had seemed to be listening, and he had told he wanted to come to see me. I had refused him using my exams as an excuse. I looked at Tuğrul, to his careless and empty expression.

"What if we don't go to Tunalı Hilmi?" I said.

"Why? Is there a problem? I have made reservation, it is a very nice place, you will like it," he said.

'As if we have never been to Tunalı Hilmi,' I said to myself. What is the big deal? I don't understand. A table and two plates all in all. Tuğrul was insisting, and he would suspect me meaninglessly if I insisted not to go there. I didn't want him to think negatively about me.

"Okay, let's go," I said.

Tuğrul seemed to be a person who liked making an appearance. The will of fascinating me was lying under the all his struggle, it was clear. Yet I didn't want to go anywhere; he wanted to spend nice and enjoyable time, but I wanted to hear his dream, his plans about life.

We were passing by shiny neons and giant sign boards. Silence was making me nervous, and he started to talk about this and that as if he understood this. His tone of voice was stressed, calm and self-confident. He was talking without smashing the letters and as if wrapping them with cotton. He was talking about where he had grown up, his family, how he had come to Ankara. Ankara wasn't bad for him, he liked here, but he preferred living in a coastal city. Once he had been to Antalya. He had found himself on the way suddenly. To see Antalya, yes, he had set off only for this. Moreover he had been wearing only his tracksuit. He was telling laughing,

"I went to Antalya but I was ashamed to get out of the car with tracksuit on me, so I drove all around the city and turned back."

He was someone who was ashamed to be among people while wearing tracksuit. It was understood that he liked living like grandees. I didn't get this, but it made no sense to ask about the details. He lived on the fly. He wanted to go to Antalya just to see there, and he went. He took life without plans and on the fly. Yet now I am as naive as not to understand this. I prefer admiring his attitude instead of understand. Everything he says makes me thought that how brave he is.

The blue luxury car stopped in front of a restaurant as luxury as it. Smart restaurant attendants welcomed us at the entrance. We passed by the people sitting at the tables on a high platform outside. Tuğrul opened the solid glass door politely. We passed through a long and narrow corridor with colourful lights, and we arrived in a large hall decorated with giant aquariums. At the entrance of the hall, an attendant was engaged with calculation work at an elegant desk. He raised his head and said, "Welcome, Tuğrul Bey." It was understood that 'Tuğrul Bey' was a regular of all luxury restaurants in Ankara. We sat at a table near the desk. We hid behind a giant aquarium. I could see the people entering and going out.

We are both much more relaxed comparing with the first meeting. At least we could speak comfortably, without stumbling. Tuğrul was looking at me with his whole being, and talking in a manner without hesitation.

"These aquariums are like the symbols of this restaurant, did you like it?" he says.

In the aquarium just next to me there are various fish, and they are really big.

"Are they piranhas?" I asked, pointing one.

"Yes, they look like so, I think they are piranhas." He says.

Tuğrul wants to make sure that I am having fun with him. However these aren't needed to be happy with him. I don't need this luxury, these giant aquariums or this magnificence... He thinks these impress me. Yet there are two things in him impressing me; his closeness to Keşşaf and this aromatic scent flowing from him to me. Perhaps the scent will lose its effect if I don't think he is close to Keşşaf. A couple is sitting at the next table, and they have a baby. I am watching them happily; I am thinking of how they met. Perhaps this woman first loved his husband in the same way of that I love Tuğrul. How happy they are now... How much happiness is close to people. The young man takes the one or two year old baby in the high chair on his lap and tries to make him eat something. The woman watches them lovingly with devoted looks. Tuğrul sees that I am watching them and says,

"Do you know, I didn't like children in the past. Children were always crying on the bus. I didn't like it at all. But one day, I read a book and started to like children thanks to it."

"Even if they continuously cry on the bus?" I said ironically.

"Yes," he said with a sincere and warm smile, "let them cry when they are small instead of crying when they grow up."

It was amazing to be with him in the same place. The closeness of his breath to mine, breathing the same air, melting in his warm and brown eyes flowing like honey... As if this brown was endless. These looks was peaching on his lambencies; he was looking as he was the master of the world. A vein appeared slightly on his wide forehead while he was speaking; that veil was like a river flowing underground. He continuously talked about something and I was tracing that veil. First it appeared on his forehead; it divided his forehead resembling a large satin into two like a fault, then it appeared his neck. This was the being of a magnificence shifting between blue and purple. A terrific spark of life.

"Well, have you cried a lot when you grow up?" I say.

He hesitates as if I uncover his fraud.

"I think you insist on being formal," he says first. He is uncomfortable of my manner of addressing him.

"Let's say I have cried as much as everybody. Life is not valuable enough to be cried only for it. Yet if this question is for the beloved, yes

I have cried."

For that moment and for all moments tonight I don't think it is possible for him lying to me. 'He has cried, he has cried for a woman,' I say to myself. He adds as if he understands what I think,

"It is not like you guess. I haven't met a woman who makes me cry yet."

We look each other upon this sentence full of hints. We both look at this sentence; the sentence remains hung in the air between us. We both think about it and load it all possibilities.

"Perhaps you will meet, don't be hopeless," I say, "if you want to cry..."

We stop talking like naughty children when the waiter comes. He puts fish in the chic plates on the table and the table is set with a green salad, warm bread, hot spicy tomato dip and some other things. "Anything else?" asks the waiter, Tuğrul thanks him. The tones of a lyrical music fills the hall.

"I think I don't want to cry. It is hard to find a woman that makes you cry," he says. "One should cry for someone who is worth for crying, not just since he wants. Yet, talking about love has become difficult for me since last week."

I am like a fish taking the bait. Yet I must be like the piranha circling wildly in the aquarium behind me, but I am still naive not to know about this. I don't know the rule that the easiest way of loosing someone you love is dancing to his tune. If I ask him what has changed since last week upon his utterance, he will think that I am in an expectation, so I give up. I look at the fish lying on the plate calmly; its dead eyes are looking at me as if saying 'don't do.' I am like this dead fish against love. The piranha in the aquarium is circling as if looking for a hunt; it meets love with bad temper. Tuğrul is talking when he starts to part the fish in his plate;

"I thought very much about you during the period we didn't see each other." When I hear this, I change place with the fish in my plate, now it's me lying dead in the plate. Two thin pieces of tomato are by my head.

"I wanted to come and see you, I even came to the campus with this thought in my mind, I parked the car in front of your dorm. However, I didn't dare and went back. I thought I could see you."

Now I am like all dead fish in this restaurant. Like all the fish cooked and about to be eaten lying in the plate all along. My hand with fork is trembling, I lay it on the edge of the plate like this fish.

All mysteries existing for people since the earth was created appear on Tuğrul's face suddenly. It looks to me like Ankara, this deaf and blind steppe, is surrounded by seas, even Ankara is an isle in the middle of an ocean. The waves of the ocean first start to hit the shores of this isle. When waves start to flow, the shores disappear, and waters rise steadily... They swallow everything until they reach Tuğrul's face. First his hair gets wet. Then the table starts to float on water. We sink in the deep waves. We just look each other in the water... Waves make us closer instead of removing. Bubbles come out of Tuğrul's mouth, he tries to say something. Piranhas patrol around us, first they bite Tuğrul's arms extended to me, then water gets red with his blood; and Tuğrul starts to look at me like a giant piranha. Something is pulling me to the bottom, deeper... Tuğrul holds me with his bleeding hands... We try to get out, "up, come on, hang on!" says Tuğrul...

I get over. Tuğrul is trying to separate the fish in my plate from its bones.

"You can separate the bones of the fish like this easily," he says. He holds the weak bone separated from the fish on the end of his fork.

"Thank you," I say, "I am pleased that you came to see me. Who knows what was I doing then?"

"Perhaps... you were thinking of me, who knows," he says.

Waters rise again, piranhas attack me this time, the blood looks like red wine poured into the water.

"Yes, I thought of you..." I say, "I thought that I didn't know you at all."

"I thought we met," says Tuğrul surprised, "and you will know in time..." His beautiful face is looking at me between these two sentences, a huge wave comes, and we scarcely wash ashore like two captives left into the water by the pirates. Fish skeletons in front of us...

He looks at me like a man in love... At that moment, I saw him, he was talking to the attendant at the desk at the entrance; Müdrik. He is wearing a comfortable tracksuit, and he seems to be contented. I immediately hide as to be just behind the aquarium like hiding in a shield. Perhaps the best thing at such a time is to learn where the bathroom is.

"We can visit Kocatepe after dinner, if you like," says Tuğrul. His voice touches me slightly. There has to be a way of walking away from here before Müdrik sees me. I immediately have a quick look around and try to understand where the bathroom is. It must be the opposite direction of the desk. The remotest corner from the entrance. Women sometimes run to that direction taking their handbags. Probably they go to the bathroom. I also ask for permission from Tuğrul and find the bathroom walking at the line of the aquariums. The same music is played in the bathroom. First I wash my hands. Again I wash my hands, and once more I wash them. The woman by me is making up carefully looking in the mirror and drawing a new face for herself. She is snuggling the mirror as if she is going into the mirror. I stand up with my hands on my belly stupidly for a while. I look at myself in the mirror at length. I try to guess how Tuğrul finds this face. About 15 minutes pass. I push the door calmly, there is the door of the men's room just opposite. I go out when I make sure that there is nobody. My aim is to reach the table following the same way again, I hope Müdrik has gone. However, the precise fate accounting moments throws its net just over me. I come face to face with Müdrik at the corner of the bathrooms. I stand there as if I score an own goal. He looks at me with an astonished expression. Perhaps this is better, it's better for him to see me here than seeing at the table with Tuğrul.

"Dilruba..." he just says.. His voice comes out like a surprised reflex.

"What are you doing here?.. I am so happy to see you. What's up?"

"Hi, I.. hmm.. with a friend.. we are having fish.. how is it going? What are you doing here?"

"I live hereabout, I have told you. My house is so close here.."

"How nice... very nice... it's better I go back.." He stops me saying 'hold on.'

"You aren't resentful, are you? We aren't cross?"

"Why should we be cross?"

"Then I will come over tomorrow evening and we can talk," he says.

I know he will insist if I tell him not to come, and I will stand here as he insists, and Tuğrul will wonder about me... In spite of this,

"In fact I am not available, shall we meet a few days later? I mean we will see." I say. These are the words said without thinking on very much.

When I get back to the table, Tuğrul says "is everything all right?" "No, no, I wash my hands for a long time."

"Is that why they are so white?" he says. The waiter has cleared the table, and two glasses of tea are waiting for us on the clean white tablecloth.

"I have ordered tea," says Tuğrul.

"I think we should leave now since we are going to Kocatepe, it's already late." Müdrik appeared upon my words, he is passing in front of us looking at us. He seems to understand who I am with and what the relation between us is. We go out hurriedly. 'Why should I be timid?' I say to myself, 'What's wrong with it? Is it a bad thing to have dinner here? Here is open to the public.' This thought relaxes me a little. If Müdrik hadn't asked me to live together and made me restless, I wouldn't have got a lather. I say that I am not a bad person, I am not.

When we arrive at Kocatepe I feel that I purify from the mess. The night *azan* is being recited. People rush to the mosque; I relax in this crowd like melting. I go upstairs, the chamber of peace, and I pray quietly after the prayer. I thank God for Tuğrul's being with me. Knowing that he is praying downstairs and being together here inebriates me. Kocatepe stands in the darkness with its crystal lights, and people filling their hearts with peace are leaving one by one.

I find Tuğrul at the exit by the stairs of the mosque. He is looking at me there, alone under the dim light, from the whistling wind. I understand how much I love him when I see him there. My eyes find his light face on the stairs washed by darkness.

"I thought you were performing *tarawih* prayer," he says.

"I keep you waiting, I'm sorry. I like this place very much..."

We walk along the wide yard of the mosque. Side by side. Kocatepe preparing for the night and we, two shadows moving in front of it. I don't want this moment to end. Never...

I feel in my cells, in every pore of my soul... Tuğrul's voice spreads on my wounds like a salve; his eyes are carrying the warm looks of a lover. His burning scent sticks on my throat here in this wide yard, it leaves me breathless, then it grants new breaths. I compare him with the Cavalry coming to take me to Keşşaf, I compare him with Keşşaf. Tuğrul's saying of 'Kocatepe' is so beautiful that I can die. Every letter of the word Kocatepe turns to an angel in his lips. His saying of Kocatepe draws me in it being an echo in syllables. The beauty of Kocatepe itself and his voice combines. The light of the crystal sparkles reflects on his face as we walk in this dark yard. How light I am. How beautiful living is. We appear and disappear between light and shadow. We play in the darkness, and we find the stairs to down as if sliding, as if flowing. We go down as if we drop on the earth in the eternity. We are pouring from the sky as drops. My chest becomes a sky when I am with him, and this sky fills with his breath. With his breath... In the light...

The beauty of this scene makes my soul blind. God, what a beautiful man You have sent to me! How did You pull Tuğrul out through thousands, millions of people? You ended all distances first with Safran, then with Keşşaf and now with Tuğrul. How Your beauty inebriates me, oh God! How You understand me, oh You, Your beauty is closer to me than my carotid. I wish You complete this. Please don't let me down.

Tuğrul lights a cigarette, and now his scent is mixing with the ecstatic air of the cigarette. The wind is drawing this magical mixture including me... Tuğrul again opens his blue car. The night is about to be over. The loser is me in the second round. Again I am covered with blood. This blood is mixing with wine, with the deep red wine of love, and I drink it voluntarily. As I drink I get quiet. More blood, more wine... Hit me more oh love! As you hit me so successively I transform to you, look! Give me a new skin, a new body oh love! Don't stop. Make me you again every moment!

Tuğrul gets behind the wheel, the key disappears in his big hands, and he leans forward a little looking at me at the same time. He is so impressive on me that if he says 'Dilruba you should die now,' I will say 'take my life.' If he says, 'Dilruba, we are going to die,' I will say 'let's go.'

He looks at me so, Dilruba let's die together. Dilruba, let's disregard life. I want to die with you. Are you in dying with me Dilruba... Your eyes are looking like a dagger on my neck Dilruba..

"Shall we go?" he says only. We set off slowly. His looks are talking slowly. Everything except Tuğrul disappears for me. I am jealous of even the window mirror that he checks rising his beautiful face slightly, of the road he is looking at, and of the letters pouring from his lips slowly as if flowing. I am jealous of even the tiniest detail that his being contacts with. I didn't know love is so. I didn't know crashing is so. If Tuğrul wanted to tie me at his door as a dog, I wouldn't object him. If he wanted to make me a mat under his feet, I would be proud of that. Tuğrul's voice tells me that heaven exists. Heaven is close. As I dive in his brown looks, the heavens that time freezes lies ahead of me. His scent resembling a magic sticks me to him, and I was racing to the pain like glow-worms racing to the fire. To the fabulous pain of love.

"Did you like the evening?" he said, he looked at me taking his eyes from the road for a few seconds. He was looking at me as if he was saying, 'I have cut your wrists, are they bleeding?' His sentence meant so to me. Or he was like saying that 'I have thrown you a hole full of millipedes, are you frightened?'

"It was so beautiful," I said.

"It is, I go to this restaurant very often."

"It is not the restaurant that is beautiful," I said. He looked at me as if saying what then?

"Your being..."

He spoke while he was moving up the gear,

"I am very pleased to hear that." He was driving so fast. The car didn't go on the road, it was simply flying. As if our emotions would have gathered speed if the car had slowed down. Tuğrul was moving up the gear steadily. He looked like that if he had stopped or slowed down he wouldn't be sure about himself. We needed to arrive at the dorm as soon as possible.

"You drive so fast," I said. I was talking to him in a more comfortable manner. I wanted him to slow down since I wanted to see him more.

"The road is empty, don't worry," he said, "are you really frightened?" He whispered without waiting for my answer:

"Dilruba... Dilruba... What a beautiful name this is... I must say this name continuously... I must call you without breathing... Dilruba... Dilruba..."

He was like murmuring by himself alone. Butterflies were flapping in my stomach; or the fish I had just eaten started to revive and move its tail after the sentence I hear. Then Tuğrul lit a new cigarette in a distressed manner. The flame of the lighter enlightened his beautiful face in the darkness. He inhaled the first sniff deeply, very deeply, and he exhaled with a distinct sighing. He threw the cigarette pack to the bottom of the front window harshly. The earth was sliding under our feet fast. The flat, shiny asphalt road was lengthening ahead increasingly. The lights by the road were reviving again on the front window in different forms.

Tuğrul's long and strong arms gripped the wheel easily, then he was dangling one arm from the window as if he was bored. Both windows were wide open. Again the same scent was mixing with the same ecstatic smell of the cigarette, and made me crazy.

"Do you know Dilruba, I have never been like this. Dilruba, you are looking like a gazelle." He said. He nailed his looks to my eyes ignoring the speed. I thought the car would go by itself. "I have no power, Dilruba.." he said.

I was turning to a wound bleeding continuously. I would have died if there hadn't been his voice. If there hadn't been his dazzling scent, purulence would have been flowing in my veins instead of blood. Tuğrul was attracting me by a terrific attraction. I was about to lose my self-confidence. His breath was making me drunk next to me, right over here.

I heard that terrible scream at that very moment. I knew these flames getting closer screaming wildly. This was the Nafs. Tuğrul's whispers and looks full of desire gave it strength. Nafs was coming to me with its ugly body resembling a hyena and with its dragon wings scattering flames blended with black foams from its mouth. Hadn't I defeated it? In fact, hadn't Keşşaf knocked it down? How had it enslaved the Spirit again and captured the throne of the land of heart?

"Please stop Tuğrul, please stop. Pull over," I started to shout. I was thinking to sit at the back and get over these dangerous moments in safe. He slowed down immediately as if something happened to me, and pulled over signalling. He didn't ask if something had happened, he understood that I wanted to move away. At the moment the car stopped, everything calmed down suddenly. I got out of the car as if running away from the fire... There was a short way to the campus. The harsh wind made me get over. I waited leaning on the front of the car for a while. He came to me. He stood just next to me and leaned on the car as if he wanted to watch the landscape.

"Did I frighten you? You will be cold.." he said. We were both standing on the edge of the cliff at that moment. We didn't lean on his blue car but something else on the edge. The earth could slide under our feet with a little movement.

"I just wanted to get some fresh air..." I was sniffing at the same time.

"Why are you crying?" he said quietly. "Did I say something wrong?" I wanted to say that 'yes, it was wrong. Your saying Dilruba was wrong, you shouldn't have say my name so sincerely, so warmly; your saying Dilruba in whisper killed me." Yet I kept quiet.

"No, no, it wasn't because of you..."

"I drove too fast and frighten you, didn't I?" Tuğrul was talking about the speed of the car. Life itself was fast.

"Life itself is fast, never mind" I said.

I was looking at the world at the end of a forked road. I would rather die having an accident than offend Keşşaf. He meant everything to me. Thousands of Tuğrul didn't worth only one word of Keşşaf. My thoughts became severe and were going to the right direction. I escaped myself from temporary and deceptive emotions in this way. Who was Tuğrul? I had met him a short time ago. How quickly I fell in with him! This was stupid... unreasonable... I again sat at the front seat next to him collectedly. If I had sat at the back, it would have meant that I hadn't trusted him at all, and myself at the same time...

However, I was again in the middle of the same burning emotions when the car started to go slowly. Tuğrul was looking at the road thoughtfully. He wasn't driving fast this time. He lit another cigarette. Again the same scent, again the same madness...

At last we arrived at the dorm, we arrived here safe and sound getting over hundreds of cliffs. When the car stopped in front of the dorm, Tuğrul leaned back; there were storms on his face. He leaned his head back completely. He hadn't finished his cigarette yet. He was smoking thoughtfully...

"Are you leaving now?" he said. As if I was setting sail, at least I was going up to my room.

"It's late, it's better I go," I said. There was nobody around. Lights were enlightening around behind the thick curtains of the dorm, but this street lamp at most that we were standing under. I got out of the car like a wire-walker leaving the wire. Tuğrul also got out of the car and he was walking a few steps behind me,

"Don't go to the bother," I said, "thank you very much."

"I see that you are at arm's length again," he said. He was smiling very nicely. It was very difficult for me to leave him there and go up. Again we stopped by the information cabin.

"When shall we meet again?" he said.

"Whenever you want..." I said.

"I will come again as soon as possible." He leaned again to my face slightly. I was drinking his voice like wine. I was inhaling his scent as if I wouldn't feel it again. I missed him even he was still with me. My heart was breaking and all the fish revived in me started to agonize. His hair got long, as long as to be fastened under his ears... A thin forelock fell onto his face. He shook his head slightly to throw the forelock back. Then he straightened it with one hand.

"To see you is very good for me, you cannot know this," he said.

"Me too," I said; I left him there and went behind the panel.

I wanted to cry as 'don't go.' I was hardly keeping myself together not to go down his knees to beg him not to go. Now there was a panel between us. Tuğrul went out by walking behind the panel and disappeared.

The angels pouring confetti over my head and looking at me with admiration when I had been last going down these stairs now were pulling me up holding my arms saying "Come on Dilruba, come on." I was resisting going up. I saw Kırlangıç when I went up the first floor in difficulty. She was standing in front of the huge dressing mirror at the entrance of the first floor. She was holding a mug.

"What happened?" she said when I went to her.

"It was a difficult night," I said.

"What do you mean, wasn't it nice?" she said.

"It was too nice," I could only say.

"Say then you have fallen over heels in love... well, tell me about it," she said.

At that moment lightening flashed in my head. Keşşaf had showed me this scene before in the world of seeing.

I had seen it in the world of seeing, yes. We had been talking to Kırlangıç in front of the huge mirror, and she had been holding this mug; I had been looking thoughtfully, even fussily. The scene I had seen was just this moment! Keşşaf had told me 'I know what you are doing,' with this. I heard a voice behind while I was still astonished,

"Dilruba!"

It was my roommate Kamuran.

"Yes?" I said.

"Your surgeon hasn't gone yet, I think. He is wandering down, I think he is waiting for you," she said.

"My surgeon?" I said, "I haven't been with him, you are wrong."

"If it wasn't his ghost, it was definitely him," she said.

"You might have mistaken him" I said.

Kamuran curled her lips meaning she didn't know then and go upstairs. Everything was spreading among girls very quickly although I didn't talk about myself to my roommates. Yet Kamuran was claiming that the one outside was 'my surgeon.' How fast Müdrik's reputation was spread. I would understand if Kamuran was telling the truth later. Now I should have told Kırlangıç everything in detail. Her thoughts were very important to me.

21
Limbo

"The ones whose soul is alive can't know, are you ready to die?"
(Amak-ı hayal)

Keşşaf was capturing my life totally. I made sure of this at one of the lessons I had this morning. Teacher of the elective course was one of the teachers I like. He handed out homework subjects to whole class and came to me and said that my topic was love. First, I thought that I was dreaming. I opened my eyes wide to see this sentence well. He thought that I didn't understand and repeated:

"Dilruba Uçmaklı, your topic is love!"

First I whispered as what love... Will I look for Tuğrul now in the pages I looked for Keşşaf?

I prattled "I couldn't understand sir, what do you mean by Love? Is it in the meaning we know?". What a beautiful department is this philosophy, one doesn't want to depart from here. I said myself that they discuss everything preying on their soul.

"Sorry?" said the teacher and then repeated "Yes you understood correctly, love!"

He was one of the most favourite teachers of this department. I heard that people line up at registration time to get courses from him. They come in front of his door with their blankets and almost camp here. There is long queue in front of his room. In fact, they are right! Each lesson with him was a therapy! My getting this course is jackpot!

Mr Altuğ! This was a name which melts in mouth like sweet! Although it is hard to admit, I take offense at the distance between the teachers and the students. I have never had a glass of tea with none of them. However, some of the friends were close to Mr. Altuğ. I don't know what they eat or drink. For me, they were living in an indefinite tent at the peak of a high mountain.

Details of love homework became clear in two or three hours. This would be homework that would deal with servant and master dialectic of Hegel as phases of love or as a love metaphor. This homework would enlighten me who was waiting in the middle of love desperately. At least it would give a clue.

In the evening of the same day, Müdrik came to the guest house to see me. We sat at the hindermost table as usual. He was a person who could realize my calmness and sadness on my face. Bad temper at our last date was disappeared. He calmed down. But his look between blue and green was inquiring me continuously. I served him tea in paper cups as usual. No matter what happens, there was a deep watershed that nobody could reach between us; Müdrik was a clever man he pushed the limits of mind. He said he developed a great interest in writing poems recently. As if he didn't want to talk about "us" anymore.

"I have been reading poems recently. I think that reality can be reached via poems. Poems make me relax. If we look into your eyes, you need to relax, too."

I said, "Do you know Heidegger also thinks like this?"

He said, "Really?"

I said, "Yes, because poem takes reality regarding human in hand. So speeches of wise person regarding poems shouldn't surprise."

I continued to ironize,

"I hope poem will restrain your mental rise and fall, neurotic intemperance. Because you will need this "

He took umbrage,

He said, "Neurotic behaviours are based on insistency of a person for turning personal choices into absolute demands; I have never considered my wishes as absolute demands. If so, I wouldn't be here."

I didn't understand what he meant. He continued,

"I am conscious enough to question how real my thoughts are. But I am doubtful about you."

Putting my elbows on the table, I looked at that scream portrait at the back for a moment. Taking my eyes away from that screaming dream, I focused my eyes on Müdrik's look.

I said, "Let's talk frankly, please, otherwise I will spent all evening trying to guess what you meant."

He steepened collar of his white shirt, turned his head right and left, we was looking like a chess master who got a shot.

He said, "If you are sure about your thoughts, you won't get off the blue streak car in the middle of the way and cry".

I was terrified. Müdrik followed me. That night, the night we had dinner with Tuğrul at the restaurant on Tunalı Hilmi, I came across Müdrik. I thought that he went away later. But he followed us.

I said, "Enough is enough! Why did you do this?"

He was talking with pleasure, heavy, hard shadows started to move around his face again. He looked with victory as if he captured the peak of the mountain he had been climbing.

"Your friend was so fast that night, I hardly caught. What was your problem?"

I must be mad to talk these with him. I remembered Kamuran. He said your surgeon was wandering around downstairs. So he came to the dormitory. What nonsense.

"You came to the dormitory, didn't you?" maybe he followed his ex-wife and led her a merry dance. Müdrik was completely disturbing me. What does he want to show me, what does he want to prove?

I said angrily, "I think you really need poem but even it may be inadequate to stop you."

My head started aching. I said, "I want you to go, you are selling down the river."

He said as if he didn't hear, "I know that he will make you sad. He doesn't look like a safe person."

I got angry. He was mobbing my life. Being patient was in the meaning of compensating unnecessarily, I was going to go. But he said something that stopped me,

"Dilruba, I have already passed saturation point in life. I discovered nearly all pleasures, I tried all pleasures. There is fifteen years between you and me, you don't miss spiritual one. I come here for this reason. Seeing that happiness in your eyes opens me a new and unknown world, doors of an alternative. I see that a different life style fits your. I come here for myself not for you." He stopped for awhile and then continued, "but I give importance to your safety. This is why I followed you. What should I do, Dilruba is having dinner with her friend. How nice. Should I say OK? You didn't even introduce me to him."

I was calming down,

I said, "You may be right, I didn't remember to introduce, because you make me scared."

He clasped his hands around his face, put his elbows on the table. He was looking at like someone who was thoughtful and who wanted goodness. He was like saying I don't want malignancy.

"You don't know anything about life. Not everybody is running after pure reality like you. You can't understand this, life is full of jackals. There are self-seeking people everywhere. When I offered you living together, I meant this. I want to protect you in every sense but you didn't understand. You break off life, you suddenly disappear and then you return swept away."

He was right, it seems as if there is something strange about me. How was I leaving everything away and attracted? Müdrik took a swig from his tea and silently put his glass.

"You say why I am like this, don't you? Because you don't have a leg to stand on, you don't have a family. You don't know who or where to give the love inside you. There is seeking in your structure, when all of these combined, this view occurs; wonderful, unplanned bodyguard. If you were in my shoes, would you take offense at the things you said? I wouldn't and so I come here. Because I know you better than you know yourself."

I lifted my eyebrows in the meaning of I don't know. I tried to free from the astonishment on my face. I was afraid of getting all the blame on me if he continued talking. He leaned back relaxedly, combined his arms at the back of his head,

"Ok let me have it now, what jobs that aren't your business did you poke your nose into again? Stop looking like you are in trouble."

Iron chair I was sitting started to disturb me or I was disturbing it. While putting my weight on my right, I pipe up with shame,

I said, "There is nothing to be afraid of as you think. His name is Tuğrul. We had a casual dinner."

Smilingly he said,

"What about Tuğrul? Is he faultless? Where has he been before? Why did he come like a creditor?". He wanted to know the details.

I said, "We must ask this to the fate"

"Let's ask to the fate then, but first let's ask the questions to ourselves, we won't lose anything."

I was losing altitude. Stress on his voice was increasing.

I said, "We met, that's it. A common friend introduced us. From Dergah."

He took his hands down from back of his neck , folded his arms in his chest and said,

"OK, Everything is clear now."

I said, "Stop speaking in the tone of seeking for a guilty, please. There is nothing to worry."

He said, "I think there is something for you. It is obvious from your look. You are waiting for him to come. Going to Kocatepe together. How interesting..."

I said, "Do you know that you are hurting me while trying to protect me?

He said, "If you don't feel the pain, you won't wake up. If you don't feel the pain, even you won't think. I want to wake you up."

"I don't demand this. You declare yourself as apron, and stand in front of me. Moreover, why do I need protection? Am I a child?"

I wasn't sure. Maybe Müdrik was covering up his desires. How can I know that there is neurotic or even more schizoid personality under the sentence of I protect you? But I have known him for many years. My father always told me he was a proper and secure man. He was a person to trust. He was a smart, single-minded and strong man to fight with life. I have heard Müdrik's name since my childhood. Sometimes my aunt also spoke of him and his family. She said they were good people. I was doing wrong or who knows? What is the best way to know a person?

Müdrik was like a symbol of patience before me. So, way of circumventing the life passes from being patient. He wasn't afraid of anything, he was determined. He could solve every knot, while acting like an unbalance, how he shows himself innocent.

I said, "Is this special for all doctors or are only you like this?". He laughed as if saying gracious goodness.

"You must also consider thing our occupation brings. A good doctor can understand how his patient is just looking into her eyes, he must understand. Especially psychiatrists are experts in this subject."

I said, "Be careful, don't have professional deformation."

A serious meaning appeared on his face.

"I know, you are not a person who can be influenced with mind, you are seeking for mystery. So you are on a slippery ground."

I asked without losing time,

"Which ground are you on?"

"I am in Research and inquiry school. I don't decide without thinking long and hard. I get my feet on the ground."

"Does this reduce your pains?"

He moved his shoulders in the meaning of what is it to me.

"My aim is to give meaning to my pains, not to reduce them."

Müdrik was talking like a poem.

I said, "Poem worked on you." The atmosphere eluded from its tension.

We were looking at the life from different corners. As we talked, we met somewhere in the middle. Despite this, words weren't telling us enough; after a point sentences defined nothing. While the words were flying, fate was staring at the people's face, it was ridiculing loutishly, in short, it was getting its own way.

A week passed over this conversation. Tuğrul was as disappeared. Maide didn't call. During all this waiting, yes this kind of waiting is a torture, I continued feeling his aromatic scent every moment I lived in the most unnecessary details of life. I was hitting the bottom slowly. Tuğrul came suddenly and then left, it was enough to turn upside-down. I wasn't losing my hope. He will come, he must come. My life veins were broken with each desperate moment I waited for him. I was like a beetle which lost its way while walking around in greenery, stuck in concrete blocks and was about to die. Setting everything aside, half-opening the shame on my face, I was asking Keşşaf: please tell me, will he come? Keşşaf was sending me the same thing every time as a response, his fragrance. This meant yes in my dictionary, my expectations become green, I was looking forward to it.

This fragrance was messing up everything in my mind. Everything regarding before Tuğrul melted away; I only remembered the moments we lived together. One night, electricity went off at the guest house I was staying. As I saw from the window, even all dormitories region was left in the dark. Residents of the opposite guest house were letting down the paper that they fired one end, there was a fantastic view. Papers were turning in the air burningly and were burning out and falling down. Everybody was shouting loudly at that moment. Everybody was screaming what they have inside them by the help of the courage taken from the darkness. All of us were hidden under a black cloth; none of us saw the others, we were just a sound. As the ones stayed in the room were shouting out of the window, the sound was echoing in the space, someone from the opposite guest house was replying randomly by shouting.

I was looking out of the window like everyone else. I had no sound. I settled back for a moment. I looked at the pathway we walked with Tuğrul, moon light was brightening our steps. This stony pathway was as wide as two people could walk. We walked there. It was like the flashy paper left from the windows, then it burnt out at somewhere there. At that moment, maybe for the first time in my life, I felt a terrible pain that was different from the pains suffered. At that moment, I turned into an indefinable, massive pain for the first time. I felt how lonely I am here. I got lost in the uncertainty of life.

However, I was unaware of the fact that darkness was something to be afraid of. A person learns being scared. Something, the things she lived make her learn fear. I didn't know that illness called fear, maybe because the pain was so new. I didn't know, because I didn't lose my hope. Hope was brightening inside of my brain and dilemmas of my heart like a lantern.

Sometime later, the heads moving in dark started to sing. These sounds were increasing like a chorus inviting to the life in the darkness. Darkness caused joy for these young people. The moon in the sky like a wafer was covering the room up to soft light. I left the people standing like extended out from the window and sat at the end of my bed. At that moment the door of the room was opened quickly. A terrific air stream started. The wind was letting the curtains fly, the reflection of the moon inside was continuously changing place. At the very middle of this stream, I stood being captured of the same fragrance at the place where darkness and wing intertwined. I was abstracted from everything around me. Wind was carrying this fragrance from outside to inside; wind became a huge hand and started to choke me. Molecules of fragrance weren't showing mercy to me, I was like a wild animal under a steel wire mesh which was captured at the end. I raised my head, I hold my neck as if I wanted to turn into this fragrance in darkness. Like a victim who was punished with dead penalty... like holding my neck to a shining sword that would cut my head. Wind was saying there is no way out, you are my captive. I am your master, understand this! Your insistence is useless! Wherever you go I will find you. I was dying on purpose, I was going to the chimney which was gathered from this fragrance on my own free will. I was pushing myself and I was glad to fall down here. Fragrance wind was slapping me until my face was in a welter of blood. Its long nails were scratching my skin wildly, it was tearing it like a cloth. It was branding me with a hot iron until all of my organs were broken to pieces. When my heart was seen naked, it was trying to beat desperately in the hands of this scent and was begging for a give it life. Then it was pulverizing my heart. First blood was leaking out of the hands of the scent. It was tightening my heart until my heart stopped beating. It was both tightening and saying you would breathe with me. Breathing without me is death itself.

Nothing was stopping the scent really. It was cuddling me with all of its "body" even under smoke. It was standing in strong meal smell, between people scent which was different like fingerprints or before all of the unpleasant scents. It was reeking me. I was continuously washing my hands. I was running away it like trying to get rid of a germ. While I was considering that the problem was me, other also started to feel that smell. This helped the situation remain a mystery.

I couldn't have visited Safran for ten days. It seemed as if Keşşaf diverged from me. Keşşaf left me in limbo. He consisted of breath reviving behind a thick curtain. He absented himself from my stage, from the lights. He was watching the events in the dark at the back of the saloon called world. Nobody except me felt pain because of Tuğrul's absence during ten days; why was I feeling a strong pain because of his absence? The question to be answered was just a question like this. I put up a thick wall of books, I wasn't joining the life if not necessary. In the late afternoon of the eleventh day, I had a call. I hadn't got dark yet. A women voice starting with buzzing crashed the empty walls of the room saying, "406 Dilruba... you have a call..." and silence that I was alone with circled for one or two seconds in this capsizing. Echo of the phone started to ring in the cabin was heard simultaneously. I thought that there was water leaking from the walls of the corridor and it turned into a waterfall. I listened to the sweet sound of the water. Then I got out of the room and walked through the cabin fast. It was ringing for the third time that I lifted the receiver excitedly.

"Hello?"

"Hi Dilruba, it's me, Tuğrul"

It was him, his very self! Again the same soft and high voice... All threat on my throat drew away one by one, I freshened, all the breath I couldn't take for ten days filled in cheerfully. Everything started smiling, everything seemed pleasant, all of the walls in the world got thinner as if it showed the other side. There weren't any dry things on the earth, everything was sopped in sherbet of love.

I was unable to pronounce correctly... I wasn't speaking. I was putting on silence stuck in astonishment. I wasn't speaking, I was looking at the sound echoing from his chest as if I wanted to drink all rain. My thirst was as it couldn't be a guide to my arid land; I wasn't speaking, my thirst was as longing of underground rivers to sunlight.

I fished out his voice again among the cotton.

"How are you?"

How am I?

"Thank God, I am fine. You?"

"I couldn't call you, you haven't resented, have you? But I will come tomorrow evening. I wasn't here, I was out of the town."

Joy including everything burgeoned inside me from the shadowy disappointment. As he talked, its green body was lengthening. I was stocking leaves with his every word.

I didn't say anything and Tuğrul continued;

"Of course if you aren't busy."

I spoke hiding the joy in my voice.

"Tomorrow evening. I don't know. Maybe." I knew that he would return; it wasn't a play having a few scenes. Your scent was a sing for your thinking me! This fragrant messenger was your call to me at every minute you thought me... It was the thing make me live during your silence, during that agonizing waiting. It was a new language between us. Nobody talked it, between existence and non-existence, invisible, it wandered around like a silent soul. It sopped me in you from my nape, tightening my hair roots!

Tuğrul became the first rule of life with this scent; he was ruining every vital reason before the air I took. I put him before everything with his scent reeked the water I drink, with his charm rubbed off my hands. Did Tuğrul know what's going on? Was he in this kind of tendency? Or what would he think if he learnt he caused a situation like this involuntarily? This was an enigma.

The next evening Tuğrul didn't break the rule. After evening prayer, while I was in a painful waiting, he appeared gliding for a short time like a falling star at night.

First the same voice saying "406 dilruba... Dilruba... you have a visitor" tripped the dark blue sky in immobility with fireworks. Lights dispersing in pieces and clenching fists fell down flowing from this dark blueness; like the paint flowing from the wall. Just then, I was looking at the mirror on my table; Kırlangıç was saying "This is your third dating, black or white, it must be clear," while I was watching crazy flashing of these lights, cracking and gliding like a seed. Pale face of Nergis appeared in the mirror, I caught her thoughtful and doubtful look. Then her expression immediately changed, hopeful clouds swinging on her face. This time, she didn't say anything. When the hope clouds became rare, she was looking like saying, life is sometimes a big, huge space.

Longing became a scream on my face; screaming, begging desperately. I went down the stairs as a person who forgot herself. My soul had got numb with the effect of the poison called love. It was in therapy that the moths running to light feel. I went back of the board slowly without knowing that I was at the door of a new transformation, a new existence. The fire started to burn my wings as I approached.

I saw Tuğrul at that time. A hand pulled me from the scenes lasting forever by turning the pages of destitution fast and put me in this unique scene. All the moments in front of and behind me, past and future were embedded in a single light. I was holding my hand to the happiness I deserved at the place I deserved. I was walking through an oasis I dreamed after a lonely childhood, time passed until now desperately, endless mirages in the desert. A possibility that he could also be a mirage when I went near him... Yes, a possibility like this... No, it couldn't be... It was against the balance in life, that unique harmony. Strong waves of life let me free on this stage like poking at a soft cost slowly.

When his eyes caught me, he lifted his eyebrows as if saying there she is. He took one or two steps towards me gently, we were walking to the single point to be walked as the last two people on the earth, to the line between us. This equator-like line was separating us like separating two hemispheres. I talked from the other side of the line:

"Welcome, What a pleasant surprise."

A cute astonishment mixed with joy,

"Thank you, I told you that I would come yesterday. Have you forgotten?"

"No, I remember, it's a surprise though."

We were at the foot of the wall a little way off the information cabin in order not to stop people. There was humming around, it became quite crowded, our voices were rolling in this humming. My soul and mind were tired of Tuğrul's scent, then they awakened to feel that scent again; it was running at full gallop in shambles continuously. The scent such blindfolded me that no stimulus that I could realize remained on the world, wherever I was, I was stuck in this scent like a fast going arrow to the target.

I was like the last princess on the world. He was like the last bird of prey on the sky.

"Shall we go?"

He looked with an expression of being disturbed by the crowd, he was like saying let's move away from the people. Crowd was breaking my brain waves, the communication between us was falling apart, was interrupted, was breaking up. Nevertheless, I said,

"Why don't we stay in?" We involuntarily walked towards the canteen. The canteen was very crowded, there were strong cloud because of smoke, the windows were wide-opened. There was a gloomy crowd.

He opened his hands like saying "There is nowhere to sit". There were paper cups between messy notes and books piled on some of the tables. The lonely ones standing aimlessly in front of the open windows were watching outside. We passed by the path among the young people sitting or lying on the grass. The weather outside was wonderful. Living was magnificent. I couldn't hold the time when I was with Tuğrul. Minutes were walking in a hurry, hours were working like the hour of a man about to die; I experienced such drunkenness for the first time.

Blue car was parked properly at the other end of the street.

He said," It's too crowded this evening. It was hard to find a parking place". He woke the car up with the same sound. The car opened its eyes wide like saying what's happening, lightened as green trees leaves before it could be seen. As the car started going on the road, Tuğrul started talking like a radio which was turned on.

"Did I keep you in suspense? But first say, what did you do? How are you?"

I was like a nightingale started singing because of everlasting joy arising from his interested in me.

"The same things as you know. Life doesn't change so much here, generally the same rush."

He said, "How nice it is. One doesn't understand how time passes. It's full of life then"

"Yeah, right. It's really like that."

While talking, he is gently lifting his and watching for the back and then wing mirrors... Then he is looking at me as if I am a mirror too. But he stops for a moment whatever he sees in the mirror. Then he again looks at the road. He is content with his situation. He again put his elbow at the window in devil-may-care manner. He lights up, I catch his eyes on the flame of the lighter. This time, I ask him not to open the window on my side. Not to be in the idle of this scent storm,

"It shocks me..."He shakes his hand in the meaning of certainly, and right after, he says,

"Did you feel my absence, you seem as if you didn't..."

"Sometimes you come into my mind but..." he looks as if asking but what?

"But you aren't that much important, right? What I hoped, I hoped you waited for me."

I said with reproachful voice,

"You didn't say wait... you only said you would come, these two are different."

"It's okay. But I obsessed you."

I said as if I don't have any idea,

"For example, what sort?"

"Your face, voice, words, how can I say, you..."

"You are so gentle."

Headlamps of the cars going on the other side lighten the regret on his face. There is some sorrow, some thought in his look. Question marks asking what will happen, how will happen disappears while talking. He is talking about the things he did during these ten days. He is complaining about not having time to call when he was out of the city. From what he told me he wanted to come immediately when he returned, he is telling those moments with "I had no more patience left."

Something breaks off me. I want Tuğrul's scent to remain for a moment, to talk with this scent, to look into the eyes of this scent, to see its hands tearing my heart out. Even Tuğrul is behind this scent, his duty is to carry it. He is carrying the words of the scent like a messenger.

The road doesn't last long. He stops by the wayside as if he doesn't want to waste time on the way. The valet takes the key of the car again. We sit at a table outside of the restaurant which is middle class. There is an artificial waterfall at the back, it caress our ears with water sound. There are greens in the decoration. They move across the high platform like ivy. Breeze is going between us like winged angels. I feel the freedom here. Pure existence being purified from all the bonds. Looking into Tuğrul's eyes. I catch myself as one who is about to die at my every look.

Minutes pass. His professional attitudes are again fascinating. He has full knowledge of everything that one who sees him thinks he doesn't have any weaknesses. One thinks defeat will not go with a person looking such strong. Worry can't shake hands of these strong hands, no sorrow can defeat him. One of the elegant waiters is dealing with our table. "Of course, Sir". Te table is set, the waterfall behind Tuğrul starts babbling, water lets itself go. Like bodies let down.

Suddenly, Turğrul's face is shadowed, he has something on the tip of his tongue. I feel mercilessness in his look. He is as he is under weight, as he is in the middle of pain. A soft tone appears under his eyes, that expression says what should I do. Aimlessness on his face starts speaking.

"Dilruba, the things I am going to tell you..." he can't finish his sentence.

"I swallow. I look as if I am in the middle of a trap.

Tuğrul waits, bites his lips, pour some water into the glass, takes a shot.

"Dilruba, I am attracted to you. But..."

But... this word that changes everything is the sparkle that starts the fire. He starts the sentence again.

"I would like to be with you, with all my heart. But you and I, it is impossible. It is impossible for me. Don't ask why. But do you know, if I am with you, you would be the happiest person on the world. But it is impossible."

He is hurling himself on me like a puma which wants to pack its prey, puma is pawing my throat and opening bloody ways. These words carry breath of rattlesnake wriggling in the river to the other side. I am continuously falling down as if being attacked, as if being jumped off a cliff. The place I fell down is Tuğrul. He continues,

"Maybe I will go abroad..."

After the first shock, I say:

"So, why are we here?"

He is speaking *sotto voce* as if he has a justified reason, as if he is going to say an important reason.

"Would I tell you this in haste or on the phone... It wouldn't be suitable, I wouldn't fit me. You would think that I disappeared and be upset." Tuprul's voice is slowing down, is becoming thin and is broken. He continues with emotional voice.

"Actually, I would like to see you for a last time."

Earth is copper, sky is iron... the floor is gliding under my feet. A crazy flame is licking my sole... his eyes are turning into dark chestnuts which are about to crack... Intensive fragrance is locked into his careless look... Under my normal circumstances, If I didn't know Keşşaf and Safran, if I didn't associated them with Tuğrul, I wouldn't be affected. I wouldn't turn a hair before this bullyboy harassing my soul... If I knew Tuğrul as anybody, "I would end this scene with a careless sentence like "Did you have to be with me?" or "Being the happiest person on the world doesn't depend on another person". But now I must go back to square one and overcome this pile-up in my soul with the lightest damage. I can't decide how long this will last.

He doesn't compromise his grandee attitude. Thanks to this. He is thinking of me. I can amuse myself with this ridiculous excuse. I want to ask why? Really, why? I understand that moment that this may be the last time I see him. I want to dig out the sentences that will eat up me; what else are there in the bottom of this purulent well?

I can't get angry, I think it is because of this scent raining to my soul. Just astonishment. That's it. How can this be? Why? Where to? Questions are setting off one after another, this road doesn't get you anywhere. At that moment, Keşşaf comes into my mind agonizingly. I tell him that they tricked me. You entrapped me. You deceived me. Oh my god, what a game is this!

Going abroad is just a bluff, it isn't too hard to understand this. But I keep alive hope regarding continuing this love. I want to say something on this, he perceives the hope in my look,

"No, Dilruba, it won't be. It is impossible for me. I don't want to upset you but I have to say these things. Otherwise, I would have given you hope." He is saying this just for fun while taking a shot from his water, he is putting his glass on the white table. I am looking at the grilled pepper, rice and *adana* kebab on my plate. The mixed salad between us. None of us can touch it. It is there like a decoration. As time passes by, as the conversation goes on the green leaves fades. The sweet corns in it turn into eyes.

Thousands of millions of reason questions rush in my look. I can't ask. It can't be helped except saying have a good trip to the one who goes.

He says, "Can I call you?"

How many times were you disappointed, Dilruba? How many times did your hopes fly away? In just the same way as your mother leaving you, as your escaping your past and coming here to Ankara. And now Tuğrul is going missing.

I try not to show my true feelings, I am smiling. A rigid, lifeless, desperate smile.

"I think if it won't be, there is no need to force. I can't do more than thanking you and wishing you good luck."

This clearly means that your calling me is meaningless.

You draw the lines Tuğrul. I don't expect you to declare your love to the one you have just met. However, I would have put up with everything with you as long as this scent hypnotizes me. I would have come everywhere with you like a shadow. As long as your eyes look at me, there wouldn't have been far-near, possible-impossible for me.

I am silent, what can be said? I mustn't be like a patient for whom all cures were used up and who was still begging for a sip of theriac.

"We said let's hope for the best, so, this is the best thing"

I feel like I was disqualified. He is looking indifferent like the one who is about to cross the border. There is no pain in his look.

"Of course, this is the best."

It is impossible to leave the one you love and pass to your side, the one who loves can't do this. Loving means leaving oneself legitimating him at every result. Running towards him leaving her own ego, being one with him... The thing called self-control is flowing like water from your hands. If he goes, he has a justified reason. He must have. If he doesn't give an explanation regarding his going, he knows something.

This is a fatal moment. Everything I have learnt until now is upside down while Tuğrul is sitting triumphantly opposite me. This calm sitting, these snoopy looks, are tearing down all sounds all images; everything I have learnt up to now become obsolete. The fireworks announcing his coming are now running defeated and sad from black, like paint in the darkness of the night. But the only winner of love is love! I lost all the signs. Which way would I follow to turn to myself in your absence? Where can I find a new flame lightening the country of joy?

This must be a strange game of Keşşaf , or a meaningless dream. I am going to wake up and there won't be Keşşaf or Safran in my life. I am going to forget this ridiculous dream and deal with interpretation of life. A half-sleepy life will surround me again. I will be unrefined unfamiliar again. Oh I wish I forgot everything...

I can't help looking at the little waterfall behind Tuğrul. All the things on the table, people's voices in the restaurant are totally nonsense. Only the water of that waterfall forms meaningful syllables for me.

Tuğrul is putting his elbow on the table, holding his hands like a heart on his cheek. Then, he is tidying his long hair. He is thinking silently.

He says, "I thought a lot, we are as different as night and day."

While he was saying this, I disturb him

"You don't have to make an explanation. Really."

Now, I want to go, to go far away from everything, from myself, from Keşşaf, from Tuğrul. To run away as far as possible.

"But Dilruba, I want to call you, please don't think that I fail you."

What ridiculous, why can't he make even a real explanation. My soul is being cut with a saw,

I say, "Really, there is no need." I am sure that he won't call me. Why does a person who wrote off me call me? For what?

"I am impressed by you, I said it frankly for many times, didn't I? But being impressed isn't enough Dilruba."

He is saying this while he is cutting his *Adana* kebab with his knife. It must be a bad joke! Joyful sounds increase from the tables next to us. Vivacious sounds of the people having dinner in crowded groups are smothering our small table. Tuğrul is looking at the laughs for a moment, then he swallows. He is looking at me with shadowy sadness in his look.

Maybe he will return although he goes. This hope doesn't go away from me. This is the hottest dish I have ever had. As if it is obligatory. As if he will understand that I caved in, if I don't seem like eating... as finishing this meal means not seeing him again, I continue eating although it is like a poison.

His leaning back comfortably is telling me so much thing: I am not from your world Dilruba. There isn't enough place for feelings in my life. I can see the life if I look from your point. Every detail of my life is planified. I have no time to idle around. I haven't passed by the dangers you have been passing all your life. I am hedonist. Dilruba, there is pain your look, it frightens me. I can't stay. You understand me, don't you? Everything I said is just an excuse. You are like a meaningless billboard that I have a look and go on the roadside. Or a silent tree on the roadside. You don't have big goal in life. Nothing is important for you. The things I want from life and your nonchalance is separating us like two legs of scissor. You aren't ambitious. But I am strong and can understand the life, you see?.. I am not interested in your meaningless theories related to existence. Dilruba, you are on the very margin of life, you look everything from the back of the tribunes. But I am in the midfield, at the stage.

I am being left without a reason. Tuğrul is going clearly, blatantly, irrevocably. The happiness am about to catch is about to turn into a mirage.

The waiter gets the tea in slim glasses to the table. He is clearing the table without knowing what a hell this table is for me. Dapperly and fast. Then he asks politely, "Would you like anything else?"

Tuğrul thanks him. I am watching the scene like a dream. I hear Tuğrul's voice as a sacrifice lying on the altar. I feel that all my body is burning up to my breath. My blood is flowing into the meaninglessness pit. Into the deep, arrogant pit...

I double up there like an athlete who is out of breath in the middle of the competition. I am breathless, in cramps. The weakness of not being able to go on, flops down on me. The others go like the wind. One of them says life is fast, you are always stranded Dilruba while passing by me. Life is so pitiless as you see! Because you don't know how to play. You are so sincere that you are always out of the game. Because people don't like sincerity; this frightens them. They have the feeling that their security is under danger instinctively. You are unavoidably sent off. You can't put on an act, you place your cards on the table. So you are boring. Even your asking as "how are you" is foul. Can you say how you are by spreading your ego to whole universe, by hugging everything, with an inclusive love? What a shame! You must stay with yourself, on your side, you must learn how to say "how are you?" without tearing down your ego. You give the shirt off your back. You are giving all the wheels to the Cartwright and you are dragging in dust. You aren't dealing with the details. You, Dilruba, are not thinking the details while buying even a simple thing, you just think about buying it. You are dying for buying it but not accounting anything. And what's more, you want it like a naughty child. You buy it without thinking whether it is broken, if it is suitable for you. You don't even ask if it isn't okay, will I give it back. You just buy it. You give yourself for everything you buy. What strange relations, similarities there are between everything. How easily people save appearance, they buy the things protecting themselves. You are unconscious, you aren't with yourself, you don't exist for yourself. You choose to be the victim yourself. The word "I" stands in the wrong place in your book. It disappears somewhere below after the word "you". You write yourself in the footnotes with small font size. Repent of your sincerity. Repent of Dilruba! Don't repent of the others' sin, don't get the others' pains on your back.

Tuğrul lights up. We are about to go. We are going to turn into two strangers when we stand up and go our ways. All the conversation will be a dream. Only this scent torturing me will stay with me. This magic darkness hitting his going my head continuously will put the gun to my forehead like a gun in his hand and then will fire away at each breath.

He is looking in my eyes deeply. I shouldn't look around so soupy, I shouldn't stand apart everything. I shouldn't make him read the meaning under my look. He shouldn't hear the line space while going. He shouldn't realize the fire on my cheeks. Oh my god, what kind of soul is swimming on the face opposite me? What a pity to mess with the darkness of that bright skin! I get out of all the figures before this marvellous symmetry. This must be the biggest strike to freedom. How can I be the slave for the deep look that chains me? I want to say him don't go. Please, don't go! How can I look myself without light of your eyes your face? I need you to see myself, Tuğrul! Please, don't go. I can't hear myself without your voice, your look shows everything like endless mirrors. Let me see myself in the endless mirrors.

Last moments. Time is running. His moving hands on the table move one more time for the bill. He is writing something short and brief on the air like holding a pencil. Whatever he writes is disappearing before being read. Like the stillborn cosiness between us. The leading letter can't catch the next letter. How fast everything finishes. A warm sweet pain settles into my throat. The remaining is melting, getting drunk in the scent with his scent.

He is looking at me with the sweetest look on earth now. I am sinking into a wave which is ebbing and flowing in brown water. His voice gets the softest melodies next to him,

"I must apologize you, mustn't I? Maybe I upset you."

I can't take off the love aba which is showing me like a poor person. Yet, a shoulder movement is enough. Careless shrugging will be enough. I don't want to do it: I enjoy the pain to death. On the contrary, I wrap myself up. "Why will you apologize? For saying you can't do? You are free to do whatever you want. Well... what kind of relation is there between us, apologize for what?"

He is coming closer and leaning against the table. I am about the feel his breath. He is slapping me with his scent. He is slapping one after the other. I realize that moment, this scent has become the breath of life, the breath without him is tasteless. The funny part is that I have this scent every time with me... His approaching me that much is doomsday. I am rising up to a wrong love. He is biting his lips, he is dropping his eyes thinking over what to say.

"I thought about you Dilruba... You can't know how much I thought. Maybe, you felt this, I don't know. This is an unexpected separation. It hurts even the reason is me." he is drawing a long sigh. Is he aware of the fact that I die for his only a single breath? My look translates this sentence.

Life is really full of bullshits. I feel the scent of a person whom I met yesterday. He was seemed to be interested in me but now he is telling me that we can't have a relation. He is sitting opposite me. And what's more, he is going to disappear. For good. There is no other data except this, I try to catch a ghost.

I am talking to him as myself for the first time. I am throwing out all of the masks, seeing that you will go, seeing that you won't come back again...

I say "I know that you think about me" implying that I learnt a secret. He squints as if saying how.

He says "Do you know that I thought about you all day without missing a moment?" At that moment, I become hopeful again, maybe he can't stand, he can't go.

"Yes, I know, every time you think me..." I hesitate, he looks at my face carefully. His brown eyes mixes with the sound of the water, the world starts turning faster, oh my god...

I say, "at all those times, this scent informs me that you think me."

He is looking at me to ensure I am saying. He is trying to understand what I said.

He says "What?"

"You got it!"

Now that you go, know this! Understand what kind of pain you leave to me. This sentence is hanging on his beautiful face forever. It is a part of his look. This is my first and the last present to him.

"I know all those moments you thought me." He is reeling as if he was caught red-handed...Then he puts all the pieces together in his mind...

All the words come to an end.

I say " Let's go. Everyone should go on its own way"

I am guilty as I killed myself, I feel like this! We are setting off in the quiet and deserted city, where did all the people disappear? As if nobody wants to share this pain. Tuğrul isn't speaking. Sometimes he is watching for the mirror with thoughtful look. A thin, as thin as to be broken music is wandering inside. Music is falling and broken without touching us. Swinging, staggering, slowing down fast, lyrics are lost in the distance between us.

While looking at the road, Tuğrul is talking.

"Is that so?"

I am playing dumb.

"About what?"

"You said you felt my scent, didn't you mean this, did I misunderstand?"

I don't speak, there is no need to speak.

The ones like you can't understand this Tuğrul. The ones who jar can't make fearless sentences like these. But do you know, I am sure of your love with this scent. This scent is a licence, a title-deed. Whether you want or not you are influenced by me. You think, you miss me. You are going over every moment one by one. You are bringing me into existence by thinking; I am reviving with a fresher body with your thinking and with your scent coming to me like a messenger. I am solving your language before you. Tuğrul, I understand your sentences before you say them. There is a link between our thoughts that can't be broken. This link is connecting us at out of sight corners. These signals flowing between our souls are explaining everything. You may go wherever you want now. You are with me!

I would like to say these, but I don't say. I fell that there is no difference between speaking and not speaking. This carries me to a harder valley;

Tuğrul is only a puppet, a tong. His existence is becoming a tongue and continuously telling me something. Whether he speak or not; whether he goes or not. The irony surrounding us doesn't permit words.

I feel Tuğrul's weakness, he is departing breaking all that strong forms.

"Despite everything should I want you to wait me..."

Should I laugh or should I cry?

"Why? Are you going to join a war? are you going to be captured?"

He understands that I am kidding. Waiting for a person failing me. I must be mad. But yes, I am mad. At least for now. He is insisting on,

"I want you to wait"

I am puzzled, I think because I have seen such selfishness for the first time in my life.

I say, "Will life wait us?"

He says, "I don't know, Dilruba, I don't know."

We are entering the campus, he is showing his ID to the information and gearing up. We are flowing into a long darkness. When the lights appear, the pain is increasing, these are the last seconds. The car stops in front of the guest house slowly. It breathes as if it wants to calm down. As soon as the contact is turned off, silence flows in. Silence leaning against the word not said and not to be said.

I say, oh life, this is enough for me. Turning to Tuğrul, I say,

"Please, don't get off. It was a pleasure to meet you. But that's all."

I understand that he is hurt from his look, without regard to my request, he is getting off the car to see me off. The crowd in front of the dormitory hasn't disbanded yet. Lonely happiness is walking around later at night. Sounds are burning my ears. We are standing in front of the information cabin where everything started.

I say, "It was a pleasure to meet you, take care of yourself."

"Dilruba, please don't look at me like that, please don't go reproachfully."

"Good bye..."

It is good to cut this scene short. But it is too difficult to leave him and go. I am deceived by an illusion, this is a nightmare I see while I am awake. Why can't I help waking up? He is looking with begging eyes. He is looking as saying if only I could do.

"Maybe everything changes, I will try for this, Dilruba. Being without you will be difficult for me."

I am smile modestly. I look like trying to console him.

"Never mind, if it doesn't go, it doesn't go. If you need to go, you will go. What did we live, we turn back at the beginning of the road."

Let bygones be bygones. Your scent surrounded me. Then your eye and after that your voice. Yes, Tuğrul, you hurt me but as I was like a branch to be broken I am broken. Maybe as I didn't have a strong body. You know, one shouldn't be hurt.

"Good bye."

As I stand there I was suffering. As soon as I decapitated my neck with separation dagger and succeeded to go behind the board, I turned into a live corpse. What a big, what a useless pain is this for a person who can't explain why we can't be together!

When you succeed to define pain, you start to deny it. But it was impossible for me that moment. I am in completely dark; I went up the stairs as climbing up the peak of darkness. When I reached the floor, I saw Nergis, she was talking to some people. When she saw me, she raced next to me curiously. Without giving her the chance to speak, I said,

"Black and white became clear. He doesn't want me, he said we were different. Moreover, he could go away." Nergis wonderingly said with sadness,

"How is that?"

"That's it."

If only I hadn't met you Nergis, you, Keşşaf, Safran, Hazel, Kırlangıç and all the others. I wouldn't have been deceived. Maybe I would have been in a different condition. I could have be lively, pleased. I could have cinched life ground with my stems. But now...

22
Keep Away from me Sorrow

"When you throw away your life, the road ends." (Attar)

Tuğrul, life wasn't waiting us. With your leaving, colours of life were also keeping out from under my feet. Fire was licking my sole. I felt the same flame as the one I felt when I stepped secrets sea. If Keşşaf doesn't save me, I will be drowned in this sea, and my parts can't be found. I am progressively sinking in the water. Furthermore, your scent left flames of which is touching my back. Your scent turning me into a bag of bones is serving life islands at the same time. Small joyful islands that only we know, surrounded by sorrow. I cannot but just hide on the island. In order to take some breath I run away to you.

What a dilemma is this? Where is this adventure started with Keşşaf going? This is a process that I can't make out the end. While clipping my wings, it is giving the message that you can exist only with me... the circle I am captured in is getting smaller and smaller. It is tightening me to turn me into a small point. Then it is gowning on my flesh and soul as if it wants to clear me from the existence stage.

I can only talk to Kırlangıç. She says he will come back. If you are patient, he will come back. I have no words to say people except Kırlangıç. There are the books I look your face and have a chat, and your scent you entrusted. These two are enough for me for now. Then what will happen, how will this unbearable sky go on? You teach me be the types of communication. Your absence forms how wide streets between hearts. I say myself just let it roll off. Life is a small disappointment at some point. However, I can't make myself listen. What should I say to your coming when I laid down my arms. Would it be like this if you came before? Maybe I wouldn't care. I wouldn't think about your absence. I want to go Safran and tell all these things to her. I want to ask where my power disappeared. I want to know where that irony which provides me to compete with life, that talent is hidden. There is sorrow in my eyes. I doesn't fit me. My arms don't belong to me anymore. My legs don't know how to walk. I don't know what having any voice means. Tuğrul, what does having gestures, implications giving of reliance, being oneself mean? Where is Dilruba looking to future with hope? Words... Words are becoming smaller, deserted; they are big for my mouth, they are difficult for me. I am heavier than before. I am so overloaded with you that I can't carry myself.

In fact, I didn't believe in love fallacies. I was unable to understand that a person can suffer for another person. I thought they were nonsense. Tuğrul, I couldn't know! I didn't know you. I was unaware of you. However, universe was kneading sorrow like this. All the love in my heart was damaged. Love for Keşşaf, longing for Safran, all of them was injured. All my loves gathered itself to an incomplete perception. My life will go on its way with suspicion after that. Time will run enlarging this suspicion. Those harbours I called trust sank into wild waves. Tuğrul, I didn't know that your absence is as painful as that. I substituted an orphan who was disqualified. They took out all my candies all my toys. I was excluded from the game called life; the life spit me like a pus. Life is shouting at me "Don't get in my way, we don't want to see you." Tuğrul, we have nothing to do with you. You represent the pain, death; but we are on the side of life. So, you are going to die, Dilruba! You can't reach the life as you are on the side of death! You will die while living, what you have inside will get out of your soul bowl!

I was preparing a love homework; what ironical! I was waking up before the birds in the mornings and taking a deep the scent of Tuğrul, I was getting up with the bitter taste of being with him all day. I couldn't help looking at the huge mirror in the corridor in the mornings. I was melting a little bit everyday. My look was fading a little bit. My head, my body were becoming a little bit blurred everyday in directly proportional to the words. I was taking my books and going to a silent place before sun rose without being seen. I was trying to learn love from the books. I was passing by the life like a ghost when the day started; my presence was extending like a shadow between all sounds and images. I was like a gravedigger digging the ground with his shovel. I was watching in cold sweat the dying of life for me. Everyday, I was burying myself alive, every night I was reviving again, then dying again and again...

I died until I had only this scent in my hand. I buried myself until I turned into this scent. I was holding hope flame at every time I felt this scent; he will come back! He may return, as he is thinking of me, he will absolutely return. When I couldn't feel the scent for a few seconds, I was burying my hopes with me.

The girls... Kırlangıç, Zümrüt, Hazel, Nergis, Hüma and the others who were revolving. They did everything to restore me to life. In fact, their effort was useless. Which one could get me Tuğrul? Which one could get his news. Where was he? Nobody knew this. Everybody was dead then. What about the others, all other people? All the children were taken out of the earth; the world was deserted, the sky was meaningless. Maide called me for a number of times and asked me how I was.

I talked to her involuntarily. Everybody was turning into only one single word; he won't return! I don't know what it meant. Everybody had straight faces. Despite all those magnificent colours that Keşşaf showed me in the world of seeing, those incredible sounds that I heard in the world of hearing, I was embedded into a colourless and silent world. I didn't want anything else except going those worlds again. The real life was there; I should have gone there again getting rid of the shadows here.

For this, first I had to take heart and go to Safran. Because, Keşşaf took me out from Safran every time. This was the only thing I could do; going to Safran, who is going to meet me with myself, who is going to take me to that deepness again. I had to run away from myself with might and main. I had to run from myself to God; this was my only option to live, and also to die.

Moreover, I should have gone alone, I should have succeeded this in this pain. I should have passed that threshold just as the first day, I should have got rid of the weight on my back as if I had never passed. I should have run away from the residues of the life, from the violence of the strikes, to that Safran's small room. I should have sat on my heels at a point between two sofas looking each other, and taken to be given headlong.

I clearly realized. The fire blowing in the middle of my heart was becoming sweet; sharp and merciless whip of the scent was becoming insensible gradually, its last strikes was messing and resolving my ego, then badly turning me into itself. A new universe was existing in my heart with each breath, I was leaving it with my each breath out, then again was banding together, the separation between these two breaths was turning into an insufferable longing. The scent captured me totally. I could neither see the future nor past. All my senses turned into a guard watching for the rest of the single scent. I should have gone out of the flames, I should have turned up Safran's iron door like a fireball. I should have stand there and hoped for help silently. All my veins should have said "Help, save me from this desperate state! Give me theriac! Give me and my breath comes back to me. Turn me away from this dream which became the pain itself while killing my pains!

I was afraid. I was afraid of Safran's touching on my sadness as if to say "Yeah, this is an illness". This possibility was preying on my mind. Or, I was afraid because I didn't know how I could bear if she lapsed into silence with sorrowfully while I was expecting her to say "don't worry about them". This could have been a deep suicide. If Safran would have been in a silence equal to "Fight your corner!", my illness would have increased thousand of time. This scent puzzle would have become an impossible load to overcome. But if she didn't say anything and just smiled, or if she said "It'll all come out in the wash!", I would have laughed away with her. Because, if she said that it would pass, it meant it would really pass.

I watched the scope desperately from the window of my room in these dilemmas. The sun was about to set. There was pinkness which was increasingly getting heavier in the scope. Darkness covering all dirt was swimming. It was becoming cool, the rambler all day out under the sun breathed a sigh of relief. All the room windows were wide open, breeze touching the soul was wandering inside. This was only giving me pain; the game was going on with all its mercilessness. The breeze strikes of which was sharpening with the scent of Tuğrul was turning into a scream for me, each scream meant one more broken vein for me; the air I was breathing like sudden impacts, some more pain, some more annihilation, some more melting.

I couldn't confess myself; I was dying for this scent. In order to feel that scent, I was looking for clean floors, life holes that fresh air enters. Although I knew that none of them prevent, I was running away from all perfumes, all food smell, all human breaths except that fascinating scent. I was just turning my head towards the direction where the smell was coming. I knew that this direction was going to an unhealthy way. As if I was examining whether Tuğrul was thinking me or not, I was looking for that scent every time I wanted. Like a newborn baby looking for her mother. I was finding the scent, like a lamb in a herd of hundreds of sheep finding its mother by smelling. I was moving away everything including my own scent and breathing it in with despair like a hashish addict seeking for hashish. As the days went on, only this scent remained from life. I was turning into that aromatic, sharp scent and I was granting my presence on purpose day by day.

I personified this scent. The things I experienced when I felt that scent for the first time, reeking of scent to my hands now turned into a permanent reality. My whole body, the things I touched. I was leaving this scent like a signature to the pencils, to the door handles I held, to the glasses I touched, to the bed I lay in for a few minutes. The scent was feeding me, quenching my thirst; I was turning into an entire love as my trachea filled with this scent. My laughter, my blubber depended on this scent. I must be mad. Who could I tell this?

The sun went down. I don't know how long I watched the scope in front of the window. It got dark, we were in the bed of the stars. I was thinking about the things Keşşaf told me while telling the light. He told me "You will take the photo of the sky on your chest". Keşşaf, what a dark sky this is! Tell me what photo I will take in such darkness! Will I take the photo of this dauntless loneliness barring? Or this steep desolateness? Will I take the photo of this scent when Tuğrul's going separated my life into two like a knife? Will I tell the pain burning me with love? You say, photograph is the poem of light and then you take all the light out of my life. With which light?

While I was drawing the curtain, a sound echoed in the room saying "406 Dilruba, you have a visitor." Although the woman at the information desk was shouting, it wasn't echoing as it was when Tuğrul came. It wasn't dispersing at the dim ceiling like a firework. It was just like a murmur, silent, shy, reluctant. It was an obligatory call, growling rolling and returning among the sizzle. I was again going downstairs curiously, what if it's Tuğrul?

It was Müdrik. He came and couldn't find me. He left me messages a few times. I threw them without reading. How could I get rid of him now? He was here hale and hearty. He was wearing that white shirt again. He was saying that he was wearing those white shirts while working. I caught a more matured expression on his face. As if his features were settled. There was slack water in his wise, blue eyes. I am approaching slowly shuffling my slippers.

He doesn't move. But he generally walks and greets me overjoyed. At the first moment, I am saying something wrong. It doesn't fit me, it doesn't fit anybody. It is a shame.

"Welcome Tuğrul!"

Oh my god, how could I do this? What kind of folly is this?

He hides his displeasure.

He says smiling "I think, you are waiting for someone"

"I'm sorry Müdrik. I was taken unawares"

He says, "Whatever is on the dervish's mind, it comes out through his mouth" but this time with a clear complaint.

"The one you are waiting for didn't come, manage with me this time!"

With a voice wanting him not to go on,

"I'm sorry, I am not waiting for someone, I just stumbled."

He says, "We are *Majnun* this evening."

As I can't find anything to say, I go towards the same corner we always sit. Müdrik is sitting in front of the portrait of "scream". I see that there is no more calm expression on his face. He resents me.

He says , "Welcome Tuğrul, haa! How important he is..."

I say, "Please don't go on talking about it, I think it isn't an important thing. Let's forget about it." It is better to shift ground.

"How are you?"

Thanks to god, he doesn't go on.

"I'm fine, but what happened to your hands?"

Müdrik is asking the spots of pen. Palms and backs of my two hands are full of spots.

"I was writing my homework..."

"Are you writing your homework on your hands, you have been in a muddle since I saw you.

Müdrik has got good jokes.

I politely say, "So I am an author writing on her hands."

He confirms mercifully.

He says "Yeah, what a beautiful author you can be, it is just for you."

I say, "What will I write, what is there good enough to write?

He says, "For example, you may write about me..."

"Okay. I promise you I will write about you if I write something."

Müdrik is leaning back and crossing his legs. The ambiance in the canteen is as usual. People are sitting on the tables, drinking their tea and the tables are full of books. There is a crowded innocuous group next to us.

He says, "You are emaciated, but women like losing weight, and the ones who can't lose weight come to me." When he looks considerately, curiosity appears in this greenish eyes,

"What's wrong with you, you have changed."

I half open the shadows on my face, I shouldn't show anything to him.

I say, "I'm OK, everything is the same."

"Does Uncle Haşmet call you?"

"My father? He has called me once this term. But he calls every term."

Müdrik is curling his lower lip. The doesn't believe in what he says later.

"Maybe he has things to do. Holiday is coming, what are you going to do?"

I say, "I am going to join summer school. You know, I failed."

"So we can see each other, I am pleased to hear this."

I want to get over those glances full of questions,

I say "What did you do? How is it going with poem?"

He says, "Oh, poem. Yeah, it is a good job to understand poem. I was abroad. I couldn't read much."

I say "Oh, really. How nice."

"Yeah, I was in France. It was good."

There is something strange with Müdrik but I can't name it. His face is clearer. There is a light shining on his forehead.

I say, "There is something strange with you but I don't know what."

He is glad that I made out this, he is lifting his eyebrows,

"Is that so? So tell me what it is? Make a guess?"

"I think you look happy, but there must be something more than this."

He says as if he doesn't want to tell, "Never mind me, first you tell, you came over, you look different, unhappy."

"You say the doctor realize."

"I don't say that, why are you so sad? Is it the thing I guess?"

"You were right Müdrik.. I got into deep water. You were right to wake me up. I think I took my measure. There is nothing else."

He is bending his head gently as if saying is that so, now he is looking at me like a father. There is a father who is worried about his daughter in front of me.

He says, "Do you know that the easiest way to learn the rights is doing wrong. But isn't it too early to say I took my measure? I think you should wait for it"

I am standing up to get tea for him and for myself. I am returning with tea in paper cups on a plastic tray and some sugar.

He says, "You are so hospitable." The vapour of the tea is rising up the surface. Clouds are passing through his eyes. Suddenly, he becomes serious,

"Look around Dilruba. How do the people live? Enjoy your days, do sports, you can do many different things, join them, look in front of you, this sadness doesn't fit you. You won't be at this age again. You are closing yourself in the sorrow well unnecessarily. What happened? Wait don't say, Tuğrul disappeared in a puff of smoke!

He is taking a swig from his tea and says,

"I won't say I told you." I wonder how he can be sure, how he makes sure everything. I am always the one who is warned and who is sad with him. I have nothing to do except approving this. Müdrik's wide angel relaxes me. He is holding my head from my chin and showing me the world again. He is doing this skilfully. But I know that this won't relieve my pain. Whatever Müdrik says, the reality that Tuğrul won't come back will make me miserable.

I don't speak. Müdrik is holding his thumb as if showing something on the table and saying,

"A kind man never goes that fast, especially if there is a woman next to him, he shouldn't go. He doesn't ride for a fall."

While bending the teaspoon out of shape, I am saying, "In fact, he wasn't that fast."

He is nodding his head as if to say you are protecting him.

I say, "He could go abroad."

"Why did he come if he was to go? Don't be sad, he wasn't a brave man. Anyway, How many times did you see him?"

I prattle, "I saw him three times, three evenings."

His pupils going between green and blue are gazing at me with astonishment.

"So, you didn't even see him in daylight. Is Tuğrul a vampire which appears only at nights?"

I say, "Yes, I didn't see him. But please don't talk about him like this"

Müdrik smiles as if to say shame on you.

He suddenly says, "Do you know my ex-wife came home a few times and left message when I was in France. She wants me to call her. He called the clinic many times."

I can't believe.

I say, "I thought she left you, what has happened? Why does she want to return?"

He is looking out and talking while sinking in the darkness,

"If only I knew... I have no idea. Maybe she regrets..."

I say, "Didn't you call her, maybe she needs something, maybe she is in a difficult situation."

"She should have thought about it before."

I say, "So the reason of your happiness is this."

He says "It's not about that. I think I became more religious than before." He is caressing his neck and then tidying his collar,

"I am trying to learn prayer. I think I am changing a bit."

"You are surprising me."

He says, "It's normal I think, everybody must do it."

"So, what are you going to do? Aren't you going to call her?"

He says, "Who? My ex-wife? I don't think so. She started a new life, she wrote off. It's too late. "

"You forget the one who doesn't come in time, Dilruba. Believe me, time works wonders. Pains stop."

I said that I didn't think so to myself. This pain won't stop. How can this be? He said as if he heard me,

"Maybe it seems impossible, your pain is too new. They will separate in time. That time it will be easier to cope with. Believe me. You will laugh away."

These words are crashing into my drum and turning back, it is impossible to accept. Longing marsh is pulling me down to the bottom day by day.

Müdrik says, "Shall we take the air?". How much I need fresh air now. We are going out. We are passing through the stony path that we walked with Tuğrul without speaking. Then, we are walking on the pavement. Fresh air is filling my heart with that scent again. I am closing my eyes for a moment. When we reach the woodland where the light of street lamp is faded and the moon light is reigning, Müdrik says,

"I bought you a present form France. I hope you like it."

I say, "You shouldn't have bought."

He is taking out a little elegant box from his pocket.

We are under the shadow of pinewood. I am opening the velvet box with bated breath, Müdrik is looking into my eyes. A little ring is shining under the soft light. I am looking at his face as if to ask what it means.

"Dilruba, Let's marry. I know it isn't a suitable time to say this."

He doesn't know what I live. He doesn't know how depressed I am. Without taking the ring from the box, I close the box.

"It's really not a suitable time." Click sound comes from the box while closing.

Müdrik says with disappointment, "In fact, I thought to take you a good place."

He says other things but I don't hear him, I only hear howling. I feel like I am to smother. I am sitting on the pavement as falling. Oh my god, what a scenario, what a merciless fiction? I can't keep calm anymore. The life's being unbalanced is depressing me. I am starting to cry, I am bursting into tears. Distress is falling down burning my face, leaving marks.

I am holding the red velvet box tight in my hand. I am starting to sob. This ring is drawing the picture of my defeat. This ring is telling me the truth that I don't want to accept, Dilruba, Tuğrul won't come back. You are waiting in vain. As you see, it is a vain hope. Life has different lens for you.

Müdrik is sitting next to me.

He says, " You are just having a bad dream. Dilruba, you will wake up. You will recover."

"But you must resist him, you must stand out, please don't cry."

Sniffing, I am whimpering,

"Yes, a nightmare. They deceived me, they are playing a trick on me."

Thousands of things are passing through my mind; Maide's calling me insistently, my paying no attention, then, Safrans attractive posture, voice, my going for seeing Keşşaf, the experiences on the way, Hevida and her group, The pools in the yard, Keşşaf's passing by like a stranger, Keşşaf's whispers day by day, his taking me out, the magnificent state of the Cavalry in the arena, those applauds, Gülistan, I see that heart Keşşaf is holding in his hand, I hear the heartbeat, then that difficult moment I came across with the Nafs, before that, the night that I felt the love of the particles. Kırlangıç's saying that Tuğrul will come back. All of them must be a hallucination. All of them.

He says, "What next? Only, your nerves are shot. You need to relax."

He doesn't know. He doesn't know what a loneliness lies under this sorrow, in what a mess I am.

"I learnt a new prayer Dilruba: For us Allah sufficient, and He is the best Guardian. Say this and get rid of." That moment, something happens. The fire licking my sole is going up to my chest like a wave. My chest starts heaving, shaking fast with the glow of that wave. I feel as if bellows. This bellows is blowing air to the fire and the fire is strengthening. This prayer is blossoming at the same time at the most sensitive part of my heart. I hear this prayer as if hearing from the God, as if the first time I heard. But I had heard it from Safran before. While Prophet İbrahim is going towards the fire after being catapulted by Nemrut, Angel Gabriel comes near him and asks, "Do you want anything from me?" Prophet İbrahim replies with this prayer, "For us Allah sufficient, and He is the best Guardian". Thereupon, the God orders the fire "Hey fire, be cool and peacefully to İbrahim"

I am closing my face with my hands and crying, breathing hard like a painful dog. I am collapsing in moaning. This time, I am crying as I am falling apart taking refuge in this prayer. The fire is burning me as I can't say this prayer. Because of this going on living is such agonizing.

Müdrik says, "Come on, wipe your tear. It is twelve o'clock. The doors are about to be closed."

I am unaware of the time. There is none on the streets, there are only one or two people walking fast towards to dormitory. I am standing up wiping my tear at the same time with Müdrik.

Saying "I am sorry, please take this" I am giving the little velvet box. He is taking it without saying anything. We are approaching to the door of the dormitory which is about to be closed running over the soft light surrounding us. The woman is grumbling looking at me and Müdrik, "You young people behave yourself, I won't take you in next time." Then, she is catching my eyes, she realizes my bleary eyes and doesn't insist.

Müdrik calls after me, "Dilruba, I will come again as soon as possible, be well, please"

23
World of Scents

> Ohh, rose, I know that I got no chance out of you,
> Others put on the attar of rose even if the bulbul dies
> (Nevres-I kadim)

Next evening was the deadline for love homework. When I knocked at the door and entered the room, Prof. Altuğ was looked at me over his eyeglasses as if to say what. Then he said "You may leave it on my table." I left the homework in the transparent file on his table without saying anything. I had to wait the afternoon to go to Safran. I had no other chance than listening to the lesson as if I was listening with headache and swelling eyes and waiting for the afternoon. When time was up, I started walking towards Safran's house under the burning sun.

When love combines with self-destructive feelings like obsession, anger, self-pity, it becomes dangerous. Man starts losing his ability to realize his feelings and ability to express them as he crumples himself. The worst part of negative thoughts and loneliness of a person in my condition is leaving the person inactive. But the most painful is that it causes self-destructive perspective. But with a nuance! While you are disappearing, love puts single subject of love into your place carefully. So, while love is sacrificing everything, it wants you to add yourself to this everything. It prefers a smooth solitude to honour the heart. And thus, love is clearly denying itself. The only way to reach the safe valley on this complicated road is to know that the love for a person never takes you to a safe valley. As loving the opposite sex will be a kind of betray to true love; illusions of figurative love will absolutely drive you into a corner. Just as the scent is driving me into a corner mercilessly. The shortest way to get rid of this is being aware of the reality that the wide range from language of feelings to body language is trying to say, in short increasing awareness.

That's why I was going to Safran. To hear what everything wants to say to me. The starting and ending points of this maze is a single place: Safran. At least, it seemed as it is from my point of view. Only she could trace the signs of this painful love compass, footprint of this thin and sharp iron foot. My remedy hand could only reach her. The starting and ending point of the clear water was Safran for me.

I reached Safran's house at about two. I felt that I dived into a clear ring. That flower, those smiling eyes of the *pelargonium* which were in front of the window just like the first day. Dead flowers of the violet, buds which started to flower, cheerful voice of the bell. All of them did good for me. Life was in its most natural course by itself as if to say life is simple. Only, I was away from them. To come closer, I rang the bell hoping everything to return normal for me.

Safran's daughter Didem opened the door. After greeting me, she invited me in. We were at the same age with Didem. Kırlangıç told me that she was going to marry at an early date. As she said she was about to marry someone she loved. I realized that how her face resembled Safran while I was getting into stepping the little hand knitted mat. In the mean time, I thought what a great felicity to be daughter of Safran, being so close to her, being her child that she was wrapping in cotton wool. It was impossible for one like me whose life is full of chaos not to envy her. She was a person who was having breakfast happily right beside her mother; all the beauty that I had never had were such ordinary for her. Her simple and meaningful life was surrounded confidently, carefully protected when she is with Safran. Didem was sometimes jealous of her mother from us suddenly, I felt this. I witnessed that her mother's showing concern for us embittered her. Didem was a happy person; it is impossible to be happy if you are Safran's daughter.

When I entered the small room, first I saw Safran's face which is equal to doomsday for me. She was sitting and reading something on the small sofa. The light entering through the window was brightening her face surrounded by the scarf, her moving lips were murmuring calmly like saying a prayer. When she saw me, she closed the book and said,

"Dilruba, where have you been? Welcome."

I perched at the end of the sofa saying "Thank you". I wished that I hadn't gone alone. The loneliness that I carry with me, my being alone with her was distressing. I was at the point where the words to be said finished in front of her. I started to pray for some people to come here and to get lost in the crowd.

Oh my god! This distance was killing me, how remote Safran's look, her attitude was! She was looking up and down considerately. I was turning over and over long and puffy feather of the key holder which looked like the tail of a squirrel. Because of the sweat of my hands feather of the key holder was getting heavy as if it got wet. Somehow, I couldn't think putting into my bag. I wasn't aware that I walked all the way with this key holder in my hand. Safran said, showing the key holder in my hand,

"Did they start plucking?" Knots overlapped in my throat with this sentence. Then, she was smiling. This was a smile disclosing the irony in my state. I couldn't say anything. I was again expecting warmth of a mother. The same attention I always attracted. Safran's wide glance watching the high seas was also involving my state; I knew this, I witnessed this for many times. Although I didn't know how, I knew that she knew my state. But I still wanted to tell, to tell with my head language... Taking my courage in both hands, I said,

"Safran. I need help." I said this with a begging voice. My eyes were filling with tears and I was biting side of my lower lip.

She said, "Tell me what happened?" She was smiling. This was a sentence saying I know what you are going to tell but if you want tell me.

Just then, Didem entered the room and sat next to her mother. I didn't want this at all, Didem's seeing my state, hearing the thing I was going to tell. She would probably feel sorry for me. But I had no other chance.

I was ashamed deadly. But I couldn't see any way out other than telling, at least mentioning with one or two sentences. I started talking looking at the patterns of the rug on the floor.

"There was a person, a Sufi. We met only a few times." I raised my gaze to Safran's eyes for a short time. She became serious. Bowing her head in the meaning of go on, she said,

"Hı hıı."

"Sister of a Sufi who you know introduced us." Safran didn't know Maide but she knew her elder sister, even she loved her and gave importance to her. She was talking about her respectfully.

She said, "Yes."

"But somehow, nothing happened." What a ridiculous sentence it is! I was failing at saying. Safran was looking at my face seriously. There was anxiety on her face, and her cheeks became clear with red informing this anxiety.

"I don't know, he may go abroad, and also ..." I was thinking how to say, I was looking for the kindest and the least harmful word for expressing my being rejected but I hadn't had such a word in my mind.

I said, "As he said, we are too different."

Safran was silent. She wasn't saying, "don't worry, you will recover or you will forget" as I was afraid. She was silent with a cold expression. Didem was looking at me folding her hands on the chest. I was looking at Didem and Safran and then I was bending my face to the patterns of the rug on the floor.

Then, the bell rang. Sharp and strong sound of the bell separated the tension of the room. Didem passed by me and went to open the door. I took the advantage of this moment and said,

"I don't know how to forget him."

Safran leaned her head forward and her expression became sharp as if she wanted to mention an indestructible reality, she only said,

"There is God." Safran was saying this sentence as if saying this to someone who had never ever heard in her life. She opened her eyes with fear as if giving a secret which hadn't come to light. She was turning the knife with her glance. Safran called me to believe in god, now she was calling me to remain close to Him and move away from myself.

It was Gül Hanım. She greeted us and sat at her usual place and leaned back to the corner of the sofa. Gül Hanım was someone from the house. She was a member of the family for Safran. Then Safran greeted Gül Hanım and then continued her speech, but this time she was murmuring,

"I can be also pushed, ha" At first, I couldn't understand this sentence. She was talking to me with my language. Safran was inviting me to accept this pushing and meeting it with maturity. I was more miserable than ever before. I was staggering as if tumbling down the stairs. Waves continuously pushing me down were rising. After Tuğrul's leaving me, Safran was giving me the cold shoulder. All of the doors were shut to my face one by one. Gül Hanım looked at Safran as if trying to understand what was happening. Safran lead forward and turned to her and said loudly,

"Melancholy"

Gül Hanım's face fell with doubt. I felt myself as I committed a terrifying offense, I bent on the sofa. Gül Hanım said looking at me as if a patient who couldn't be recovered,

"May God heal you" Horrible humane sentiment appeared on her cute face. Was I ill, was I mad? Was this melancholy something like Black Death, leprosy or cancer? Was I really in such trouble? Then, Gül Hanım said showing mercy,

"For God's sake, don't worry, everything will be fine." And Safran confirmed her.

"Don't worry princess, don't worry, if god let, everything will be fine."

Didem held the floor and said,

"Everything will be fine but it hurts you so much"

The place called Ground zero must be a place like this. But I was lower than ground zero. I was celebrating the victory of defeat at the bottom. All of the defeats were flying at me, everything will be fine, nothing will be fine, heal, melancholy, being pushed, sentences were circling on my head. The sentence "There is God!" was rescuing me from the impacts of these sentences. I was dying, was death so much painful? I was hurt as much as a woman suffering child-birth pains. Then Safran said something I didn't expect,

"But please don't be alone with him, OK?"

Tuğrul had published everything already and went saying no. What did this mean? I said that he had gone just a while ago!

I was about to say this I heard that unknown voice again,

"Oh love student..!"

This calling voice... Cavalry was standing in front of me with his hazel eyes, white head-dress and green clothes. He was on his white horse and holding headstall of my black-maned red horse. It was the white horse that he took me to the Cabülka, to love or world of hearing and then to world of seeing, the horse we passed over the secrets sea, and reached to the arena, the horse I flowed from country to country, we passed through the forests, the horse jumping over the rivers like an antelope... the horse flying from a valley to valley like an eagle. Cavalry is smiling scattering the sparkles in his hazel eyes in the same way when he was throwing javelin in the arena. He is burning me with piercing look behind his veil. There is dagger in his waist as usual.

"I thought that you missed your horse. Come on, get up the horse. But before it, clean your eyes from that sorrow. It's not you."

Hey Keşşaf, do you think that sorrow remains if you look at me in such a way, if you come me! I am ready to go to the last point, the last valley, the last world that soul can step with you. Keşşaf, my reason to live! How all the loves melt with your existence! Tuğrul or the other people drop the map beside you. Take whatever I had, my entire existence, my entire soul! My head is yours! Take out whichever you want, if you want, my heart beats in your hands as it was beating in the world of hearts! Order me to come, the world will burn with only a letter of yours. Only you can interpret the world we are in! This magic will only be solved with your single look! Grow me up, make me sleep in your compassion lap, then make me walk wherever this road goes!

In fact, how much I missed my red horse! I last left it in the arena! I suddenly remembered that night. I remembered that we were running full gallop under the heavy rain, under the flashes crazily. I visualized the magnificent yeast at the arena and the mercilessly struggle at that night. First I caressed its black mane. Then I inspired its smell. Long afterwards, I realized where I was. This was a face land. Thousands of ten thousands of faces were hung around. There were all kinds of the expressions, gestures and shapes of a person. They were like pictures; eyes of all faces were looking at me but I wasn't afraid. There was a broad mirror under my feet. This was a mirror which was shining as far as eye could see and where the hung faces were reflected. Cavalry was shining with a different vitality among these faces. Without getting mixed with these faces, he was looking at me and smiling.

He said "Don't look at the faces, they are just picture" and added "Come on, Keşşaf is waiting for you, we are going to the world of scents"

This time, I hold the headstalls skilfully. Thoroughbred white horse of the cavalry was opening the way to me among thousands of faces like a light. We were running full gallop like flying. These faces, these expressions, the faces of women and men were like real. They were even like alive. Moreover, there were beautiful faces. I was afraid, what if Tuğrul's faces had been among these faces? I was trying to see him. I was looking at the faces passing by me fast if I could see his brown eyes. If I couldn't see him, I was watching for the next one hopefully. Blond faces, brown tufted faces, the ones with blue eyes, dark-skinned... Oh my god, it was as if faces all of the people on the earth had been here. Faces of old people, faces of clear skinned teenagers, smiling faces, the ones looking sad, the ones crying, the surprised ones, happy expressions, meaningless faces with glassy... What the hell is that supposed to mean? Who were those people?

After a while, I felt a deep shame for trying to see Tuğrul's face while going after cavalry. The thing I did wasn't fidelity. But whatever I did I couldn't get rid of seeing the faces, their faces reflected the road which was a huge mirror; where could I look? Then, I started to look at Cavalry's white horse. We two were flowing among these faces, his existences was cutting the faces like a light and opening the road. As we gained speed first the faces started to flow and then to melt. I couldn't choose the expressions, the shapes of the faces. I could only see a light, the white brightness behind the hooves of the Cavalry's horse.

Son after, faces turned into a long line because of the speed, a long line flowing under and by me. This was like a photo taken from a car going fast. Then, we started to through straight lines and moving mist. Later, these lines and mist disappeared; we started to go on a pure white mirror. The mirror under us was just reflecting us now. Just then, I couldn't see my own reflection. He was the only one on this endless light! I must have been lost among the flowing, melting faces.

Later, cavalry pulled his magnificent image over me. He was looking with his big and dark hazel eyes. I could see him from every corner, he said,

"If you look at the faces in such a way, you will get lost in them. Do you know what the punishment of looking at a different face other than the beloved when you are with him is? Who are you looking for when you are with us?"

I went as red as a beetroot with this sentence, this was shameful. I shouldn't have looked at the faces. Cavalry said with glory "You are the person who you are looking for in this world!"

I could see myself nowhere. However, there were mirrors at all four sides. Where did I, my face get lost? I tried to speak, I couldn't find my voice. I was in an absence. I was trying to see my hands holding the headstalls dismally as if I was having a nightmare and couldn't wake up. My red horse was in the absence with me. Then suddenly something unexpected happened. I started to hear only my heart beats, my heart was beating crazily to exist again, it started to make point strikes in my larynx. It was pumping blood to my invisible body with each shot, my veins where blood was passing started to appear in the mirror one by one. At that moment I existed as only conscious; I didn't have my eyes seeing the mirror! I was in pain as if every part of my body was being cut, I was trying to find my way in veined absence. Every vein reflecting in the mirror was existing with pain. Despite this pain, I was begging to exist, to become visible again! Absence was an unbearable pain! I said to myself, please, if I could see myself again!

Cavalry who was on its white horse called me,

"Do you want to see yourself? First know yourself!" He stopped for a while and then continued,

"Keşşaf is waiting for you, go!

Then, an unbelievable thing happened, as all these things are believable? When cavalry disappeared, I stood lonely with that scent I felt very often recently. This was Tuğrul's scent! What was he doing here? He found me here. Melancholy was such a thing. But this scent was petrifying me. I was indescribably dragging me. How come I could be captive of this scent? I was again drinking that magic elixir that I filled with each breath. My veins which became apparent in the mirror with my heart beats became more visible. Then I saw the skin that those veins wear. I was slowly existing. And what's more, I was existing with this scent! I was in eternal happiness. Keşşaf was creating me with this scent. I said to myself, so that's the truth. I closed my eyes, I started to think that Tuğrul was my fate; I was existing with his scent. However, the mirror was drawing Tuğrul's face instead of my image at that moment. When I opened my eyes, I saw reflection of my image: Tuğrul! Every beat of my heart drew Tuğrul to the mirror instead of me.

That moment, I understood that I was in disastrously trouble. I was afraid of seeing Tuğrul for the first time. He was on the red horse, he was holding the headstalls with his strong hands. Moreover, I was smiling him. That moment, I realized that I had missed Tuğrul very much. A hand was throwing coal to me with a shovel, that coal was continuously being blew, it was flaming up. Then I looked for myself again. I just saw him. I told myself "but no way out". The image in the mirror was saying "but it's impossible": Tuğrul. I was saying, "it's impossible!" it was repeating at the same time "it's impossible!"

Cavalry left me as Tuğrul in the middle of the immense mirror and went. So, the punishment of looking at a different face other than beloved was this:

Being imprisoned an endless loneliness in the face you looked, on top of it being as him, being alone being sentences to live in this loneliness that can't find its own face! Staying as the face you looked at a place where any images, any sounds weren't. Being sentenced to what you are looking at other than beloved! So punishment of every sin was in its kind! Oh my God!

Before disappearing, didn't Cavalry say, "Keşşaf is waiting for you, go"? Where could I go in this situation? I made my horse bad-tempered by turning the headstalls from side to side in a state of fear and despair. No! The horse got used to Dilruba found Tuğrul strange! It was rearing up, scattering its mane left and right, neighing and trying to throw off me, in other words Tuğrul as if to say who is on me. It turned into a raging bull. I was holding the headstalls tightly, leaning towards its head, and was saying "It's me, calm down" trying to subdue my fear. What the hell is that? My voice is Tuğrul's voice. When the horse heard Tuğrul's voice, it was sure that the one riding it wasn't Dilruba. It reared up and threw me, in other words Tuğrul away at once... Red horse was saying me with this action that I couldn't keep going as Tuğrul.

This downfall was more than the pain I felt when I fell of the horse at the very beginning of the way to Cabülka. I fell off as myself, Dilruba and when I lifted my head I saw Cavalry. He said "Are you OK?". Now, I couldn't see anybody pitying for me. Furthermore, when I fell off, I wasn't in melancholy yet. I was deemed to be at peace with myself. I hadn't rejected myself yet. I opened my eyes before lifting my head on the place where I fell off, it was me! I saw myself everywhere. Dilruba! I said Thanks to God. It is again me! What a beautiful thing being myself again is! But the road that I had to pass for being myself was too long.

Although I hadn't seen myself at the place I fell down, this huge mirror cleared out under my body and my head, the reflections around were cleaned. It got dark as if its foil fell off, lost its brightness. It remained only as a glass. I couldn't see my red horse anywhere. Now, everywhere an eye could see was entire glass. I tried to stand up, meanwhile, I saw the shadow of that palace which was reflecting on the window under my legs. While I was lifting my head with astonishment, I was saying "Can such a thing happen?" The thing which was impossible to believe was this! A glass palace! This palace was so big that there weren't sides, corners of the columns; it was so high that end of the dome wasn't seen. Maybe there were hundreds, thousands of balconies, bay windows; all of them were made of glass. There were bottles which were over my head in the wide yard of the gracious palace; they looked like tear bottles. They had thin and curled bodies and narrow necks; their top was in oval shape made of crystallized glass. There was a golden inlaid wide long glass door. When I approached to this mysterious door I caught various types of scents. They are marvellous scents attracting me like a magnet.

As I approached to the golden inlaid giant glass door, its wide wings which were at least ten, fifteen meters high moved slowly. As I approached it, it was being opened. When I reached at the door I got the idea that this door consisted of the scent. Later, the scent turned into incense and started to pull me into the palace. When I entered the palace, I found myself at a wide corridor consisted of the scent; the scent was turning into two stairs which were inter-penetrating each other and wriggling upwards, then it ended at a stage upstairs. Wherever I turned, I saw big rooms full of glass bottles, scented tablets, tulip vases scenting, dove bottles, musk and amber censers. All sides of this palace were transparent, so everything was like coming over people and fragile but nothing was moving. As I continued walking at the wide corridor consisting of scent, I started passing by camphor and henna smelling transparent and substance-less walls. These walls also looked like smoke or vapour. Substance-less shelves with hundreds of little bottles and smelling tablets made me think that here was a giant store. It seemed to me that these hundreds of little bottles were in the air by themselves. Each scent was opening the door of a little palace. Various types of aromas, various balsams, perfume and essences, smelling oils, fumes, pomanders... None of scents was preventing me from catching the other and also they weren't making my breathing difficult. Even none of them was mixing each other. Another censer door opening to a wide saloon appeared ahead. In the same way as I was entering the palace, the door was half-opened as I stepped and as I approached, it was opened. That moment I saw him: Keşşaf was there. Smelling resins and burned aromas were giving off their smell as if to say "welcome" to the people entering this wide saloon. Then, smelling balls, incenses, balms, rosemary, *nerol*, honeysuckle, sweet basil, thyme, clove and lavender shells... all of these scents, the magic injected to my soul were turning my head, was doubting my consciousness. After passing these scents, I found myself in a department full of hundreds kinds of perfume bottles. I saw Keşşaf, but everywhere was mirror so it was making my perception difficult. As I tried to approach him, the road was getting long. In which room was he in?

This part looked like a scent archive. All the walls of the room where are colourful perfume bottles were full of these little bottles. There were cream vases, face powders, foams, lotions, even pomades. When I went ahead some more, I understood what the thing in my visual space was; they were scented candles. These candles constituted a long twisting pathway. Their scent was different from each other, some of them has basil, some of them has saffron, some of them has pure rose, some of them has violet scents... After passing the twisting pathway, I saw Keşşaf more clearly. I passed by sandalwood and jasmine scents, nightingale's eye vases and bowls, smelling sticks, breeze consisting of all these scents. Then I saw Keşşaf at the big table next to musk and amber scents behind rose water flask and scented pastes lined up in rows. He was sopping quill pen in the ink mixed with musk and amber and was writing something on the tissue paper and putting it into thick books bound with silk and damask. He was wearing a silvery cotton collarless shirt. His amber hair was falling on his shoulders as he leaned, his forelocks on his forehead were moving with the scent breeze.

I watched his beauty for a while. He was finding the thing he was looking for easily among hundreds of little bottles which were like hanging in the air. When he opened the bottle, a new note was being added to all the scents music. Then Keşşaf wrote some more lines sopping the quill pen in the golden ink. I was under the impression that Keşşaf was writing the poem of that scent. This was a long poem written on the thin colourful tissue papers first with musk and amber and then with gold. There were scents that I didn't know in the little diamond and ruby inlaid brass boxes among the thick books bound with silk and damask in front of him. I was catching them but I didn't know what they were. There were many other things like scented glass rosaries, scented jade rings, scent jugs ruby inlaid decorated with topaz, old pumping perfume bottles made of crystal, scented cotton in oysters on this table where was vapour consisted of scents...

Keşşaf left the quill pen into the ink bottle, lifted his head slowly and we caught each other's eyes, and he said,

"Welcome to the world of scents Dilruba, come closer!" I moved one or two steps towards the table where the scent incenses were rising. When I came closer to the table, I saw that the table was made of scents. Everything on this substance-less table was hung in the air. I said quietly,

"Thank you". Not catching his eyes wasn't easy. His look was making my heart beat fast, my entire soul was surrounded with excitement. I felt like jelly when dazzling scents were added to the piercing look in his eyes. His eyes were turning into hazel because of the sparkling glass around. Scent as cold as ice passed from his thin and slim face. This scent was such hard and cold that it was almost crystallized before this face, it was frozen. Keşşaf wasn't looking at my face now. He was taking his eyes away from me, he was still as if to say "something came between us." A few seconds later, he said,

"Do you know, Dilruba, the best way to obtain the scent is distillation. Just like the perfect man is reached by distillation."

I said, "I didn't know that."

"Well, do you know what parsing , stilling him is?"

I shook my head as if to say no. I was just standing there among thousands of scents in a glass palace in the world of scents.

He said, "The thing distilling man is pain."

This sentence was hurting my heart. I hung my head, and again said,

"I didn't know." I must confess that, I was looking for Tuğrul's scent since I came to this glass palace. All the scents on the earth were here so his scent must be somewhere here. Then I remembered how I disappeared suddenly while coming here, how I got lost in endless mirrors, then how

I turned into Tuğrul and I tried to keep them out of my mind. But, no matter how much I tried, The Nafs didn't stop following me, he was following me scattering flames out of his mouth. Keşşaf understood the situation.

He said, "Are you looking for this?"When I heard this sentence, Tuğrul's scent started to burn my nostrils suppressing hundreds of scents in the room. However, there wasn't anything! What a shameful moment it is for me? Then Keşşaf took a little bottle from the shelves behind him and showing me, said,

"You have been looking for this since you came to the world of scents. Here it is." He put the bottle slowly on the table incenses rising. It was Tuğrul's scent. As I couldn't do without breathing, I had to breathe this scent. Tuğrul's scent surrounded me like a hoop, like a circle, left no place to hide.

Keşşaf stood up slowly. Everything on that magic table took their places on the shelves. Every object appeared on the glass shelves consisted of scent as if they knew their places. First the bottle Tuğrul's scent was in, damask and silk bound books, all perfumes, oysters, scented rosaries, ink bottles, ruby inlaid boxes, jugs, quill pens. Then the flying incenses diminished. Now I could see more clearly. Keşşaf was wearing a long dress. He came towards me a few steps through the scents, suddenly a pool made of glass like a circle bathtub appeared between us. The water of this pool was such clean that I realized the things swimming in it were fish. But they didn't look like fish we knew, they were like made of colour glass; they were transparent. As all the things in this palace they were made of glass! But they were alive. There were pink rose petals on the surface of the water. Keşşaf caressed the water with his hand. The image of his beautiful head, his brown hair was reflecting in the water. His cheekbones were becoming more evident than it was when caressing the water. While Keşşaf was caressing the water, a hypethral dome appeared at the top of this glass palace. The hypethral of the dome was two or three times bigger than the pool. After a bit, a thin moon light started to reflect from the dome; the water shone with the reflection of the moon. Then the glitter of the scented glass shelves around us decreased; scented oil-lamps appeared above our head in a way that they surrounded the pool. These colourful oil-lamps were scattering different colour and scent, there was an unbelievable view on the pool as their reflected on the pool. On the top of it, colourful glass goblets were in the air in a silver tray next to Keşşaf. So, this glass palace could get into the shape it wanted.

"Do you know Dilruba, sense of smell gives an independent kick than the other senses; however, scent is transient. And scent is more personal sense than the other senses. Do you know who the scent addresses to most?"

I shook my head in the meaning of I don't know. As it turned out, scent lesson was starting. Every word from Keşşaf's mouth was very important. As Keşşaf talked, I could see the moon light reflecting to the pool on his face.

"Scent addresses the sensitive people the most. The scent both fascinates and contains disappointment as it is short. But the thing makes us feel our uniqueness is mostly the sense of smell. Because the closest organ to brain is nose."

The pool smelt rose. I think it was rose water pool. This smell of rose was suppressing Tuğrul's scent. Then Keşşaf put his hand in the water and hold me his palm which was full of rose water and said,

"Drink it!" This was like an order. I drank the water of rose water pool. It was so sweet, charming like sherbet.

He was going on telling,

"Scent I more subjective than other senses; it leaves distinctive reflection at every one. Scent is momentary but it whispers us that there is a better world. A good scent contacts heart and mind again. It integrates human and nature, it whispers the hidden corners of ego because a good scent crystallizes the soul of the person." He looked at my face to understand what I thought and continued,

"Sweet scents are like medicine. People used to believe that wearing fragrant oils would protect them from plagues."

As the moonlight reflected to the rose petals in the pool their colours were becoming thin. Then flames of the reflection of the moon on the water were reviving on Keşşaf's face; I caught a light pacing around in his pupils.

"Dilruba, every people corresponds to a scent on the earth. Like fingerprints, everybody has a special scent."

Keşşaf nailed his look on me now.

"But smell of rose is different. Would you like to learn how rose oil is made?"

I had never thought such a thing. I didn't know anything about rose oil or rose water. Keşşaf pushed the rose petals aside slowly. At that moment, a rose garden appeared on the water. I took a few steps back with astonishment because of the liveliness of the view. I was both looking at this view and wondering about the things he was going to say.

It was like reflecting a film to the surface of the water, the rose garden in the film was approaching. Big petals of the rose became more eligible. Pink, red roses were swaying in the twilight of the morning with breeze. Then hundreds of women and men came to the garden with sacks. Even the embroidery at the end of the kerchiefs of women could be seen. They started to carry the roses they put in the sacks; they emptied the sacks and returned and then they filled and emptied them again. Keşşaf said,

"A kilo of rose oil consists of three hundred and five hundred or four thousand kilos of roses." This time, besides the pinkness of roses, shining colourful lights of the oil lamps hung on our heads. Then, hundreds of people loaded the roses they gathered on the carriages to take them to the distillation factories. All these petals were laid flat at a shadow place in the storehouse in order to be dried in the distillation factory. They were like a pink carpet on the huge square. Then, they put the rose petals into big copper boilers, in other words in the distilling apparatus, they started to boil them by giving steam. Even the inside of the boilers were seen in this film; the boilers were boiling profusely by stem injection, the rose petals were nearly melting. Finally, the liquid in the boiler started to transform into an oily-water. This boiling water carried to the condenser crossing over distilling apparatus. Then the steam got cold with the effect of cold water in the condenser and turned into liquid again. Later, water and essential oil were put into Florentine bottle. Then only then it appeared as a layer on the beautiful attar of rose Florentine bottle.

Keşşaf said, "Yes, as you see attar of rose produced from tones of rose petals is jut this! Sometimes sorrow applies this distillation process to people. We are hurt because of that." Then, while the people were filtering the attar of rose, Keşşaf touched the water with his hand and the image disappeared; there were water rings instead of the image now.

I was saying to myself, "what would happen if they remained as rose? Is it a must? Keşşaf talked again with that moonlight appeared on his face,

"Love melts all contrasts, all discriminations, differences of people in its own pot, like the melting rose petals in these copper boilers. It burns the lover until it changes everything to beloved."

It looks like he was mentioning that steam of love would burn me for a long time. I couldn't speak before Keşşaf. I couldn't even speak a word. I wanted to break the silence. He continued,

"Dilruba, you were wondering about the inner eye that fronts you everywhere, weren't you?"

I could only say “Yes”. Finally I could break the silence.

“You must have understood it; it is the sky on your chest. Let’s say it the mirror in us, when it is dirtied or broken, the harmony between body and soul is broken. When an image or message doesn’t reflect the mirror, the body starts collapsing. Various kinds of illnesses hinder. When the harmony between body and soul is broken, both body and soul are plunged into loneliness. Love steps in at that moment. When it captures body and soul, it connects them again... Remember the lesson I taught you about heart! Heart is in a special place that is carrying common fascicles from body and soul.”

I remembered the heart lesson, but I was looking as if I didn’t understand anything, I shook my head as if to say I didn’t understand.

“Love integrates while distilling. It is the secret, while it is separating you into pieces it makes you the world. The pain you are suffering is showing you the power of your soul, you gain strength in the ratio of your pain. You are being distilled, separated into pieces and you turn into a precious thing.”

Right after the shelves full of bottles behind Keşşaf brightened up as if a lantern was held. As he handed, that little bottle which that certain scent was in came to Keşşaf’s hand. Then the silver top of it was slowly opened and he dripped a single drop into the rose water pool. Surface of the pool burst into flames as soon as the drop touched, it bubbled and boiled up. The fire was sizzling as if water was poured. The rose water pool interacted with a single drop of Tuğrul and it started to spit up black smokes. After burning for a while, it calmed down and went out. The power of the moonlight reflecting on the water decreased, the shadows became heavier. Keşşaf took the blood-red goblet on the silver tray hanging on his head, immersed it into the pool, filled a little, handed me and said,

“Taste it, what would you say?”

I couldn’t feel my hands, I took the red goblet and I took it to my lips instinctively. Then, Keşşaf turned the bottle down as if he wanted to pour all of them in it, but nothing poured out. I saw all the bottles melting at that moment. The glass bottle in his hand turned into water and flowed.

He said, “Glass is originally liquid, it hardens when it gets cold, like heart.”

The liquid in the goblet burned my lips at first. My mouth was filled with a poison like nitric acid. But I liked this. Then my mouth was filled with a taste of sour, I couldn’t swallow. I couldn’t gulp down. I was with this gradually getting hot scent liquid in my mouth...

Just then the trip in the abdomen ended and I found myself in the little room of Safran. The time didn't pass, it froze here. Gül Hanım was nodding her head and saying " of course, don't be alone with him". Then Safran turned to Didem and was saying,

"Make some tea for us, it is good for melancholy."

24

The fruit of the tree of love is not achieving the dream.
Whoever has a dream, has a desire,
tell him to go away by himself! (Şeyh atar)

The next day I thought about Keşşaf all day. I was trying to understand his words and all meanings I interferred was carrying the hope of that Tuğrul would come back. Keşşaf didn't refer anything negative; so Tuğrul would come back.

It was a bright Sunday. I had breakfast with Kırlangıç and Zümrüt; and we all holed up. They reproached since I hadn't told them when I had been going to Safran during the breakfast. I told them that I had decided suddenly. Then Zümrüt asked what had Safran told about and I told them she had said that 'tea is good for blind love.' They looked at me strangely. Then Kırlangıç, "Is that why we always have tea? It must be true, I felt it!" Safran didn't blow smoke, there was always a hidden cause and it appeared at that moment or later.

The extraordinary scents of the world of scents was still right under my nose. Keşşaf was right; the scent was standing on a private perception area. The sense of smell was presenting an independent pleasure, and it was instant. In spite of this, it was the scent to contact heart and mind again; scent was whispering us the existence of a livable world.

I was watching outside from the wide open windows in my room. I was there, but as if my perceptions had stayed in the world of scents. The weather was so hot that people were walking around half-stunned; the heat in them was being read from their faces. In this hot weather at the stone path I had walked with Tuğrul... I saw him suddenly. First I thought it was a dream. It is not difficult to dream for someone in my situation. Two seconds later, a sizzle getting higher filled my room, then the sound deepened and turned to the voice of human; "406 Dilrubaa,

406 Dilruba, you have a visitor!" I was shocked with this announcement but then I gathered myself up. It must have been Müdrik, who else could be except him?

I headed the stairs dragging my slippers. When I held the handrail, I wished that the visitor was Tuğrul, then I drew myself from this hope with all my strength, because hope is an absolute torture. I went down the stairs to the panel. The world would enlighten or get dark behind this panel. When I came behind the panel, I saw that there was none there. I was looking around, and at that moment the attendant woman took his head out of the cabin and told,

"Walk towards the canteen." I went to the canteen excitedly, stood by the door. I couldn't be brave enough to go in. My looks were getting flu. Then I saw him at the table I had had breakfast with Kırlangıç and Zümrüt in the morning: Tuğrul!

He stood up when he saw me. He was like a giant. The table was squashed under his feet. He passed this squashed table, came to me; I saw him alive before me but my mind was telling me it was a dream. This illusion continued until I heard his voice.

"Hello." His face was bended down slightly with a look full of modesty. I didn't know what to say, but then I gathered myself,

"Hello, I see you have returned. I haven't expected to see you..." I said with irony and trying to stand upright.

"Shall we sit a little?" His tone of voice implied that he couldn't talk on the run.

"Of course," I said, "but I don't have much time." He had brown under eye bags and his face was tired and exhausted.

"I wanted to see you," he said.

I wanted to say that 'Tuğrul! I'm not such kind of a person that you go letting down and you can find at your elbow whenever you want to see.' However my heart was suppressing this voice. And at that moment I felt that I stepped on the peak of a mountain with his return. All difficulties of life were sliding under my feet. I revived with his return like a patient seeing the daylight after long and breathless nights.

"How did you go and come back from the other end of the world," I said trying to hide my feelings and with an artificial astonishment. I was implying that I knew he hadn't been anywhere but I had assumed that he had.

"I don't remember I told you where I was going," he said laughing. I caught the magic circling around his face. His tone of voice that I know almost better than my own name, his scent and the faithful expression of his face hadn't changed at all.

"You haven't told, but don't you think everywhere is the other end of the world at the moment you go out of the borders?" He laughed again thinking I was joking.

"Yes, you are right actually." He hesitated. I wondered why he had come. He hadn't even phoned. I didn't think it was about me!

"I have needed to see you, I have understood that I can't live without seeing you." This confession poured before me with a dangerous splash like broken glass. The whole hardness of life melted in this sentence, and the crystals in his voice swept me off my feet transforming to a wild wave. I was the happiest person among billions of people leaving their trace between earth and sky. Even the heavens hadn't seen one happier than me. Thousands of stars were passing through Tuğrul's tired eyes, and I was plying between the east and west setting up swings.

"I am pleased to hear that," I said. I was smiling from ear to ear. Everything had been getting better slowly, and the meaning of the scent appeared in this way. Scent was a kind of communication way between me and him.

Tuğrul visited me a few times after that day, even he was calling everyday. Now, I was transforming to Tuğrul actually. I was wandering as if I had forgotten everything except him and I was always thinking about the future I would construct with him. All faces were fading away except his; his voice was as lively, real and extraordinary as the ones that I had heard in the world of hearing. Now this huge campus was more beautiful than ever; I had never loved people so much, I understood this now. I couldn't thank God enough! How much I owed to Keşşaf , and of course to Safran. I was swarming with love thanks to them. What a beautiful thing loving is; the sky on my chest was about to crack of happiness.

Kırlangıç, my dear friend was proved right. She said, "Didn't I tell you he would come back?" I was looking into Kırlangıç's eyes with a crazy happiness. When one love so much, worries about the past and future fall from his shoulders like an old jacket, and he wears a new and fresh hope. Almost he can forgive and love people who did wrong to him in the past even without any offence. This love was sweeping all offences from my heart, and it was destroying even the tiniest weirdest emotions. It placed all positive emotions instead of them and turning me to a person feeling competent in everything. Life was opening its arms as if it wanted to hug me, and said "Dilruba, run to happiness, don't stop!"

Every part of my being swarmed with the breezes coming from Tuğrul. Love was climbing over my head and rose to the clouds like a spiral. Both of us, he and I were having the most beautiful week of our lives perhaps. I must confess that I forgot what Keşşaf had told me completely. Only Tuğrul remained from those extraordinary images, sounds and scents. I didn't know anything else any more. However man sometimes learns without being aware but remembers nothing when he looks back, all knowledge was caved in his soul by an indelible writing.

How meaningful the songs were, I understood this now. How blue the sky was, how green the trees were. Universe was placing vocal in its words for me to read more clearly, the flowing life was nothing short of a total love. I was walking as if I was hypnotized like a person standing up in his sleep and doesn't know where he goes during this one week.

And one day... That day I went to Safran's like a needle drawn by a magnet, without knowing why I went. I just wanted to tell her how beautiful everything was while I was on my way. This was an irresistible will! I wanted to tell her looking at her eyes that blind love hadn't knocked me down and life had planned everything for me slowly and beautifully. When I arrived at Safran's, firs I felt that how much I had been far from this clear atmosphere. The small room was very crowded. Since I didn't want to be in the crowd in this hot weather, and also I think I had been involved in Tuğrul's love of luxury, I sat on a table at the entrance and waited the room to be desolated. I was watching the activity in the house more clearly from this point. I was witnessing everything, those going into the kitchen, going out of the kitchen with trays and the plain and far from the luxury state of the iron gate opening and closing steadily from the point I was sitting more closely.

After a while people started to leave, and I started to listen to Safran very carefully sitting somewhere near the threshold like a soldier keeping watch. Safran clasped her hands in her lap with respect and told the crowd listening to him, "in fact metaphor is a bridge." I hadn't looked at Safran's magnificent face shining like a pearl among the soldiers of hearts, then I heard that voice again;

"Hey, the captive of the metaphorical love!"

I froze when I heard this. The Cavalry was calling me, but what a calling! When I raised my head towards the voice, I found myself in the mist waving before the Cavalry. I was buried until my belly in the mist resembling like a colourless fog. When I saw his face clearly at last, he gave me his unique voice again,

"Dilruba! Hurry up, Keşşaf is waiting for you!"

He took me on his horse's pillion. I found myself on his white horse being swept away like flying as soon as his strong, brunet hand grasped my wrist. So I became the captive of the metaphorical love, his voice turned to and echo in my ears and it was tinkling.

The road wasn't too long, I found myself in the world of scents again in the blink of an eye this time. Moreover I was just before Keşşaf by the pool of rose water in the same scent workshop. I was looking at the scent bottle turning to liquid in the hand of Keşşaf being astonished how I came so quickly. Oh my God, I said murmuring, time hadn't passed in the world of scents.

"You see Dilruba, actually glass is liquid, it solidifies when it is cold," said Keşşaf; so this scene in the world of scents hadn't ended yet. That bitter scent was again in my mouth, it was burning my throat, acetifying my tongue and clouding my mind. Keşşaf raised his delicate face towards my face. I saw the reflection of the rose water pool and the moonlight reflected from the open dome in his eyes. This was time in time! In fact there had been a very long time since I left here, at least one week or more. However, it seemed that time didn't pass here.

"Do you still have the same bitter taste in your mouth?" Keşşaf asked. Keşşaf was standing on the bastion of a divine magnificence through thousands of scents, and his back was in a light beam. Immediately I gathered myself up,

"Sort of," I said.

"I think you still have it. You are here since you still have it," he said.

Now Keşşaf's tone of voice was bitter. He was looking at me as if he would say something important to me and he was kneading my ego by his eyes. These lanterns hung over my head, these colourful glasses hung in the air were there as I had left. Keşşaf was again pouring musk into my marrows. I was fermented with patient and pain like rose oil. Here, in the world of scents everything was moving in a sweet drunkenness. Everything related to the scent I smelled, yes, Tuğrul's scent, all mysteries were becoming mysteries in this glass palace. I was passing from the land of absence to the land of existence by Keşşaf. He was taking me through the worlds; he was tambouring me on a scent frame.

"Dilruba..." said Keşşaf. This voice, this tone walked like a sword taking my heart out of its place.

"The world is not a permanent place, so we cannot expect loyalty from it. Am I not right?"

"You are right, of course it is not sir," I said.

"Everything except God's reign is temporary. In this world illness and health are removed; sadness and joy are wiped away; youth will fly like a bird, and the elderliness will also... We will leave the world eventually, Dilruba... You also think so, don't you?"

"Yes, of course, who doesn't think so?" I said.

"Then don't throw the seed in an arid land!"

What did he mean? I didn't understand anything from his words. He continued,

"We, the saints, have left our will, we don't want anything for ourselves. Every step we take is by the order of the Almighty God's order and decree. You know that, don't you?"

"Yes, of course it is so," I said.

"Dilruba, if it is so, I want you to give up Tuğrul."

This sentence stroke me like a lightening! It woke me up in pain from sweet dreams. I wanted to cry as why, but I couldn't speak. My imagination went too far to think that this was a joke. This could only be a joke, but saints didn't make jokes, I should have learned this. Keşşaf went on when he saw my face turned to ice,

"I can help you if you want. I tried to tell you about the meaningless of the matter and time during all those timeless breaks. I wanted you to have a grasp of the secret behind the material."

He continued after a moment of silence, I felt that he was going to say something important,

"Metaphorical love captured you Dilruba! And the solution is not giving Money and saving the hostage in the events of capturing. Even if fate gives you Tuğrul it doesn't mean will save. Saving you is only possible by capturing and holding the metaphorical love, neutralizing it and transforming it to the true love. This was only a short performance including you to teach you what the love is. Yet, if you are insistent in staying there, I'm afraid a loyalty seal won't appear on your forehead and your sufistic training will be left half finished. You will remain as a rosebud at the step of the metaphorical love."

I wanted to die when I heard these. I wanted to run far away from everything. I wanted to run my life back and reset everything. When he saw my frozen looks,

"A pain like this is needed to develop the skills. We need you."

How could I serve to whom any more? I existed in the world as a nimiety. Here he was saying, fate wouldn't give me Tuğrul. I wouldn't be! My heart turned to a child stamping continuously when what he wanted wasn't done in my chest. Keşşaf went on; the lights of the hung lanterns lighted his face and the shadow of the moon fell onto his forehead.

"Sinking into the flood of the emotions is the work of thoughtless people. This is not Dilruba that I know. Do you remember I told you about the dark room?"

I stood there like an icon that couldn't move between escaping or staying there. Then the warm tears of despair started to run down slowly as it might have happened to everybody learning the ugly truth. I was crying. I was simply crying smelling only one scent among the thousands of scents and sobbing. When Keşşaf saw me crying, his tone of voice changed, it softened,

"Dilruba! The dark room is your cage, your cave. It is the pain of love to reveal you how much the cage is dark and to put the hat of fate on your head. If you want to see the light stop sticking the rebellion handle! This trouble coming splitting and cracking the dark is the light going into your room. You were asked what your desire was in the beginning. And you wanted love. See it Dilruba, the real owner of love is sifting you, cleaning you out, filtering you out, shelling you, unravelling you. He is distilling you."

Then he paused. Keşşaf was catching me as a hawk was catching its hunt.

"We need both light and darkness to see because light is not enough to see, our eyes should touch darkness also. In fact not seeing is realized when you see black because black objects absorb all the light hitting it and they don't reflect light just like the situation you are in now. Now you are in the dark room. Light eventually come into this dark room definitely. Then you will start to see the sky on your chest. Now you are experiencing only a sudden blindness since darkness prevents seeing just like intense light."

I was crying like the flood flowing under my feet when I had been crying in the stadium under the heavy rain as bent double in the beginning of the way. I fell down on my knees and I was trying to suppress the sobbing covering my face with my hands as I had done at the moment of pray. Again only my shoulders telling that I was crying as if I turned to a spot. Again I returned the place where I had started. My lips opened slightly, and I talked getting rid of the flame burning my face; my voice was coming out brokenly finding a way from the quakes in my chest,

"Your desire..." I couldn't breathe properly to complete my sentence. Then I sighed deeply, "is an order to me!" I said but Keşşaf was hearing all reproaches and groans in my heart.

"I have never been doubtful about you, Dilruba! Yet I know you, you are still cursing, you will. And know this that you are not sort of a person that one can pass in a narrow and limited area; metaphorical love is a very small area for you. Are you aware that you pull a gun on the sun crying and cursing? Remember! What has Safran said? The power of love is destroyer, you can't stand and yield eventually, and when you melt away you reach your real identity."

I stopped crying. I was wiping my eyes on one hand, sniffing on the other hand. I saw the world like a child just starting to learn prayers at that moment, there were poems in my heart, 'know that there is no union in Islam, reaching ones are infidels!' said the poet. I was telling these two lines tirelessly, singing it as if I had been hearing for the first time.

"Come on, rise and don't have a fright of my words! You are still at the first one of the testing valleys. If you manage to pass over this valley, you will face more difficult tests. You will fight with the bottomless cliffs and wild oceans flowing as being flood."

It isn't possible to stand before saints without being frightened. I rose trying to resist crying about to start at any time, my knees was trembling terribly.

"What if I can't pass over this valley?" I said sniffing. It was impossible for me to pass it, I knew that.

"Succeeding the tests is not important, the important thing is participating the test, being on the way and trying," he said. Now Keşşaf was looking in the affectionately like a father. He was smiling that almost his front teeth would be seen. Sweet breezes of the moonlight were wandering in his eyes and a warm pity appeared in his looks while the sparkles of the rose pool were reflecting his face. He caressed the surface of the pool backhand, he pushed the rose petals looking like spreading. Then he shook the water as if he had wanted to clean it, rings occurred in the water and the water cleared. He sank his hand in the water as much as his sleeves lightened by silver sparkles and he poured the rose oil he took out. Rose oil was pouring in my hand like delicate milk solidified slightly.

"Smell this, it is good for you," he said. This sweet scent slid down my throat. I was touching the rose oil on my temples starting to ache and I was inhaling it like a remedy.

Then Keşşaf stopped talking. I felt again that he was going to say something important. Now I could estimate what his silence would mean. He walked getting rid of the lights dancing in the pool while I was trying to keep my steadiness.

"Follow me!" We started to walk along the breeze wall consisted of scents and sweet aromas. All those breezes were flying as if they had wanted me to faint as his long dress was flying and I was walking behind Keşşaf . We were leaving behind everything I had passed by when we had come to the scent workshop. Scented tablets, musk and amber censers, tulip vases, dove bottles... everything was remaining behind us as a breeze. Then we came to the entrance of the solid glass palace. We arrived at the first step of the stairs starting at the entrance of the palace and going up spiralling and ending up with a high rostrum. Here the particles of scents rising like a smoke until my waist were so strong that they could faint one as if he smelt ether. Keşşaf checked me turning his whole body back. Then he started to go up the smoke stairs constituted of scent one by one. As if he was rising in a mist on the very spot. I did the same; it was like standing in the air. I was wondering very much what was there on the rostrum at the end of the stairs. I saw a bell glass on the rostrum. However, Keşşaf stopped after a few meters and called on without looking his back,

"You are permitted to go up here for now. Come to me."

When I reached the height he was, I saw him sinking his hand into a glass cube. This glass cube spread its dazzling scent generously with the touch of Keşşaf's hand.

"This," said Keşşaf, "is the scent of the aloe. It is necessary for one who is in the valley of testing."

I found myself in a desert just before Keşşaf finished his sentence. My feet were stepping on the ground, hot sands; he continued; his face was so close to me that I could see it clearly.

"Aloe grows up in deserts at most. Now tinge it your eyes like kohl, it will give you strength in the desert of absence. I will lighten around with patient." This scent burning my nostrils was tinged my eyes becoming kohl by itself.

I realized that moment that the stairs of scent had been vanished. I was in an endless desert. Moreover there was not only the scent of the aloe but itself under my eyes. Aloe was a hard plant with its flat leaves resembling a triangle with a sharp end. Its leaves were thick and plump. While I was examining the plant, I couldn't see Keşşaf's face but hear his voice.

"You can run away from the desert of absence only by fighting with Nafs because metaphorical love throws one to the desert of absence finally. If you pass over the desert you reach the door of absence, but first you need to pass the desert of absence!"

The sun was as hot as boiling my brain in the desert I was looking around lonely. The yellow colour of the desert was curtaining the blueness of the sky. I was walking desperately stepping on the sand flowing like yellow hot flood under my feet. How it was difficult to walk on this sand sea! Here, in this place that I thought life had never visited, sand was pulling me from my ankles down turning to strong hands. I thought that if man walked in this heat for a few hours his death would visit him. There were dunes resembling yellow butter bars. Perhaps I could find water or shade down there if I passed over them. I rested in the shadow of a dune. The situation seemed so hopeless; I needed hundreds of lives to pass this desert. Then I started to climb the dune hardly but I was rooted to the spot and sank into the sand to my knees. I gave up and let myself go down, I dragged to the shadow of the dune. Sand shaping like sea waves was lying before me. Further the sand took the shape of a crescent. I walked travelling around the dunes. I was exhausted. At that moment I saw the tent. I didn't know why I hadn't seen it before, I must have walked a lot. It was a state tent with a big dome. At the top of the dome the flag of Spirit was waving. Camels and horses were waiting in front of it, and noises were coming from inside. I understood that it was the headquarters of Spirit when I got close to the tent. Spirit had gathered all its staff and soldiers and they were discussing about an important matter.

I crept in half-opening the thick and heavy curtain of the tent. The only thing I wanted was some water; thanks God I found what I had been looking for. I quaffed a bowl of water left at the entrance of the gate. I realized when I gathered myself up that the soldiers of Spirit had weakened and they had been all as skin and bone; in spite of this they were determined to fight with Nafs. However the worry penetrated in their looks was peaching on them. I saw Spirit for the first time at that moment. It was sitting cross-legged in the centre of the large tent and had a worried expression on its face. His face was white and his looks were clear. He had left his armour just over there, he was drawing something on the ground with his sword and talking at the same time.

"My people! Nafs and his soldiers are about to capture the country. I have heard that fearless soldiers are getting close to the headquarters. We need to exile them from this land girding ourselves with swords. Unless the owner of this body land takes sides with us, defeat will be inevitable for us."

Spirit must have referred me by saying the owner of the body land. I was so sorry about this tragic state of Spirit and his soldiers. To help them became my duty. I immediately interrupted, and the soldiers hearing my voice turned their heads back with astonishment;

"I think you are looking for me, I am here, with you," I said. Spirit stood up quickly when he saw me, came towards me among his soldiers. He came by me, shook me from my shoulders and,

"I can't tell you how happy I am since you are here, but we don't have much time. If your soldiers don't obey the commands, Nafs whose breath is like a lightening will destroy your country and dispossess it. He will inundate you and us into an eternal sorrow. I will not be possible for us to see the honourable face of the Sultan of Sultans. A little later, the riders of Nafs resembling true fire terrorise this desert. Unless our swords that are about to become blunt dazzles their eyes, we will scatter like dust particles in this desert of absence."

My heart was sinking deeply, I didn't know anything about fighting. Then Spirit turned to his soldiers, the skirts of his kaftan were sweeping the floor.

"Hey, my people! Tell me, will we stand by while the enraged soldiers of Nafs are darkening the sky?"

The soldiers responded:

"No, my Sultan, No!" Spirit went on,

"Oh, my people, don't praise the bandits of Nafs. Is there anybody doing this here?"

The soldiers again cried,

"No, my Sultan, no!"

"Then my people, will we drive away this trouble we have had?" Now the soldiers were silent as if they were dump. When I saw this silence I completed His words,

"With the Almighty Allah's blessing," I shouted. Then I went on, "your swords have forgotten how to cut, how long will you wait like a delicate lady? Shake the sweet sleep from your daffodil eyes, shake yourself!" I said. The soldiers were moving half-heartedly; Spirit walked among the soldiers with light and helpless steps like a commander of an army having defeated already,

"My people, why are you so loose, why have you ceased the swords, why have you accepted the defeat?" A dark man stood up among the soldiers,

"The owner of the body land has remained at the step of the metaphorical love after so much love and journeys through pure and clear worlds. So the soldiers of Nafs became stronger day by day, they have been fed by the poisoned food of lies. Isn't it the reason why we have stuck on this desert of absence? We have got weakened as they have been fed. We have given everything to them. We are as hungry as eating our shoes! Yet they are drinking water from all of the fountains of the country resting their demon mouths on them. All fruitful lands we own have been dried by the purulence coming from their throats. Perhaps even only one among the thousands falling into this desert of absence couldn't survive from this fight. Will we survive then?"

I took a deep breath when I heard this.

"It isn't the time of deploring, but fighting now. They must be ten thousands, and we are only a handful of people, but it doesn't matter, love is with us. True love is on our side. Our wings of sense are as wide as filling between the east and west. Isn't it enough? Do they know where the oasis of peace is better than us? They are just idling around a mirage and wandering as their tongues out. The most important thing is that why should we wait while God defends us?"

I had just let myself go; the warrior in my soul was running at full gallop riding on the horse of words. It was the high time while the sitting soldiers were grumbling between each other,

"Then pull yourself together, gird on your steel armours, and rise like dazzling suns over the enemy spreading sparkles from the hooves of your horses! Let the heart of the enemy fire with the blood flowing from your swords, give no quarter to the cruel, make them a sawn ear field with your paws!"

The soldiers hearing these words seemed to be soothed a little. They ran to the horses going out of the tent with the cries of 'Allahuekber' and 'long live my Sultan.' When I went out, I saw him among this weak crowd; the Cavalry was here. Moreover my red horse was standing by him. He was like a light with his green cloth and his white horse in this blasting weather. The mane of his horse was like a foaming river.

"I have told you, I am with you whenever you call me." I smiled to show how I was happy to hear this, my eyes was filling with tears by happiness. I felt self-confidence and courage in my heart. Then the horses got move, and I pulled the bridles while the cries of 'Allahuekber' were mixed with the warm breaths of the horses: Giddy up!

We were galloping as Spirit and the vizier were leading this small, weak army and we were flowing like water against the heat cutting our look. The soldiers were wearing their armours and they were dazzling with their swords and shields; arrowed troops, the ones swinging iron maces and skinning swords fearlessly... Suddenly the army of Nafs loomed up from afar. They covered the sky in their black armours like a dark night. Riders got close waving the flags looking like shades over them. There were Nafs and his vizier on the front, drums, kettledrums and horses running as bursting were by them. Spirits drummers and kettledrums on the camels were added to this rumble and all hell was breaking loose deafening. Nafs had disguised in human but he couldn't hide his ugliness even in this state. He was heaving ignoring his black face, exhaling flames again screaming wildly and extending his pitch black wings to the sky. The shadow of the waving flag was falling over the wide shoulders of the steel armour he was wearing.

Two armies came across like two rivers overflowing their beds. The horses on the front reared up with their bridles being pulled hard. Kettledrums stopped. I could see Nafs' face clearly; the drunkenness of a certain victory was seen in his eyes resembling a black light. He grinned like a pig looking at the vizier by him; he was pulling the bridles of his rocking black horse,

"Hey Spirit, are you confronting me with this weakness? It's a wonder!" said he and raised a demon laugh.

Spirit didn't condescend to respond him; he knew that Nafs' challenge demoralized his army that had already been weak. Then Nafs stepped forward leaving his army behind. There was a silence of death in the air. He swivelled a few times on his horse becoming vicious and addressed his army,

"Hey bad-eyed brave men of the land of malice! Hey the sons of instigation and evilness!" Naws was crying spreading saliva from his mouth and giving courage to his soldiers,

"Hey the helpers of Satan! Now it's the time! The desert of absence and all valleys are ours and will remain ours. As the desires of the people wandering on the earth continue, all worlds of heart are condemned to belong to us! Whisper them ambition, greed, arrogance, endless desires and every kind of lust; they will be lulled as they are slaves of their passions and angers. Come on lions, go for it!"

Nafs cried terribly flying his sword and again went back to his army. He seemed contented. He was looking at the direction that I was standing as if he had been looking at an insect. Then Spirit also left his soldiers and took a few steps forward and started to shout as his veins in his neck would be seen,

"Hey the pearls of the heaven! Hey the men of love rotating as burning! You have become the respondent of the Beloved, then both defeat and death are forbidden to you! How can one die reviving by an eternal life coming from Him? Attack this cursed army with a faith expelling the darkness! Fear only from Allah, if He desires victory for us, who can oppose to Him? Defeat is for the ones who turn away from the word of Almighty Allah. That is true that God is with us!"

The soldiers hearing his words were saying 'Allahuekber' raising their swords to the sky, and the clanks of their swords and shields were screaming the place down. Then Spirit raised his milk-white hands to the sky and prayed. What he said wasn't heard in this noise. He wiped his palms shining with the acceptance of the skies on his face like a silk satin. The attacked started.

The soldiers of Nafs started to attack swinging their sword with rage; horses were running at full gallop, one cannot see beyond the end of his nose. Fight started like doomsday. Naf's soldiers' arrows were pouring upon us from the sky being trouble. The arrowheads of their swords were piercing our shields, soldiers of the enemy were slaughtering Spirit's army cruelly. I was raising my sword fearlessly and swinging it randomly while I was trying to protect myself. When I saw a soldier with flaming eyes and whose face couldn't be seen clearly because of his helmet under my nose I hung my sword with my all strength; the red horse had never been panted of air. However, sword didn't work on his shield. Man with flaming eyes was swinging the mace over my head; the mace turned to an iron top in the heat, it circled, circled and fell into my chest like an iron mountain. I fell off the horse to the feet of the enemy with a great pain. The red horse was neighing wailfully and it was raising its front feet as if it was running to the enemy. I was done. The soldier of the enemy dropped the shadow of his sword on my face, a little later blood would drain away from my carotid. At that moment I saw my face in the mirror of the sword. I was waiting for the moment of death desperately. Then at that moment the Cavalry coming from the back of the enemy was running breathless raising his bejewelled dagger. Only the eyes and the neck of the soldier appeared. His eyes spreading fire was looking at my face as if they were saying 'say your last prayer.' The Cavalry stabbed his dagger in his right hand to the neck of the leaned soldier. First his helmet fell off his head and his eyes turned in their sockets. He fell on me with groan not understanding what had happened. The Cavalry saved my life once more. He pulled the corpse of the soldier out and let me stand.

After he said "there is no time to lose," he slipped the bow and arrows in his saddlebag. The brave soldiers of Spirit had attacked to the enemy and they were attacking with their swords. They would either become martyr or gain a victory; the way to be taken was one of these two! The cries of 'Allah' was mixing with the heat of the desert giving no quarter, and we were fighting in order to defeat the enemy to the bitter end, to the last drop of blood. Then something happened that I hadn't expected!

I was learning that there was no pity in the war in this tumult. I didn't know how the war was going while I was swinging my sword with my eyes half-opened and throwing arrows. However the soldiers of Nafs had surrounded us and were repelling us. Some soldiers of heart became the target of the enemy arrows and became martyr, and some was giving up as wounded during this retreat. I found myself by the Cavalry in this retreat and panic. I looked into his eyes covered with dust,

"Why are we going back?" I asked breathlessly.

"That's why," he said snapping the bridles of his horse, "Soldiers of Nafs spread a net of rage over us, this rage filled our heart made us move away from the commitment and war and we were defeated and frightened. If the rage is not for Allah, it reveals fear and it is revealed by fear. So swords are not needed any more, rage is a deadly power, they know this very well!"

"So what will we do now?" I was talking out of breath while running away from the black army flowing onto us, my eyes were full of desert sand.

"We must protect Spirit strictly, the peace of the land of heart depends on His life; if he dies Nafs can rule this country for a long time, and this can be an endless road!"

Immediately I looked for Spirit restlessly. He was waiting on his horse ahead out of the tumult and watching the fight. A few soldiers charged with protecting him were keeping a sharp lookout but if the fight went on so, he would be captured easily. I pulled the bridles severely, I turned the face of my horse back. Then I attempted to take an arrow from my saddlebag. However, I touched something soft. It was the feather that the phoenix, the love bird, had given me. Once when I had held the feather not to fall, it had told me "it is yours." Then I raised this magnificent feather to the sky. The feather transformed into a giant wing suddenly, and it flew over us like a shade. Its lights was dazzling the eyes of Nafs' soldiers and making them blind. The soldiers of the enemy were dispersed by the light of the wing; love was wiping them off this desert and making their bodies flow like black water. When brave men of Spirit saw this, they turned back and passed over the flowing black water with the cries of 'Allahuekber.' The unfortunate army of Nafs fell apart and they turned to a handful of tar.

It was our victory, the fight was over. Spirit came to the square as he had a crown fading the light of the sun. There was a confidence in his holding his horse's bridles, the worry had been erased from his eyes and love had taken the place of it. He looked at the men of love remaining as a handful, and he addressed them with his crystal voice;

"Victory is your conscience!" he said. "Your conscience tells you how you will win the war!"

Just then, while we were in the euphoria of this unexpected victory, the vizier of Nafs came close to us as he was wearing his steel shield and with his helmet on his head. He didn't seem to be like defeated. We were all looking at him carefully wondering what he would do. He reached out his hand to his helmet confidently and attempted to take off his helmet. Then one of the men of heart shouted,

"Hey cursed, take off your helmet and I will behead you!" Yet the Cavalry stopped him with his looks. The vizier took off his steel helmet and firs his thin hair waved at the edge of his ears. When the steel helmet was taken off his beautiful face appeared like a ruby. At that moment I thought my heard would go out of my chest. The vizier before me was Tuğrul! The clearness in his brown eyes... The lines of his face jogged my memory... I just stood there as if I was under the effect of a magic. Tuğrul first touched each of us with his eyes, these eyes were more burning than the heat of the desert for me!

"Dilrubaa!" he called me. I passed the men of heart one by one and went to him. Again his aromatic strong scent made me an exhausted slave. As I got close to him this strong and cruel scent was locking into my soul like a bond.

"Tuğrul. It is you!" I could say with astonishment.

"I came to take you Dilruba," he said. At that moment I was determined to go with him. I forgot everything, all difficulties we had endured for the victory.

"I long for you very much." He said, "here I am yours!"

What could I think anything else than going with him while I was under the effect of the scent penetrating my lungs? The Cavalry caught me like a scream when he saw I lowered my colours,

"Beware Dilruba! If you go with him Spirit will be captured. Your land of heart will become Nafs' plaything forever! Think carefully, don't do it upon our victory!"

When Spirit saw that I was giving way to the vizier of Nafs that was the devil's voluntary servant, the light of the crown on his head was dying away. His face was clouding as the dying away of the light, and his looks was being covered with a shadowy mist. I was on the horns of a dilemma. The wing of the phoenix in my hand didn't work with the vizier. Love was weak against the metaphorical love, it was ineffective.

At that moment Nafs blew in masquerading as the two-headed dragon spreading flames from his mouth. His bellows were shaking the ground, and horses were getting restless. The dragon was raising his both wings to the sky and he was screaming wild cries of victory, then I was like coming to my senses. The Cavalry said,

"Don't listen to this bandit's vizier. If you listen to him you will remain as a prisoner in the dragon's destroyed land!"

Tuğrul was looking into my eyes. He extended his hand when he saw I was hesitating,

"Let's go as soon as possible! Don't listen to these feeble people. What will you do if you stay with them? Isn't it me that you want? Come on!" he was saying.

Dry knots in my throat were overlapping and the boiling sun was making me suspicious. What would I say to the men of heart looking at me like begging? What if I stayed... I could do neither of them. Spirit came to me through the crowd with his cloudy face, he was holding a dagger: the dagger of regret! I had wounded Nafs with this dagger. At least I had thought so. Then I had understood that it had been Keşşaf's beautiful face to wound him. This dagger of regret brought me myself. I took this rusty dagger which had lost its sharpness and I got close to the flaming, old and ugly body of Nafs as I had done before.

This time it was a one-to-one fight! Spirit, the Cavalry, men of heart, Tuğrul the vizier of Nafs, all of them was looking at us. This time I was determined to knock Nafs down. I got close to him quietly. The desert turned to a destroyed land suddenly, bloody rivers were flowing under a black sky between me and Nafs; snakes and centipedes were everywhere. However these didn't frighten me; the dagger of regret was giving me strength and it was lightening my way. Nafs was coming towards me screaming wildly, shaking the ground and the black sky and he was spreading fire from his both heads swinging back and forth. I kept going stepping on the ruins of this destroyed land. I started to climb his back going behind his huge tail that he was hitting on the ground with rage as I had done before. He was swinging his wing as if a fly had been settled on his back. He was trying to throw me off turning to a raging bull. I climbed holding his wild wings and I stuck the dagger on the base of his neck as I had done before. He writhed crying with pain. I was holding his black wings so tightly that I didn't fell down this time. At the back of Nafs, at the beginning of his wings a black bloody river developed. I wounded him! But just as this!

Long afterwards Nafs fell down as bent double and vomiting

purulence. So I had stuck the dagger this much strongly; I was proud of myself. However, I understood the truth when it lightened.

What was happening to this destroyed, black country and it was filling with colourful rainbows and dazzling lights? Bloody rivers, snakes and centipedes had disappeared and the land of disaster had turned to a paradise. I turned my head before I had understood what had happened and the groans of Nafs had still been in my ears. And I saw him:

The Cavalry had taken off his veil, and all colours in the world of seeing, all wonderful sounds in the world of hearing and all overpowering scents in the world of scents had come here due to the beauty of his face. I had seen him without veil for the first time. I fell on my kneels out of my senses, I thought I was dying, my last breath was almost flying out. In fact I couldn't see anything because of dazzling! An intense, pure light covering everywhere was preventing me to see him!

At that moment I found myself before Tuğrul, the vizier of Nafs again. The Cavalry was by my side and he was covering his face with the veil swallowing all dazzling lights. This niqab swallowed all lights, sounds and scents while covering his face and turned this desert into its former state.

Vizier Tuğrul staggered when he saw his sultan was being racked with pain. A fear settled in his looks. When he understood that he would be captured, he started to play his last card on my side,

"Dilruba," he said with his pleasing voice. "Remember what we lived together! What about our future, what about us? I am here it doesn't matter what happens, what is important is this, isn't it?" The tone of begging appeared clearly.

"No!" I shouted with my last voice. I was so exhausted, sweltered and weak that I couldn't speak. Moreover the pain of the mace I had had on my chest was deepening every moment.

"There is nothing as us! I am no good to you as you continue to be the vizier of Nafs, of this bandit. Neither your beautiful face nor this magical scent means anything to me!" At that moment I had been fighting with the scent for the first time, I hadn't yielded. I revolted the scent penetrating all my cells and I thought it as enemy. I ignored the longing in my heart; I broke off one of the chains of the metaphorical love at once. However that was what I felt that pangs of love didn't leave one at once.

Tuğrul's looks were hurt when he heard my words, his beautiful brown eyes were just melting, a gloom settled on his delicate skin. His state was heart-wrenching. Perhaps if the Cavalry hadn't taken off his veil and filled the earth and sky with solid gold from his light, I would have upset the apple-cart by submitting the defeat upon our victory and gone with him. Yet thanks God, the Cavalry was with me, he was the epitome of Keşşaf, I didn't know, perhaps he could masquerade as hundreds of different forms.

Now the victory was ours in real terms. Spirit's crown started to shine again and clouds on his face disappeared. He came to us,

"We can pass over the desert of absence with the mercy of God." He said. I was looking at Tuğrul's expression out of the corner of my eye. It wasn't difficult to understand the pain filled in his brown eyes. Then this clear face and the scent flowing from him to me started to melt. Tuğrul's face was melting like soap under the sun. It melted until an ugly face appeared, and it disappeared completely. Now Nafs' vizier regained his real face! I gaped with astonishment. One of the brave men of the land of heart stretched his bow and targeted him before my astonishment had disappeared. The arrow passing over my head like a sharp whistle hit Tuğrul's chest. The vizier spurred his horse holding his bleeding wound and even without taking out of the arrow and he disappeared through the yellow lights of the desert being a dream. When Spirit saw him he said,

"We didn't kill Nafs and his vizier, just wounded them. This gave us power and time to recover. Yet don't be afraid, they can prevent us only until the satisfied hill and after that hill they will get off our back. Even if their weakened voices is heard by human, they won't be effective."

I widely opened my eyes with joy,

"I am very happy to hear that. Well, does it take long to the satisfied hill?" I said.

"Yes," he said. "The way there is too long, you need to pass hundreds, thousands of valleys." I was disappointed, so I would struggle with Nafs much more. Spirit went on,

"There are such men, such undefeated brave men that they can pass over the satisfied hill in the same breath. They keep going with unique pearls in their saddlebags." As if I saw my conscience on the beautiful face of Spirit. I asked curiously while I was wiping the sweat on my forehead,

"So what is there beyond?" He must have excused my curiosity so he smiled,

"After the satisfied hill, the stages of being saint begin. If the almighty beloved desires He takes his man further. You take off your human features and dressed up with divine features. If it is in his destiny, one reaches perfection, gets lost in the light of the pure truth with perfect and complete purgation at the end of this long and difficult journey and exists in a new state. He abandons all doubts about existing, and all curtains are taken off for him." While Spirit was telling these I was looking at the Cavalry. The puzzle in the Cavalry's eyes was solved with Spirit's words to some extent. I could understand why his blessed face filled the whole world with solid gold in the least.

At the early hours of the evening victory celebration started with the weather getting cold in the desert. The tent turned to a funfair. Candles and fires were set, the voices thanking God reached to the sky. The Cavalry came to me during the celebration, he was holding Spirit's dagger of regret in his hand,

"Take this! You are the real owner of this. You have learned where and how you will use it." I took the dagger of regret, kissed and touched it on my forehead. Then the Cavalry said,

"Come on! We're done here! It's time to go!" Yet I hadn't enjoyed the victory festival fully yet. The sparkles of the huge fire in the desert were lightening the Cavalry's eyes and the fire of the candles was reaching to the stars. So in the darkness, a door resembling a transparent cloud half-opened in the distance. The Cavalry pointed the door,

"That is the door of absence, we will pass there!" he said.

He got on the horse of which mane was washed by the lights of the stars. His beauty was wiping all my tiredness and decreasing the pain on my chest. I was travelling behind him on my horse that had been dyed red by the balefire in the darkness of the night. Dark blue clouds over us were lightening the sand resembling sea waves and the sough of the wind just started to blow were hitting my ears. Night at the desert looked like outer space, we seemed to be passing over the craters that didn't have any signs of life. The door of the absence before us that seemed that I could touch if I extended my hand was moving away more and more. I called the Cavalry,

"You know that I am an impatient person; when will we pass through this door?"

The Cavalry talked without turning back but turning his head to one side,

"It's not easy to pass through that door, let the morning comes!"

I couldn't believe my ears. How would we travel in this utter darkness and while we were so tired and hungry? While I was travelling very closely to the clear moon in the sky I lost sight of the Cavalry suddenly. Had he gone very fast? I was looking at the left, right and back, but I couldn't see him. In the middle of the desert of absence, and while very close to that door... I shouted out,

"Heeeeyyyyyy, where are you? I can't see you!" I thought I was dreaming that moment. Whatever I had lived was flying out of my mind and mixing with the wind. At that moment everything I had seen until then was remained as a few meaningless seconds.

My emotions, desires, rages and hopes took off all their meanings; all of them became rootless and baseless dreams. Everyone I had known was flocking into my mind and then they were flying becoming dreams one by one. This state went on until no one remained. There only remained me. Then, even I was broken into pieces, and split up to my tiniest particle. Darkness and the wind was cutting me into pieces, I was feeling that. In the middle of a dumb desert, I had forgotten my own voice, my front and back was a dark nothingness, there was neither a living creature nor a movement... I was dragging in a deep, bottomless meaningless. From time to time my mind was looking like waking up from this dream, then at that moment the idea of that my life was an unacceptable dream was hitting my mind, then I again fell into the same sleep, the sleep of supposing. I looked at the moon resting in the sky like a wafer. It was lightening the sand waves in the shape of crescent, it informed me about the dunes in front of me, and it provided me to turn the bridles to the flat places. I was thirsty, and I was exhausted as much as I couldn't carry my head. I examined my saddlebag, I found some water in my water-skin. Drops were flowing down my chin when I was drinking the water and they fell on my chest had been aching because of the mace.

When I felt the pain of my chest, I started to be frightened. I thought to go back and spend the night in the tent. However, since the Cavalry said "we're done here", the tent must have been a dream already. Then I remembered the words of Keşşaf coming from the dream of the past:

"If you want to take the photo of the eye in your conscience, you should take it as sharp as the retina in the eye. It must be unique, it must be different, you are able to reveal its strong aspect and make it speak. That is the photo of the sky on your chest must be revealed together with you and everything, the whole universe, all seas, event the nothingness. If you try to look at the sky I am talking about from up, down, right and left as a separate individual, as a separate creature, this takes you far away, and in fact this is a strike for your freedom. You move away much more as you try to look at it. You should look at both the lens and the sky you are looking at; you should both see it starkly and you should also see your eye that sees. If you try to take the photo of the sky on your chest in this way, you will understand that there has been nothing called loneliness and the concept of loneliness exists only as you keep yourself behind the lens." And he had added,

"The sky on your chest is so active, so slippery, endless, so complicated and in so different shapes... The more you try to be free the more worried and weak you will be, because the idea of being free isolates you."

I remembered these sentences word by word. Keşşaf meant becoming a total mind, being a seeing eye, being a consciousness apprehending the symmetries and asymmetries in life in the sharpness of a razor. At that moment I realized how self-pity made me move away from the true images. As I tried to cover the face of my helplessness, I was moving away from understanding it. Loneliness was in my perceptions. The thing leaving me alone in this desert was that I had separated myself from everything and put it in a corner. However human was soul breathing with the whole universe, moving with it and transforming with it! Then my chest started to widen and the pain of the steel mace started to relieve. All shapes, all colours, all sounds were in my soul; living was in my chest. Everything was happening there!

It was interesting that there was connection between the words of Spirit about the satisfied hill and these words of Keşşaf! Your look was changing depending on which step of the consciousness you were and which valley you were in. I started to understand why the Cavalry's beautiful face turned that destroyed land into a paradise. It was his blessed soul, pure conscience and mature being that shined on his beautiful face!

I could understand that much from Keşşaf's words yet. Then suddenly the clearness in my consciousness made the door of the absence visible again. So I was upon the right scent. I was getting close to the huge, light, oval door. Moreover morning was coming, the darkness of the sky choking one was lightening stringy. So I had travelled all night. I spurred the red horse effusively, then at that moment, I didn't know what happened, but all swords in my chest cage started to go away one by one; I felt this extraordinary airiness. My chest was being opened, cleared and filling with the pure light of the door of absence lightening the sky. I just understood that it was the light breaking the dawn! This solid light was attacking to my chest, drawing me like a magnet and I was adapting this irresistible drawing between the arms of a spiral circling in this flying. In this giant helix, in this nothingness resembling the outer space and through the whishes I heard that sound. This sound must have been coming from the world of hearing; it was caressing my ears with delicate touches accompanying the wonderful melody. The rhythm of this melody that made everything obvious took me and threw to the other side of the door.

At that moment I opened my eyes in Safran's small room. Safran's voice resembled a soft velvet.

"The metaphorical state of love opens a door the real love." She said and added, "the important thing is to save the foot of hope from the bond of this metaphor."

25
Whatever I kept quiet I heard it

"For example you, although you are Jacob, they won't give you Joseph."
"I lost a Joseph in the well... of course I will find him sometime!"
reply of hoopoe to wagtail (Mantık Al-Tayr)

Those were the last days of May... We were all upstairs of the guest house in Hüma's room. We were about the end the year and next term Hüma wouldn't be with us, she was graduating. We all knew that we wouldn't see her again. She was watching the shadowy sad expression on our faces calmly and saying "Life is full of separations as well as coming together." I was throwing silent glances at Kırlangıç; she was as innocent as a school girl. While Hazel was hiding her sadness behind her laugh, Zümrüt was saying "I'm gonna tell you right now, I won't call none of you after we leave here and go different cities." Nergis was surprised to this and just saying "that's alright but..." Hüma was right. Life was surrounded with separations as well as coming together. I know that the name Tuğrul would also take its place among the separations page of my life, I felt this.

It happened such as I hoped! While showing concern for me every day, he disappeared in a puff of smoke. I couldn't hear his voice nor get news, he went to the earth. Nobody including Maide knew where he was. I called Maide at the fifth day of Tuğrul's absence with the hope of getting news. Trying to persuade me, she said "Believe me, I don't know". I was like someone who fell off a fast going car. I rolled to a deserted, an arid side headlong from the sweet dreams. This time the voice coming with worried taps was saying that he wouldn't return, hope for lover is like a lamp which is always on. I was consoling myself with various excuses. Keşşaf said "I want you to give up Tuğrul, but that's all. He didn't say anything in the meaning of he wouldn't come back, you couldn't do with him! I was saying myself, even if a person gives up, the thing to happen would happen. Maybe he doesn't give up. I couldn't create a strong "I" from "we" which came into being in a week with this kind of salves. The moments I had with him captured my mind; I was getting into those magic moments at any moment.

Seven days! It was a marvellous period when the door of the heaven half-opened and a cute hand reached me. I remembered the day he came back after saying he couldn't and going away. He said, "I had to see you, I understood that I couldn't live without seeing you." Then he sat at great length and told that he would settle permanently to here, he understood the value of his country. He was like a sad and ashamed cat which was lost and came back. While talking, his face fell, chubby lines were tangling in his face. He was sometimes bending his pink cheeks and saying, "What a beautiful thing being here with you is, I won't go again." However, a clever one could understand the terrifying process in this situation. An endless process. After a few meetings, he disappeared without saying the reason, then suddenly he came back and was telling like trying to find a leg to stand. But love has nothing to do with mind! Mind becomes so weak that it can't read the data regarding love. It can't foresee or return. Because no matter how hard it tries it can't see the end of love, deductions isn't the job of mind. Mind says everything is perfect but the circle called "we" starts tightening, strangling the person because of a simple reason. In order to take a breath, the only way is to go out of "we". Experiences that the mind defeated by love remain from the smashed "we".

Of course I was in the deep so as not to see the reality. The darkness of the drunkenness barring me was making it difficult to have an idea regarding where I went. My senses were deaf my perceptions were blind. After Tuğrul said, "I won't go again," we had a conversation like this,

"There may be a new desire kernel under I won't go shell, be careful."

He said "I cracked that shell and broke that kernel. I tasted the separation fruit. I say let's turn our face to a new future." His voice was offended and distressed because of deception of leaving.

I said "Let's turn" being in doubt of this turning being an illusion. Because I saw insensitivity which didn't stand firm and was watching for the scope in his brown eyes. Ours wasn't a self-assuredness situation. It was idling around sand basis which was established on possibilities. Love was like a strong whirlwind; it required protecting, not hurting the other while being with compassion. But I understood now, there was never a pure relation between two people. There were so many variables of love so many premise and inference of love that a person was spending himself or the other in this shambles. Metaphorical love was a total illusion, it had an absolute ending, it was ending before starting. But I said like sipping poison "I wish we hadn't come to this ending that much early.

How I was transforming while talking like this. I was reviving with a precious identity which I couldn't succeeded before, I was feeling myself like the others. I could cope with the life as at least the others, I was becoming as important as the others by writing his name in the blank place next to my name. The certainty of being as a couple was penetrating into my heart. Now his going overthrew all these preciousness and captured me in a worst loneliness and insignificance. I existed when I was with him, my precious existence was swinging on the end of doomsday with his going. Then Tuğrul said that day, I mean the day he came back,

"Let's have dinner for my coming back tomorrow evening, let's start everything again." He said these sentences as if he was a veteran coming back a war, as if he had victory epaulettes on his shoulders. He was inviting me to struggle in an absurd net arising from all those going-coming backs. He really came the next evening.

Life is full of sharp signs for the one who can read them. The ones who can perceive the further of the moment they live won't omit these signs. The evening that he was to come, one of my roommates cried on the bed all day. We three tried to console her but we couldn't succeed. How long could a person cry? Unbelievable. After an hour or two, heart gets tired, the chest breaks down because of the shakes, the head starts aching. But as if her crying wouldn't stop. She was shouting out, she was roaring, then she was embedding in her bed and was hiding her body shaking with hiccups. There was a little hill of wet handkerchiefs next to her pillow. Her situation was like the first phase of mourning process. How I had mercy for her. But the one to be pity was me. I didn't know the unique balance in each part of life; I didn't know that the events around us carry signs about our state.

I took my bag and went downstairs leaving this gloomy scene when Tuğrul came. I hugged the night in joy while running away the sorrow that this cry left to my soul. As I opened the door to go out, the same scent was snowing on me with all its body, I was ambling with the happiness of knowing that the owner of this scent was downstairs. I was doubling the stairs.

That night, Tuğrul came with that blue car again. We walked through the stony pathway in endless happiness again, we again passed under the shadow of the trees which were shaking up their lights. Tuğrul woke the blue car up with the same "vcıvv" sound. Everything was same, the seatbelt sounding when not fastened, Tuğrul's arm hanging down the open window of the car carelessly, his controlling the steering with his one finger, the music and the scent... Everything was a copy of the previous nights. But with a single difference! This time, there was the feeling that was unobjectionable because of overcoming the obstacles and that gave confidence to the person. An outsider looking in would think that we were a couple who solved our problems, and reached the coast safely. And the sparkles of intimacy suddenly appearing in his eyes... They were the marks of love that I couldn't read its back and that seemed absolute. Now in his absence as I remember them, I realize that separation was sharpened dagger. How difficult it is to survive! Maybe I hide behind the past to run away from pain. Tuğrul was talking easily along the way as if he wasn't the one who went and came back, he was looking at me as if he had known me for years. He was leaning back, stepping on the gas. He was sure about the happiness of his decision with the music in the car. Then there was silence for a while. There are moments when words stop but eyes talk, it was one of those moments. I was watching the lightness between us on his face; the shadow of the passing cars was sweeping out his looks. Then, he turned with a sharp, smooth look. He was like in the centre of the life where I looked, everything was turning around him, he was attracting everything to him, I was taking my share from this attraction.

He said, "I don't know why do you catch that scent." I think a person must be deaf to all sounds but must live just hearing this voice.

I said " Really? Why?" What should he say? The scent I caught wasn't related with him, in fact, OK he was wearing this scent but that's it. This scent was like a jig baited, I was stepping into the metaphorical love with it. To tell the truth, Tuğrul was only a jig.

"I was thinking you from morning to night, night to morning. I was stunned because of thinking you. I was forgetting the things I had to do. This is the reason! In fact, if I had thought someone more important, like the Excellency, instead of you, I should have already sat on the fur."

In the forthcoming minutes I would realize one more thing. How indifferent and carefree he was sitting at the restaurant we had dinner that night at the place where the elegant waiter were hovering around. He was speaking sweet nothings in a way that he wasn't finding anything valuable to care about. I understood that, nobody, including me, can step on his uninterested plane, but may touch slightly. You can't share anything with him because all the whole and parts is his. Due to his comfort, everything is at his feet. Including me. The image reflected from you slams the wall of a dark ego in him; then, he adds your image to his image, kneads and that ego wall grows, increases more and more. Only it? Most of the people on the earth are like him. They live only for themselves and even they die for themselves, everything is for their benefit. No other probability is possible for them. They are like the yeomen who can't be held a candle, can't be defeated; everybody is only "cropper". All these croppers are poor workers who have to work for them. Body lands of these people retains life water, it runs dry. But man is blind so as not to see the selfishness or utilitarianism of the others. I was tailoring this blithe profile to him, this was one of the details making him special. I think being carefree was a curtain to trouble. I gave place to him with various kinds of faces in the scenarios I wrote: Tuğrul must be an angel.

That night, I totally forgot Safran's warning "But please don't be alone with him, OK?", I fell into the Nafs' trap. But hours ran out of the night in such a bottomless blindness that I couldn't realize this, after the dinner I returned to my room.

Now Tuğrul went again, moreover he didn't make any explanation and disappeared. This was a fate that suits Keşşaf's strict order "I want you to give up Tuğrul". I lost my was at this guest house, then in this campus and in this city as if I got lost in absence desert. I didn't remember the experiences I had with Keşşaf and Safran, I was just wearing a cardigan of loneliness knitted with Tuğrul's scent. This time the pain I felt on his going was hundreds times more than pain I felt on his first going. Going of everything that much strange and unreasonable was clipping my wings. The order was strict!

I was at a very sensitive place between being broken and giving in. In the middle of that dark room Keşşaf mentioned! What about that thin light, which direction would it come? Sometimes my being hurt outweighed and I was turning my face away everything, sometimes I was forcing myself to give in fate. There was no comfort in both situations! My being hurt made life unbearable for me, at the moments I tried to give in, I felt at peace for a short time. I felt the thin, very thin light at giving in. But this giving in didn't last long, being hurt was throwing me to absence desert again. Known darkness took the place of light appeared in the middle of this absence desert. Time was frozen for me when I couldn't see myself on the way to world of scents. If there hadn't been Keşşaf's whisper, I would have been in that frozen time for years.

Whisper that I mentioned came while I was trying to sleep in my room later at night, while I was about to meet that obscurity called sleep, at the critical moment I tried to return to foetal position. When my perceptions regarding the world were about to be broken, when I was only breath, Keşşaf whispered: "change the focal point of the photograph and don't kill the background!". I fell asleep without understanding what was happening, even without opening my eyes, at the unknown between hearing or not hearing this hoarse voice. Next morning, when I remembered this sentence word for word, when I was sure about the certainty of it, I decided to live as if I hadn't heard it. I was waiting at the threshold of giving up everything.

I said "Don't say me anything!". But my mind was worrying about understanding the message in this sentence. Then with astonishment, I said to myself, but which photograph, there wasn't a photograph I could see!

I realized that a thin light was filtering into the darkroom at every strip I was swaying about between being broken and giving in, this light was making the things, although I hadn't chosen yet, visible. Moreover, there was complaint, the desire for turning me from my way in this sentence. I put Tuğrul to the focal point of the photograph that I couldn't see in the middle of the absence desert. I deleted the background in the photograph, in other words Keşşaf, Safran and the reality they took place, with Keşşaf's words I killed the background. As I learnt, "Killing the background" is a idiom in photography. Background, in other words world of reality was about to lost its sharpness in my photograph. Because everything I looked and saw was only Tuğrul. What Keşşaf wanted was my changing this focal point. The only factor which was clear at the acceptable level in the photograph was Tuğrul; it occupied the depth of field with his entire existence, he crowded out to an object or a person except him.

Now that the photograph started to appear; it must be accepted as hopeful. I had to change the focal point of the photograph immediately. But how? I decided, I wasn't going to go Safran, I was going to keep my hands off. I didn't know yet, the one who was going to give the clue would inspire how it would happen. Even though I didn't want to hear!

26
"Who didn't fall while learning to walk?"

Life is always around these two words and it takes form with them: Yes and No! These two words take you where you are. Not being able to use even one of these words will leads into a dead end. Especially the people who don't know to say no never stop fighting with themselves. People, who can't say no because they are afraid to lose, generally don't realize that this attitude is rasping their life. But someday this word no faces them as an indestructible wall; although they say everything yes, life replies them with a "no" which is turning in a scream. The echo of "yes" turns as a hard "no". I heard the "no" screams of life at one of the wide and clean streets of Kızılay which is considered as the middle of Ankara while I was trying to cross to street in the continuously flowing crowd.

That day, the guest house inhabitants were in rush of the last exam and drowsiness of the coming holiday. It was Saturday, Kırlangıç was going to meet her fiancé. We had our breakfast at the same place, at the canteen at a very early time. While drinking our tea, we watched outside from the wide opened window and dread of staying at the same room during the summer school. The loneliness I felt after Kırlangıç went after breakfast, started to tighten me like a steel cage. I wanted to go out of the campus and move away at least for a few hours. I got on one of the collective taxis, I was thinking that I was unfair to Müdrik. It would be a good idea to go to Tunalı Hilmi and say a friendly hi to him.

When I reached Kızılay, I looked around the florists' behind the place I got off for a while. The colours of the flowers reminded me of the brilliant harmony I saw at the world of seeing. A person could stay here for hours without moving among these flowers and could be full of joy of life again. I passed by orchids, *liliums, gillyflowers* and daisies, bouquets of *gerbera jamesonii*. Bouquets of roses next to the colourful arrangements reminded me of the rose water pool in the world of scents. I couldn't pass by the red and white roses callously; I stopped and bought pink roses for myself. The colour of its petals was as the same as the petals at the surface of rose water pool in the world of scents.

At first I intended to cross the street and idle around at the bookstores. I approached the crowd waiting for crossing the street. Although the pink rose didn't smell, it was enough to make the person happy. I was looking at the running traffic as the others and watching for the traffic lights. After a few minutes, the crowd started to enlarge, steps were about to run over the road, the crowd couldn't wait to cross the road. At those moments I felt as if I got rid of the boring campus and joined a real life. Crowded streets of this city were growing maturing the person.

The cars slowed down with the light allowing the pedestrians cross the street. The street in front of us appeared like a free field because of the hot weather. Everybody started to walk at a trot, the women with their babies in their stroller, young girls and boys, the old ones walking more slowly... At that moment, at the moment which didn't seem like very important, I saw him at the other side of the road in the flowing crowd. He was wearing a leather jacket although it was hot! At first I thought that I was dreaming or I was mixing him up but it was him! Tuğrul! I could only see his head because of the crowd. At that moment, I was only in need of hiding suddenly, he wasn't supposed to see me. I tried to hide my face with my hand, on the other hand I was looking at his direction. When the crowd became less frequent I saw him more clearly. He was talking happily with the women whose hand he was holding tightly, and he was trying to cross the street at a trot. I caught the happiness in his eyes, and then in the eyes of the one next to him. I felt myself as the most unlucky person on earth, I was shocked. Life must have been joking. At that moment, I felt certain that everything related to Tuğrul finished for me. The pain I had been suffering for months turned into misery at only a moment. While I was standing still like a target board, the crowd was elbowing me, some of them were commending me to walk.

An old man said, "Missy, please walk". While he was saying this sentence, I noticed the newspaper under his arm. I was standing like a scarecrow, people were bumping into me unconsciously, some of them were trying to apologize. I didn't realize that I dropped the pink rose in my hand. I tried to run away from Tuğrul's sight at once, to pass right pushing the people. It was like swimming in the current. I realized that I dropped the rose at that moment. I saw it under the feet, it was crushed.

I was short in time, but I still thought to turn and get the rose. My effort to hide myself like a null subject could make me cross the street.

When I crossed the street, I had difficulty in breathing. A hand, merciless hand of life, was tightening my throat and wasn't giving permission to the air pass my trachea. Life was looking at my face as if it was saying you are extra in this life. All these joy of life is too much for you! Life cloth doesn't fit you! As you see, it's difficult, too difficult. I was looking at the dark face of life fearlessly and saying "What's difficult, I don't know". The signboards screaming with big fonts, blessed crowd flowing through the street and humming of life were saying "you are learning". Even the models in the showcase must have been laughing at me. You skinny! I told them "What do you know?" Happy people were passing by me as if they were saying "Tuğrul will never be with you". While I was taking deep breath and I was trying to turn to life, a lollipop dropped at my feet. The owner of the sugar started crying. Her mother said "no! I will buy you another, leave it." The child was trying to take the sugar from the ground, her mum was trying to take her away.

The light was green for the cars, the impatient drivers were sounding the horn for the people trying to cross the street. At his moment I turned back and looked at the rose lying in the middle of the road. Then I watched the flowing traffic over the rose. I was standing there as if I was waiting for someone. I didn't know how I passed this side of the way. I was drifted with the current and got here in no time flat. What a difficult moment it was! All my hopes were dashed in a couple of seconds. My belief regarding his coming was broken, was dirtied like that rose crushed under the feet. A single sharp moment finished me off like a sword in the crowd. Tuğrul turned into a hangman and decapitated my head.

I don't know how long I stayed there. I must have waited there until I was brought low. I was looking around. I took the lollipop which was about to melt and stick to ground, threw it to the dustbin with all my future, my dreams and my being tricked. I started to walk. In fact, being rejected was good. Being beyond the love, being defeated by yourself. I was walking and apologizing from myself at the same time.

First, I said "I am sorry Dilruba!" Dilruba didn't reply, I think she wasn't listening me.

"I am so sorry to cause the things you have gone through. I shouldn't have accepted Tuğrul when he came back for the second time."

Dilruba said, "Yes, you shouldn't." she was looking the scope sadly.

I said "But you can never know." As if I wanted to justify what I was doing.

Dilruba said, "You should have known, you should have known. There were too many clues but you didn't want to see them."

"Yes, you are right. I accept my faults. I never wanted to give you pain."

We were falling out with myself. Somehow I must have begged me off.

"I was so light-headed, wasn't I? Believe me I learnt my lesson. It won't happen again."

Dilruba stopped, looked at my face, and said,

"I hope so and I hope you won't get conned again." That moment, I remembered the arena. I thought about the moment when Cavalry met with his enemy under the heavy rain in the arena. That mysterious moment that he forgave his enemy who was approached him enough to make rule violation. I understood now. There was no other sound other than groaning of the sky and everybody was wondering about what the cavalry do. At that very short scene, Cavalry's forgiving his enemy in the short scene was corresponding to this day in my life. Cavalry head off his horse. I must forgive myself as if Cavalry did. I knelt before Dilruba.

I said, "Getting coned? Give it to my youth Dilruba, I perish as I made you sad, believe me." Dilruba wasn't looking at my face, her tense features were veiling the mercy in her heart. I continued,

"I know how merciful you are" her face touched my face, with a tone implying there was nothing left to say, she said,

"God forgives you as you torture yourself! Beg God's pardon!" I walked begging pardon. Nobody would do the things I did myself.

I didn't understand that I arrived Tunalı Hilmi. I was taken back when I was the signboard writing Müdrik's name. I put myself inside in a relieved state as if I found a close friend. Thanks to god it wasn't crowded inside. I remembered that I last came here at New Year. I had drank herbal tea and waited Müdrik self-satisfied. I sat at the same armchair next to the window. The secretary took a glass of water I wanted and said that the doctor was busy and I needed to wait.

I said, "I will wait, no matter, but could you please inform him that I came?"

She said smilingly, "Of course." I waited for Müdrik for about two hour, I read newspaper and magazines, I viewed around. The office became simpler than I last saw. Accessories that I couldn't understand were reduced, it returned to normal. At the end of two hours, when there was nobody left in the office, Müdrik came out in white uniform.

While taking off his uniform he said "Dilruba, I am sorry to keep you waiting. Welcome!" and sat against me perplexedly. His hair got longer, his eyes decided on blue.

I said "Don't mention it. Thank you"

He said "I was thinking of visiting you this evening. How nice of you to come. I thought you had forgotten me," while touching his hair.

He just smiled without saying anything. Müdrik was the second person after Kırlangıç that I could open my heart, I could complain about my problems, he was a friend. Whatever he said was for my sake. Moreover everything he told until know were all on target. He folded his hands in his chest sagely, crossed his legs and said

"You look as if you have seen a ghost?" and he shook his head as if to say what happened.

I said "No, I'm OK. It was too hot today."

"Let's go to our café. Tell me the ghost you saw there!"

While standing up, I said "Is that the café with jukebox?"

He said "Yes, I promise I will play the most arabesque son!"

The café Müdrik called our café was at the end of the street where Müdrik's office was. Although I had been there before, I didn't realize that the café was so close. There weren't empty tables in front of the café but as the door and windows were all opened inside was like outside. We sat the first table at the entrance. Müdrik ordered two white coffees, then said,

"Tell me what happened?"

I changed the subject saying "Please don't ask me anything. What about you? How are you?"

"If you tell, I will order you a good meal. And what's more? At the restaurant with aquarium near here!"

He was putting out feelers. I would prefer dying instead of going there.

I said "I will never go there! I would prefer staying here and having a toast."

He talked pedantically "Grilled meatballs and garlic walnut and bread crumbs sauce (Cevizli tarator) is good here. And spiced mutton liver (Arnavut Ciğeri) and dried fried aubergines in tomato garlic sauce (şakşuka)..."

I interrupted Müdrik,

"I don't want to eat anything. Let's drink coffee." Sometimes speaking got ahead all humane needs. The only thing I want was speaking, revelation of troubles in the shape of letters in a way that reversing my inside and getting rid of it forever.

When I took a shot from my white coffee the waiter left t the table, I said "You were right, I was out of my depth."

Müdrik nodded his head saying "hıı hıı" and added some sugar into his coffee. There wasn't a shadow of his former self.

I said "I saw him, there was someone with him, they were hand by hand" and told him Tuğrul's coming back after saying we couldn't be together and then his disappearing again a week later, I short I told him that he disappeared in a puff of smoke. Müdrik listened me calmly without saying anything. I was sure that he was going to start speaking rigidly, he smoothed collar of his green shirt, pushed back his hair again and said,

"Dilruba, it isn't difficult to guess all these. But if you are a person who can easily be hurt, you must buy a new life to yourself. And you know, a new life isn't sold anywhere!"

I said "Easily hurt?" "Does it look like that from there?" Müdrik's hard broaching the subject was staggering me. I was also staggered now. I didn't say anything. I didn't want to be tensed again. I waited his speech.

He said "He will come again Dilruba, even if he doesn't come, he will call you. But this will be good for nothing but will increase your pain. Keep away from him!" I said bewilderedly,

"What gave you that idea?"

After saying "Let's say a wisely guess." He changed the subject.

"Do you think that only you had these problems? Nearly everybody suffers from this kind of pain. And then he forgets about it. He didn't remember even the name of the person giving him this pain." I said bewilderedly,

"Really?" But sun of hope regarding Tuğrul's coming back had already started to shine. I remembered the Keşşaf's words under this sun of hope. His saying "I want you to give up him." This sentence was going up like a wall in front of me.

"Of course, everybody experiences this at a certain extent, first love is like the first step of life! Who learnt walking without falling down?"I couldn't tell how I was relaxed. Thus, everybody experiences them.

I asked "Does everybody suffer from this pain, really?" Müdrik pushed his cup which was in front of him kindly towards the middle of the table. He was like looking for a place to put his hands. Then he put his elbow to the place emptied, he reached out his hands as if he was carrying a magic ball,

"Dilruba, everything in life, every action, every existence is for balance, for watching for an organization. You will understand this in time. It is as natural as the things that a living organism does for surviving; life is also like a living organism, it wants to watch for itself, to balance its existence." I took a deep breath, I shook my head in the meaning of no, I said,

"Hearing them doesn't decrease my pain." He talked to me looking into my eyes,

"Because you are a human being!" he stopped speaking for a few seconds, as he saw that I didn't speak, he continued,

"I have watched an impressive documentary. While a man is hiking with her daughter at a canyon they are attacked by a mother bear. A terrible attack! The mother bear is scalping the man with its claw, it is tearing the daughter's face starting from her mouth, nearly all of their bones are broken, they have a medical operations for many times." I was listening curiously, I said

"How horrible!" He continued,

"The attacked didn't say like this. Do you know what he said?"

"What..?"

"He said 'I saw the magnificent harmony of the nature in his power and his cry' or something like this. Then he repeated "amazing, amazing," he was like fascinated."

I said "Unbelievable!"

"But this is the one to be believed! Blessing the pain! Then do you know what her daughter said? Scar starting from his mouth was becoming evident. She said mother bear only wanted to protect its children. In other words, she didn't accuse it, even, she recognized it."

I took a sip of my hot white coffee.

I said "Maybe she found herself lucky as she could survive and she talked like that."

He said "I don't think so, the father and the daughter were professionals, that to say, they had a job on wild animals and they knew them well. I think life also wants from us this; this professional and real view." Müdrik was looking as himself than ever before. I understood that he was freed from all masks by looking at the sparkles.

He said "Do you remember my last arrival to you? You cried on the pavement. I told you that your had a dream and you would wake up. You see this pain is because you don't want to wake up." Then he stopped speaking. The waiter who was again and again passing by us, who was serving the customers came near us, Müdrik ordered something to eat and continued speaking,

"I dwelt upon after that day. I needed to give you time. You were learning the life. You weren't answering my telephones. I left you messages for many times. I realized that I had strangled you. I stepped back. This was the best thing to do."

My heart was sinking. I felt guilty and full of remorse. What should have been said?

I could only say "I know that I was unfair to you, even I may have behaved badly."

His voice was becoming thin, falling in strips "I don't say these to you to confess your sins." At that moment I realized that how I bored him with my problems, and omitted him. Pain was shot to my stomach,

"Dilruba, I thought that I know woman. For the sake of my job I am with them for many years, and also I had a bad marriage. But all these weren't enough to know a woman."

I had my heart in my mouth. We were at the end of our rope. God knows what he would say.

"You know, comparing is immorally. But I take the risk of this. I never took a woman to a luxurious restaurant to influence her, I never passed myself off as an artist to deceive her, I preferred wearing my heart on my sleeve. I never disappeared after saying to a woman that I was going, and then never came back as I wanted. As far as in me lain I acted honestly. But I saw that women don't like the one who is honest." I was hitting the bottom. What was he accusing me of?

"I can't believe you, you are surprising me. Do you really think that I was fooled with these?"

"Yes, you were! Moreover, the one like you whom I thought that was running after the realities believed them! Because every woman believe these! Even a nun!" Müdrik seemed so hardcore that it was impossible for him to accept that he was wrong. Later, in order to change the environment he laughed,

After saying "As you see, I can be bad-tempered, too. I can complain about the things," he stood up. He walked towards the jukebox. The waiter was serving meatballs, tarator and liver. The lonely young woman sitting next to us took her bag and went way elegantly. There were only Müdrik and I and the tired waiter. The howl of the crowd was becoming thin until it came us. I looked at Müdrik, he was trying to choose a song at the jukebox. Finally the apparent and strong tones of music started echoing inside, and effusing outside from windows and doors. While sitting to his place, Müdrik said,

"I choose the most painful song for you!" I wasn't laughing. I wanted an aspirin from the waiter taking water to the table. I leaned forward him in order to make him feel that I was going to say very important things.

I said "Maybe the women also behave in accordance to the balance you mentioned to protect themselves."

He said "Yes, you are right, their effort for guaranteeing the lives of their children can't be ignored."

I said "Let's leave this subject away. I will tell you why I was affected by him" When I said this people in me were running in haste.

"As you know, I found myself in a new and different world in recent months. While trying to understand the events, I explored the existence of love that was new and blessed. I had never experienced before. It was a holy attraction. This is too difficult to tell." Müdrik was filling in the glasses with water, and was shaking his head in the meaning of I am listening.

"When he came, I was as if I had lost my self-control, as if I wasn't on this world. If it had happened at a normal time, everything would have been different." Keşşaf came into my head, my tongue touched cinder, I couldn't continue. I only said again

"I was out of my depth." We couldn't eat our meal on the table.

He said "It is also out of my depth, I don't know, you may be right. Can we say that it is a testing? Can all these coincidence refer to this?"

I said "Possible." I was about to double up because of my stomach-ache. Müdrik left the fork in his hand on the table and said

"Our life is totally wrong Dilruba! You found a light resource and went towards it willy-nilly. But it doesn't mean that you have corrected your life. Nevertheless, if you found a light don't lose it. Because, there are so much faults in our life. We spend our life offending the Creator, showing ingratitude to him. Then, we roll on the ground like an empty sack. The life ends without understanding."

I said " How sorrowful"

He continued "My grandfather visited us when I was a child, whenever I got up I found him performing the *salat.* He prayed silently. One night, when I got up, I found him again praying on his rug in the middle of the room. I snuggled him. I asked what he was saying. He said, I was praying for you to realize everything, for you to be clever. Do you know he gave me my name?"

Something was happening to me, my face was burning. Müdrik continued,

"I woke up with his lament one night. He was sitting on the ground and was crying his eyes out. I had never seen him like this before. His white beard got wet, I could even see how his eyes were swelled up in the dimness of the room. I was afraid of his lament, I thought that there was something bad. I got out of the bed and shook him from his shoulders. I was saying, "Are you Okay?" anxiously. He lifted his head, he was smiling, he made me sit next to him and said "Don't worry, I am OK. I am weeping for joy. I got good news. I got a letter from afar. They are calling me a beautiful place." He was hugging me, kissing me as if he couldn't see me again. He smelled so good..."

I was resisting for no crying. Trains were passing through my head. Then, he said

"My grandfather died that morning. He was a person of hearts, may he rest in peace." He spoke without knowing how important his last words were for me, he just said it.

"My grandfather saw his own photograph in the eternity before dying." His eyes filled with tears, blue waves were about to come down from his eyes.

Then Müdrik let himself go, it was the first time I had seen him like this. Tears were falling down from his cheeks but his face wasn't moving.

What was happening to me? The number of the trains in my head increased, my chest started to tighten, the pain in my stomach turned into a nausea. Keşşaf came into my mind. I felt like a germ, I wanted to disappear. All my perceptions were dragging in the paws of misery, everything around us started to circle. First, Müdrik realized the cold sweat on my forehead and said,

"Are you OK, you look pale, you are also sweating..." This sentence exploded in my brain like a bomb. The meal on the table, the howl of the people outside were all as if they were stuck around the wings of the fan turning over our head; everything was turning with the fan out of breath, fan was burning out everything stuck it.

I left the table with the look of a death who wanted to revive. I was about to turn into a volcano, I was closing my mouth tightly in order not to erupt the lava which was about to brim over. I walked as if I was holding the thin thread between life and death, as if my steps were going between death and life indecisively. I hit the door of the toilet, I had no staying power, I bent over the big dustbin next to the door as if I was falling and started to vomit whatever I had.

Thousands of ants are climbing my trachea, and as soon as they reach my throat they are jumping. They are mixing with black water and they are poured out. I am looking for a single breath among fitfully growling, among water as black and peevish as petrol to return to life. I hold the dustbin with my two hands which are as cold as ice and I am composed of bellow without a head.

I hear Keşşaf's voice. He says "You will remain at the stair of metaphorical love as a rose bud which hasn't opened yet." I take the rose the girl gives me when I turned to the arena. Then I find myself in the secrets sea on the land of heart way. The rose water pool, that fierce battle under the desert heat, aloe plant. Then Tuğrul's scent. The spirit says " Satisfied hill", "You don't know how far it is!" I hear Safran's voice, her voice saying "Come!" is echoing. I turn into a rose and am crushed under feet. Tuğrul's delighted look is killing me from pain. I tell to Safran "I won't come. The heart beating in Keşşaf's hand is flowing like water, he says "all of them are only images Dilruba, the originals are here !" a woman is screaming "Oh my god, help!" Müdrik says "Even you are fooled Dilruba, even you!" he is saying this with vehemently. No I am not fooled. But I am being fooled. Safran, where is living, I can't find it. What is the reality? Tuğrul says " Reality is me" while striking over me. That is the reality! The rhythms in the world of hearing are groaning in my chest. A voice says melancholy. Müdrik says, No. I hear the voice of the Spirit. "Hey my servant, Don't gush over the bandits of the Nafs. Are there anyone who does this?" "God forbid! Never" No, Dilruba! Dilrubaa!

I am lying down on the ground as fitfully growling. The trains in my brain are passing over me now. Their sirens are moving away slowly. A woman is looking at me dreadfully and shouting as "oh my god help. Müdrik is holding my head, breathe Dilruba, breath! Our life is totally wrong Müdrik! Will it be useful to breath, I hear the lightening, the sky is furious like a raging bull. You see, I am incapable of coping with.

27
Keşşaf!

So this is speaking without using letters! Revealing without images. Pouring a drop of elixir explaining everything severely to the perception where the tongue is absent! Oh, Keşşaf! My endless scar!

My life veins break one by one when I cross with you, my soul falls down to every moment separately. I am dying quickly, quickly and endlessly. I am dying for not to revive again, if a soul like this revived, it would revive only in torture, it would wake up in the great confusion in order to be consumed by itself and to be grieved continuously. There is nothing without your name, nothing exists! All moves freeze, the flow haven't stopped from all eternity freezes in my window. Don't stop, save me from this distance as you saved from this skin suddenly. Save me so grant me breath from your breath.

I make small mistake because I am hurt, because I want to get rid of this tie, this chain. Then I understand that this is an unbreakable tie, it doesn't matter whatever you do, if you fill a glass with the oceans, if you turn back as much as you fire the sky, or if you struggle in the marshes as if you fell in a bottomless well, this eternal look between us doesn't break. I know you find me it doesn't matter whatever happens. You destroy that high wall suddenly after I wait in the dark rooms for years and thousands of sun come inside. You make me wait on an island in the middle of the deep black waters for hundreds of years and watch me; then suddenly, almost at only one moment a sail in the colour of sky lands at the moment of death rising from loneliness. All crew is you, the masts of that big ship are your words and the deck is your wiles.

I die suddenly when I cross with you.

I become paralyzed slowly but suddenly. All moves go away from the breaths, the whole humanity dies; time becomes meaningless brokenly, the rhythms empties, I go blind when I fall apart from your kingdom.

My ears don't hear, even if they hear, the universe sinks in a sound called deafness. Time so agonizes in my hands when I fall apart from you that I hold it in my hands like an ice bar. It doesn't flow. Wherever I go, whatever I do, whatever I say the heart of the time has stopped. Space doesn't work on me, people cannot console me. Spring has gone away taking all seasons on its back. Only darkness remains everywhere I look.

I have run away from you thousands of times, you know. I have tried to break these ties thousands, ten thousands of time. I have made a lot of plans, I have made a lot of mistakes. Then I have arrived at the same place every time; everything has submitted you crazily, knowingly or unknowingly, everything is derivative to you. Some falls for your name for knowledge, some peels the skin of the fame, some falls for a human and trace you. At a beautiful face, a dimple, a smile. Some completes his life with the worry of material, but only trouble and only cure of everybody is you. Some finds this, and some sleeps the sleep of life deeply.

How can face smile unless heart smiles?

Come on soul! Revive me with your breath, pour that sherbet called eternity on my face! This time let my face covered with its taste. There is nothing abundant in this world except your sweet and rose; the entire world is full of your name's petals blossoming continuously and buds. Wherever I look boozily let me see your deeds, let me hear all the time how your being covers the entire horizon...

This is the labour of giving birth to yourself! That beautiful mother called love leaves you down from her womb that she has hold tightly. She is such a mother that if she doesn't suckle us, we will perish. How does blood reach to our baby heart beating fast? How do we move our feet in the mother's bosom? How do our hands touch her merciful hair? If that mother called love weans us and tells us 'you already grow up, let's take a step', we will be very miserable. We want breastfeeding insistently. How can we walk unless she holds our hands? Darkness suckles us unless she smiles to us and caresses our head. Grief suckles us, the hand of gloom caresses our head. This is the crying of the soul, this is the origin of all troubles. What can we do anything except waiting in blood, purulence, vomit and urine unless the ball of compassion called love mother cleans us and washes us in clean waters? Neither our tears stop nor we can sleep well.

Sometimes love mother turns her head on the other side, the sun doesn't touch on her beautiful face; we hug loneliness; or we mistake supposing the beautiful women or attractive men the bosom of the love mother. Whatever happens, whoever we hold on to, it only blows the suffering. Yet, thanks God, the beautiful mother of the love suckles us in the darkness of the night during deep sleeps. Love mother is unable to get to sleep. If her child wanders about the face of hunger as if he is in a desert. We fill from her clean breast until morning. If she wants...

28

How can you take step and proceed through this passage unless you waive the being? (Attar)

I opened my eyes in the hospital. I felt relieved. As if my soul had been fined down and purified. Then I saw Müdrik. He was engaging with the serum bottle on my bedside. He was talking to the young doctor with white cloth by him. Müdrik left the serum bottle and walked to the door with the doctor, "Let's do all examinations until being sure that there is nothing serious," he said. The doctor nodded his head meaning OK, put his one hand on Müdrik's shoulder, "Don't worry, I don't think there is something serious. She is so tired, she recovers when she has some rest," he said. Müdrik thanked to him.

I tried to gather myself after the doctor went. I raised slightly, I felt a little dizzy. "What's wrong with me?" I said, "Have I gone mad?" Müdrik came close slowly when he saw I had waken up.

"You don't say," he said, "you have got tired a little, that's all." His face looked so tired that it hadn't been before. His eyes had dimpled and his fine features had been shadowed. He took a chair and sat by the bed.

"Don't worry, I haven't tell uncle Haşmet anything," he said.

"I am glad to hear that," I say. "How long have I been here?"

"Since mid-afternoon." I could remember what had happened a little; I had put my head in the dust bin in the end. Afterwards wasn't very clean. Müdrik crossed his hands wisely again, he was biting his lips, it was obvious that he was very tired. His long hair had been dispersed. Yet especially on his face, yes on his face, there is an expression of regret.

"How do you feel?"

"I am quite well, but tired a little. I think it is because of lying, I feel a little dizzy, that's all."

"It's because of me. I have pushed you around too much. You weren't already well when you came to me." He said.

"Don't talk nonsense. It's not about you." I was getting tired as I spoke. "Take me out of here as soon as possible, I don't want anything else," I said.

"We'll think about it when the serum finishes." He said. "We are going to have a look at the analysis results."

"Will you also serve tea?"

"Why not?" he said.

"You will have a look at them after I go," I said, "the girls must have been worried about me."

"Today is Saturday, I don't think anybody is aware of your absence, don't worry." My consciousness was recovering slowly. I didn't remember how I had come here, but I remembered what had happened. I was twisting the ends of the coverlet on me and I was moving my feet. I was quite well! I started to move. I needed a shower, I was smelling to high heaven.

"I am smelling very bad," I said. He crossed his arms on his chest and leaned back,

"Well, you puked in the dust bin! You did this so, then why did you fall on the floor in the bathroom?"

"Did it happen so? Ah yes...!" Now I remembered everything. First I had started to sweat coldly. Then I hadn't been able to breath and emptied whatever in me like a wild river. I had puked something resembling black water, then I had been knocked down as if I had been punched.

"Well, I wish you had made a bed on the floor, how did I know?" Then I asked the question prepossessing my mind,

"Why did you bring me here?"

"In order to learn if there is something serious." The door was opened, a plump nurse in the middle-ages came in. Müdrik said "I'm coming," without giving her the opportunity to say anything, and he went out with the nurse.

I raised in the bed. There were syringe traces on my arms, so I had given blood. Müdrik must have gone to see the test results. I stood up and headed to the window dragging the serum bottle with its hanger. I tried to see where I was between the blinds. I saw the flowing traffic flowing in a sparkling wide street. Here must have been a small hospital by the road. The hour hand of the clock over the door indicated nine p.m. I sat on the coach by the wall. My handbag was on the night table by the bed. There were various papers and fruit juice in small boxes.

About fifteen minutes later Müdrik came back with some papers and a bag in his hands. "Have you raised?" he said.

"There is nothing serious for now but if it occurs again more detailed tests will be needed."

"Why does it occur again?" I said.

"I might not occur again. I told only a precaution. I hope it won't occur again."

He tidied the papers in his hand and put them in a big envelope,

"I will keep them for now," he said.

"Keep them," I said in murmur. "Since there is nothing serious, let's go." He took out a sandwich from the bag in his hand,

"First eat this, we will think." I got the sandwich involuntarily. Müdrik looked at me as if he was about to say something serious, I knew this way of looking.

"Throw the sorrow from your heart please. Your body and soul is getting exhausted Dilruba. You are worried about unimportant things." He said. I nodded as if I understood the seriousness of the situation.

"I will do my best, I promise!" I said. Müdrik seemed to be avoiding speaking, he was selecting his words very carefully and he was trying not to reveal that he had been worried about me. He stood up,

"Serum has already finished," he said, "now you can eat contentedly."

This cold sandwich made me gather myself up. How nice being sick was.

"I can't thank you enough," I said, "I can't forget the things you have done for me."

"Yet you don't know my worth," he said with an air of smugness.

I was as weak as swinging in the lights of the city when we went out of the hospital. Yet, I was as light as a feather at the same time. Müdrik didn't want to send me to the guesthouse alone. When I told him that I had been able to go alone, he said "impossible, I will take you. Don't worry my car is over there. We won't walk a lot." It bothered me to be forced to go with him, I thought that I was a trouble for him. When we set off towards the guesthouse Müdrik said,

"Don't pull a long face, what's the big deal? I told you that I was going to visit you this evening."

"OK," I said, "all right then." I watch the road trying not to think anything for a while. Then I made the mistake that every girl at my age could make because of her not knowing; every time Müdrik changed the gear, examined the window mirror, holding the wheel in a natural way and in a lot of other details I remembered Tuğrul. Then I started to think how I would get rid of this trouble. Müdrik said,

“Don’t worry, everything will be fine in time,” as if he heard me.

“Why do you say so?” I said turning to him.

“Life teaches itself to you in forcible.” He went on talking while he was taking the bend, “but be a good girl as soon as possible. Your blood pressure was so low, you were about to fall into a coma!” I was shocked when I heard the word ‘coma.’

“What do you say?” I said in a stew. The lights of the oncoming cars were sweeping the dim darkness inside. He spoke as he was looking at the road,

“Don’t worry! Just be careful from now on!”

“What is going on when the blood pressure becomes low so that one can fall into a coma?” I said. Müdrik half opened the window on his side touching a button.

“You know, the thing we called as blood pressure is the pressure by the blood onto the veins. Blood coming to the heart is inadequate when the blood pressure is low; it means that heart doesn’t feed the organs properly, that is it cannot pump the blood properly with enough amount. When this occurs body mechanism comes into play to protect itself, especially the brain and other vital organs. For example the heart started to beat fast to increase the heart pressure, and arteries restrict the blood flow to the hands and feet.”

“Well, that’s why my hands were very cold!” I said.

“Yes,” said Müdrik, “so if the blood pressure drops too much all organs started to deadlock and a shock is inevitable.” We were about to go into the campus, the lights of the city symbolizing the natural life was diminishing. He went on,

“The self-protection mechanism of the body is extraordinary. However, if you go on to upset and knock about yourself this situation can be repeated in time even if you don’t have a sickness. So, be a good girl!” I was like seeing the heart beating in Keşşaf’s hand in the land of heart. He had told me the contractions, ventricles and valves of the heart in detail. Then I remembered the heart captured by Nafs, how it had been looking miserable. I had been trying to beat hardly. Perhaps my heart was in the same state today. Thinking that perhaps I would learn new things, I said,

“Why do you think it is because of sadness? Don’t you think that have happened because of heat or tiredness?” Then as if I knew what he would say,

“Ah, yes, you have told me about it several times. One think with both his body and soul, doesn't he?" He nodded his head meaning 'yes.'

"This is a so complicated question! You asked a question that the entire humanity is looking for an answer. One is not made up body, Dilruba. We don't consist of only blood, bones and veins. Our soul is so impressive on the body that they are almost as like as two peas. Soul and body are in interaction each other one to one; one is almost handcuffed to the other from the wrist. Yes, they are different but their impressions on each other go on all the time. They follow each other like a shadow; they take the same shape together as if a wave is curling." Müdrik stopped here, gave his id to the attendant at the entrance of the campus and went on driving,

"Soul gives the order, Dilruba!" he said. "Haven't you heard about the old people living only two or three months after the death of their partners? And what about the children whose all essential needs such as feeding and sheltering are met but cannot grow up properly because of the absence of love?"

"What a pity!" I said, "but then heart can think!"

"It absolutely senses, it is aware of everything as if it had a mind! But thinking..." He stopped speaking as if he didn't know what to say. He didn't want to say something wrong. He talked as decreasing the volume of his voice as if he was going to say something top secret,

"It is possible that it can think because it can sense!" I interrupted quickly,

"If it can think, then it can see, even it can hear." Müdrik looked at me as if he didn't understand my rising.

"Are you talking about a perception like the seeing of the eye or hearing of the ear?"

"Yes!" I said, "Remember that your grandfather told that he was called from a beautiful place that night? Perhaps he heard this by his heart." He looked at me as if he understood what I meant,

"Yes," he said, "it is possible to hear and see in that sense, but for who? This is the question needing to be answered! I don't think it is for people like us. It needs to move away from the material for that kind of hearing. I don't think it is easy." He said.

"Perhaps we don't rest the ear of our hearts on such kind of sound, how about?.. Perhaps this possibility is not far away?" I said. Müdrik said,

"You started to ask difficult questions again, believe me I don't know anything about this topic, but I think I will be interested in from now on." He parked the car in front of the guesthouse properly, and when the noise of the engine stopped he said,

"Aren't you sick, young lady? Why are you talking so much?"

"Believe me I speak in difficulty," I said jokingly.

"It isn't clear..." he said.

"What a long Saturday it has been for me. Thank you very much for everything."

"You're welcome," he said when he saw me to the door, "at least don't do anything without telling me nowadays, for your health."

"Of course," I said, "what will I do?" The press of the evergreen shirt on him had been gone and its colour had become dark. He gathered his hair dropping his neck with two hands. I had realized how wide his forehead was for the first time. His fine features of face as if they had been drawn were advising me silently. There was somewhere on his face far from me, a place like the hidden corners of life that I hadn't seen before.

Müdrik accompanied me to the panel inside. I felt the pleasure he had being with me under this light. Hope was wandering in his looks slowly.

"I don't know what would I do without you today?" I said. He responded without hesitation,

"You would do what everybody does. You would go on rising after you fall." This is a response just for Müdrik. A tongue which is always witty and wandering at the end of a quick-wit... His eyes changing between blue and green were now flowing like a green river. They were flowing as if they wanted to carry out the coldness between us, they were waving. This river had been so clear in his face framed with maturity for the first time. So helpless, so burden-less for the first time... But something was missing: scent! There was no scent in Müdrik that made him himself at every breath, to express himself continuously...

He fixed his green eyes into mine, he thinned his voice,

"I was so frightened Dilruba! When I saw you so... I felt so sorry about the things I told you..."

"What did you say? I have forgotten all of them. I don't even remember."

"Go now, have a good rest. Take care of yourself."

While I was going to my room I knew that a terrible loneliness was waiting for me in that dim and gloomy room. The room had been choking me since I became cross with Keşşaf, since I turned away my dirty face from him. Me myself hadn't taken that love coming as flowing in my room. So the four walls of the room had lost its all fluidity and hard, airless tar had filled its stomas. I headed Nergis' room perhaps because of escaping the loneliness or seeing the face of a friend. I just pushed the leaf door opening to the first floor and I caught Kırlangıç's eyes. She was talking about something to Nergis and Zümrüt on the run. "I was coming to you" I said.

I'm so lonely Kırlangıç. I'm lonely as much as a dumb person that there is no sound to touch whose ears on the earth. Nergis, I'm lonely as much as an innocent person who has learned he has been sentenced to life. Can you understand this? Is there anyone among you to talk about Safran to me? Anyone who lend me a word from her? Is there anyone among you to know the word that can defeat my patchy and coward resentment in one move? Or anyone who can stop my feet desiring to turn back to the beginning giving up everything? Anyone who will smile at my remaining in limbo like a theriac... Can you understand as if you are tearing the walls of the ego? There are thin membranes between each other, they separate us from each other forever. We are all turning back to our wells after a greeting. There are limited thin bridges between us constructed with deficient perceptions. We touch each other's heart for a while holding that bridge. Afterwards disengagement... Afterwards darkness, afterwards heavy...

"You look like you have beaten" said Nergis. "Are you all right?" Here the stillness beyond reach that I have never had and I will never have... This simplicity, this extraordinary satisfied look... This happy voice implying the gladness from every shot of life.

"I'm OK," I said, "I have walked too much in hot weather today. I have had heat-stroke a little."

"Well, what has happened? Have you dropped by Tunalı Hilmi?" said Kırlangıç. We had talked during breakfast, I had told her that I would go to Müdrik.

"Yes, I have," I said, "I'll talk about it later."

I cannot talk about it Kırlangıç. If I tell you will also get frightened of me. You will move away then. How I effuse a well of purulence from my heart... If I tell you how one falls prostrate after seeing a face resembling heavens... When your hands touch the other side, touch a very different love, they freezes here Kırlangıç. They cannot touch even themselves. You also know that nothing is enough here. May be you have also experienced these, why doesn't anybody talk? Why don't they tell that they have been there? I want to know how you can keep pace with here. I need to hear what is going to cauterize this black loneliness here. Which hand spaces it? They don't give me Tuğrul, is the land of testing arrived by this way? Why? Will separation hit my head as if it is smushing the steel on a stithy until it reveals that there is nothing as separation?

Zümrüt spoke with her tone of voice making velvet jealous;

"Is there any news?" I understood what she meant. She was asking about Tuğrul.

"No," I said shortly with a short and deep voice as if I was preventing all other questions.

"But I think I saw him today. He was with someone." Zümrüt understood what I meant and she could only said,

"Why!"

"It was just one of those things," I said with a neglectfully, "it's not necessary!"

"Of course, never mind!" they whimpered with sympathy.

"There is no one in my room, let's go in," said Nergis.

"Has anybody seen Safran recently?" I said after I sat on a chair throwing my handbag to a corner. Nergis perched on the bed by the window and put her hand on the heater.

"I and Hazel went to her yesterday," she said. This sentence lightened my heart like a lantern.

"How was she? Was she all right?" I wanted to know if she asked about me.

"As you know," she said, "she asked about you and asked about the school." Nergis was talking slowly. I couldn't include myself into her slowness.

"Did she ask about me?" I asked in a cheeky manner. First Nergis couldn't remember,

"She asked about you generally," she said. I would accept as call Safran's asking especially about me. It didn't happen, and it wouldn't happen also. I wouldn't have peace until I accepted Tuğrul's absence voluntarily and with a full acceptance.

When I woke up on Sunday morning light-headedly after the long Saturday, I was only thinking to go to Safran. I wanted to go and break the ice. It wasn't easy to turn back to her as a small person. As I was running after her breathlessly she was moving away from me. When Tuesday came I hadn't known what would happen that day. I walked to the faculty in a deep silence, after settling my affairs I came to the dorm and threw myself on the bed tiredly and I woke up at about four o'clock after a sad and fitful sleep. During the last three days Müdrik had called me to ask how I was, and he added "I will visit you when I find an opportunity." I tried to gather myself so that he would see me in a good state if he came. Although he had said “Don’t worry, I haven’t told anything to uncle Haşmet,” at the hospital I was still full of doubt about it; I couldn’t help thinking that he had told my father about me. My father, Haşmet Uçmaklı was a strange man. He liked to control things from remote, and I knew he had been calling Müdrik instead of me since this seemed him to be a safer way.

On the other hand, I hadn’t got rid of the scent under my nose yet. I must confess that even the thought of getting rid of the scent gave me an unidentified pain. This scent meant to me hope while it increased my sorrow.

The scent was telling me “Nothing has finished yet. As long as you feel me, as long as you submit me I will be with you!” It surrounded me at any time and said, “We are going to burn together Dilruba! There is no escape from me!” I had already submitted to this scent. I felt that there was no escape like a person who had a mortal disease. Sometimes I was breathing deeply, and to extend an inhale as much as possible to fill my cells with this oily, aromatic, sliding scent. “Okay, I have no other chance, we are together, you and I. As long as we stay close to each other, we will reach beyond the pleasures.” The scent became my breath. I decided not to talk about this scent to myself although I smelt it clearly. I was thinking that I could overcome it by ignoring, and I thought that someday it would go away from my breath. Every time I sipped this scent with pain, I remembered what Keşşaf had told me in the world of scents. In the world of scents Keşşaf had showed me the bottle containing Tuğrul’s scent and said,

“You have been looking for this scent since you stepped on the world of scents. Here it is!” Then he had poured only one drop of this scent into the rose water pool appearing in the scent workshop suddenly, and he gave me the red glass filling it with the water of the pool. So I always remembered this scene every time I felt the scent. Then the sour taste of it in my mouth... Afterwards Keşşaf had asked me, “have you still felt the bitter taste in your mouth?” and he had given the answer himself,

“No, you are here because you still have that bitter taste in your mouth!” Dark room, aloe, desert of absence, Nafs... I was trying to combine everything that had happened so far and to find a way out. Spirit, the real owner of my land of heart, was captured by this scent. The scent was so powerful that it could have Spirit’s soldiers do whatever he wanted. All ammunition that Spirit had in the land of heart was powerless and ineffective against Nafs’ power.

Even if my tongue didn’t tell me anything, the scent was burying me alive mercilessly every new day that Tuğrul was absent. The sweetness of the scent was sweeping all tastes on the earth, it was playing with me overthrowing all images, and it was making me a person whose all faculties and senses became blunt except the sense of smell.

There was a short time to the evening. The gloomy hot weather felt in the air all day and make one stewed was the sign of the rain. I was tidying my room and thinking about the events in the desert of absence in my room. I was telling myself "I must ignore the wild whips of the bitter net knitted by the pleasure given by the scent." Yes, it was there. Then a moment would come that the scent would go away anyway. Yet thinking about this was equal with death for me. How could I live without it? It had tamed me, and it had captured and domesticated me as if a master was doing with his slave. How could I keep standing without the scent? What if my breath would become an empty breath again? What if this drunkenness would finish one day? So I was drawing the scent to me worrying about such things. When I felt it here, at my elbow, a new meeting was happening between us. I couldn't live without this silvery fire from now on. All my being was tied to its existence, and I couldn't think, see and hear without it. I needed to drink it until it burnt my throat, and I needed to test its existence until its charms made me faint. I was nothing without the ordering breezes of the scent. Existing was meaningless before its wild paws broke me into pieces. An eternal life was hidden in its oily and arrogant pertness; the scent gave me the eternity in every breath even if the deadly pleasure that the scent gave me destroyed my mind quickly! All rhythms, all colours and all sounds were moving their moribund bodies with the scent and they joined in life. I was an undefined and unclear meaninglessness stuck in the middle of absence. I was expanding through the aromatic flames of the scent, and I surrounded the entire universe with this fire. I became the universe itself in response for its surrounding me. The scent I was covered of which elixir, the sweat of love was giving me the love itself totally. It inspired me the elusive privates of love and it disclosed all hidden seals of it.

The moment I had seen Tuğrul on that way! I had told myself it had been impossible, how? While I had been feeling his scent every moment, how had it been possible? What about the scent penetrating my soul? How had I been able to scrape off it from the bottoms? I had remembered what Müdrik had told me before, "We must bless the pain, Dilruba; we must take it realistically as much as possible." Then I had told myself that this scent had obviously been real. What had it been there more real than that? A hidden hand had put that little bottle under my nose. It hadn't been an illusion that much! Then I had remembered Keşşaf's words, "Scent is temporary. It contains disappointment due to the magic and the shortness of it." Then I remembered his words in such pain; "pain is the thing distilling one."

I sat at my table, I saw my face in the oval mirror on the table. I looked at myself as if I was looking at somebody else. How I got lost on the way going to the world of scent through thousands of face and then existed again as becoming Tuğrul. Watching myself in the mirror as if I was watching somebody else remembering everything... It was feats of bravery to look one at himself. I looked at my eyes. I looked at my defeated looks in which hope appeared as a weak shadow. I was trying to find my own trace. Finding my own trace was only possible with the scent; I examined it taking a deep breath, it was here. This time it came like a slave that was called by its master. I was waiting readily as if it was waiting for my orders and saying 'I am here, by your side.' I closed my eyes. I called it by isolating from everything again and again. It poured into my heart tearing my veins like a sharp dagger. I was getting close to me until nothing but only it remained in my lungs. The scent was choking me transforming into a hand; it was shouting as "breathing without me is forbidden you." It was dragging me from my hair, then it started to scream holding my neck. It takes me at the end of a cliff; I know it is going to push me down without mercy. I ask myself that if I want to die or live with this scent. Afterwards... Afterwards a new desire of living sprouts in my soul. No, I say, you won't be able to kill me. You won't manage it. I start to bell like a wounded animal; only one breath will mean escape! My hands are looking for a space to breathe among its thick fingers. I examined myself with severe pain; the iron feet of the chair I am sitting on are moving with noise.

"No!" I say; "you won't be able to kill me." I open my eyes in broken breaths. I examine myself with my hands on my neck as if I examine life. Then the most unreasonable thing among all these experiences happens; my hands are so big, they are not my hands! First I see long thick fingers in the mirror. My neck, my stubbly beard... Oh my God. I look at my eyes. They are Tuğrul's eyes. This skin is not mine! This big, boned face! I take my hand to my face, I must have died. No, I see Tuğrul taking his hands to his face in the mirror. The scent must have transformed me to Tuğrul at last. Oh my God! I enjoy this situation in a terrific way. I am him! Here everything I want is me. This pleasure doesn't last long, shouldn't last long; I jumped with a terrible attempt like running away. The iron feet of the chair make noises as if they were breaking the ground. I find myself as Dilruba again when I stand up. I am Dilruba. Everything is over. This must me a nightmare I have dreamt awaken! Gather yourself up, you are all right, it's over, I say to myself while perching at the edge of the bed.

I wait everything to be normal as sitting. I look at my hands steadily. Then I start to think that this is a gift given to me. Here, I say to myself, you reached the furthest place you can go, you have appeared as Tuğrul even if it has been a few second on the earth. How happy you are Dilruba! How many people among the ones who love can reach such a pleasure? The main point is that to be him, not to be with him! I try to remember what I felt during those a few minutes; in fact I try to experience it again. First I felt that my back widened during those moments I lost the feeling of self and experienced a different body. After I felt a back widened in four sides, my hands got bigger in this unexpected feeling of giantism. Then my face got harder and my head got heavier. Yet there was something different, something indescribable. While I was just staring at the threshold of a existence that was impossible to describe, while I was in unendurable pains of being Tuğrul, I... Yes, I discovered that Tuğrul was just a person as limited as me and far from capable of anything at that moment. In fact there was no difference between being Tuğrul or being Dilruba! The scent that I had been feeling for months, yes, actually a scent he used, and it was all about me. At this moment that I was thinking of thousands of things, my room shined with the announcement of, "406 Dilrubaaaa, 406 Dilrubaaaa, you have a visitor." This voice took me out of the halos in which I had been struggling between the dream and reality. Only Müdrik could save me from this madness, thanks God he had come. I looked at myself in the mirror without losing time: I was Dilruba. I boggled at the noise of a lightening. I seemed to rain. When I went down the stairs slowly and arrived by the panel downstairs I couldn't see Müdrik. The woman in the announcement cabin told me to look around the canteen extending her head out of the cabin. It was about to be dark. The light of the day was about to give its place to a thin darkness. The residents of the guesthouse had been relaxed with the end of the term, they were walking around in their slippers, and some was trying to change money for the biscuits machine. I walked around the phone cabin, I stopped at the door of the canteen from where a noise was coming from.

I was looking for Müdrik among the sluggish crowd. He couldn't be outside. At that moment I saw him at the table he had sat when he had came to me before. Tuğrul! Again he stood up when he saw me and again he got smaller as much as he was smashed under the feet of the table. He took a few steps towards me,

"Dilruba!" he said. He was looking at me as if he had never gone, as if we had just separated. As if it hadn't been him going away without giving a reason... He was so relaxed that as if he had a valid reason to be here. His smile was like taken from pure children. He leaned to me with happy looks. I saw the hot torches which were about to flame up in his brown eyes. He was in a state as if he wanted to celebrate his coming back. His looks were as if they were saying 'look, how I honour you with coming to you.' Tuğrul, I had been transformed into him a while ago was before me; he was so close that I could feel his breath! He was alive with his blood and soul. My will was melting while he was looking at me so and I was transforming into a creature without conscious and mindless. For a moment only two of us remained in the crowd, just two of us existed until we didn't hear a noise. His looks were so beautiful that they can give life even a dead planet. The place he occupied here, the stones under his feet, the table he put his arm, all details his eyes touched... There was a magic in these things spreading from him. A black magic...

Without understanding what had happened I was staring at him bewildered. The distance between two faces was getting closer; Tuğrul was coming closer to make me hear his voice. At that moment the very itself of the devastating scent was standing before me like an indestructible statue. The scent was telling me that "It is impossible to give up me, Dilruba." The wind coming in was dancing around the scent deadly; all moves of the dance of the wind, its bending and rising, its selfish and ambitious flying was transforming me into a gazelle shot by an arrow. The meeting of the scent and Tuğrul's eyes in the same frame meant an inevitable death.

So you see Dilruba, I am defeating again. No, said Dilruba! No, you haven't been had again, have you? You have promised, haven't you? Müdrik's voice was circling in my mind, "he is coming again Dilruba, but it doesn't make you any good except giving pain; keep away from him!" No Müdrik, the pain itself means love, your words are useless! Then Keşşaf's words were sticking into my heart. "I want you to give up him." I could remember what he said word by word:

"Metaphorical love has captured you Dilruba! And the solution in hostage events is not giving money and save the hostage. Even if destiny gives you Tuğrul it doesn't mean you will be saved. To save you is only possible with capturing the metaphorical love, making it ineffective and reforming it to the true love. This was only a performance including you to teach you love. However, if you insist on staying there, I'm afraid a loyalty seal won't appear on your forehead, and your sufistic journey. You will remain as a bud at the step of the metaphorical love."

A bud... I have dropped that bud Tuğrul. I was crossing the other side of love. You were coming back from the way I was walking on. We were going to different directions. I got so excited when I saw you, you couldn't understand. I dropped myself, I lost it on halfway. In fact I dropped myself, do you know that?

Now Tuğrul was standing before me like Nafs' vizier in the desert of absence. Now it was time to ignore and give up him. Tuğrul leaned his head backwards, he pushed the forelocks falling his eyes back. A thoughtful expression waved on his face.

"Hello, how are you...?" I couldn't answer. Saying something opening my mouth... Müdrik is going to proved right again Dilruba, don't do that... Everything will be over, if you believe, everything... Tuğrul extended his hand as if he had given an un-tasted fruit from heaven being aware of my astonishment.

"I want to talk to you... Dilruba..."

The darkness fluttered with the vibration of a deafening lightening. When the rain started to beat the windows, it was putting out the torches starting to fire in Tuğrul's eyes. I was feeling a spontaneousness and simplicity bringing me home as the bare arms of the rain were coming inside. I was gathering myself, I tried to build up my voice, at first a meaningless wheeze came out of my mouth, but then,

"Welcome. You bothered coming here." What a historic moment it was for me! A moment that could change my destiny! I went on,

"But please don't come again." I could only say. What was it remained to talk about? I left his astonished looks there. I turned back; I was running away like a gazelle running away from the hunter. I threw myself out not to strangle. I was walking in the dark without knowing where I was going at a trot, and I wanted to go away from myself. If I had stayed, I would have been defeated by myself. I wanted to go away from all lies. I don't know how long I walked outside under the rain. My hands got sticky due to rain. I walked to the stadium where I had said the prayer that had started everything feeling that I was purifying as I was soaked to the skin. I knelt on the grass resembling a giant wet carpet. I waited silently like a butterfly waiting for going out of its cocoon holding on a thin branch in the air under the black and starless sky.

"If you don't lighten me, I will remain in the dark, in this dark net." I could say whispering. The wind hitting my face and my ears was passing by me leaving a crazy howl. This rainy wind sweeping the air freely and then turning around me crazily carried my whisper to the skies. Carefully... Without wasting even a letter of it... Then the scented net surrounding me, this transparent cocoon was torn and cracked by the hitting of each drop. The big drops making noise as hitting my head was thinning this scented net, tearing it and untying the knots. I stayed there as if I submitted my neck to the rain for a few minutes. I was waiting for a clear and definite answer from the skies. I waited there as all my clothes were wet and until my knees got the colour of the green grass. Until I saw a lightening overflowing the darkness as cracking and boiling up over the stadium...

29
The food of a lover is fire

"I became such a soul that there is no far, near, strong or nice! Materiality is the prisoner of my order, spirituality is victim of my self-control. Nevertheless why I am hungry!"

(Amak-ı Hayal)

I knew that I had to go. All signs were calling me. The next day in the afternoon I looked in all the rooms one by one and searched the girls in their rooms, only Nergis was in her room. I asked her whether there was a group to the *dergah* or not on that week. She was shocked with this question. She slipped a paper saying "I don't know but if you call this number, they may inform you." When I called the number, the voice on the phone said "Yes, there is a group this evening." the voice on the phone... I was sure that I had heard this voice before. But until I saw the owner of the voice, I couldn't remember who it was.

I must have called Müdrik and said I wouldn't be there for a while. I didn't want him to think that I disappeared and to get angry with me. I sauntered at the ground floor for a while thinking how to say this to him. Finally I screwed up my courage and dialled the number of the office. After the secretary said "I will make you wait a little", I could hear Müdrik's voice.

"Hello Müdrik"

"Dilruba, what a beautiful surprise. How are you?"

"Good, thank you. I wanted to call you this time."

Müdrik said "I am so glad. I will visit you this evening." At first I couldn't say anything as I didn't know how to sum up.

"Hello, Dilruba Are you there?"

I said "I think I am busy tonight. I am going on a short trip"

He said bewilderedly "A short trip? But how, where? I last told you to be good. Did you get better?"

"Yes, I'm fine. Really. I will tell when I come back. I called you to thank you, and also not to go without informing you."

Müdrik said "You're welcome, but thanks for what? What's up? What happened? Your school finishes a week later, doesn't it?" Although he was asking this, I knew that he understood. Luckily, he didn't insist.

I only said "Yes, that's right. I will try to call you when I am back. Take care of yourself, bye." But Müdrik lashed out,

He said "I guess where you go, let me come with you. What's bad?" He was trying to convince me. I thought that I had gone with him for a while, I tried to guess how possible it was. I couldn't forecast anything. Then this idea made me afraid.

I said "I must go alone Müdrik. At least this time."

"Dilruba, could you tell me from what you are running away?"

"Believe me I don't run away from anything."

"Then, why are you in a hurry? At least wait for finishing school."

"What will change? If I stay here a little longer, I will smother."

He said "OK, you know. But please call me when you go there, if possible, I want to know you are fine" His voice was sad, as if he was disappointed. I couldn't tell that I wouldn't call him when I went there. I couldn't air a grievance. I was afraid of making him sad but I had to go.

The group was going to leave in a few hours. I was thinking about every detail in case there would be a problem and I wouldn't go. I arrived at the meeting point of the group. I appeared like a shadow next to the women waiting. As the time passed, the number of the shadows in front of the old small mosque increased, the wrecked street became more crowded. Then an old bus stopped in front of us with a tired and long hiss sound. A man with a cap got off the bus from the front door, he was looking at the list in his hand and counting the crowd. He came near me looking at his toes without looking at my face,

He said "What's your name?"

I said "My name is Dilruba, I have enlisted my name before."

It got so dark that I couldn't perceive the face of dervish, but I was sure that I knew him from somewhere. He looked for my name in the list.

He said "OK your name is in the list." At that moment I remembered where I had seen him. He was the one who met me in front of the palace of love, he told me to follow him after the gold-leaf door of the palace was wide opened. It was him. Then, he said "Enter one of the spheres and wait" While I was watching him bewilderedly, he checked the names in the list one by one and disappeared.

Before the group left, we crowded into the old small mosque where we were waiting as the first time. Thin wood were squeaking as our foreheads touched the ground. We heard transformation of the squeaking into the melody as we were fidgeting. Then we went down the stairs in doubled up state and crowded into the buses. This time I didn't know anybody in the group. It got dark, faded lights and weak voices started to lash at the window of this old bus. That moment when everybody took their place and we started our journey! The wheels were turning under us slowly, we were going by sweeping out the darkness. I felt a glow of happiness when I heard the voice of the bus driver, I remembered him. He was the wise bus driver talking joyfully and enthusiastically at our first trip. I hear the same sentences as in the first time. "Don't forget the intentions, may Allah accept. Bismillah"

I am sitting at one of the seats in the middle of the bus. Someone is asking for "We are going to take some people on the way, tell the bus driver to go slowly." I say the same sentences to the ones at the front seat. Some others get on the bus onwards. Greeting us, they are filling the empty seats joyfully. We are looking at each other. At first, I am trying to read the peace on their faces. Then lyrics of a chant are going around us. Plates are being passed on from behind, stuffed wine leaves, cake. I remember my first trip, Kırlangıç. I say I wish the girls were me too. And also Safran. Although they are not with me, I feel the same family emotions that I first felt. I feel that all these people are as close me as sibling, I am set at ease.

The bus is shaking us like a crib singing love lullabies. We start talking with the girl next to me. She shows the little bag in her hand and says "I didn't get anything except this. I have my gastric medicine in it." I can't understand why such a young girl uses gastric medicine. While she is telling, faded lights touch her face surrounded by an elegant scarf, she says joyfully

" I am going to stay there for a while inşallah" I pay attention to her immediately and say

"I wonder if I could also stay?"

She say "I don't know, you should ask" The one sitting in front of us starts flapping lie a bird. I say to myself "the conversation started" While the woman is flapping as if she wants to fly, I turn to the girl next to me and ask,

"Who should I ask?" With the confidence of having knowledge on this kind of subjects, she says

"There is a head servant, when we reach there, ask him." I say to myself that I must find the head servant. The road is flowing under us like rebellious rivers again. Our wise bus driver starts telling the rules to be obeyed there one by one in order not to return empty-handed. The people on the bus are listening to him carefully, some of them are nodding their heads as if there are approving. He is saying

"Try to placate everyone. Don't hurt anybody. Don't hustle, the thing in your destiny will come and find you. Do not even look hostilely." These sentences remind me Safran's sentences on the road.

When the *isha azan* is being recited, we give a break in front of a deserted mosque. I remember this mosque. I read the statement of esteem and respect from heart on the faces under the street lamp at the place we get off. The women find a trace in the darkness and go to the lavatory in groups. I go behind them. I remember our smoking with in front of this wall, having our heart in our mouth in case Safran would see us. When we crowded into the mosque, the ecstatic scent, which is implying that time hasn't flowed since I came here, choke up. I feel the energy in the mosque, the brightness of the mosque is mirrored to our faces. As we leaned down, we look at our faces of our hearts closely, more closely. All of our dirt is washed under these lights. How strange! The peace here at this moment, the atmosphere turning us to our internal cycle. Fantastic. The peace taking you out of all shambles and fatigue duties of life, a distance one can reach at once are turning around us like a prayer relieving the person. Aureole is visible. It is embedding you in it and laying down its ground cloth.

I return to my place at the bus with the group after leaving some of the peace at mosque. The bus starts flowing like water again but this time more purified, it is going on the land knowing that it will purify more as it flows. As the minutes pass, stillness that I girded myself starts breaking, eluding in pieces. My thoughts start being sharpened with blunt saw. The doubts withdraw their ugly and rude heads slowly. I say Tuğrul. I remember the last scene with him. "Please don't go once more!" This sentence goes in to pieces like a broken glass. Safran's saying melancholy, the things that Keşşaf told in the world of scents come into my mind one by one. I remember all of them as if I am sipping a bitter medicine.

I am saying to myself "You are running away Dilruba." Dilruba answers it,

"Yes, I am running away, as I said you before, I am running away from myself."

"Maybe everything changes, maybe forgetting will win this time" my imagination is fixed at a base place.

"If I didn't say like that everything would change. Maybe a new fate was going t be written."

I whimper "Oh Dilruba, don't do that. It won't happen. What have we spoken with you?" I take a deep breath. Again the same thing! The same scent! It finds me here, too. I understand that this testing hasn't finished yet. I am waiting for a strong hand which can take out this scent form my nose; that strong hand which will save me from this oily and fragrant scent which is falling on my head like a cutter made of loneliness.

My seat-mate is sleeping. Reflection of my face is seen on the window, the bus goes fast through the night, as if it isn't going to pass again the same places it passes, as if it is flying. I say "You said that whenever you call me I will here you." Calling you with your voice. I don't mind telling you that I can't hear my own voice. I squint and start watching the blue light decreasing. They are handing their indigo-blue colours to blackness. Then they are hardened wherever they touch, they freeze. I lean my head on the window. The cavalry passes at full gallop from the openness of the window. The whiteness of his hands holding the headstalls sparkles. Mane of the white horse passes erasing the deserted lights of the city. This time his green cloth is so close to the window as to touch it. His thin body touches reflection of my face. The images mix, it takes away my face. Its skew-back is shining and its silhouette is lengthening. His white head-dress is touching the shadow of the bus slightly. He is showing his back as if to say I am here.

I call him from before it lost the heat of the image at the window,

"Keşşaf, your beautiful face is spread over my life! Tell me where this going is? How far from me can my heart house go?"

Cavalry is turning his head with a look that doesn't leave a life in the heart,

"If we became a single eye by ourselves, if we didn't immerse the words in dark colours, if we didn't believe everything we heard, we could smell a mystery behind the things we saw. We could touch our wings to the speech of secret, at that case we would understand that there is nowhere as far... If we didn't care about ourselves that much, we could plow through the seas. We could make ourselves happy if we put strength in the dough of the days coming like tongue twister. If we thought the wishes as sacrifice, at that case we could understand that this going to ourselves, this going is to unity..."

I am giving a hand with my voice,

"Then tell me on which sky does face of an un-beloved woman pace?

Where can her look fill into? Who holds the hand of dismissed, who holds her breath, while going barefooted? Who is proved right from this sleep? Or who hears the infinite who finds live whenever he says it's over? Where is the nook to hide? Where is the good news that I deemed trouble and I ran away from my corner? Broad and pure reality that leaves no room for doubt... how close or how far? How active, how live and how real this boredom in this life shield... which is the hand holding me? Which invisible rope is on which wrist?"

I hear his voice, with an eye looking like jasmine in my chest,

He says "Dilruba, you are now in the presence, you are right here. Understand that the hand holding you is making you smell a secret. Scent is only a tool to purify your conscious. You can't become one with love without your conscious is sharpened with purity. You are going to smell it until your consciousness is consciousness of whole universe. Neither fear nor worry touch your face, Dilruba! Do you understand me? Hearing me isn't enough, you must understand."

I say "Smelling a secret... drinking it until you suffocate because of poison... drinking it until you are erased from yourself. All I understand is this, and also unfailing reality of your existence. Save me from this poison!"

"Dilruba, we are on a long trip, it is so long as not to end. These are your first steps at testing land. You gain insight into a situation late. You will enter the scene where that old story ended. You must leave the lonely called ego to the hand of water in which scene the reality flows. Move your mouth when it's your turn to speak, cut the head of the sentence when you are told to stop speaking. Where is ruined, where is the palace, where is the vagrant, where is the king? Be purified from all of your identities. Make your all wishes follow you. If you do this, door of a new world will be half-opened to you. At that moment, you can ask your soul mixed with love when you hand a clean heart: What is existence, what is absence?

You are a *cemre* (any of three radiations of heat falling in succession from the sun to the air) touching yourself and take an astrolabe to look at your own sky, that will teach you the language of the stars and show you their reflection in your chest. And it will fill in your breath with the Milky Way, it will reflect you a sky which is yours and it will draw whiteness in the blackness of your eye. When you find the sky in your chest, the world will stay behind. There won't be even a point in the white part of the sky. The place you stepped will not glimmer. A way will be found for the things that happened, that will happen, as long as you fall down like a *cemre* to the place the secret starts."

My hearing is getting out of focus at the last sentences. Voice of the cavalry is goes out of me. it is mixed like a soft dough. I resist until I have no staying power. I am pushing the sleep in that armchair until my head falls down like a scarecrow. Finally I fall into the arms of deep but painful sleep.

I am in a sleep full of enthusiasm and wishes but away from them as far as possible. I see that all our enthusiasms are illusions. All the enthusiasm I extended a hand is in the wish pool. They are pouring out one by one like the scent bottles in Keşşaf's hand. Only my mind remains, batting around freely on the surface of this wish pool. Then I get rid of that mind and go up. This is the freedom of zooming out myself! I can see the chaos in my mind explicitly, what kind of a conflict is it? What kind of a conflict is there in the middle of my mind? I look into the fear nooks hidden, future and past are unravelling knot by knot. The hand of now is being twisted at the timeless moment. I clearly see the now including all times. Myself, my conscious are away from all times.

I don't know how the whole night finished. I open my eyes to voice of driver Mahir. The group stops with a tired, long *tıss* sound in front of a mosque lightened by the *azans* before the sun shines. The passengers are looking around bleary-eyed. They are trying to understand the moment that life took them. The breaths are increasing with the opening of the back door, life joins us. We get off the bus like still, sleepy rivers. Col weather cuts our sleep like a sharp sword. I remember the trees, we pass by the dark green shadows with prayers.

In this little mosque, everybody lives his birth again. As the foreheads touch the coldness of the ground, the load of living falls off our shoulders. We turn back to our seats with light and cool breaths. We set off again. There is an action in front of the bus, the bus driver is speaking among the buzzing, "We are going to have some soup, we have a little time for the break." When it is dawning, we reach to the *dergah.* This building with two or three rooms is as I left. Big cooking pots are here without moving since I last saw them, as if they are lifeless. The big rounded cooking pots are the symbols of eternity. They are turning with fruitfulness. Piping hot soups are put on the tables, travel-sore wrists are reaching the thin slices of bread.

Sharp end of the loneliness is still on my head. There is the pain of not tearing the transparent cloths and not going beyond them, my look is all out confused. What difficult it is to understand, comprehend! I ask myself where I was! Where is here? Where are these people, this road, this group going? In reality all of us are trying to go beyond the ways in us. All of us have put our ears to that single music, to the enthusiastic melody of existence. We are trying to separate this unique melody from the sounds of life. The spoons are plunged into the bowls. We hear these enthusiastic melodies among the secret tones of wooden spoons. This is the drift of persistent existence. A musical turning in front of the heart. It makes us listen the majestic existence of the universe, it is taking out us from duality. These are the pains of going to the oneness. This drunkenness, this drunk obscurity turning between us, is flowing through the fingers cutting the bread. The spoons moving from the bowls are following that unknown way, at that short distance.

The group sets off while the warmness of the soup is wandering in our veins. We are passing through a bright new day with joy. There is motion inside. There are signs of going towards hope on the faces. The beauty of reaching at last is half opening its claw. Life means going without stopping. All of us are going without stopping in this life in a group. Life is changing as moments are added to moments; each moment is different from the previous. What remains the same?

Despite the things I experienced, this road is going to a distance now. I feel the strikes of not belonging to nowhere, nothing which is first cutting my flesh then deboning, which is peeling me. These are moments Tuğrul is thinking of me. The same messenger is saying that he is thinking of me. I say to myself it can't be. It can't be like this. All of these are illusions Dilruba! What nonsense the things I experienced with him. Those elegant restaurants, that fascinating atmosphere. This shouldn't have happened. One shouldn't stay alone with him even in crowd. I say I wish there was someone with us. This was the right thing, maybe I shouldn't have fallen in that much...

The group was going through the alcove of love, to the most untouched land of seclusion. The weather was getting hot, the coolness of the morning was giving place to joyful lights of the sun. The ones in the group were drawing the thick green curtains from end to end, the chants pleasing the people greatly were hymned. At every moment of this blessed way, all of us were turning our heads towards a distant like sunflowers reaching to the sky. We were half-opening the curtains and trying to see where we were on our own way. After a while, we reached to the desert flowing like yellow water. The group was walking in the middle of very yellow carpet where no living creature was. We were getting ahead on the asphalt road as if we were yellow saffron flowing from stomach between arid silent droughts. While passing through here, a person felt that he was passing through a forgotten, an adrift place, the place where is no sound, in the middle of a fearful silence. Chunky tragacanths appearing locally and birds of prey diving into the space above us caught my eye.

Thin dust clouds were rising between the seats because of the heat, the hands reaching to the backpacks were disturbing this dust cloud. Then an addressing was tearing the sounds inside, then a prayer, a shout was cutting us like a knife. We perspired suddenly passing our faces licking up to our neck.

Keşşaf said "the road to soul passes from house of heart, from love Dilruba! This is the road to be obedient! Be obedient!"

The group was going through destruction for me. I said "I don't know what being obedient means, Keşşaf? When metaphorical love took an arrow from its quiver and put it to the bow rigidly, it was quickly finding the target, I was suffocating in the same scent. Oh Tuğrul, I wouldn't be with you, would it... Then a separation catapult threw me away from the group. Then Keşşaf was calling me,

"There isn't reproach, condemning any kind of separation in the land of love." Whenever I opened my eyes in this old and weak seat I was going back from land of derogation as I was contemptible and worthless.

I said "My duty is to admire you love-locks. I don't have any job other than this, Keşşaf."

Keşşaf said "Then clean your house of heart from couch grass..." As Keşşaf talked, the beats of loneliness cutter were increasing instead of decreasing. But didn't I have to be at the place loneliness ended? In failure of understanding it,

I said "Why is this loneliness increasing? Why?" Cavalry was turning up as if he wanted to cut the head of loneliness. Skew-backs of the galloper were shining and chattering. It was going on the asphalt road which was almost melted, white male of the thoroughbred was crystallized and flowing. The group was going on the crooked way, it was trying to get rid of the flaring hands of the desert, it was turning all around as if it was playing hide and seek.

A narrow, rough, arid way started at the foot of the high rocks. The cavalry was going like flying in the dust cloud as if teaching the way to the bus driver. We were flowing through a sand and dust shower. I heard the same tambourine sound at the foot of cliff rising like sword. Drum beats appeared like heart beats at the foot of the cliff. It was echoing like fast-beating pulse at the peak of the rocks. Rich sound could be heard from obscure, smooth, bright yellow pain. Love was reducing me with every beat of the knob, how faulty and far away from maturity I was. Keşşaf said,

"Loneliness is inability of the lover. Understand, all the beauty belongs to the loved. When love tree turns green in your soul like Tree of life, the fire becomes the food of the lover Dilruba!"

When we entered that narrow as impassable village road, earth-sheltered roofless houses met us. When some shrubs, very low houses stayed behind us, we stopped with a thick and long *ptıss* sound at a nook. We turn into hearts drunk because of thirst and are flowing to the steppe like Bedouins found oasis in the desert. Breath of the flame licks and passes my face. The one taking his backpack starts waiting like a comma. I remember the sounds of naughty birds nested in the woodland. We walked from the thing road towards the high and majestic wings of this hidden city which were like doors of a castle.

When the iron doors of this firm city in the middle of a desert are half-opened, we glide into calmly. When we walk down the concrete slope, I realize the wooden bay window that Keşşaf watches the ones who come. I have a lump in my throat. This is the place where discoveries stay close to the realities, where the dreams turn into fate and revive. We reach to the yard passing the low houses. These thick fountain pools are like from the time I left. Newly washed stone ground is shining, it is all out wide. The group goes towards the stairs curling up. We enter one of the narrow iron doors, we let ourselves go the dim coolness of the *dergah.* It is too difficult to stop after such a journey. Even if our feet stop, howling of the road is in our ears.

I watch the ones who came and settled in to room before us. I remember Hevida. I wonder if she is here? I watch the women wearing colourful clothes like Hevida and her group. Their joy and care free mimics are notable. There are tattoos on their faces, dark hennas in their hands, long indigo-blue dolman on their head. They are as comfortable as they are at their houses. They are like rings which can't be broken around the wide table. We, the ones who has just arrived, are opening our backpacks, some of them takes water from downstairs, from the yard. The other one is putting the untidied slices of cake which was in a plastic container. Although the faces, bodies are tired, the souls are alive. It is hitting the time like a harpoon. I must have understood; here both the hunter and the hunted are us. The thing we are running after is our own heart. Because nobody can take the thing he owns from the other. We are all aware of the substantial meal set inside us. We reach our hands to the bowls full of wine timidly, we are here to get the wine served us with the hope of drinking. There is a wedding dinner at the invisible corner. This can be seen on each face. Although nobody talks about it, the bubbling sound of the sherbet and the top-full *halva* can be heard.

What an extraordinary thing to live here, in a crystal time. It is such extraordinary that realizing this scares me. Feeling the energy mixing with the breaths, curling itself up is turning one's head. It is as if after a breath every mystery will come to light. We are helpless people waiting at the threshold of mysteries, whose food is fire. Having food of fire is only for a lover!

The sun will obey the order given to it fastidiously and is going to deploy at the hill in a little while. It is going to come to the place it meant to be in the endless blackness. The world is turning, the sun is turning, all galaxy is turning... nothing stands firm. There isn't a trouble in the order of the universe. How can this be when a hand organized everything steadily?

The rush starts in the little room, the table is cleared quickly. Although I don't understand anything from the speech of the other groups, I guess it is for the *azan*. They are walking around jiggly their colourful long skirts, in glory and harmony. The beauty of the clothes of these women terrifies me. How is it looking to the world in these colours. What kind of a fashion is this different from everything, every region? How can a person carry these heavy clothes, these long covers while travelling like a voyager? I look their wide and embroidered belts for a while. There are sparkling cut glasses, colourful mirrors, light chaos and various patterns in every span of this long dress. This colourful and sparkling pattern is the same on the sleeves. They are like peacocks. They are so glad that they are as if they aren't interested in how other people live. Their body language says that there is no other turnout. They have the first state of being a woman on them. A little intervention to this state will be artificial and factitious. It will throw away all the things in orbit of femininity, it's a bit wild but it will turn this order upside down. But there is being crushed besides all this beauty and naturalness on their faces, and also adaptation of life as so. They are looking as if to say "life is painful, I know and accept this," behind the smiling eyes. Here, it isn't important who you are, you only belong to that universe, that order...

The brunette woman in tattoos next to me is putting her parcels one after the other neatly with her thick strong wrists. Contrary to her other fellows there is no make-up on her face. She has got mingled tattoos going back to her chin instead of it. They become visible as washed, become live as got wet. I suddenly remember the moment Hevida washed her face. The patterns on her face freshened, almost activated. I say to myself they are as if the revolution writings on the stairs of the stadium that I prayed at the beginning. It is like that becoming evident of writings written by the students in a way that they cover all stairs instead of disappearing.

I find myself in a little Armageddon again when we go downstairs to the ablution room. Existing in such crowd is just huddling, waiting until being permitted to move in a small space you are in. I go upstairs quickly pressing the back of my shoes with wet feet. I crash the people meanwhile. But nobody cares about these crashes here, even they don't have a look. The *azan* is breaking off in the silent sky like doomsday: *Allahuekber!* The crowd upstairs is coming together like water filling in a hole. Heads are on the same row when the *azan* finishes and the microphone is turned off. The ground is hidden under the feet. The same voice is shouting, " Sufi, please move a little bit back, for the God's sake." The steps are moving back like a ring locked each other.

Squinted eyes because of the brightness of the sun are closed. A voice says, *ecce homo.* "He is coming!" my heart is beating fast as if it wants to tear my chest and fly. Peevish and impatient beats go up to my throat. World becomes meaningless against the hope of seeing him. The scent of rose coming bleeding the silence of this waiting deploys itself at the peak of loneliness. Tottering in failure here. Being nothing before him. There is scaring mercy smell in the air, he is seen from the end of the yard! Keşşaf! Because he is passing, looking at his toes again like a stranger. The lovers are hurt in his beauty. I am out of breath in ring of fire, at the first moment I see him. My body is a wound salted down! He steps on me and passes, his existences is salve, a theriac. He is going with his crook in his hand sweeping his long skirt. His face becomes invisible because of his light. He is leaving the scream in his larynx to the women as silence, a guttural weak prayer.

Oh my god! This is the unbelievable affectation of the loved, all we have is prayer. Seeing the face reflecting the rose water pool in the world of scents now. Oh My God, Keep my mind! Keşşaf is none other than Cavalry in the army fighting against the Nafs in the desert of absence. The owner of the voice saying "I want you to give up Tuğrul." The voice always whispering me, the hand masterminding me. I watch him until the stairs at the end of the yard. He calmly goes downstairs like climbing the sky. What kind of a drunkenness that I have, how can find my mind again, Oh my God!

When the crowd starts to disband, I am at the foot of despair. I say how far you are. Was everything to know that distance rising like an indestructible wall. We are dispersing like pollens scattered by the wind, learning that we don't have anything other than helplessness. I reach in front of the big pool downstairs, wash my face in this water once.

Insignificance and being nothing I felt when I first came was descending upon me in a heavier way. It became a misery and it was eating me. It was teaching me how empty and temporary this heart I had against the loved. Children, young and old people were passing through the middle of the yard again. And seriously ill people whose shadows are on the brilliant stones were being taken. Some of the women were walking quickly, they were holding their skirts. I saw this kind behaviour here much. That sign of devotion on the faces of woman! The thing I had never reached. I was like a couch grass here. Keşşaf told me "Clean your heart from couch grasses, be the obedient" I was the couch grass, then how could I be an obedient? I was a person who was tripping up herself, the one who was trying to take share from the absolute love raining here despite this. Conditioned love on the earth was giving pain. All the humanity was saying If this happened I would love you. However, Keşşaf and the blessed way he represented was saying "Whatever happens I will love, you will love." The thing carried me here was this natural flow! Whatever happens to love and to be loved! A person could only understand the value of loving without barrier and conditions when he was troubled with conditioned love. As I know, only a mother would love her child unconditioned, except her many feelings called love couldn't go beyond delirium, an illness or a reason! Setting out a condition to be loved was against the endless nature of heart. In a universe where everything exists due to love and where everything stands up to love, conditioned love had to be finite, finite, limited and a painful illusion.

I could just understand the most important thing while watching the people passing by the yard. Keşşaf said me "Understand, all the beauty belongs to the loved. When love tree turns green in your soul like Tree of life, the fire becomes the food of the lover Dilruba!" so in order to love tree turn green in me, I had to realize the conditioned loves until the bottomless space took me to the soul land. Then he said "There isn't reproach, condemning any kind of separation in the land of love" He said this while trying to vomit the bad luck like reproach in the stomach of the separation, when the separation flowers of metaphorical love bloomed like oleanders. But now I understood that there wasn't coming together or separation in the book of love...

I saw my seat-mate at the beginning of the yard, the one who sat next to me during the journey. After speaking with the crowd around her, she realized me and smiled. Her silk scarf was neat. It was the same as at the beginning. The face surrounded by this scarf was smiling. She came closer with cute look, in a hurry as if she was going to say something important. I had just realized the freckles under her eyes, her face was so small and thin.

She said "Do you still want to stay here?" I stood up at from the side of the water, sides of my skirt was wet. All the thought flying in my mind dispersed with this question,

I said "Of course, I do!"

"Then come with me, I will take you to him." She started to walk quickly without saying anything else. She passed the ablution room choosing the dry places without stepping the small paddle in the stony yard which was washed in the morning. I started to walk next to her. We entered into a small building like a workshop, went downstairs and reached to a small room. She talked something with the head servant who was about her forties and who wasn't from here. The woman called the head servant was in whites from head to toe, the irritable expression in her eyes was shining in this whiteness. There were some sacks and coaches in the room. While my friend was talking with the head servant sitting on the Seljukian style coach, she was bending towards, she was speaking so respectfully. Referring to me, my friend said,

"She wants to stay here." The head servant fixed her look on me, she laid her eyes on me, and asked only,

"Where have you come from?" without asking anything else, she said,

"Find Nedime, she will tell you the place you will stay and the things you will do. You can only stay here for a week, then you are going to return with the group." I was very happy that she let me stay there. Even it was for a week, I would be close to Keşşaf in this time. I was going to breathe the same air with him, I was going to drink from the same water. Then the head servant turned to my friend and said,

"Renan! Show her the way!" I learnt my friend's name by this way. Renan thanked with the respectful expression on her face and we left the room. We were walking towards the yard following the same road we came, the dark, colourless, dull expression on the face of the head servant disturbed me, I said

"She looks like a stern woman." Renan said,

"Yes, she is. But don't be afraid, she has to be stern in order not to delay the jobs here." I didn't understand anything from this sentence, I curled my lips in the meaning of I don't know. Renan continued,

"You can find Nedime in that small *dergah,* she is there at this time of the day."

It didn't last long to find Nedime. She was calm, a caressingly talking woman who wants to help in every subject, when compared to the head servant. As I understood, she was only a few years older than me. While she was talking, she was busy with other things, she was taking notes into the thin cover-less notebook in her hand, she was giving answers patiently to the ones coming and asking question. She didn't have time to speak looking at your face. I understood she was happy from her first sentence which you could feel the tiredness. Nedime first showed me the place I was going to stay. This was a big room behind the interwoven houses away from the yard. Temporary servants were staying here. There was a small place for ablution, some blankets and rugs on the floor. It was more comfortable than the other rooms in the *dergah.* Then she told me my job.

"First day, you will wash all the stairs going up from the common yard and dry it until there is no water."

I said "Of course, I will do with pleasure." I liked washing the stairs. Because Keşşaf was disappearing from the end of that stairs. As washing the stairs was my duty, then I would see the continuum of the stairs.

She said with a sweet and sincere voice "Then, I will ask you the cleaning of the big yard overflowing all day. I don't want even a single dust on the floors. That's all for now, have a rest today. You can start tomorrow."

As it could be guessed, I spent the all day with the happiness of staying here. I was dispersed in the crowd bursting at the seams with the *azan,* I was trying to help people with the honour of being a servant here. I roamed around until the late hours of night, I was going up and down, I was looking how many floors that the stairs went up. As I understood, there were a lot of stairs enough for four floors in this building rising between low houses. I was full of an incomprehensible happiness, I was continuously smiling, I was turning around Keşşaf's orbit without feeling tired, I was watching for his steps and his breath. It was such an extraordinary experience that I had never lived. This felling of freedom I felt here made me believe that I had wings especially at the first days.

The other servants retired to posture tiredly when I went to the room at a late hour. After greeting them I also retired to posture and leaned back to the wall. The most comfortable and cheerful one greeted me first. This modern cool woman was like she came here by mistake. She was a warm person in her fifties, she was thin and she was getting pleasure out of life.

"My name is Iraz. What's your name?" she said sitting on her feet as if she was cold.

I only said "Dilruba"

"Dilruba. I haven't seen you here before. Is it the first time you came here?"

"No. I came here before." As if I wanted to say that I wasn't inexperienced. I was going to love Iraz as I knew her. Maybe she was older than me but we were going to be god friends with her. Her voice was clear. She was talking freely as if to say I had no sharp corners sides.

She said "Let me guess. You came here whether from Ankara or from İstanbul"

I said "Where did you know, I came from Ankara." She was an enthusiastic woman, she was chanting clapping her hands, beating time, she was shining out. How much she told me at our first speech. She was telling happily about their happiness with her husband, how they travelled and worked at different cities, then their coming here after saying to their friends that they were going on a holiday. As she said her husband was here, in the *dergah* for men. When one became familiar with someone like Iraz, she remembered how beautiful and worth living the life was.

She tied cross her kerchief on her neck and said,

"Where could I know, it is obvious from your state, only the ones who came here from metropolitan look so strange." Then she folded her arms in her chest,

She said "Here is a desert, a desert but a green one. A person can understand what the greenness in her is."

I said, "Yes, while coming here, one can realize it, the group passes through a desert." Iraz looked as if to say "There you are" then asked

"What duty did Nedime give you?"

I said shortly, "Cleaning." Iraz called the tired girl over there,

"Dil□ad, look, an assistant has come for you!"

Iraz was humane as well as smart. I was going to see her in the kitchen while working dapperly during my stay here. She was putting the big cooking pots on fire at once, putting the meals in order, was preparing them at the time they had to be ready. Then she gave a break for smoking, was talking with the people at the door, she was enjoying every moment. She was controlling the life, at the same time she gave in knowing that she couldn't be in the driving seat. She was the proof of Keşşaf's saying "Be obedient!" She was a live document showing how to be obedient. She chucked off sorrow from her heart, laid down her heart like a simple rug under the foot of her lover. She was like saying whatever comes from you I don't know anything better than gratitude. Her look her mimics were disclosing this. Iraz didn't know thoughts, tiredness, pulling a long face, being cross with somebody, getting angry. As she said, her four sons got married then one of them was divorced. She said while talking about her daughter-in-law "But we are still like mother and daughter. She says that I love you so much that I divorced your son but I can't leave you." It was impossible not to justify her daughter-in-law, Iraz was a friend that can't be stayed away.

Next morning, at an early time, Dilşad and I appeared at the highest step of the stairs. We were ready for the job. While she was telling me how to do the job, she was imposing the hose to the fountain of the pool of the yard at the top floor which I was wondering that how I didn't realized. She said "We have to finish before it gets crowded." We were running in the water with slippers on our feet, it took at least an hour to go down the first floor. Then we were starting over and washing each step with clear water one by one and finally we were having rest at the last step. Then the real job started, I was drying all stairs, turnings, the yard from end to end with the thick mop I took. I was again having a rest at the last step, then starting over and going down drying everywhere. Finally I was I was drying the steps Keşşaf passed. As there wasn't a pool here, we were carrying water with bucket from upstairs, after washing, we were drying. These stairs were going to the part for men. So Keşşaf was swinging and going down these stairs, after a wide yard he was passing the other side from a big gate. Every stone he stepped was valuable for me as a jewel. I was cleaning my heart with the flow of the water, with the mop touching the floor. I was cleaning myself, all the dirt, rust and hold-up making me sad were cleaned by this way.

At each step washed, every span cleaned, the yard was turning into a daisy garden. We were running up and down in this daisy garden. When we were tired, we were going to the department for the servants for breakfast, then coming back to the yard and collecting the garbage in the yard. When we were sure that everywhere was clean we were having a rest for a while. When the sun was walking to the hill and it got hot, crowd started to pour down in the middle of the lowest yard. The crowd was closing together until there was no place to step.

I was under the impression that cleaning was a game, I wasn't doing anything. My all effort was cleaning my own dirt with the mop in my hand. Dilşad. She didn't want to say frankly but I felt that she didn't like the job I did. She said that I did "shallowly" once, then she added "You can do better" Here cleaning was more important than I had seen ever before. It wasn't enough to wash a place once, it must have been washed at least three times, it must have been rinsed and dried. The women cleaning without stopping were riding off all directions. It was impossible for someone like me who wasn't rigorous to understand this.

After a short break, Dilşad and I were starting our cleaning duty. There mustn't have been even a butt or fruit stem on the floor. It seemed as if it was easy. But it wasn't. It could only be understood when the crowd was considered. We were running after even the small children eating bread and walking, there mustn't have been even crumb. We were catching the plastic bottles almost before they fell down and throwing them to the dustbin. We were collecting even the seeds of the fruits when we saw that they were being eaten.

As the minutes passed, I started to understand. If people had paid attention to his heart, as we tried to keep this yard clean, it would be enough. How much dust, stain, mark was filling in the mirror of the heart. Then these marks became darker, were cutting the light and were darkening the mirror. Cleaning was granting life to every particle, was making it breath, changing it into its first shape. Stones of the yard must have been cleaned until they shine as if they were just furnished.

Before the evening, on the last leg of afternoon, we were washing all the stairs again. The steps were getting eluding from the load of the day. I was washing the last step that Keşşaf's lucky feet touched until I saw my face on it, until every particle of the stone was reviving, were speaking in their own language, until they hugged the sun. Then I mopped for many times and then again ...

The next day, all these rush went on in the same way. I was tired and sitting on my corner. Suddenly Iraz came in and said "You didn't go to the dinner, they are waiting for you." I forgot going dinner. When I went to the kitchen, the head servant was sitting at the table. I tried not to make an eye contact. I sat as far as possible. There was nobody left after the dinner. ı was about to start eating that she said,

"We can't wait for you all night, you have to come on time." She was reproofing me. She was looking at me like a little child that she bent her ear without caring about her. I spooned up the soup without lifting my head. I had my dinner without saying anything and left the kitchen silently.

The head servant who didn't even ask my name was bringing me to task. She was expecting an excuse for being late for dinner, she was inviting me to obey her authority. I felt that she was developing an attitude towards me. I should have told her "I have nothing to do with you." But my duty here was avoiding me. Then I was saying to myself, how Keşşaf could accept such a person here? I sat near the room I stayed out of the yard sadly, I could see the people here. Iraz, Dilşad, and the others. I looked at the sky for a while, Why was I here? At this time, in the middle of this desert, what was I doing here?

Next day, Dilşad and I ran up and down and washed the stairs again. We again kept watch in the yard under the burning sun. Whenever I heard the azan, I was burning with the desire for going upstairs with the group and seeing Keşşaf, then I met with Dilşad's preventing. At the first duty day, she stopped me saying "The servants here don't see him." Despite this I was trying to slip through her fingers, to get lost in the jam-packed stairs and to see him for just a second. But as long as Dilşad was with me, I wouldn't succeed it.

When the day ended, I decided to disappear and not to go dinner. I ran the risk of staying hungry. I ran the risk of many things for Keşşaf being interested in me. Hunger was so worthless. I was curled up in my room when Iraz came and said,

"The head servant got angry with you, you were again late for dinner." I didn't show any interest. I said "Iraz I decided not going to dinner tonight." Iraz was so astonished that she wide opened her eyes and said,

"Then go and say this by yourself". I went out. The sky was suffocated into stars. I found a stone an sat on it in the coolness of the desert. I watched the sky on my own in this hiding place. I was thinking. I wondered if Tuğrul ever called me? Did he realize my absence? Or did Maide try to reach me? Drawing in the cool weather, I sounded whether Tuğrul thought me or not. I should have felt his scent which was agonizing but was granting life. Even I should have found him when I got back and should have started everything from the beginning. Even if it was possible I should have got back with the group tomorrow. I waited news from him for a while under the starlit sky with my eyes closed tightly. At last he was here, this was an obvious proof of his thinking of me! That oily perfect tune of existence which didn't leave strength in my soul was mine! It was again surrounding me like a net, it was capturing me, it was whipping me until everything the name Tuğrul lost their meaning. I sat still there until the black night vomit all the scent in its stomach first into my nasal passage, then to my heart. So the time slowed down, all the motion was balanced for me.

I walked through the yard like a voyager whose eyes were pacing in the scope of an unknown country. There was a agitative brightness because of the stars and lights shining above. The yard was silent, everybody took a back seat, the night became heavy. I passed by the ablution room, I started standing up under the penthouse of one of the low houses. I could see the lights of the yard from here. The women leaning to the stone safety rails of the yard upstairs where Keşşaf walked were watching around silently, they seemed as if they were content with their situation. The ones who came out of the ablution room, the ones going down stairs in this cool desert night... They were all as if they jumped out of a fairy tale country. That yard, that stone floor shining like the centre of the world and the brightness on it was making me peaceful. I was like a stranger who didn't know what to do under the penthouse. There was nobody including myself that I knew.

Keşşaf told me "Whenever you want I would here you. Just call me" he said it many times. It's high time for calling him.

First I said, "Here I am, near you." The words weren't turning into sound, just echoing in my chest. "I came here running away from everything especially myself. I am tired and hungry. I am a voyager who wants to learn whether the things I am looking for are in this world or not. Leave me sign, a mark from you. Let it be as obvious as shaking off those hurtful feelings called delusion. I have no one Keşşaf! Change my duty here. Please, make me closer to you." My face was burning, I was biting my lips and looking at the yard in despair. A hot tear fired my skin and shed like a deep well calling the light, like a dummy's missing for the words.

"If I say that I loved you more than everybody, more than my father, more than my mother whose face I didn't remember. If you cut my head here, it won't bleed. Say something nor or..."

I hadn't finished my sentence that the big gate under the penthouse half-opened. A girl who was trying to hold tightly the round tray full of various foods on her belly came out. I got out of the way but instead of going she stopped and looking into my eyes she said,

"Please eat. This is his meal." First I didn't understand what she was saying. But after a second she repeated. An inlaid cover was surrounding her slim face as if it was drawn by a master artist. This face could only be a face of an angel under these lights.

She said "Come on you should eat." Someone who didn't know me was giving me banquet and saying me that I should eat. What a strange place is this. I wonder if she was aware why she said this. Why me in the yard where are hundreds, thousands of people?

This was absolutely a reply from Keşşaf to me that didn't allow any delusion. But when lover sees interest from the loved, she doesn't know what to do. I couldn't touch my eyes to the food as if the lover couldn't have the strength to look at the love-locks of loved. Although I was sure that this was coming from Keşşaf, it was sent me by him, I said, maybe because I was shy,

"I am not hungry." The young girl was standing still in front of me with the heavy tray on her thin belly, and she was tightening her loosened hands in order not to drop the tray she sometimes took in her arms.

"If you don't eat, you wouldn't do a good thing. At least taste it for fruitfulness." She was saying this as if she was begging in a tone which was making me understand that it was my last chance. I wish the ground would open up and swallow me, being swallowed was a honour here. I regretted the things I had said to Keşşaf a little while ago, my playing hard to get as if I had a value. I wanted to reach one of the plates in the tray randomly, I should have taken even a bite, the young girl was right. Who was I that I was refusing the meal of a holy person, a beautiful person?

While I was wavering in a incontestable astonishment being petrified because of the sign, while I was full of pleasure, I was unravelling, I reached the tray. Without knowing what I got although I didn't deserve, small round things touched my hand.

I said "Thank you, it's enough." The young girl bent her head in the meaning of alright, she went down two or three stairs of the stony place and walked towards the upper yard. I still didn't know what that round thing was. I knelt down and hardly leaned my back to the cold wall. I was like a volcano which was about to explode. I let myself in an endless space, I started to cry first silently then sobbingly there. The things in my hand were two black grapes. While my hands holding the grapes were like bleed, totally red, I popped them. What unforgettable moment it was!

This time the entire yard was full of scent of rose! I went to my room like a butterfly which was flying happily between colourful flowers. Before sinking into one of the happiest sleeps in my life, I gave my thanks for many times.

30
Rose Water Pool or Keşşaf

"The amity made in the name of Allah and in the name of truth is permanent between the guide and his follower, and nothing in the world can spoil it." (İnayet Han)

The next morning I woke up Iraz's voice. She was trying to wake me up leaning towards my head. "Get up sleepyhead!" she said first. She was smiling as if she knew everything I had experienced, as if she hadn't meet sorrow. "Your duty had changed," she said with joy. I came to my senses, "Really? What is the new duty?" I said curiously. "They had been entrusted with the pool in the top yard." She said. I didn't understand anything from her words. I got up excitedly and told her I wanted to hear all details. "First breakfast!" said Iraz. "The pool is difficult!" Changing the place of my duty was the second sign. I had asked Keşşaf personally in the previous evening. My mood lifted with this surprise, I became as light as the birds wandering among the branches.

As she said, the duty of the pool started at 12 at night. During the day I would help Iraz in the kitchen and at night I would work by the pool. I started to help Iraz after breakfast. I peeled potatoes and chopped onions all day. I prepared small dates for dessert taking out their stones. I sang along with Iraz in the beautiful hymns Iraz sang. It was very entertaining listening to Iraz's life story for long hours and watching her teasing the attendants circling around her. In addition, Iraz was teaching me a lot about this big *dergah* that I hadn't know. She could even guess which group would come at what time. According to her a new Ankara group would be here in the afternoon today. Here was a heaven in the middle of the desert!

I had found a unique oasis in the middle of the desert! I was learning a new thing at any time. One of these things was that the prayer rugs had been ready for the prayer without any space between them at every *azan*. The people of all ages living here was ready for the prayer before *azan* finished. It seemed to me so fascinating... Once I had been taking a pinch of parsley Iraz had handed me to one of the other kitchens. I had looked into the open door of one of the rooms between two kitchens. Women had been waiting for *azan* by the inlaid prayer rugs in rows.

My mind was trying to understand all goings-on. I wanted to see where I was standing. However, my mind was helpless to understand. I was trying to see the whole picture combining all clues. The picture was always blurred, it was left unfinished every time. Then I was thinking of the head servant trying to being away from her. I remembered Safran's words she had said when I first departed to come here. "Propriety, absolutely propriety," said Safran, "don't you dare to hurt anyone there, be polite to everybody without discriminating them as patient, elderly or child. Look down yourself than everyone. Don't despise anybody, or you just visit like a tourist, mind you don't!" Now I understood what she had meant. Here the ego of the person, Nafs ordering the evil, Nafs was getting out of control. Then Safran had said,

"Don't think ill of anybody. Don't open the door to the Satan in any case. Satan will bring your mind into doubt, it pours dirt into your words. Don't push and shove anybody, take only your share. There are hidden saints in the public; perhaps the one you look down is Allah's friend; be respectful to anybody."

With these thoughts in my mind, I went to the yard to smoke when there was less to do in the kitchen; I also wanted to see Ankara group which was about to come, perhaps I could see someone I knew. I leaned somewhere as not to prevent the way of the people, the surroundings had livened up. Women with colourful clothes and with tattoos on their faces were engaging with their small brunette children, and they were trying to cool washing their faces with the water coming from the fountain. I was looking at the woman wearing necklaces with big stones and with a nice dress in pastel colours. She had crouched among the snowy women having left their packs or bags alongside. She had come here wearing her most beautiful clothes like the other women with tattoos on their faces. Caring.. Then I looked for Dilşad, she must have been around; then I found him coming out from the ablution room. At that moment I saw the head servant coming towards me opening her legs like a pair of long scissors. She appeared in the crowd suddenly, there was no time to run away. She glared at me, got closer, and put her hand as heavy as iron on my shoulder,

"Here attendants are not allowed to smoke, put it out immediately!" she said. She was overstepping. I was looking at her as if I told "what are you doing here?" and she was looking at me as if she told "in fact what are you doing here?" My being here started to be a threat for her. On the first day during the meal she had asked me "Why did you come here alone?" I had said "It just happened so." Coming here alone meant that I hadn't been a trustworthy person. Then I had realized that she looked up and down me during the meal. Everybody had come here with their friends. It had boded no good to come here alone for her.

At this very moment I had an irresistible will to push her hand resembling a pile of hot and meaningless iron on my shoulder. As I was going to open my mouth to tell her "I'm not charged here anymore"...

I looked at the crowd moving two or three meters away from me, I saw Safran there. So she was in the group of Ankara. I could hear even her whispers in the howl of the crowd. She was looking at me longingly as if she was saying 'don't speak', as if she wanted to protect me, as if there were only two of us on this short way appeared only between us.

I told the head servant, "I'm trying to give up, it's poison in the end." First an astonishment appeared in her tough looks, then she turned her head to the other side as if she was saying 'I don't want to engage with you.' She took her fingers resembling dry branches out of my shoulder, she turned back and moved away with the wobble moves of someone who didn't know how to walk.

Now I was trying to understand how I had been able to get out of myself by keeping quiet here. How I had transformed.. Seeing how my deeds had become irrelevant to me made me sink in a deep despair. I was transforming to a puppet whose limbs were attached with ropes, my will was going away from me, my choices were being taken from me. It meant that somebody who trusted his mind wasn't able to choose in any way and decide even for himself.

When the nightmare of the head servant finished I looked for Safran in the crowd breaking slowly. She had just been here . A few seconds ago. Everyone in Ankara group I asked about Safran was shaking their heads meaning they didn't know. Then I remembered *dergah;* I went up the stairs curling upstairs on the double in the same breath hitting people. I couldn't accept a possibility that she hadn't been here. What if I had mixed someone with her? Impossible! It was impossible to mix somebody else with her since she was one of a kind.

Safran wasn't in *dergah* either, I went down to the ablution room on the double and looked for her. I waited to see her beautiful eyes for a moment but the waiting lasted too long. Safran wasn't here. That moment that I had thought that I had seen her was just a dream.

I could reach the night barely looking around in despair that day. I arrived at the pool at the upstairs yard at exactly 12 at night. This pool looked like the pool that Keşşaf had made me watch the film revealing how rose oil had been made in the world of scents. It was round just like that pool and the moonlight reflected on the water just as it did on that pool. My duty was to clean the pool and fill it again. First I told myself what an easy duty it was. I went into the half-full pool and I put a cloth on the mouth of the groove to stop the water coming from the fountain. I spread soap powder to the brimful pool and foamed it well. I wiped the edges of this big circle as no dirt would remain on the white tiles of the pool. Then I looked for the drain leaning on my knees. I was holding the edges not to fall into the pool but my fingers could only touch the ground. I needed to find the drain and drain down the foamy water. I was pulling the foams and looking for a drain in the cold water. There must have been a drain somewhere in the bottom of the pool. I couldn't find it although I examined very well. I decided to go into the pool. I gathered my skirts and went into the foamy water. The level of the water was about to exceed my waist and reached my chest. I wasn't able to find a drain even if I examined the bottom with my hands and feet. The ground of this round pool was a flat, quite smooth wall. A blind and deaf wall...

The shadow of the moon was shining in the foams of the pool; the yard was lightening with the lights of the stars. Sometimes somebody was going up the stairs curling down, walking towards the corridor at the corner of the yard and disappearing going into one of the rooms at the end. While I was waiting not knowing what to do in the pool, thanks God, Iraz came.

"How beautiful the view here is, isn't it?" she said first. Her delicate shadow was lengthening under the weak light of the lamp in the yard. She got close to the pool dragging her slippers, "how is it going?" she asked and leaned on the rail of the yard just behind me.

"Iraz, I can't find the drain here," I said disappointedly. She smiled thinking I was joking.

"Who told you there was a drain here, there isn't one!" she said. "You will drain down the water of the pool. You will clean it until there is no foam at all, you will rinse it several times, when you make sure that it is clean you will fill it again," she said.

"It will take hours," I said as I was in the pool. She came to me, she found a tankard in the buckets and gave it to me,

"Then, it'd better you start immediately!" she said and added, "The water of this pool will be drunk, so it must be very clean. You won't go away when the pool is clean, you will wait until a Sufi comes and takes over the duty." I took the red tankard she gave me and started to plunge it into the foam and throw it out of the pool. There was no time to waste. Iraz went out again dragging her slippers after she said "good luck with that."

Water lessened every time I plunged the tankard. It decreased to my waist first, then to my knees. I went on until the foams looked like butterfat which was about to overflow. When there was no water at all finally and the white tiles appeared clearly, I thought what I would do the foams remaining there. First I wiped them with a cloth and wrung outside. Yet the foams were going on to froth as if soap powder was poured over them every time I wiped. There was no chance than taking out the cloth I put on the mouth of the fountain and filling the pool a little. Once I took out the cloth the pool started to fill quickly. I let the pool fill until the water covered my feet first and then raised my waist. Afterwards I put the cloth on the mouth of the fountain again. Foams were growing as I was trying to rinse everywhere of this deep circle. I started to drain the water with the tankard again. However I started to feel desperate. The water lessened but the foams didn't go. Moreover since I hadn't been able to put the cloth on the mouth of the fountain properly, the pool was filling steadily. I told to myself that there must have been an easier way. Absolutely there must have been! I went out of the pool holding the edges, my clothes were all wet. The water I took out of the pool was lengthening like a river and poured into the loophole in the end. I decided to try a new thing; I would take out the cloth turning to an ingot because of getting wet from the mouth of the fountain and let the pool brim. So the water in the pool would overflow and it would rinse by itself. I had no chance than trying; the hour that the Sufi who Iraz had told about would come and take over the duty was coming. The pool must have been cleaned and brimmed before she came.

I was more alarmed as the noises coming from down yard stopped. Now there was no one coming to this up yard. The magical shadow of the moon reflected on the wet ground and white tiles of the pool and it shined the foams flowing under my feet like snow-white butterfat. I took out the cloth from the mouth of the fountain and the water started to pulse and to fill into the pool noisily as if it had wanted to tell something. The gurgle of the flowing water interrupted the silence of the yard; I was waiting for the pool to rinse itself overflowing ignoring how much I got wet and cold. However, I had made mistake, this method didn't work. As the water was rising it was foaming much more, as it was overflowing the foams remained on the surface of the water insistently, and only water was pouring out of the pool.

I put the cloth which got as wet as being about to start to be mossed and torn to ribbons on the mouth of the fountain as tight as I could do this time. Again I started to drain the water with the tankard more quickly. I was going into the pool, circling around, and struggling in the waters until there was no water in the bottom. When it was empty I filled it again, then until I made sure that there was no sign of soap powder I repeated the action.

I didn't know how long it took. There was almost no sound around. Only the gurgles of the flowing and draining water were being heard. After a while the pool was totally empty and rinsed. Its white tiles were shining and lightening around like a lantern. I took out the cloth I had put at the mouth of the fountain for the last time. The water draining its groove started to run with a gurgling sound. I stood aside as wet to the skin and watch the pool filling with the content of an artist watching its work. I looked at the rising of this water as clean as a love purified all its obscurity. When the water filling the pool to overflowing as running by singing and not repeating the same melody, tirelessly and continuously, I put the cloth on the groove again and stopped the water. I was wet almost to my hair as much as I had swum in a river. The Sufi Iraz had talked about came with slow steps finally. She had sleepiness in her eyes and buckets in her hands. This slim woman was wearing a thin waistcoat, handmade. She put the buckets on the ground noisily and pulled the waistcoat to her breast as if she was cold,

"I'm taking over the duty, you can go," she said. I felt very tired.

"I'm glad to see you," I said, "what time is it?"

"It's about four," she said examining the pockets of her waistcoat as if she was looking for something. I was so tired that I couldn't watch what she would do with the pool. I walked towards the room I stayed slowly and tiredly. Everybody was in a deep sleep. I changed my clothes and put on something dry and I lied on my bed consisting of a thin blanket on the ground with the happiness given by the completion of my duty successfully.

I was so puzzled in my first pool duty that I couldn't understand anything. There were only three days to finish the week and I had been able to see Keşşaf only once. "It isn't important to see him or not," said Iraz, "just try to do your duty here, this is enough!" And I did what she had said.

When I woke up next morning the breath I inhaled told me that Tuğrul was thinking of me. I rose on the ground and thought what it meant at this time of the morning. Then I went to the kitchen to Iraz as if there was nothing extraordinary. I found her placing the supplies in the kitchen. She was trying to fill the empty jars with lentil, rice and bulgur. She was as comfortable as in her own kitchen while she was working on that wooden table. I started to peel potatoes taking a stool. Iraz asked while she was tightening the caps of the jars she had filled,

"You are so calm today. Are you tired or are you thinking of your darling?"

"Darling? What a cute word it is!" I said while aligning the jars.

"You can tell me, I listen," she said. Then she wiped her hands with her apron.

"I don't have a darling, Iraz. There was someone but nothing happened," I said. She stood up and talked while she was extending to the shelf;

"Don't worry. If a plate of fruit was presented to you and if you didn't eat from that plate, it means that a more beautiful and fuller plate will be presented."

"How nice!" I said while I was trying to take out the rotten parts of the potatoes. "Well, why can't one eat from that first plate? What if it is difficult to forget about the fruit in the first plate?" Iraz turned to me while she was washing the big bowl she had taken from the shelf as she always did and she was smiling,

"It means that the one who is presented the plate has not been hungry yet. It isn't time to eat. Perhaps she is being tested with a fad."
"Fad" I said whispering. Yes, fad. Iraz was right, mine was only a fad.

I spent all day trying to help her, and tidying up the mess in the kitchen when the there remained a little to do. I was by the pool at the upstairs yard when it was twelve o'clock at night. I put the same cloth on the mouth of the fountain again and started to pour soap powder into the full pool. This time I was very careful with foaming as much as I could cope with and I waved the water leaning. I was thinking that in fact this job was very entertaining while the water was foaming making fizzy sounds. I wiped the edges of the pool very well. Then again I started to drain the water with the tankard leaning. After a while I went into the decreased water. I was playing with the water, struggling with the foams and trying hard not to leave even one dirty tile in the round pool. Then the level of the water decreased and went down from my knees slowly.

At that moment, I meant the moment that the water left my knees, my foot touched something. An indistinct, thin and delicate object, an object circling in the water not finding something to hold... First I thought it was a trash falling into the water. Then I leaned, I looked for it in the foams, how come I hadn't been able to see it before? It was appeared on the surface continually. I couldn't understand what it was but it was certain that it was a glass object. Then I put my hand in water as holding it, that was impossible! This glass bottle was the same as the one that Keşşaf had poured a drop of rose water in the pool and containing the scent of Tuğrul! I recognized it from its silver cap. What was it doing here?

Then I remembered the rose water pool in the world of scent. When Keşşaf had poured a drop from it to the pool, the pool had tried to vomit the scent by throwing off demon smokes and bubbles. Afterwards Keşşaf had made me taste the water of the rose water pool. What a bitter taste it had been! Now my face took a sour and unpleasant form as if there had been the same taste in my mouth. My cleaning of this pool without a drain was about Tuğrul! My emptying the water, struggling in the foams, filling and emptying the pool several times, all of them was for me to get rid of the metaphorical love. How this moment was deadly now! I took the bottle to my nose, I was sure that I would smell the same oily and dazzling scent. Even if the water of the pool hid the scent there must have been a little of that on the mouth of the bottle. I rose the bottle to the weak light of the lamp of the yard for a moment, there was no liquid in it. I shook it again and again violently... Then I held it on a line with my face as if I had wanted to kiss it. The starry night had left all its light into my arms and gone. At that moment I could beg that this would be a sign that I would be with Tuğrul. Every passing second was growing my hope instead of destroying it. My knees were shaking and thinning steadily, like they wouldn't keep me standing. I held the bottle far from the light of the lamp a little more and hold at the end of my nose as if it had whispered me an ancient secret. That moment was an unbelievable shot that I hit the marks and all possibilities was upended. Yes, this was Tuğrul's scent! Actually I was scratching out Tuğrul from my heart together with this pool. All struggle to clean it was for getting rid of his shadow. This pool, these foams, missing of the drain, my struggle to make the pool ready on time, everything, everything was a game.

I got out of the pool. I remembered what Keşşaf had told me in the world of scent at the moment that the glass bottle had become water and poured into the pool; "In fact, glass is liquid, it solidifies when it's cold just like the heart." At that moment I started to understand the point of the pool game here. Keşşaf had given me the duty of taking Tuğrul's scent out of my heart. This difficult moment that I felt this into my skin... I got closer to the sparkles waving on the surface of the pool and winking whitely. All the water of this pool consisted of Tuğrul's scent.

I crouched by the pool and held my head with two hands. Now the entire pool released its scent freely. And unfortunately all these were a sign that Tuğrul wouldn't be with me. Moreover, he must have been only a dream for me... I thought everything was over for a moment, I was angry but there was nothing to do. I got to work like a soldier understanding the order given him totally ignoring the scent burning the end of my nose and knocking me off my feet. I drained the water of the pool all night, added some more foams thinking it wasn't clean enough. I wiped the tiles until they were worn. I filled it again, then put the cloth on the mouth of the fountain and drained again. I was thinking of only Tuğrul while I was doing all these. I rinsed the pool until it became shiny, until the scent came off the end of my nose and my veins.

The Sufi came with buckets in her hands and sleepiness on her face towards morning. She was from this city or somewhere around here, I could understand it from her way of speaking. She swallowed most of the letters, smashed them and her words became incomprehensible while she was speaking with an accent. There was an expression of focusing on only her duty on her sunburn face. She looked at the full pool and then to me while she was leaving the buckets on the ground noisily.

"You can go and sleep, I am here," she said. She examined the pockets of her handmade waistcoat and looked around as if she couldn't find it again. I held the glass bottle as it was seen clearly and said,

"Are you looking for this? I think it fell into the water, but thanks God, it hasn't broken, if it was broken it would be difficult to clean the pool." She wasn't surprised when she saw the bottle in my hand, contrarily she was pleased and she whimpered something. Even if I didn't understand what she said, her face was saying that she was pleased clearly and in a way that I could understand. She got close to me while she was gathering her skirt made of her flower printed cotton,

"But it's empty," I said, "what was there in it?"

I could see how much her face had got wrinkled at such a young age despite the dim light. She thanked while she was taking the bottle,

"There was rose water in it," she said.

I must have guessed it. I smelt the scent that everybody smelt as the rose water as Tuğrul's scent especially at some distinct times. I would be tested with this mistake until a determined time, it wasn't difficult to understand it. When the test ended for me my perceptions would become normal and everything would start to smell as they were.

When I cleaned the pool again in the same way next night, my duty was over. I was astonished when Nedime came and told me that biting sentence,

"You are going back tomorrow. Help Iraz in the kitchen during the day and get rest at night." "So I am going back," I said. Then I could see Keşşaf for the last time since my duty was over. I went to the yard leaving the kitchen toward noon and I looked for the group I would go with. Then I went to Iraz again. I needed to be in the yard where Keşşaf had passed by walking slowly when the evening *azan* was recited.

I wandered about the yards in this big *dergah* toward evening. I swayed from side to side in the crowd scratching every stone into my mind and memorizing every corner. I didn't want to leave, I was desperate. Going back was barring me like a high wall. Roads to be walked on ended and only going back remained. I thought of the head servant. What sort of a world she was living in although her duty was so hard! Perhaps she could be a little more affectionate to all of us, I said to myself; but who cared if she wasn't. Then I watched Nedime and Dilşad for a while. I witnessed the peace on their faces again.

Everything ended when it was time, even life! The weather started to be cool while the day was taking its light. The sky over us was being unravelled to put on an untouched darkness. I left behind the stairs curling up to the middle yard one by one. As if it was the flowing crowd swallowed my steps and my shape was getting thinner, being wiped away. So I was being pushed back and forth in the feeling of worthlessness. A voice was telling the crowd, "Back, back..." Yet I had been accustomed to this voice also. When the whiz of the microphone that would put the sound of *azan* to the ear of the heart, the lamps of the yard started to light and the crowd was moving steadily in that crystal light. *Allahuekber!* Allah is great! Admitted. The voice of the muezzin was snuggling into us, among us cracking the sky and gave the good news of a new meeting. I wish I had held the time in my hands, why is it rushing so? Where is it going in such a hurry?

I'm waiting at the point where words fail. The crowd shakes as if a storm broke out and stopped suddenly. "He's coming" says a weak breath. Heads are leaned and they fall to the shoulders like ears which are touched by a violent wind. First his scent and light surrounds me. Me and the others whose hearts are shaken... Our freezing in the blinding halos feels his quiet steps. 'Love,' I say, 'what it is like to love so much?' "Our togetherness is timeless and placeless Dilruba!" Let me be with you even so. "No, you should go back."

The scent of rose fills my heart as being words. It is poured down my throat gurgling. Here he is! He is passing by floating, flowing in the same strange aba. What if I throw myself in front of him and go down on his knees saying don't send me away! "Don't do that Dilruba!" Then don't send me away. The world is revolving due to your beauty, night hides all its lights. It remains in shame. At this moment of swaying about, fire snuggles into my soul with its all heat. Thousands of suns are hung on his baton. I don't have the backbone to look at his face. I don't have that power. While I am in a bloody red fire... Please, please don't do that. Don't go. Don't go.

I am defenceless in the darkness falling after his going. The women are moving away from me slowly. A meaningless me in the space... I am in the distant as far as I can find myself. Actually I forget what I have known now, Keşşaf! Teach me again. Again!

I am walking on his threshold. Again the sparrow net on the point that the opposite wall connects with the ceiling... Birds are twittering with joy freely. I crouch leaning my back to the wall, I get smaller a little more. I wish I turned to a spot here. I take a deep breath, deeper, and deeper afterwards. Ah, please give me a few days more! I close my eyes tightly, lightnings are flashing in my soul.

I open my eyes in a place where the loved shows mercy to the lover. My God! This time I found only my red horse before me, I am looking for the Cavalry. He must be looking at me behind his veil. But he isn't there! There is no one calling! The red horse rears up flying its black mane, and again it rears up. It calms down when I go by it, I kiss it from the white sign resembling a comet on its face, I caress its black mane.

Then when the fog surrounding my horse and I realized where I was, as if there was a rug knitted from strings under my feet. This cool softness opened, opened and at last some other lights from far away under the yellow lights appeared. Then only then I gathered the bridles and held on the saddle with the fear of falling, I mounted on my horse stepping on the stirrups in difficulty and in a hurry without understanding what was going on.

My hands holding the bridles were shaking, I was spurring the horse, I couldn't look down and I commended it to go wherever this road went as soon as possible. It was clear that the red horse had come to get me, but where? Then I realized that even if the silvery shiny strings loosened steadily, we didn't fell down. Then I found the power to look down. The lights of a city were flowing underneath. I wasn't able to look any more, and I spurred my horse as if I had wanted to cross over a cliff in speedily: Dehhh!

When my horse was started to be pulled up as if it went into orbit, I had my heart in my mouth. The steps of the horse weren't heard in the space any more, there was only an echo hitting my ears, a sound like a flapping of a bird. The echo was hitting my face sweeping the air and lightened wherever it touches like a torch. This rhythm! I remembered this rhythm! It was the terrific sound that I had heard in the world of hearing. In this echo looking like pulsation while I was about to die of pleasure I realized what the silvery yellow strings were that were moving away from us underneath. They were the yellow light that Keşşaf had tied my eyes with tightly! When my eyes had been tied by this light it had looked like a swirl or a whirlwind, but I could see what it was clearly. Keşşaf had said, "Close your eyes so the embroidery of love can be drawn into your eyes," and he added,

"Here one learns how to hear the sounds of jewels, he hears the unravelling of the stones, the sound of an arrow piercing the air, the sound of the blood messed with the arrow, the quiet steps of the destiny on the mountains, and learns the language of a flame." So we were passing close to the world of hearing.

Then here was a familiar place, there was no need to worry! After a while the yellow silvery lights started to turn to brown as they had in the world of hearing. Then I saw the huge palace of the world of hearing consisting of solid melody, and the horse gained more speed with the opening of the two golden inlaid doors.

I started to understand what was else beyond this road going in the sky. The red horse elevated a little more, until all the yellow and brown lights disappeared. After a while the sound resembling flapping of wings stopped also and weak tunes of a deep howl started to be heard. This was just what I had guessed! The turquoise door of the world of seeing at the end of the long and light road was spreading its colours generously. I remember how wonderful inside was when I go by the light spirals and colour whirlwinds. The journey beginning in a dark night is going on through a strong light. Everywhere is so light that one mistakes that everything here, all creatures are white.

My diminishing mind tells me where I am, but the one to understand must be my heart. The glass palace of the world of scents is seen to its domes, afterwards the desert of absence... I am sure I have experienced the same moment before. The sweet scents in the world of scents were reaching to the desert of absence, moreover, I understood from the lightening of the road more and more that we were getting close to the oval door: the door of absence! I spurred the red horse once more, we were almost there; at that moment I was experiencing again that the swords in my chest was falling one by one. My chest became clear and it widened with the pure light overflowing this oval door. An arm of light pulled me up quickly and pushed into a spiral as it had been happened at the first time I had passed this door. I started to fly; I heard the wonderful music coming from the world of hearing in the helix circling steadily, in the middle of nothingness. This delicate and fragile but getting stronger rhythm took me and threw to the other side of the door.

I opened my eyes with difficulty at the place where I fell. When the silver powder flying in the air, on me and everywhere was opened part way I understood that I had fallen on his feet. First I thought it was Keşşaf or the Cavalry was the owner of the feet, but it was neither of them. Everything was seen clearly in this strange place as it had been in the palace of love. All my veins in my hands on the moving silver rug, the flowing of the blood, even the thinnest capillary vessels, everything was seen. Yet the strangest thing of all was that I wasn't disturbed by this! My skin became a transparent light steadily and it was floating before me. Again I had fallen in the middle of an extraordinary world, the person I didn't know called,

"Where have you been Dilruba?" I could see the black haired and beautiful faced person covered with the silver powder rain surrounding everywhere raising my head. He was looking with a bossy look in his big black eyes.

"We had been coming so fast!" I said. Now the silver rain shining in his black eyes lessened, and became rare. When I stood up,

"I'm □agaf," said he, "I've been waiting for you."

"Where is Keşşaf?" He understood from my question that I got worried.

"Don't worry, of course I will take you him!" he said. "But first you need to know who I am. I am the blind love inlaid in the membrane of the heart, I am the final point of the love. All metaphorical loves reach to me, but cannot go into the heart."

"But why?"

"This is the order of the heart's owner! The heart is an eternal mansion reserved only for the owner of the eternity. So, since the heart is the home of the eternity it cannot take something limited into it, it doesn't include anything that is not in its nature in it. It waits for the look of its owner." Şagaf stopped for a moment,

"The lover in the metaphorical love doesn't actually love the loved one but himself. He wants himself by desiring the loved, cut the head of the love you feel for yourself with the sword of wisdom. All hopes and consolations wasting your time with metaphorical love make your feet heavy and delay your arriving at the land of heart."

Şagaf stopped for a moment and soon after the rain of the silver stopped and the large engraved turquoise doors of the huge palace behind him appeared.

"If you became separation wholly you can go into the land of love pouring the existence figs in your skirt. Yet clean the signs of the metaphorical love from your breath!" I isn't necessary to say that I don't know how to do it. Şagaf must have understood the severity of the situation, and he went on;

"Separation exists only until it turns to a sherbet separating you from itself steadily, then it doesn't exist. Metaphorical love has taught you drunkenness. You have discovered how you can be fed from the loved without him. You have learned that the real place of love is heart." Then there wasn't a lot of things to do! Şagaf talked turning to the door of this huge palace,

"All worlds you have seen so far exist inside!" I understood from this sentence that I needed to go in. The wings of the large turquoise doors opened with my one step, and these rhythms and melodies reaching my ear at the same time... I had known them. It seemed that all the worlds of seeing, hearing and scents had been collected in this huge palace. Scents from inside as nice as they could make one faint were circling in a colour spiral.

First I thought my eyes would go blind because of the aliveness of the colours when I went to the doorway. One could die of happiness in such a palace. I could hear extraordinarily beautiful sounds showing me the way. All colours that had been seen on the earth and all music that had been heard, and more were here. Thousands of music I didn't understand where they were coming from filled in my ears together with the stringed, percussion, bow and wind instruments. And thousands of birds were singing songs all together; it was weird that I could distinguish each sound separately again.

When I walked a little, everything appeared more clearly. Colourful mosaic pendants vibrating over a large mirrored hall... The breath taking lights of the chandelier flowing over me in the centre of the colourful glass ceiling like a waterfall... These crystals, colours, mirrors, stained glass... I had last left them in the world of seeing. I'm attracted to the milk-white lights, I trace my consciousness in an extraordinary colour flowing and eternal light motion flying from colour to colour. I'm lost in the dancing flames of the red, and astonished again how black can shine so much.

A smoke rising nearly to my head calms me while I am thinking that I will get drowned in a colour storm, a basil scented smoke... It makes me walk on passing the white peonies circling around me, crystal particles beating like a heart, white roses and the others. Now I watch all the colours of which every corner poured into my soul in the mirrors around me. Pastel colours extending to the invisible points are coming to me again in these mirrors.

While all these things are happening, the smoke rising to my head turns to a steam. I feel every scent dispersed through the colours. I catch scented tablets, tulip vases and the scents of musk and amber censers in these colour halos. Transparent scent walls smelling camphor and henna are buried in a colour spectrum as I walk, and appear again with the disentangling of the music. I pass by the substanceless shelves constituting hundreds of small bottles. Every scent opens the doors of a new world to me. It is impossible to go! Yet here there is no other way that looking around for one who doesn't know even what he is looking for like me! Again various kinds of perfume and fragrance, scented oils, incenses, scent sachets and this palace growing steadily! Here the stairs interlacing each other and curling up in the world of scents. Last Keşşaf gave me aloe on these stairs! Just on this step!

The melody in my ear changed when I got close to the stairs of scents and all colours over-set. Now the magnificent rostrum appeared at the end of the snuggled stairs rising in curves. That mystical glass box at the end of the stairs! The rhythm of the music was increasing and colours were circling around madly. Only this mystical glass box remained in a fog now! Then the fog lifted, lifted and my beloved Keşşaf appeared!

"Welcome to the world of love, Dilruba!" Keşşaf pulled the magnificent colour helix as if he was sweeping the air, all scents and colours and even music stepped back due to the beauty of the glass box, and they weakened. Despite this retreat, every living thing, every colour, every scent was trying to get close to the glass box as if they were taken their lives from it. I heard moans and cries as I got closer, I heard the sound of the scents and smelt the scents of the colours. All melodies started to unravel and melt as being a fainted body.

Keşşaf was looking at me with the smile on his thin delicate face. While thousands of colours were passing through his hazel eyes all together his nice voice dazzling me becoming a musk,

"I have never doubted you would manage to reach here!" he said. So the place I had reached was very important even if I hadn't understand its importance yet!

"You understood how much you were faulty and how much you were far from the maturity while love was diminishing you from yourself. This was the reason of your loneliness Dilruba! You realized that you had no power. The helplessness of the lover is to understand finally that all beauty belongs to the loved." Now the shape, colour and scent of the glass box started to change eternally. This huge bell jar started to circle like a planet, like an invocator... It circled and circled swallowing all colours and transforming into a shining light; as it was circling, it started to draw everything inside due to its scented wind. It became a whirlwind and swallowed up everything with an eternal power, everything became a lover who couldn't get enough of watching the loved one. Yet I was still hearing the magical voice of Keşşaf even during this drawing.

"There is no closeness in love; its name is faraway-ness here! Close and far are the same unless you break off yourself! This is only possible to submit the loved one!" I was breaking into thousands of pieces at the moment that I heard these words. I flew to pieces, split up and fell apart. The bell jar was drawing me like the scents and colours; who could be strong enough to cope with this irresistible drawing? I was falling into a light spectrum;

"Submit Dilruba! Submit and lose yourself! Burn until there remains nothing from you. All veins will open if you submit, the thing that makes you reach the beauty is submitting."

I was drinking wine from the bowl of eternity. Keşşaf voice reached every piece of me separately,

"You have learned what it is to get rid of yourself. From now on you can deserve the whims and torture of the beloved, and the endless rigours of love! All truths you have discovered so far will lighten your way and prove that your being is a sign of separation!"

I was circling together with every particle, sound, happening and ending in the universe as one of them and as a part of them. I was nearly falling into the world of atoms! I nearly disappeared! Keşşaf's voice slowed down the circling and at last it stopped,

"The way going to the soul passes by the house of heart, by love. The eyes of the soul don't open before passing the land of heart."

I tried to open my eyes rapturously, it was strange that I couldn't open my eyes but still I could hear and see as it had been in the world of hearing.

"I wanted you to see the golden ratio existing in every structure, atom and sound," said he. Now my heart beatings slowed down and everything started to become normal again. Keşşaf was standing by the bell jar among the steps of fog, and the light reflecting on his face nearly made him invisible.

"One can see the sky in his chest only by this way. Actually, do you know, man can see the photo of his sky at the clearest and most distinct way at his last breath, so it is impossible to change the photo, time is up then. Yet there are some to reach it while they are alive, and I wanted you to see this photo while living because it means being at the way going to the salvation."

When I opened my eyes I was looking at everything from inside of the photo of my chest. I was there both as seeing and the seen. The photo was changing and transforming with my every breath. I saw there Nafs and Spirit. All sorrow hiding in my heart was competing with hopes. When I saw the sorrows staying like black tar there,

"Watch for the light and don't make any sorrow go into your heart, if you do so you will see that the sorrow going into your room is actually light! Look for the perfect shot among infinitely many shots,"

Now I could see all circles, ellipses, hexagons and all diagonal shapes in the photo of my chest. Each was taking place of the other continuously, combining like the rings of a chain then breaking again. Keşşaf went on,

"If you balance the light to see the particle in the whole and the whole in the particle, then symmetry will set and obscure points will lighten. The rhythm of the photo is the rhythm of your heart, its harmony in itself depends on your mind. The tissue there is your words, discover the excesses unbalancing and get rid of them as soon as possible, before the last breath!"

There was no space in the photo I was watching,

"All sounds, scents and images that you perceive are in your chest, not outside. Knowing that they exist only here equals with having a treasure. All those long lessons were for you to understand this. Now look at yourself coming out of your photo!"

I felt that I was going out of a kind of energy, I was looking at myself with an eye opened in the middle of my chest like a jasmine or rose. I saw how my thoughts and feelings were changing the colours of this sky, and I understood how a feeling moving unrestrainedly to all directions ruined the symmetry in this photo and offended the light. When I was in a state of a solid eye, I heard Keşşaf,

"Take this!" He was holding my picture machine in his hand, that small box I had been playing with fondly and that had showed the pictures in it successively as you had pushed the button on the edge with a click sound. "Now you have learned that you only need to hold it to the light. One can see the photo of the sky in his chest clearly only at his last breath. Yet, as I told you before, you can look at your sky for thousands of times with this small picture machine..."

I got the small picture box he gave. I rose it as I could catch the light in my own sky.

"You must always stay as pure and clean as a child, your dreams must be untouched like a child."

Now all colours moved over at the place where I was looking from the small box, and the frame showed only that mysterious bell jar. There was something strange. Keşşaf hadn't told me what was there in the bell jar. I didn't know when I would take the photo of that perfect shot while I was watching the disappearance of everything around the bell jar, I watched for the light and I was trying to open a way for myself through the continuously circling spectrum. It didn't take too long to understand that I had become the eye on my chest. Now everything started to move including the picture machine in my hand, the eye opening on my chest and the mysterious bell jar; I was examining the light again and waiting for that perfect moment.

"In that mysterious bell jar," said Keşşaf, "there is the scent of the Sultan of the two worlds where everything was created for Him. I understood why everything was drawn to this glass bell jar when I heard Keşşaf's words. Then the bell jar on the focus of the photograph disappeared, and I could see only the light itself in the shot I had been looking at. This eternal light widened and widened as it could take everywhere and also me in it. It grew until it turned every point it passed burning into a blue, clear sky. Every creature that the light had swept enlarged endlessly, a different life appeared in each particle. Come on, I said to myself, it's high time! I pushed the button of the small picture machine. I languished against this extraordinary shot, I fell onto my knees, the moment that the light took my soul and body in... At that moment...

I opened my eyes on the threshold I had sat. Iraz was shaking me from my shoulders and trying to wake me up. Yet I was sure that I hadn't been sleeping. "What are you doing, get up!" said Iraz. I couldn't help looking at the small sparrow net on the point that the opposite wall and the ceiling intersected. Little birds were playing joyfully.

I went to down yard like a drunk. Women constituted a big circle and they were circling jiggly and slowly. I recognized the woman holding a rose in her mouth in this big circle, she was the woman who had whispered the secret to me. "Do you want me to give you a secret," she had told me, "the one who has come here for the first time reaches the eternal secret of love." We caught each other's eyes, her looks seemed to be cinder flared up. I leaned under the locked arms, stayed at the centre of the circle swaying in harmony, and I started to revolve; as the circle gained speed, my feet also accelerated as if they dependent on the movements of the circle. I started to revolve speedily with their wind, until I turned to a fire ball...

Water blue lights were pouring on the stone ground. As the rhythm gained power I was flowing in the circle, I was melting in an extraordinary dance. At this state the women in the circle became invisible; their weak and blur bodies couldn't be seen clearly and only a moaning sound remained from them. When the moaning consisted of murmurs turned to an echo, I lost my consciousness and I fell down.

Next morning was the end of my one week here. I found the group with the steps of a traveller. "Ankara group, all aboard!" a voice said. "Okay," I said to the owner of the voice in a hurry, "I'm coming, just five minutes!" I wanted to see the pool in the up yard for the last time. I went to the pool that I had struggled with the foams until morning and I had circled around to clean. The pool brimmed, and the groove of the fountain was again closed with the same cloth which had been torn to ribbon and nearly mossy. Thin water was leaking from the neck of the fountain escaping from the imprisonment of the cloth and was flowing freely. I leaned, I wanted to kiss the water and drink a little. I trembled with the scent of rose filled my throat at the moment the cool water touched my lips. "Allow me," I said to the water, "let me go with a piece from you." The pool was shining with the generous lights of the sun as if it granted life to man...

After a short time Ankara group departed. I couldn't describe the sadness of returning. The group passed by the roofless earth-sheltered houses and got out of the village road. After a while sharp rocks rising as if they extended their heads to the sky appeared when we arrived at the dry and narrow road. We were passing through the sand and dust clouds as the group got speedy. I could hear the sounds of drums and tambourines from the peaks of the rocks when we got closer. We were going through the desert under the impassable heat flowing and curling. Then the Cavalry appeared. He caught my eyes suddenly turning his head on his bloodstock running at full gallop. The stirrups of his horse were passing shining, the light reflected on the dagger on his waist dazzled me, the skirts of his clothes and the end of his head dress were flying due to speed. I felt an irresistible desire to left the group and go with him. However, "No," Keşşaf had said, "you had had to go back!"

I was chained by the heaviness of returning. I let this painful returning capture me during breaks along the way. The group arrived in Ankara when the day turned its face to the night, and I was again stepping on the land of this city as if I was becoming sick.

I threw myself on my bed when I arrived at the dorm getting my pack which had nothing important. I thought if the things I had experienced were real. Yes, they were real, I said then, but everything happened so quickly!

Next morning was Friday and the last day of the term, and it was time to go packing up everything. Moreover, Nergis, Zümrüt and Hazel had left before Friday and they had returned to their hometowns. So I could find only Kırlangıç. "What have you done?" she asked immediately. It was so long to tell! "I have waited for you to depart," she said. The city we were going to leaving here was the same, so I could told her everything on the way.

This time I found myself in a new journey with Kırlangıç before I hadn't rested yet. I was going to my aunt's, and she was to her family. It was always nice to travel with Kırlangıç.

When I arrived at the house of aunt Reşide, I was weak. I looked like sick. Seconds later I came together with my aunt, I couldn't find the power to stand. In the later days I had a temperature and I thoroughly weakened and got a hoarse voice. Yet, I don't know why, I didn't feel bad. I could speak whisperingly when I was able to get up a week later, I started to regain my voice again.

One evening at the end of the week Müdrik phoned. Aunt Reşide was calling me as lifting the receiver,

"Dilruba, Müdrik Murathanoğlu is on the phone!" she said, then she asked "Is this Müdrik that we know?" keeping her hand on the receiver. I nodded my head meaning yes and I said hello to Müdrik with my husky voice.

"Hello, Dilruba, it's me Müdrik. Is it Dilruba? I can't hear you!" he said.

"Yes, it's me, hello. Where did you find this number? I just have a husky voice."

"I got this number from uncle Haşmet, I'm very worried about you, I hope I haven't disgraced her. You haven't called me." He said with a reproachful voice.

"I'm sorry, I couldn't, I haven't had time." I could speak with difficulty; letters were going out of my throat hardly.

"What's happened to your voice?" he said anxiously.

"Don't worry, I will be fine" I said trying to sum up.

"I have something to do there next week, can I see you if you are available?"

"Of course," I said, " I think I will get well then."

I faced with Müdrik when I made a full recovery a week later.

****

I get a small and old photo shop of which window is full of colourful photos all along in no time flat. Inside the shop is quite cool in spite of the heat of the outside. There is no other voice than the television's at full blast. There is a Far-east movie on the TV with a fuzzy image on its screen. A woman's voice is tinkling inside. There is a beautiful, slim Japanese woman on the screen. She cries to a slant-eyed man with a strong look that "If you do not accept my help offer you will remain as a slave forever" with a manner of empress. The man looking like a samurai with an old, mealy beret on his head answers that "I know, but I prefer remaining as a slave rather than coming with you."

This small and a little gloomy entrance of which walls are covered with photos smells cigarette ash. There is a small young man with grey hair behind the table ahead at the furthest end. The suffering expression of the steppe is fixed on his face. His face is colourless as if it lends all its colours to the photos on the wall. He says "Welcome" unperturbedly and turning his eyes away from the TV at a moment and then he looks at the TV with curious eyes.

I cast my eyes on the photos. Most of them are from 80's. They are photos of old couples side by side. I look at a black and white photo of a young woman whose forelock is about to go in her eyes. She looks at the objective over her one shoulder. She smiles like flirting. Who knows where this woman is now and what she is doing. She became a housewife most probably, even she put on weight. There is a photo of a child just under it. How he smiles happily with a football team t-shirt on him. I look at the photos of the brides and grooms. In a shot the groom takes the bride on his lap. The face of the woman is barely identified because of the make-up. There is another shot of another young couple just next to it. There is a man with a moustache, a happily smiling woman beside him, probably his wife, and only their heads and shoulders are seen.

"Hi, I want to have a photo taken." I say. "It will be a portrait. Can I get it instantly?" He stands up and comes to me.

"Of course" he says, "how many do you need?" The voice of the woman on TV is tinkling, it carries on tinkling, the woman cries angrily:

"I order you to come with me. The soldiers will soon be here, then they won't leave both of us alive, what are you waiting for?"

The samurai answers recklessly:

"I am waiting for dying, please, please go your grace..."

"Six is enough" I say to the photographer. He lifts the curtain with flowers on my right off and shows me the way. He points at a small mirror lightened by a cylindrical fluorescent lamp at the far end of the dark room and says "Make your hair here, I am coming, there is a comb over there." He goes out of the dark room. I look for the comb staring around. I get a quite dirty pink plastic comb. I had better to make my hair with my hand. I gussy up in front of the mirror for a while. I look around. My eyes catch an old, abandoned wing chair on a side. There is an old pouffe a few steps away from the wide plates. I go and sit on it. Minutes are passing. I look at the photographer sitting at the table lifting the curtain. He stares at the TV without gloating with a cigarette in his hand and his camera in front of him. He stays calm as if there is a mould layer between the World and his body.

I say with a low voice:

"I am ready."

He stands up immediately and starts to do his job.

I sit on the pouffe of which cover worn off because of sitting on again, but this time I sit up straight. The photographer turns off all the lights and two separate plates, both of them, start to shine with a white light. The photographer, who is behind the plates in the dark, takes a few steps to me, he raises my head a little with a timid manner and then he turns my chin to the right slightly. He pulls my collar completely to my neck. After he tidies my hair with the same timid manners, he says "Don't move and look into the objective soulfully." He walks back without hitting the bright plates and watches me still with the camera in his hand for a few seconds. "Don't hold your breath otherwise you look nervous. Please smile."

I feel a kind of anxiousness that I have in hospitals in this nervous moment. Just sitting there still... "Please smile," the photographer repeats. I force the edges of my lips to smile. At the same time the woman in the movie continues talking.

"Oh my God, the guards are approaching, I beg you Sadu, please come with me..."

A pair of hands blocks the lights of the wide plates first, I can see strong wrists are reaching out into me. The fingers of the hand starts to tighten my throat with hatred and rage, they press upon my veins to take me away from the life with all his power. On one hand I try to understand what is happening and on the other hand I catch his wrist with my two hands, I prick my nails into his skin, my breath dies away, first brokenly, then it turns to a growling. The owner of the unknown hands who understand that he cannot kill me tightening my throat now starts to hit my face with all his power, squeezes my arms leaving a great pain everywhere he touches. I tumble down with his last strike, he starts to kick me. There comes blood from my mouth.

The woman on TV start to scream,

"Guards, nooooo!" The clanks of the swords are heard, besides the painful moaning of the woman, the samurai cries: "Bastards! Leave her!"

The photographer calls from the darkness for the last time:

"Please stay still."

I am still dragged on the floor like an animal. Then, at a moment I get back my power, I don't know how, my eyes shine with a last will of life. I stand up, my fingers clasp the fingers of the unknown hands, squeeze them unceasingly, first my finger joints crunch, the power in my body well gets out after these strikes. I try to shake him pushing and bending my arms, I strive to run away from him. Once again he attacks with kicks, slaps and fists. I haven't got hurt like this before, I have fallen into a fire like this fort he first time. He punches me again and again, what kind of rage this is, this time he starts to squeeze my throat crying, the floor slips under my feet, everything starts to circle around me, I realize that I am at right beside him trying to save my head. He doesn't forgive, he starts to drag me holding the back of my neck, putting my feet down is useless, we come to the edge of the cliff. I understand his intention, he will push me down. I come with an ace of falling, and I realize at that moment that a man can do anything to survive, pain of life is not like anything. Desire to survive ignites all power in the soul. I start to bell like a wounded animal as my neck is dangling from the cliff, the only thing I want is to breath, my hands are looking for a space among his thick fingers for only one breath. His hands get more powerful as I scream; he tightens my neck much more.

The woman on the TV starts to cry.

"Sadu, oh my God, blood... Sadu, we will survive, won't we? Please don't give up, hold on!"

My shoulders dangle from the cliff; I must get rid of his hands before dangling from my waist. You cannot kill me, I say to myself. I resist his hands squeezing my throat with my whole body, I resist as if I rear up. I am helpless like a rodent in a beak of a bird of prey...

I hear the voice of the photographer:

"I am takiiinnngg!"

My eyes are drowned in a shining, puking light. A burning light crashes on my face. The time freezes for a moment, it covers everywhere as if it wants to swallow every lived thing. After a moment the light is drawn away, the photographer says:

"But we couldn't make it. You moved," and he comes to me. First he wipes away my eyes burst into tears due to pain without caring about my body about to dangle from the deep yard. He says "I am taking it again, you didn't smile," cleaning the fresh blood running from my nostrils.

He finds his place again without hitting the light plates in the dark room and he hides as if he takes shelter. The hands squeezing my throat with their all power grab my hair roots. My shoulders slide towards the bottom of the cliff some more. During the bitter struggle I do not even realize that my hair is torn from the bottom. Only a sharp pain cause my head lean towards the back. It doesn't seem that this unknown person, who ties his hands resembling paws to my hair, will free me. My eyes catch the eternal blueness shining over my head while my heart carries on beating as if it rushes out from my taut throat. For a moment I think that the sky will survive but this is my end. Two drops of tears runs towards my ears, as if they begging. They manifest as the fluid forms of begging. Once he frees my head, I will get down in no time flat. If he doesn't free my head, he will find my hair in his hands with my scalp. I grab his hands gripping my hair with my two hands; I grip him as much as his grip, may be more. I hear the voice of the photographer once again.

A little bitter, a little ironic smile is set on my face. I look at the blue sky forgetting everything. The camera flashes once more while the hands are dragging me to the blueness, my face is parallel with the sky and I am breathing deeply.

The voice of the TV fills the dark room; Sadu answers with a moaning and with his last breath,

"Yes, my darling, yes, we will survive, forever..."